D1311417

COMPLETE DIGITAL
PHOTOGRAPHY

SECOND EDITION

COMPLETE DIGITAL
PHOTOGRAPHY

SECOND EDITION

BEN LONG

CHARLES RIVER MEDIA, INC.

Hingham, Massachusetts

Publisher: Jenifer Niles
Production: Publishers' Design and Production Services, Inc.
Cover Design: The Printed Image
Cover Image: Ben Long

CHARLES RIVER MEDIA, INC.
20 Downer Avenue, Suite 3
Hingham, Massachusetts 02043
781-740-0400
781-740-8816 (FAX)
info@charlesriver.com
www.charlesriver.com

This book is printed on acid-free paper.

Ben Long. *Complete Digital Photography, Second Edition*.
ISBN: 1-58450-231-2

Library of Congress Cataloging-in-Publication Data

Long, Ben, 1967-
    Complete digital photography / Ben Long.— 2nd ed.
        p.   cm.
    ISBN 1-58450-231-2 (Paperback with CD-ROM : alk. paper)
    1. Photography—Digital techniques—Handbooks, manuals, etc.   2. Digital cameras—
Handbooks, manuals, etc.   3. Image processing—Digital techniques—Handbooks, manuals, etc.
I. Title.
    TR267 .L66 2003
    778.3—dc21
                        2002012911

Printed in the United States of America
02 7 6 5 4 3 2 First Edition

Contents

ACKNOWLEDGMENTS xv

CHAPTER 1 **INTRODUCTION** 1

Whom Is This Book For? 4
What Counts as "Digital Photography?" 6
What Else Do You Need? 6
Digital 101: A Few Basic Ideas 6

CHAPTER 2 **HOW GOOD ARE DIGITAL PHOTOS?** 11

A Word about the Images in This Book 12
What's Wrong with Digital Cameras 13
    Did You Hear Something? 13
    Color Troubles 15
    Detail and Aliasing 17
    Exposure Problems 18
    Too Much of a Good Thing 19
    "Reason?! We Don't Need No Stinking Reason!" 19
Why You Want a Digital Camera 19
    Why Digital Cameras Are Better than Point-and-Shoot Film Cameras 20
Next Steps 21

CHAPTER 3 **HOW A DIGITAL CAMERA WORKS** 23

Something Old, Something New 24
A Little Color Theory 24

How a CCD Works   28
    Counting Electrons   28
    Arrays   30
    "One CCD, Hold the Interpolation"   35
    Some Assembly Required   36
Compression and Storage   37
Meanwhile, Back in the Real World   39

CHAPTER 4   **BASIC PHOTOGRAPHY: A QUICK PRIMER**   **41**
Lenses   42
    Focal Length   44
    Zooms and Primes   45
Exposure: Apertures, Shutter Speeds, and ISO   46
    Reciprocity   49
    Lens Speed   50
    ISO, Or "Try to Be More Sensitive"   50
Mostly the Same   51

CHAPTER 5   **CHOOSING A DIGITAL CAMERA**   **53**
Basic Anatomy   54
CCDs, Resolution, Image Size, and Compression   55
    Resolution Categories   57
    Image Resolution and Compression   64
    Aspect Ratio   67
Camera Design   69
    Point-and-Shoot Cameras   69
    Prosumer   71
    Prosumer SLR   72
    LCD-Only Cameras   76
    Professional SLR   77
    Body Design and Construction   78
    Status LCDs   80
    Tripod Mount   81
    How to Choose   82
Lenses   82
    Lens Features   87
    Digital Zoom   89
    Focus   90
    Shutters and Irises   91

Viewfinders   92
    LCD Viewfinders   93
    Optical Viewfinders   95
    Electronic TTL Viewfinder   97
    SLR Viewfinders   97
Exposure Control   99
    White Balance   99
    Metering   100
    Exposure Compensation   101
    ISO Control   101
    Exposure Locks and Panoramas   102
    Preset Exposure Modes   103
    Sharpness and Saturation Controls   103
Shooting Modes   104
    Priority Modes   105
    Image Buffering   105
    Continuous Shooting   106
    Movie Mode   106
    Black and White   108
    Self-Timers and Remote Controls   108
Camera Performance   109
Flash   110
Playback Options   112
Storage and Input/Output   113
    Transferring and Viewing Images   114
    Storage   115
    How Much Do You Need?   120
    Media Tips   121
What's in the Box?   122
    Batteries   123
Special Features   125
Compare for Yourself   127
What Should I Buy?   127

CHAPTER 6   **BUILDING A WORKSTATION**   **129**

Choosing an Operating System   130
    Macintosh   130
    Windows   131
Building Your System   131
    RAM   132

Processor Speed   132
Storage   133
Monitors   134
Software   138
Image Editing Applications   138
Panoramic Software   142
Wavelet Compression   143
Image Cataloging Software   143
File Recovery Software   144
Accessories   145
Ready! Aim!   146

CHAPTER 7   **SHOOTING**   **147**

Initial Camera Settings   148
Choosing a Mode   149
Image Size and Compression   151
White Balance   153
Metering   157
Sharpness, Saturation, or Contrast   157
ISOs   159
Framing and Focusing   161
Focal Length   162
Focusing   166
Metering   176
What Your Light Meter Tells You   177
The Right Meter for the Job   181
Simple Flash Photography   186
Flash Modes   186
Flash White Balance   191
Power and Storage Management   192
Feel the Power   192
Media Baron   194
And That's Just the Beginning!   196

CHAPTER 8   **MANUAL EXPOSURE**   **197**

Motion Control   198
Depth of Field   202
Shutter Speed and Depth of Field   205
Tonal Control   207

Don't Know Much about Histograms 212
Details, Details 217
Adjusting Exposure 220
Exposure Compensation 220
Priority and Manual Modes 222
Automatic Reciprocity 223
ISO Control 223
Exposure Practice 225
An Intentional Underexposure 228
Another Underexposure 230
Manual Override 231
Of Brackets and Histograms 233
Exposing to Avoid Purple Fringing 235
Taking Control 237

CHAPTER 9   SPECIAL SHOOTING   239

Macro Photography 240
Finding the Optimal Macro Focal Length 241
Macro Focusing 242
Poor Depth of Field 242
Black-and-White Photography 244
The Zone System 244
Infrared Photography 247
Shooting Panoramas 251
Preparing Your Camera 253
Panoramic Exposure 256
Shoot with Care 257
Shooting for the Web 260
Image Size and Quality 261
Consider the Legibility of the Image 263
Finally, a Use for That Digital Zoom! 263
Shooting for Video 263
Using Filters 264
Types of Filters 266
Lens Extensions 269
Shooting in Extreme Conditions 270
Dirt, Dust, and Sand and Digital Cameras 270
Water and Digital Cameras 270
The Camera That Came in from the Cold 271
Hot Weather and Digital Cameras 272

Halfway There 275

CHAPTER 10 | **PREPARING YOUR IMAGES FOR EDITING** | **277**

Moving Pictures: How to Transfer and Organize Your Images 278
Make the Transfer 278
Organize Your Digital Media 279
Preparing Your Image Editor 281
A Little More Color Theory 281
Color Management Systems 283
Color Management Workflow 283
Configuring Your Color Management System 285
Soft Proofing in Photoshop 7 295
Preparing Your Image 296
New Image Resolutions 297
Resizing an Image 297
TUTORIAL: Understanding Resolution 300
Step 1: Open the Image 300
Step 2: Open the Image Size Dialog Box 300
Step 3: Resize the Image without Resampling 301
Step 4: Resize with Resampling 302
TUTORIAL: Cropping and Resizing an Image 303
Step 1: Open the Image 303
Step 2: Evaluate the Image 303
Step 3: Perform the First Resizing 304
Step 4: Crop the Image 305
Step 5: Resize Again 307
Why You Should Resize First 308

CHAPTER 11 | **CORRECTING TONE AND COLOR** | **311**

Histograms Revisited 312
TUTORIAL: Correcting an Image with Brightness and Contrast (Or Trying to, Anyway) 314
Step 1: Open the Image 314
Step 2: Adjust the Image's Brightness 314
Step 3: Adjust the Contrast of the Image 316
Step 4: Give Up 317
Levels 317
TUTORIAL: Using Levels Input Sliders 318
Step 1: Open the Image 319
Step 2: Adjust the Black Point 319
Step 3: Adjust the White Point 321

Step 4: Play with the Gamma Slider 322
Should You Worry about Data Loss? 323
TUTORIAL: Real-World Levels Adjustments 325
Step 1: Open the Image 325
Step 2: Set the Black Point 326
Step 3: Set the White Point 327
Step 4: Adjust the Gamma 327
Step 5: Readjust the White Point 327
Step 6: Save the Image 330
Curves 331
TUTORIAL: Correcting an Image with Curves 334
Step 1: Open the Image 334
Step 2: Set the Black Point 334
Step 3: Set the White Point 335
Step 4: Adjust the Gamma 336
Step 5: Make Another Adjustment 337
Step 6: Adjust the Sky 338
Levels and Curves and Color 338
TUTORIAL: Using Both Levels and Curves to Correct Color 341
Step 1: Open the Image 341
Step 2: Take a Closer Look 341
Step 3: Make a Curves Adjustment 344
Step 4: Make a Levels Adjustment 345
Don't Touch That Dial 347

CHAPTER 12   BUILDING YOUR EDITING ARSENAL   349

Brushes and Stamps 350
Brushes 350
Airbrushes 352
Rubber Stamp or Clone 352
TUTORIAL: Cloning Video Tutorial 354
Masks 354
Mask Tools 355
Selection Tools 356
Mask Painting 357
Color-Based Selection Tools 358
Special Mask Tools 358
Saving Masks 359
Sort of Masked 361
TUTORIAL: Creating Complex Masks 362
Step 1: Open the Image 362

Step 2: Create a Mask 363

Step 3: Load the Mask 363

Step 4: Fade the Background 364

Step 5: Assess the Change 364

Step 6: Create a Gradated Mask 366

Step 7: Try the New Mask 366

Step 8: Create Yet Another Mask 367

Step 9: Fade the Background 368

Layers 369

Some Layer Basics 370

Adjustment Layers 374

Layer Masks 375

Other Editing Tools 376

Hue/Saturation 377

Selective Color 377

Unique Tools 378

The Right Tool for the Job 378

CHAPTER 13   ESSENTIAL IMAGING TACTICS   379

Workflow 380

Initial Cleanup 382

Removing Noise 382

Identifying Noise 382

TUTORIAL: Selective Blurring Video Tutorial 388

Removing Dust and Blotches 393

TUTORIAL: Cloning Video Tutorial 394

Correcting Barrel and Pincushion Distortion 395

TUTORIAL: Correcting Barrel Distortion 395

Step 1: Open the Image 395

Step 2: Create Guide Lines 395

Step 3: Expand Your Canvas 396

Step 4: Correct the Image 396

Step 5: Try Again 398

Step 6: Crop 398

Color and Tone Adjustment 399

TUTORIAL: Color Correction 400

Step 1: Open the Image 401

Step 2: Remove the Blue Cast 401

Step 3: Desaturate the Background 403

Step 4: Adjust the Levels of the Background 403

Step 5: Adjust the White Point and Black Point 403

TUTORIAL: Color Correction Video Tutorial 405

Removing Red-Eye   407
Removing Color Fringing   407
TUTORIAL: Desaturating a Chromatic Aberration   408
Step 1: Select the First Fringe   409
Step 2: Create a Hue/Saturation Adjustment Layer   409
Step 3: Target the Offending Colors   410
Step 4: Desaturate the Fringe   410
Step 5: Target More Colors   411
Step 6: Check the Results   411
Adjusting Tonal Range with Layers   412
Correcting White Balance   412
Correcting Vignetting   414
Saturation Adjustment   415
Increasing Contrast and Saturation with Layer Stacking   416
Decreasing Contrast and Saturation with Layer Stacking   417
Editing   417
Scaling   418
Scaling Down   419
Scaling Up   419
Sharpening   421
How Sharpening Works   421
Not All Sharpness Is Created Equal   425
More Tools to Come   426

CHAPTER 14   **SPECIAL EFFECTS**   **427**

Simulating Depth of Field   428
TUTORIAL: Shortening Depth of Field in an Image   428
Step 1: Open the Image   429
Step 2: Prepare a Gradient   429
Step 3: Apply the Gradient to Your Mask   430
Step 4: Apply the Blur   432
Step 5: Alter Your Mask   432
Step 6: Apply Your Final Blur   433
Converting Color Images to Grayscale   440
Conversion Methods   440
Creating "Hand-Tinted" Images   443
Adding Texture, Grain, and "Film" Look   446
Adding Grain   447
TUTORIAL: Adding Grain to an Image   448
Step 1: Create a Layer of Noise   448
Step 2: Change the Blending Mode   449
Step 3: Lower the Noise Opacity   449

Compositing   450
Preparing to Print   451

CHAPTER 15   OUTPUT   453

Choosing a Printer   454
    Laser Printers   454
    Dye-Sublimation Printers   456
    Inkjet Printers   457
    Media Selection   459
    Ink Choice   460
Printing   461
    Choosing a Resolution   461
    Choosing a Resolution for a Laser Printer   462
    Choosing a Resolution for an Inkjet Printer   464
    Using Your Color Management System When You Print   465
    Correcting Your Image for Print   466
    TUTORIAL: Targeting an Image   470
    Step 1: Open the Image   470
    Step 2: Talk to Your Printer   470
    Step 3: Target the Image   471
    Step 4: Evaluate the Image   472
    Web-Based Printing   473
Web Output   474
Conclusion   476

APPENDIX A   SUGGESTED READING   477

APPENDIX B   ABOUT THE CD-ROM   479

GLOSSARY   483

INDEX   499

ACKNOWLEDGMENTS

This book could not have been written (at least by me) without the help of a number of people, who offered their advice, opinions, and modeling, including: Rick LePage, Paul Winternitz, Kalonica McQuesten, Michael Wyman, Regina Saisi, Beverly Forsyth, Tom Penberthy, Ron Miles, Don Byron, Reed Kirk Rahlmann, Dean Cook, Mark Patron, Adele Shaw, and my dad.

INTRODUCTION

In This Chapter

- Whom Is This Book For?
- What Counts as "Digital Photography?"
- What Else Do You Need?
- Digital 101: A Few Basic Ideas

One hundred and fifty years ago, when photography was first developed, most "serious" artists considered it a curiosity—a mere novelty that couldn't compete with "real" art forms such as painting and drawing. Although these debates waged well into the 20th century, today photography has not only been accepted as an art form, it has become one of the most successful forms of communication ever created. Look around the room you are in right now and consider just how many photographs you can see—from book covers to food packaging to advertising circulars.

There have been many important technological breakthroughs on the way from daguerreotypes to 8" × 10" glossies. Color film, sophisticated light meters, zoom lenses, autofocus cameras, Polaroid-Land photography, simple point-and-shoot cameras, and one-hour photo processing are just some of the technological milestones that have helped to make photography both a powerful and ubiquitous medium.

Despite all of these changes and improvements, today's typical 35mm film cameras are not fundamentally different from the cameras of 100 years ago. Sure, the optics in a camera's lens, the metering and control systems provided by a camera's electronics, and the chemistry available in modern film and processing technology allow for higher quality and more creative control than ever before, but today's film cameras still record an image by exposing a piece of film to light, just as cameras have done for the last 150 years.

Digital photography, therefore, represents the first fundamental change in photographic technology since the mid-1800s. Although the lenses, metering systems, and controls on your digital camera might be identical to those found on a film camera, the simple fact that the camera does not record images on film makes digital photography a very different process—both technically and creatively—from traditional film photography.

Practically, the digital photographer has luxuries the film photographer can only dream of: the ability to instantly view images and delete unwanted exposures, the lack of film processing and scanning, and the elimination of the environmental and financial concerns presented by film and film processing chemicals. Artistically, the digital photographer can take advantage of unique in-camera features such as panoramic shooting, automatic image processing, and the ability to shoot and shoot and shoot, trying many different settings, framings, and exposures without worrying about wasting film.

Even with all of these advantages, most photographers have been waiting for the answer to one question: Can digital cameras produce images that are comparable to film? (Some digital photographers are even asked if digital photography is "real" photography, just as their analog-based predecessors were harangued by stodgy painters and illustrators.) Until recently, the answer was "Yes, digital can be as good as film, but it will cost you upwards of $20,000." But finally, after years of waiting, film-quality digital cameras have gotten down to the $1,000 range. They're not perfect, and many of them lack features that experienced photographers have come to depend on. However, whether you're an occasional hobbyist, dedicated amateur, or serious professional photographer, if you've been waiting to make the jump to digital photography, now is the time, and this book will help you take the leap.

If you've spent much time around computers, you might have heard of Moore's Law, which states that computing power doubles every 18 months. In the year-and-a-half or so since the first edition of this book, the resolution of high-end consumer-grade digital cameras has, in fact, doubled from around 3 to around 6 megapixels. What's more, as vendors have continued to improve the resolution and image quality of their cameras, they've also improved on everything from ergonomics to features, and typically managed to deliver more power for less money.

In this updated edition of *Complete Digital Photography*, you'll learn about the latest cameras and technologies, as well as the most recent updates to the software and hardware that you need to edit and print your pictures.

In the intervening year-and-a-half, many vendors, programmers, and photographers have found ways to work around some of the problems that digital camera users typically face. We discuss such new techniques in detail throughout the book.

As in the previous edition, the book's image editing examples and tutorials are built around Adobe Photoshop. Although Photoshop is the premiere image editing application, there are plenty of other good editors out there and in Chapter 6, "Building a Workstation," you'll learn how to pick a package that provides the tools typically used by digital photographers. Fortunately, most image editing programs provide the same basic tools and interfaces, so you should have no trouble adapting the lessons described here to other editing packages. All of the tutorials have been updated for the latest Photoshop (version 7 as of this writing). While most of the screen shots are from the Macintosh OS X version of Photoshop, the program's interface is the same whether you use Mac or Windows.

ON THE CD

In addition to the tutorials from the first edition, three new video tutorials are included on the CD-ROM. In these QuickTime movies, you can watch "over my shoulder" as I perform a number of imaging and adjustment techniques. Because many image correction processes are "interactive" rather than strictly procedural, these movies allow you the opportunity to learn techniques that cannot be explained in a written, step-by-step form.

ON THE CD

The tutorial movies are included in the Video folder on the CD-ROM. You can watch them in any order, but it would be best to view them when mentioned in the text, as some of the techniques assume that you have already learned certain concepts.

Finally, with the addition of full color throughout the book, all of the tutorial and sample images now provide better examples of many of the color theories and concepts discussed herein. As with the previous

ON THE CD

edition, full-color versions of many of the book's images are included in the Images folder on the accompanying CD-ROM. Access to these images affords the opportunity to study them in detail on your monitor or printer.

WHOM IS THIS BOOK FOR?

Complete Digital Photography covers all of the technical details that you need to understand how to produce high-quality digital photographs. This book is for photographers of all skill levels who want to use digital cameras to produce images. If you're an amateur or hobbyist photographer who wants to take better pictures and have decided to use a digital camera instead of a traditional film camera, this book will explain the fundamental technical concerns of shooting good pictures. If you're an experienced film photographer who is interested in making the switch to digital photography, and you want to understand the new technology, this book will help you learn what is different about working with a digital camera.

Using a film camera is really a two-step process. First, you shoot your pictures—with the goal of getting as much color, contrast, and tone into your image as you can manage. Then, you develop and print the images in a way that takes maximum advantage of that information. Shooting digital photographs is no different. As with a film camera, you first shoot your subject—after carefully calculating the proper exposure. Then, you digitally process and print your image.

Although cameras might change, the physics of light remains the same (fortunately!). Consequently, digital and film photographers share all of the same concerns over apertures, shutter speeds, and metering techniques. Chapters 2 through 5 and Chapter 7 address these questions and show you how a digital camera works. This information will help you choose a camera, and will form the basis for much of the practical shooting and editing information that will be covered later.

All of your additional shooting concerns, from choosing the right exposure to using filters and flash, are covered in Chapters 7, 8, and 9. Although experienced photographers might already be comfortable with much of the information presented, they'll still want to take a close look at these chapters for information on the particular idiosyncrasies of shooting with digital cameras.

Although it is difficult to separate the artistic and technical concerns involved in creating a good photo—after all, it is your technical control that allows you to achieve your artistic goals—this book does not cover certain "artistic" issues. Composition, artistic intent, photographic narrative, and many other concerns are not discussed, mainly because there are so many good books already available on this subject. See Appendix A, "Suggested Reading," for a list of valuable resources.

Just as a film camera requires a good darkroom, a digital camera requires a computer and a few select pieces of software. Chapter 6 helps you select and assemble a computer system that's right for your photo processing needs.

Chapter 10, "Preparing Your Images for Editing," gives you some tips on transferring your images to your computer and shows you how to keep them organized and archived. Chapter 10 also helps you configure your computer's color management system and prepare your images for editing.

ON THE CD

Adobe Photoshop is used for all of the image editing examples and tutorials in this book, and demo copies of Photoshop for both Macintosh and Windows are provided on the CD-ROM. Most of the tools and functions used in the tutorials are fairly generic, so you should be able to follow along using any image editing program, provided it includes a reasonable assortment of editing tools. Your editing efforts will start in earnest in Chapter 11, "Correcting Tone and Color," where you'll learn about histograms, and make your first tonal and contrast corrections. Editing continues in Chapter 12, "Building Your Editing Arsenal," when you will be introduced to some of the basic editing tools that you'll need to touch up and adjust your images.

Chapter 13, "Essential Imaging Tactics," details the image editing workflow that you'll typically use. It also expands on your editing know-how with discussions of color and saturation adjustment, resizing, and sharpening. In Chapter 14, "Special Effects," you'll perform some of the more complex edits that digital photographers often face—correcting distortions, simulating depth of field, stitching panoramas, and converting images to grayscale.

Finally, with your images corrected, massaged, edited, and tweaked, you'll be ready to output them using the techniques presented in Chapter

15, "Output." Whether your final image destination is print, the Web, or video, Chapter 15 covers the details of getting your image out of your image editor and into the real world.

Because *Complete Digital Photography* is intended for users with a variety of experience levels, many terms have been defined in the Glossary rather than within the main text.

WHAT COUNTS AS "DIGITAL PHOTOGRAPHY?"

Many people use the term "digital photography" to cover any photographic process that involves correcting and editing a photograph using a computer. By this definition, shooting with your film camera, scanning your film or prints, editing them digitally, and then printing on a desktop printer counts as digital photography.

In this book, digital photographs are photographs taken with a digital camera. This is an important distinction because shooting with a film camera and shooting with a digital camera involve different concerns and practices. The simple fact is that there are many things you must do differently with a digital camera. But don't worry, this book covers them all!

WHAT ELSE DO YOU NEED?

ON THE CD

You'll need a digital camera, computer, and some editing software to follow along with the tutorials and some of the examples in this book (Chapters 5 and 6 will help you decide which camera and computer are right for you). None of the tutorials or examples in this book are platform specific, so you should have no trouble following along, whether you use a Macintosh, Windows, or Unix. Most of the editing and correcting tutorials are built around Adobe Photoshop, but you can use a different editing package as long as it provides equivalent features. Demo versions of Photoshop, as well as many other handy utilities, are included on the CD-ROM in both Macintosh and Windows formats.

In addition, all images necessary for the tutorials are included in the Tutorials folder on the CD-ROM.

DIGITAL 101: A FEW BASIC IDEAS

In the old days, photographers made their own photographic papers, films, and *emulsions*. Whether it was to achieve a particular style or texture, or to gain more control over their printing processes, photographers such as Ansel Adams, Alfred Stieglitz, and Eduard Steichen had to know a good deal about chemistry to create their prints. Similarly, to really understand how to get the most out of your digital camera, it's important to understand some of the technology behind it. Chapter 3, "How a Digital Camera Works," covers the details of how a digital camera works, but a basic understanding of the *digitizing* process will make things easier.

The "real" world in which we live is an *analog* world. Light and sound come to us as continuous analog waves that our senses interpret. Unfortunately, it's very difficult to invent a technology that can accurately record a continuous analog wave. For example, you can scratch a continuous wave into a vinyl record, but because of the limitations of this storage process, the resulting recording is often noisy and scratchy and unable to capture a full range of sound.

Storing a series of numbers, on the other hand, is much simpler. You can carve them in stone, write them on paper, burn them to a CD-ROM or, in the case of digital cameras, record them to small memory chips. Moreover, as long as you don't make any mistakes when you're writing them down, you'll suffer no loss of data or quality as you move those numbers from place to place. Therefore, if you can find a way to represent something in the real world as a series of numbers, then you can very easily store those numbers using your chosen recording medium.

The process of converting something into numbers (or digits) is called *digitizing*. The first step in digitizing is to divide your subject into distinct units. In the case of an image, this is a simple process of dividing your image into a grid of *picture elements* or *pixels*. How fine your grid is (i.e., what *resolution* it has) varies depending on how sophisticated your equipment is.

Next, each pixel in the grid is analyzed to determine its content, a process called *sampling*. Each sample is measured to determine how "full" it is; that is, a corresponding numeric value is assigned that represents that pixel's contents, a process called *quantizing*. Finally, these numeric values are stored on some type of storage medium.

Figure 1.1 is a simple image composed entirely of *black and white* pixels. As you can see, it's very easy to assign a one or a zero to each pixel to represent the image. Because it only takes a single *bit* to represent each pixel, this image is called a *1-bit image*.

In the example shown in Figure 1.1, our individual samples can only be 0 or 1 (i.e., they have a very small *dynamic range*) because we are only storing one bit of information per pixel. If we want to record more than simple black and white, then we need to be able to specify more colors; that is, we need to have more choices than just 0 or 1. By going to a higher *color depth* (*bit depth*)—let's say 8 bits, which allows for 256 different values—we can record more information, as seen in Figure 1.2.

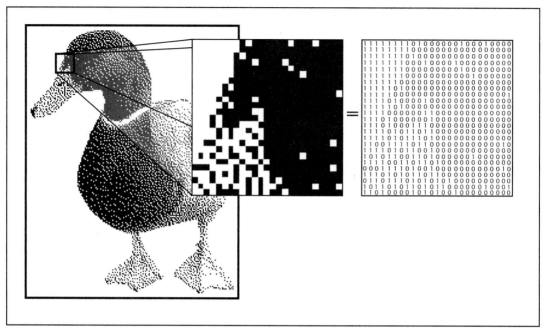

FIGURE 1.1   Each pixel in this 1-bit image is represented by a one or a zero.

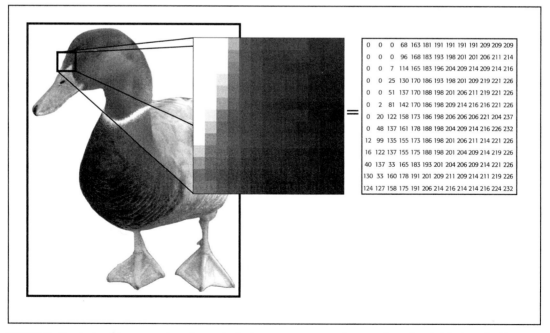

FIGURE 1.2   By storing bigger numbers for each pixel, we can store much more than simple black and white dots. With the ability to use gray pixels, the image looks much more realistic.

With 256 shades from which to choose, we can represent a finer degree of detail than we could with only two color choices. To store full-color images, we must go to an even higher bit depth and store 24 bits of information per pixel. With 24 bits, we can represent roughly 16 million colors, allowing us to store photo-quality images.

To sum up, two of the factors that determine the quality of a digitizing process are resolution (the size and number of your individual pixels), and dynamic range (how big a range of color choices you have for each pixel).

Many other factors affect the quality of a digitized image, from optical quality to compression. Before exploring these questions, though, it's important to consider what makes a good image.

HOW GOOD ARE DIGITAL PHOTOS?

In This Chapter

- A Word about the Images in This Book
- What's Wrong with Digital Cameras
- Why You Want a Digital Camera

Many people are still wary of digital photography—they question the claims that digital cameras can produce results that are competitive with film. Given the rapid advancement of the technology, and the low level of quality produced by the first few generations of consumer-level cameras, these concerns are often valid, particularly if one is up against a deadline or shooting for pay. These days, though, with an "average" digital camera packing 2 or 3 million pixels, and with advances in lens, sensor, image processing, and printing technologies, the question of "film versus digital" is becoming more and more irrelevant. Since the last edition of this book, there have been few—if any—revolutionary advances in digital camera technology but plenty of positive evolutionary change.

In the next few chapters, you will be spending a lot of time reading about the technical details of how a digital camera works. These concepts will help you better understand how to choose—and get the best results from—a digital camera. Because of their underlying technology, digital cameras are subject to very particular imaging problems. In this chapter, you're going to learn what those problems look like, and how to identify them. This should make your technical forays a little easier to understand.

A WORD ABOUT THE IMAGES IN THIS BOOK

Although a lot of hard work went into ensuring that the images in this book are accurately printed, some of the image quality issues discussed herein are very subtle and might not be easy to see. The printing process and paper used in this book are not what one would normally choose for a high-quality photographic reproduction, so you shouldn't take the prints in this book as examples of the best that can be done with a digital camera. Rather, think of some of these images as reference images that will, hopefully, help you understand the concepts we discuss.

ON THE CD

For closer, more accurate examination, many of the images in this book are included on the companion CD-ROM in the Images folder. Images are organized by chapter and are stored in both TIFF and Photoshop formats.

Although examining the images on-screen will be very informative, for the truest understanding of image quality, it's best to look at the images using your chosen output device. If that device is your monitor, then by all means, keep looking at the images on-screen. If you intend to print to a particular printer, however, then it's best to judge image quality by studying prints from that printer. In addition to providing a "real-world" sample of image quality, you'll begin to get an understanding of what your printer is capable of, and how its colors differ from those produced by your computer screen. You might be pleasantly surprised to find that *artifacts* and other problems that are very annoying on-screen don't appear on the printed page.

We discuss printing in great detail in Chapter 15, "Output," and the tips in that chapter should help you get better printed results. Until then, simply printing the images straight off the companion CD-ROM should at least help you follow the concepts in this chapter.

ON THE CD

WHAT'S WRONG WITH DIGITAL CAMERAS

This section is not about how digital cameras are a bad choice for your photographic pursuits. Rather, you'll simply learn about some of the problems that digital cameras face and how those problems show up in your final images. Just as film photographers have to worry about everything from *reciprocity failure* to the color balance of their film, digital photographers have their own set of concerns.

In this section, you will learn what types of problems digital images are prone to, and you will get some practice in learning to recognize them. In addition to providing you with a vocabulary for discussing these issues, studying problems will help you train your eye to be more discerning, making it easier to select a camera, avoid problems when shooting, and correct your images later.

Did You Hear Something?

One of the easiest problems to identify in any digital image is *noise*. Unfortunately, all current digital cameras are susceptible to noise, and they manage to produce many different kinds. Some noise is more acceptable than others, but even if you are not bothered by the noise in your image, it's still important to pay attention to how it can affect certain editing operations.

Figure 2.1 was shot with an Olympus C2100 UltraZoom using the camera's default automatic settings. No exposure adjustments were made and no edits were performed.

If you look closely at any of the shadowy areas, you'll see that they are fairly noisy. In fact, even some of the middle tone areas have a marked amount of noise in them. Although noise can sometimes appear as a grain-like texture, in this image, the noise shows up as light-colored speckles—mostly magenta or green—spread throughout the shadow areas.

FIGURE 2.1   Like many digital camera images, this street scene has some trouble with noise, particularly in the shadow areas.

Noise typically occurs in darker parts of an image, although even some of the lighter shades on the pink building are suffering from a little too much noise. Note that this particular image is free of noise in the sky, a problem that plagues some digital cameras.

Different cameras produce different amounts of noise, and some digital cameras produce "prettier" noise than others. In some cases, the noise has less color in it, and almost looks like nothing more than film grain.

On the positive side, depending on the quality of your printing process, this noise might not be a problem. If you're using a somewhat coarse, noisy printing process—such as what you might find on some inkjet printers—then the printer might produce enough artifacts of its own that the noise in your image will be obscured. This is a bit of a gamble, though, and it's better to try to get a camera that produces less noise, especially since you might one day upgrade to a higher-quality printer.

Although you can reduce noise with some simple editing tricks, it's difficult or impossible to get rid of all of it. Moreover, because certain editing operations can actually make the noise more pronounced, it's a good idea to stay aware of any noise in your image.

Color Troubles

There are many different types of color problems that can occur in any image, whether digital or film, but digital cameras have a few problems all their own. Learning to spot them will give you a better idea of where and how to start making corrections.

Downright Incorrect Color

Figure 5.42 shows the same scene shot with three different cameras. Each camera was set on full auto and no exposure adjustments were made. As you can see, the three cameras produced very different interpretations of the colors in the scene.

Color reproduction is a subjective characteristic, and while some cameras might be more accurate in terms of color reproduction, they might not produce an image that you find as attractive as another model does. Some cameras, on the other hand, can produce color that is simply wrong.

With a film camera, your color concerns are a factor of the type of film that you use, and you can always change your film choice at any time. With a digital camera, you have to consider image quality when you choose a camera, and you can't change it later! Fortunately, many of today's digital cameras are capable of excellent color reproduction.

Color Casts

Some cameras have a tendency to produce images with particular color casts—overall color tones that make the image appear as if it was shot through a colored filter of some kind. Sometimes a camera will have a tendency to cast only the colors in a particular range. For example, shadows might appear too blue or yellow while the midtones and highlights are fine.

Although color casts aren't very attractive, they're usually not too hard to remove, as they typically present themselves in just one range of colors in an image. You'll learn more about removing color casts in Chapter 13, "Essential Imaging Tactics."

Bad White Balance

As you'll see, before you shoot with a digital camera, you need to calibrate it to your current light source, a process called *white balancing*. If improperly white balanced, the camera will not be able to accurately reproduce colors.

Images with bad white balance are similar to images with color casts, except that white balance color damage usually goes through more areas of the image. Figure 7.2 shows the same scene shot with a variety of white balance settings. Notice the shift from red to blue throughout the image as the white balance changes.

Color Artifacts

You're probably familiar with the *red-eye* phenomenon that can turn people's eyes into demonic red circles, but there are many other types of color artifacts.

Figure 2.2 shows a weird color artifact. If you look closely at the pen in the middle of this image you can see that's it's very strangely fuzzy. For some reason, the camera got very confused when it was rendering the red of the pen and produced a weird halo.

FIGURE 2.2   The fuzzy red pen in this person's lap is the result of a strange, unpredictable color error on the part of the digital camera.

Note also the weird color noise in the denim of the jeans as well as the high noise levels in the flesh tones.

Digital cameras that have resolutions over 2 megapixels are susceptible to a type of color artifact that you don't have to worry about with lower-resolution cameras or film cameras. Sometimes referred to as *sensor blooming,* the weird *purple fringing* that you can see on the edge of the building in Figure 8.30 is actually the result of a computing problem within the camera. In Chapter 13, you'll learn more about these artifacts and how to avoid them.

Many color artifacts, including sensor blooming, seem to occur along boundaries of high contrast change, or in areas of sharp color change. When you are evaluating a camera, or when you are assessing the quality of an image, pay attention to these types of areas.

Detail and Aliasing

After bad or weird color, lack of sharpness or detail in an image is one of the most easily recognized problems faced by any type of camera. The amount of detail visible in an image is the result of several factors:

- How much resolution your camera has (a camera with more resolution will be able to resolve finer details).
- How good your lens is (a better lens will be able to focus more sharply and produce better image detail).
- How good the sharpening algorithms in your camera are. As we'll see later, all digital cameras employ sharpening algorithms that help improve detail and sharpness. Some cameras are better at this than others, and some can even go too far, producing images that are *over*-sharpened. Detail is very closely related to sharpness in an image. The sharper the image, the easier it is to resolve fine detail. We'll spend a lot of time discussing sharpening later in the book.

An image with poor sharpness and detail will have a "soft" look. However, digital cameras are also susceptible to *aliasing* artifacts that film cameras are immune to.

Figure 2.3 shows an example of bad aliasing in an image. The characteristic star-stepped pattern of an aliasing problem usually shows up along areas of fine detail, and, very often, such artifacts only appear in areas of high contrast.

Aliasing problems can often be avoided by lowering your camera's sharpening setting, but it is very difficult, if not impossible, to eliminate them using image editing software.

FIGURE 2.3   Aliasing—the stair-stepping pattern visible around this woman's glasses—can be a common problem with lower-res cameras. However, even high-end digital cameras can suffer from slight aliasing under certain conditions.

Exposure Problems

As with a film camera, if you set the wrong exposure on a digital camera, you'll get a bad image. Although modern automatic light metering systems are very sophisticated and often do a very good job, they can still make mistakes, particularly if they aren't used properly. The meters in most cameras have tendencies, and experience will usually help you predict how your camera's meter might respond to a particular lighting situation.

Figure 8.7 shows three different exposures of the same image. The lower-left image shows the camera's default exposure, which yielded an *underexposed* image. As you can see, there are no visible details in the shadow areas of the image. Exposure and detail is a matter of taste, of course, and one could easily argue that it doesn't matter that there are no shadow details. However, if you were hoping for a different level of contrast in the image—one that might reveal some detail in those dark areas—you'd be out of luck with this picture.

To try to correct for this underexposure, two additional images were shot. The lower-right image is *overexposed* and suffers from lack of detail in the bright, highlight areas. The upper image was overexposed to a lesser degree, resulting in an image with good detail throughout the highlights and midtones. Again, you might prefer the darker or lighter image. The point is to recognize how a camera's metering and exposure choice can affect detail and overall results.

Too Much of a Good Thing

Most cameras perform some type of sharpening on their images. Sharpening improves detail and the sharpness of edges, and tends to boost the contrast of an image. It's important to realize, though, that too much sharpening can be a bad thing. Better cameras offer a choice of sharpening levels that let you adjust the camera to your sharpening taste.

"Reason?! We Don't Need No Stinking Reason!"

Sometimes an image just looks bad, and there's no real reason why. Sure, you can look for color casts and *aberration*s and contrast troubles, but often there are simply indefinable combinations of all of these things that cause an image to just look "wrong." Similarly, you might have an image with bad contrast and horrible noise and find it very compelling.

The point is that, when you judge image quality, an image might be full of technical mistakes, but still be a good image. Before you spend too much time obsessing over technical details, step back from the image and examine it as a whole. You might find that your technical concerns are irrelevant.

Nevertheless, it is important to know a camera's technical shortcomings so that you can work around them or, sometimes, exploit them as in Figure 9.19, a low-resolution, grainy, technically bad image that is still nice to look at.

Why You Want a Digital Camera

Don't let the previous discussion discourage you. Yes, digital cameras have their idiosyncrasies, but so do film cameras (you could easily come up with a list of "What's wrong with film cameras?").

Many of the problems discussed here are infrequent and won't necessarily be pronounced enough to show up in print. What's more, as you'll see later, all of the problems can be fixed with some simple image editing techniques.

The fact is, unless you're a professional photographer with very specific, high-end concerns, today's digital cameras can provide image quality that's every bit as good as what you'll get from film. Certainly, not *every* camera will deliver such good results, but if you choose the right camera and learn how to use it, there's no reason why going digital should feel like a compromise.

Whether or not you already have a camera, if you bought this book you probably investigated digital photography enough to understand the practical and creative advantages of shooting digital photographs. From the immediate review of images, to being able to delete unwanted pictures on-the-fly, digital cameras offer creative flexibility that film photographers can only dream of.

One of the biggest advantages to digital photography is the elimination of the scanner. You might have a great film camera, and a very good photo lab, but without a good scanner and the knowledge of how to use it (and the patience to do it right), then all that extra film quality might not count for much.

Yes, there are hassles and concerns when you shoot digital photographs. If you have any experience with photography, however, you know that there are also plenty of hassles and concerns when you shoot film. With the current level of digital camera and printing technology, it's safe to say that once you go digital, you won't go back to film!

Why Digital Cameras Are Better than Point-and-Shoot Film Cameras

It can be difficult to perform a straight comparison between digital and film, mostly because there are so many variables on the film side—How good is your camera? Your lens? Your processing? Your scanner? Not to mention the issue of how much skill you might have with all of these technologies. Certainly, if you compare a decent digital camera to a high-quality medium-format film camera outfitted with a $5,000 lens, the film camera will win out, particularly if you have professional processing and a $20,000 scanner with which to work. However, if this is not the type of film camera that you would normally shoot with, then this comparison is irrelevant.

These days, most people use a point-and-shoot 35mm or APS film camera. If this sounds like you, then you'll be happy to hear that a moderately priced ($300–$500) 3-megapixel digital camera is capable of producing much better images than a typical point-and-shoot film camera is. This claim usually shocks most people because they believe that film must be higher resolution than a digital camera and, therefore, must be inherently better.

What this assumption ignores is that fact that, just because a piece of film might have a tremendous amount of resolving power, the camera's lens might not be able to take advantage of it. The fact is, most—if not all—point-and-shoot film cameras have really bad lenses. They're good enough for simple snapshots, but they're far from able to take advantage of all of that "resolution" that a piece of film might have.

Mid-range (and even some low-end) digital cameras usually have lenses that are far superior to point-and-shoot film cameras. This is mostly because it's much cheaper to engineer and manufacture a high-quality lens for a digital camera than for a film camera. As you'll see in the next chapter, the image sensor in a typical digital camera is substantially smaller than a piece of 35mm or APS film (Figure 3.9)—usually measuring roughly 3/4″ diagonally. It is much easier to build a lens that can focus down to this small size than it is to build a lens that can focus to the larger film sizes. Because of this, digital cameras usually sport much higher-quality optics than point-and-shoot film cameras do.

Even if you normally shoot with a 35mm SLR, if you haven't been willing to invest in high-dollar lenses, then you might find that the optics on a better $500 point-and-shoot digital camera are much better than that $200 lens you bought with your SLR body. When building a lens, image quality gets harder to maintain as the lens length and diameter increases. In other words, building a high-quality 100mm lens for a film camera is much harder than building an equivalent lens for a digital camera, simply because of the size of the lens. Therefore, unless you're willing to spend a lot of money for high-end lenses, you'll probably get better optics on a mid-range digital camera.

Lens is not everything, of course. Light meters, image processing algorithms, and many other factors affect the quality of your image. We'll discuss all of these factors in the next few chapters.

NEXT STEPS

Now that you've seen what a digital camera can do, you're probably ready to start shooting. Although we won't get to any actual shooting for a while, the next few chapters will give you the groundwork and understanding that you need to get the most from your camera. Whether you have a camera already or are still shopping, Chapters 3 through 5 will help you understand just what's going on inside all of those silicon chips.

HOW A DIGITAL CAMERA WORKS

In This Chapter

- Something Old, Something New
- A Little Color Theory
- How a CCD Works
- Compression and Storage

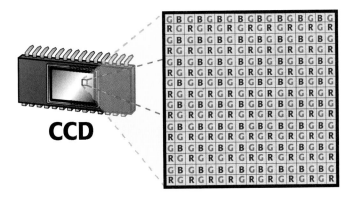

CCD

As we discussed in Chapter 1, "Introduction," the only real difference between a digital camera and a film camera is that a digital camera does not use film to record an image. However, this one fundamental difference affects all of the other systems on the camera, from the lens to the light meter. Consequently, just as the great film photographers have a deep understanding of the chemicals and emulsions that they use, it's important for digital photographers to learn just what exactly is going on inside a digital camera. Knowing how your camera works will help you select the right camera, and help you understand how to get better results when shooting.

Something Old, Something New

Just as a film camera, your digital camera records an image by using a lens to focus light onto a *focal plane*. In a film camera, light is focused by a lens through an *aperture* and a *shutter* onto a piece of film held on the focal plane. By opening or closing the aperture, and by changing the amount of time that the shutter is open, the photographer can control how the film is exposed. As we'll see later, exposure control allows the photographer to change the degree to which the camera "freezes" motion, how well the film records contrast and color saturation, and which parts of the image are in focus.

Your digital camera works the same way, but instead of a piece of film sitting on the focal plane, there is a special chip called a *charge-coupled device* (CCD) sitting on the focal plane. (As we'll see later, most digital cameras don't have an actual mechanical shutter.) When you take a picture with a digital camera, the CCD *samples* the light coming through the lens and converts that light into electrical signals. After the CCD is exposed, these signals are boosted by an amplifier and sent to an analog-to-digital converter that turns the signals into digits. These digits are then sent to an on-board computer for processing. Once the computer has calculated the final image, the new image data is stored on a memory card (Figure 3.1).

To thoroughly understand how a digital camera functions, though, you need to know a little color theory.

A Little Color Theory

In 1869, James Clerk Maxwell asked photographer Thomas Sutton (the inventor of the SLR camera) to take three black-and-white photographs

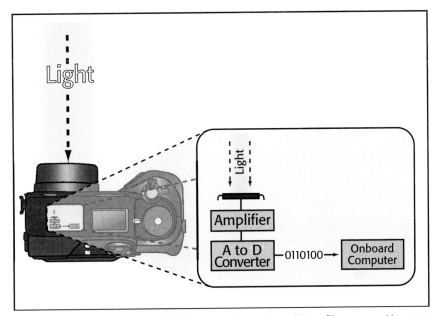

FIGURE 3.1   Light passes into a digital camera just as it would in a film camera. However, instead of hitting a piece of film, it is digitized by a computer chip and passed to an on-board computer to create an image.

of a tartan ribbon. Maxwell wanted to test a theory he had about a possible method for creating color photographs. He asked Sutton to place a different filter over the camera for each shot: first a red filter, then green, and then blue. After the film was developed, Maxwell projected all three black-and-white pictures onto a screen using three projectors fitted with the same filters that were used to shoot the photos. When the images were projected directly on top of each other, the images combined and Maxwell had the world's first color photo!

Needless to say, this was hardly a convenient process. Unfortunately, it took another 30 years to turn Maxwell's discovery into a commercially viable product. This happened in 1903 when the Lumiere brothers used red, green, and blue dyes to color grains of starch that could be applied to glass plates to create color images. They called their process "Autochrome" and it was the first successful color printing process.

In grammar school, you probably learned that you could mix primary colors together to create other colors. Painters have used this technique for centuries, of course, but what Maxwell demonstrated is that, while you can mix paints together to create darker colors, light mixes together to create lighter colors. Or, to use some jargon, paint mixes together in a *subtractive* process (as you mix, you subtract color to create black), while light mixes together in an *additive* process (as you mix, you add color to create white). Note that Maxwell did not discover light's additive properties (Newton had done similar experiments long before); he was just the first to apply the properties to photography.

Figure 3.2 shows a simple example of how the three additive primary colors of light can be combined to create other colors.

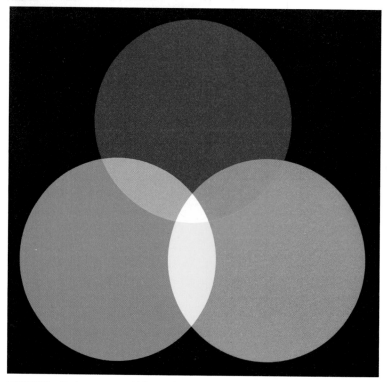

FIGURE 3.2   Red, green, and blue—the three additive primary colors of light—can be mixed together to create other colors. As you combine them, the resulting color is lighter, eventually becoming white.

Your digital camera creates a full-color photograph using pretty much the same process that Maxwell used in 1860: it shoots three different black-and-white images and combines them into a color image.

The image shown in Figure 3.3 is called an *RGB* image because it uses red, green, and blue *channels* to create a color image. As we'll see later, it's possible to perform sophisticated corrections and manipulations by editing the individual red, green, and blue *color channels* directly.

FIGURE 3.3 In a digital image, three separate red, green, and blue *channels* are combined to create a final, full-color picture.

 YOU SAY "BLACK AND WHITE," I SAY "GRAYSCALE"

Although film photographers use the term black and white *to denote an image that lacks color, in the digital world it's better to use the term* grayscale. *As we saw in Figure 1.1, your computer can create an image that is composed of only black and white pixels. Consequently, it's sometimes important to distinguish between an image that is made up of black and white pixels, and one that is made up of pixels of varying shades of gray.*

In the century-and-a-half since Maxwell's discovery, many other ways of representing color have been discovered. For example, another model called *L*A*B color* (also known as Lab color) uses one channel for lightness information, another channel for greenness or redness, and a third channel for blueness or yellowness. In addition, there is the Cyan, Magenta, Yellow, and Black (*CMYK*) model that printers use.

Each of these approaches is called a *color model* or *color space*, and each model has a particular *gamut,* or range, of colors that it can display. Some gamuts are more appropriate to certain tasks than others are, and all of these gamuts are smaller than the range of colors your eye can perceive.

We'll deal more with gamuts and color models in later chapters. For now, it's important to understand that digital photos are comprised of separate red, green, and blue channels that combine to create a color image.

How a CCD Works

George Smith and Willard Boyle were two engineers employed by Bell Labs. The story goes that one day in late October, the two men spent about an hour sketching out an idea for a new type of semiconductor that could be used for computer memory and for the creation of a solid-state, tubeless video camera. The year was 1969, and in that hour, the two men invented the CCD.

Roughly a year later, Bell Labs created a solid-state video camera using Smith and Boyle's new chip. Although their original intention was to build a simple camera that could be used in a video-telephone device, they soon built a camera that was good enough for broadcast television.

Since then, CCDs have been used in everything from cameras to fax machines. Because video cameras don't require a lot of resolution, the CCD worked great for creating video-quality images. For printing pictures, though, you need much higher resolution. Consequently, it wasn't until recently that CCDs could be manufactured with enough resolution to compete with photographic film.

Counting Electrons

Photographic film is covered with an emulsion of light-sensitive, silver-laden crystals. When light hits the film, the silver atoms clump together. The more light there is, the bigger the clumps. In this way, a piece of film records the different amounts of light that strike each part of its surface. Color film is composed of three separate layers, one sensitive to red, one to green, and one to blue.

The CCD in your digital camera is a silicon chip covered with a series of small electrodes called *photosites* (Figure 3.4). Arranged in a grid, there is one photosite for each pixel in an image. Consequently, the number of photosites determines the resolution of a CCD.

FIGURE 3.4   This Kodak CCD is typical of the image sensors found in most digital cameras.

Before you can shoot a picture, your camera charges the surface of the CCD with electrons. When light strikes the CCD, the electrons cluster together over the grid of photosites. The more light that strikes a particular photosite, the more electrons that will cluster there. After exposing the CCD to light, your camera simply has to measure the voltage at each site to determine how many electrons are there, and thus how much light hit that particular site. This measurement is then converted into a number by an analog-to-digital converter.

Most consumer cameras use an 8-bit analog-to-digital converter. That is, the electrical charge from each photosite is converted into an 8-bit number—or, a number between 0 and 255. Some higher-end cameras have 10- or 12-bit analog-to-digital converters, meaning that they can use values up to 1024 or 4096, respectively.

However, an analog-to-digital converter with a higher bit depth doesn't give your CCD a bigger dynamic range. The brightest and darkest colors that it can see remain the same, but the extra bit depth does mean that the camera will produce finer gradations *within* that dynamic range.

The term *charge-coupled device* (CCD) derives from the way the camera reads the charges of the individual photosites. After exposing the CCD, the charges on the first row of photosites are transferred to a *read-out register* where they are amplified and then sent to an analog-to-digital converter. Each row of charges is electrically coupled to the next row so that, after one row has been read and deleted, all of the other rows move down to fill the now empty space (Figure 3.5).

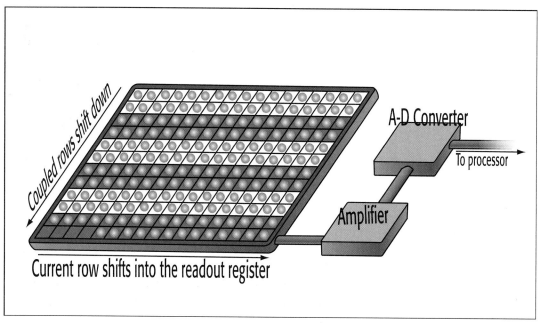

FIGURE 3.5   Rows of photosites on a CCD are coupled together. As the bottom row of photosites is read off of the bottom of the CCD, all of the rows above it shift down. This is the *coupled* in *charge-coupled device*.

After all of the rows of photosites have been read, the CCD is recharged with electrons and is ready to shoot another image.

Photosites are only sensitive to how much light they receive; they know nothing about color. As you've probably already guessed, to see color your camera needs to perform some type of RGB filtering similar to what James Maxwell did. There are a number of different ways to perform this filtering, but the most common is through a *single array* system, sometimes referred to as a *striped array*.

Arrays

Consider the images in Figure 3.6.

If asked to fill in any "missing" pixels in Figure 3.6A, you'd probably say "What are you talking about?" If asked to fill in any "missing" pixels

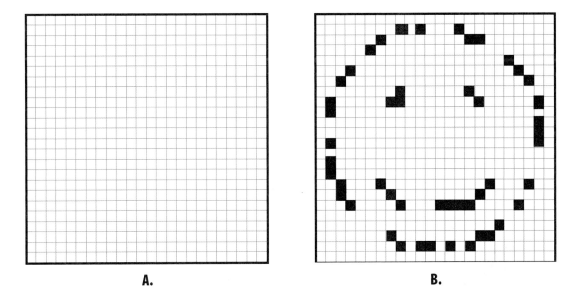

A.   **B.**

FIGURE 3.6   Although you have no idea what pixels belong in Figure 3.6A, you can probably hazard a guess as to what the missing pixels are in Figure 3.6B.

in Figure 3.6B, though, you probably would have no trouble creating the image in Figure 3.7.

You would know which pixels you needed to fill in based on the other pixels that were already in the image. In other words, you would

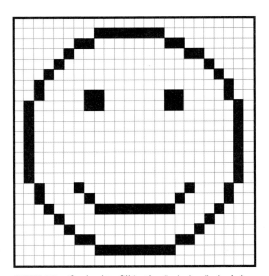

FIGURE 3.7   If asked to fill in the "missing" pixels in Figure 3.6B, you would probably come up with an image something like this.

have *interpolated* the new pixels based on the information that was already there. You might have encountered interpolation if you've ever resized a photograph using an image editing program such as Photoshop. To resize an image from 4" × 6" to 8" × 10", your image editor has to perform many calculations to determine what color all those new pixels should be.

The single array system in a typical digital camera uses a form of interpolation to create a color image. As we saw in the previous section, the CCD in your camera is able to create a grayscale image of your subject by measuring the amount of light that strikes each part of the CCD's sensor.

To shoot color, your camera performs the same type of RGB filtering that Maxwell used in 1869. Each photosite on your camera's CCD is covered by a filter—red, green, or blue. This combination of filters is called a *color filter array*, and most CCDs use a filter pattern like the one shown in Figure 3.8.

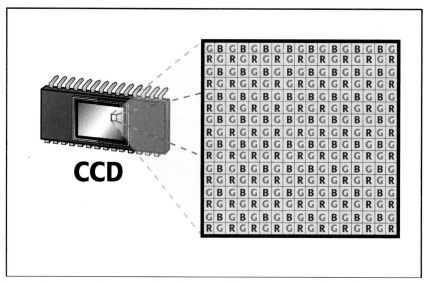

FIGURE 3.8 To see color, alternating pixels in a CCD are covered with a different colored filter. The *color filter array* shown here is called the *Bayer pattern*.

With these filters, your CCD can produce separate, incomplete red, green, and blue images. The images are incomplete because the red image, for example, is missing all of the pixels that were covered with a blue filter, while the blue filter is missing all of the pixels that were covered with a red filter. Both the red and blue images are missing the vast number of green-filtered pixels.

An incredibly sophisticated interpolation method is used to create a complete color image. Just as you used the partial pixel information in Figure 3.6b to calculate the missing pixels, your digital camera can calculate the color of any given pixel by analyzing all of the adjacent pixels. For example, if you look at a particular pixel and see that the pixel to the immediate left of it is a bright red pixel, the pixel to the right is a bright blue pixel, and the pixels above and below are bright green, then the pixel in question is probably white. Why? As Maxwell showed, if you mix red, green, and blue light together, you get white light. (By the way, if you're wondering why there are so many more green pixels than red or blue pixels, it's because the eye is most sensitive to green. Consequently, it's better to have as much green resolution as possible.)

Needless to say, this type of interpolation is incredibly complex. Figuring out a single bright white pixel is one thing, but calculating all of the subtle shadings required to make a photograph involves a lot of really complex algorithms. Differences in these algorithms are just one characteristic that separates the quality of different digital cameras.

This process of interpolating is called *demosaicing*, and different vendors employ different approaches. For example, while many vendors' cameras look at only immediately adjacent pixels, Hewlett-Packard cameras analyze a region up to 9×9 pixels. Fuji's SuperCCD eschews the grid pattern of square photosites in favor of octagonal photosites arranged in a honeycomb pattern. Such a scheme requires even more demosaicing to produce rectangular image pixels, but Fuji claims this yields higher resolution.

Other companies use the familiar rectangular design, but use a different color filter array. Canon, for example, often uses cyan, yellow, green, and magenta filters on the photosites of their CCD. Because it takes fewer layers of dye to create cyan, yellow, green, and magenta filters than it does to create red, green, and blue filters, more light gets through the CYGM filter to the CCD. (Cyan, yellow, and magenta are the primary colors of ink, and so don't need to be mixed to create the color filters.) More light means a better signal-to-noise ratio, which produces images with better *luminance* and less noise.

STILL MORE INTERPOLATION

In addition to the interpolation a camera performs to calculate color, some cameras perform still more interpolation to achieve a higher resolution. For example, the Fuji FinePix S602 has a 3.1-megapixel CCD, but can interpolate the image upward to produce a 6-megapixel image. We'll say more about this kind of interpolation in Chapter 5, "Choosing a Digital Camera."

CCDs are often very small, sometimes as small as 1/4 or 1/2 inch (6 or 12mm, respectively). By comparison, a single frame of 35mm film is 36 × 23.3mm (Figure 3.9). The fact that CCDs can be so small is the main reason why digital cameras can be so tiny.

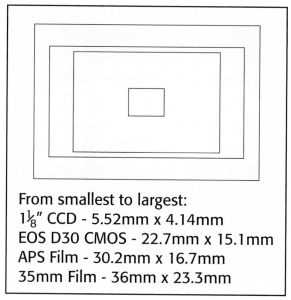

From smallest to largest:
1⅛" CCD - 5.52mm x 4.14mm
EOS D30 CMOS - 22.7mm x 15.1mm
APS Film - 30.2mm x 16.7mm
35mm Film - 36mm x 23.3mm

FIGURE 3.9   Most CCDs are very small, particularly when compared to the size of 35mm film.

The only downside to this CCD scheme is that it doesn't work right all the time. For example, if too much light hits a particular photosite, it can spill over into adjacent photosites. If the camera's software isn't smart enough to recognize that this has happened, you will see a *blooming* artifact—smearing colors or flared highlights—in your final image. Blooming is more prevalent in a physically smaller CCD and in higher-resolution CCDs because the photosites are packed tighter together.

As you might expect, interpolating the color in a camera with millions of pixels on its CCD requires a lot of processing power. Such power (and the memory needed to support it) is one reason that digital cameras have stayed so pricey. A lot of fancy chips are necessary to make a digital camera.

EXTRA PIXELS

Not all of the photosites in your CCD are used for recording your image. Some are used to assess the black levels in your image, while others are used for determining white balance. Finally, some pixels are masked away altogether. For example, if the CCD has a square array of pixels, but your camera manufacturer wants to create a camera that shoots rectangular images, they will mask out some of the pixels on the edge of the CCD.

"One CCD, Hold the Interpolation"

The system described previously, which is used in most digital cameras manufactured today, is called a *single array system* because it uses a single CCD to image all three color channels. Although this scheme is the most prevalent, there are other ways of getting a CCD to see color. Many high-end, medium-format digital cameras use a *three-shot* array that takes three separate exposures, one for each color. These three shots are then combined into a full-color, RGB image.

Because they use no demosaicing, three-shot arrays are free from some of the artifacts of a single array system. Unfortunately, taking three pictures in succession can take a few seconds, so your subject has to be stationary and your light has to be constant. Consequently, these cameras are only useful for shooting inanimate objects in a studio situation.

A *linear array* system consists of a single row of sensors that make three separate filtered passes over the imaging area. Because there's only one row of sensors used, manufacturers can pack a lot of resolution into the sensor without greatly increasing the price. Obviously, as with a three-shot array, the linear array is only good for studio work. Like the three-shot array, however, no interpolation is used.

Trilinear arrays are a simple variant on the linear array, consisting of three linear arrays stacked on top of one another. With each array filtered separately, the camera only has to make one pass over the image area. However, because of the single pass, some manufacturers have actually been able to create trilinear systems that are fast enough for shooting moving objects.

Finally, some cameras use *multiple arrays*, a collection of three separate CCDs (Figure 3.10). As the light enters the camera, it is passed through a prism that splits the light into three copies. Each copy is sent to a separate CCD that is filtered for a different color. Multiple array cameras have all the flexibility of a single array system, but with none of the interpolation troubles. Unfortunately, because they have three times the number of CCDs as a single array camera, they often cost three times the price.

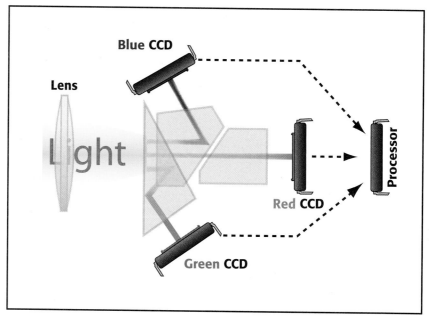

FIGURE 3.10   In a *multiple array system,* separate CCDs are used to record separate red, green, and blue channels. This system eliminates the interpolation required by single array systems.

Unless you're planning on spending tens of thousands of dollars, you'll be looking at single array cameras.

Some Assembly Required

The preceding description might sound complicated. In reality, though, the process that a CCD employs to capture an image is even more complex.

First, the light coming through the lens is passed through several filters, including an infrared filter (some cameras use a very slight infrared filter, making them ideal for infrared photography as we'll see in Chapter 7, "Shooting") and a low pass filter, both of which help ensure better color and fewer artifacts. After being processed and interpolated by the CCD, the image data (which is now in full color) is passed to an on-board computer that makes a number of adjustments. For example, the image is adjusted according to your camera's *white balance* and *exposure compensation* settings (we'll discuss these in more detail later).

Next, the camera might perform adjustments to the image's contrast and brightness. Most cameras now provide user-controlled settings for how much brightness and contrast adjustment to perform.

Finally, many cameras perform some type of noise reduction algorithm to reduce unwanted noise in your image, and almost all cameras perform some type of *sharpening*. All of this processing takes place inside your camera, and is one reason why it can take a while for a digital camera to store an image.

 RAW IMAGES

Some digital cameras, ranging from the prosumer Canon G1 to the high-end Nikon D1, let you download raw, unprocessed data from the camera. This is the information that comes right off the CCD. Through special software, you can specify how the raw data should be processed, with full control of white balance, sharpening, and contrast. This is a great feature for the user who demands a high degree of control. In addition, because raw images are not compressed, your images won't suffer from the compression artifacts sometimes found in JPEG images.

CMOS

CCDs are not the only type of image sensor available. A few vendors are beginning to work with Complimentary Metal Oxide Semiconductors (CMOS) sensors. Because these chips can be manufactured in the same way as most other computer chips, they are much cheaper than the difficult-to-make CCDs found in most cameras. CMOS chips also consume much less power than a typical CCD does, making for longer camera battery life and fewer heat problems. CMOS also offers the promise of integrating more functions onto one chip, thereby enabling manufacturers to reduce the number of chips in their cameras. For example, image capture and processing could both be performed on one CMOS chip, further reducing the price of a camera.

Although CMOS used to have a reputation for producing rough images with inferior color, Canon's excellent EOS D30 and EOS D60 SLRs—both CMOS-based—have shown that CMOS can be a viable alternative to CCDs.

COMPRESSION AND STORAGE

After your image has been processed, it's ready to be stored on whatever storage medium is provided by your camera. There are currently a number of competing storage options, and we'll discuss these in detail in Chapter 5. All of these options have one thing in common: they're finite. Consequently, you'll want to make the most use of your camera's on-board storage, and the best way to do that is to tell the camera to compress its images before storing them.

To do this, most cameras use a form of compression called *JPEG*. Created by the *Joint Photographic Experts Group*, JPEG is a powerful algorithm that can greatly reduce the size of a photo, but at the cost of image quality. Consequently, JPEG is referred to as a *lossy* compression format.

Most cameras offer two forms of JPEG compression: a low-quality option that visibly degrades an image but offers compression ratios of 10 or 20:1, and a high-quality option that performs a good amount of compression—usually around 4:1—but without severely degrading your image. In most cases, you'll probably find that any artifacts introduced by higher-quality JPEG compression are obscured by your printing process. For those of you who are very particular, many cameras offer a completely uncompressed mode that stores your images as very large TIFF files.

JPEG compression works by exploiting the fact that human vision is more sensitive to changes in brightness than to changes in color. To JPEG-compress an image, your camera first converts the image into a color space where each pixel is expressed using a *chrominance* value and a *luminance* value.

Next, the chrominance values are analyzed in blocks of 8 × 8 pixels. The color in each 64-pixel area is averaged so that any slight (and hopefully imperceptible) change in color is removed, a process known as *quantization*. Note that because the averaging is only being performed on the chrominance channel, all of the luminance information in the image—the information your eye is most sensitive to—is preserved.

After quantization, a non-lossy compression algorithm is applied to the entire image. In the *very* simplest terms, a non-lossy compression scheme works something like this: Rather than encoding AAAAAABBBBBCCC, you simply encode 6A5B3C. After quantization, the chrominance information in your image will be more uniform, so there will be larger chunks of similar data, meaning that this final compression step will be more effective.

What does all this mean to your image? Figure 3.11 shows an image that has been over-compressed. As you can see, areas of flat color or smooth gradations turn into rectangular chunks, while contrast in areas of high detail gets boosted too high. Fortunately, most digital cameras offer much better compression quality than what you see here.

FIGURE 3.11   This image has been compressed far too much, as can be seen from the nasty JPEG artifacting.

MEANWHILE, BACK IN THE REAL WORLD

If the information in this chapter seems unnecessary, it's probably because when you buy a film camera you don't have to worry about imaging technology—it's included in the film you use. However, if you're serious about photography, you probably do spend some time considering the merits of different films. And, just as you need a little knowledge of film chemistry to assess the quality of a particular film stock, the topics covered in this chapter will help you better test a particular camera.

Your camera is more than just a CCD, of course, so in Chapter 5, you'll learn about the other components and concerns that you'll need to weigh when choosing a camera.

BASIC PHOTOGRAPHY: A QUICK PRIMER

In This Chapter

- Lenses

- Exposure: Apertures, Shutter Speeds, and ISO

f you worked through the technical details of the last chapter, you saw how radically different a CCD is from a piece of film. So, why do we keep saying that there's little difference between a digital camera and a film camera? Because no matter what type of camera you use, the physics of light always work the same way. Consequently, all of the mechanisms that a camera uses to measure and control light work the same way, whether you're shooting digital or film.

In this chapter, therefore, we're going to take a quick trip through the basics of optics, apertures, and exposures. Simply put: To understand most of what follows, you need an understanding of a few photographic principles. If you don't know an *f-stop* from a hole in the ground, you'll want to spend a little time with this chapter. Those of you with more experience will probably be able to skip ahead to Chapter 5, "Choosing a Digital Camera."

In its most basic form, a camera is really a simple apparatus. A lens focuses the light from an image onto a focal plane where it is recorded by a piece of film or a CCD. An aperture and shutter placed between the lens and the focal plane allow the photographer to control how much light reaches the focal plane and how long the focal plane will be exposed to that light.

An understanding of lenses, apertures, and shutters is not necessary to take simple snapshots using a modern, fully automatic camera. However, if you want more creative control over your image, knowing how these systems work together is essential.

LENSES

If the name Willebrord Snell doesn't sound familiar, don't worry; most people aren't too familiar with Snell. Nevertheless, he got things started for digital cameras in 1621, when he performed the first experiments with *refraction*.

Light travels through space in straight lines. However, when it passes through a transparent object such as water or glass, it gets slowed down and bends, a process called *refraction*. How much the light bends is measured by the *refractive index* of the transparent substance. Air has a refractive index of 1, water 1.3, and most glass 1.5. In other words, glass bends light more than water does.

A lens is simply a piece of transparent material (usually glass or plastic) shaped to bend light in a particular way. A convex lens focuses light inward, while a concave lens spreads light rays apart (Figure 4.1).

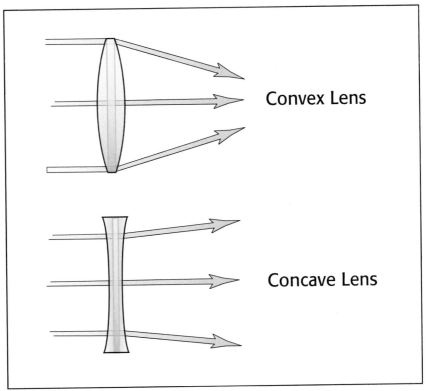

FIGURE 4.1   As you might remember from science class, *convex* lenses bend light inward, while *concave* lenses bend light outward.

Unfortunately, making a perfect piece of glass or plastic for a lens is impossible. Consequently, the surface of a lens might have defects and irregularities that can result in a number of different types of problems, or *artifacts*, in the resulting image. Further complicating lens-building matters is the fact that not all frequencies (colors) of light bend the same amount as they pass through a lens. For example, a lens might bend red light more than yellow light, resulting in color aberrations (or *chromatic aberrations*) in your final image.

A camera lens is actually an array of concave and convex lenses, called *elements*, that are engineered to produce a specific magnification (Figure 4.2). Lens designers continuously add elements to correct for aberrations in other elements until they eliminate as many problems as they can. Some elements are cemented together to form *groups*. Although you might think that more elements and groups are inherently better because they will remove more aberrations, be aware that each new element increases the chance of reflections within the lens. These reflections will make the lens more likely to create *lens flares* in your final image (see Figure 5.24).

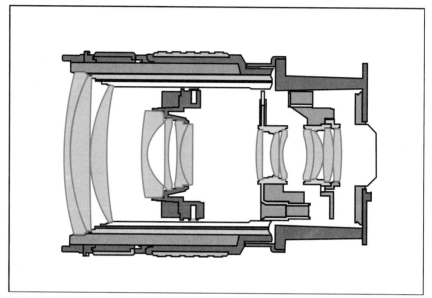

FIGURE 4.2   If you look at a cross-section of a camera lens, you will see that it is not a "lens" at all, but a complex series of multiple lenses.

In the next chapter, you'll learn how to test and examine a lens to determine its quality and how to recognize different types of aberrations.

Focal Length

Focal length is a measurement of the magnifying power of a lens. Technically, focal length is the distance (usually measured in millimeters) between the lens and the focal plane, the area upon which the lens is focusing. The longer the focal length, the more magnification a lens will provide. However, as magnification increases, *field of view* decreases (Figure 4.3).

If you've ever used a 35mm SLR camera, then you're probably familiar with a 50mm lens, a lens that provides a level of magnification, and a field of view that is roughly equivalent to the human eye (50–55°). A lens with a smaller focal length, 28mm for example, produces a *wide-angle* image, while "long" lenses—say, 200mm—are considered *telephoto* lenses.

FIGURE 4.3   As focal length increases, field of view decreases. Therefore, a long lens has a very narrow field of view.

That is, they provide a lot of magnification and a very narrow field of view.

Zooms and Primes

Prime lenses are lenses with fixed focal lengths. *Zoom lenses,* as you might already know, are lenses whose focal length can be varied. When you "zoom in" on a subject, you are increasing the focal length of the lens. A typical point-and-shoot 35mm camera will have a zoom lens with a range of around 35 to 110mm (Figure 4.4).

Until eight or nine years ago, it was pretty safe to say that prime lenses were always higher quality than zoom lenses. Today, advances in design and manufacturing techniques have so improved the quality of zoom lenses that they are almost indistinguishable from prime lenses.

FIGURE 4.4   Same image shot with a 35mm and 110mm lens.

However, if you're shopping around at the high end of the lens market, you will see a difference in quality between zooms and primes. In general, quality prime lenses offer better sharpness, while zoom lenses offer greater flexibility.

EXPOSURE: APERTURES, SHUTTER SPEEDS, AND ISO

As we saw in the last chapter, a CCD—like a piece of film—is sensitive to light. Although not as sophisticated as the human eye, it still takes only a fraction of a second for the CCD to get all of the light that it needs to create an image. By changing the amount of light that falls onto the CCD, you can control a number of characteristics of your final image.

For example, Figure 4.5 shows four different images of the same subject. Each image was shot using a different exposure on a Nikon Coolpix 990. The first image (A) is a straight snapshot with everything in the image—both foreground and background—in focus. In the second image (B), we used a different aperture to cause the background to be rendered out of focus, bringing the viewer's attention to the foreground. In the third image (C), we chose an exposure that enabled us to blur the motion in our subject's hand. Finally, in the fourth image (D), we chose an exposure that would allow us to use a little post-processing to increase the contrast and color saturation in the image. Later, you'll see which exposure controls on your camera produce these different effects.

As with a film camera, if you subject a CCD to too much light, your image will be overexposed. If you overexpose an image enough, it will turn completely white. Conversely, if you don't expose the image to

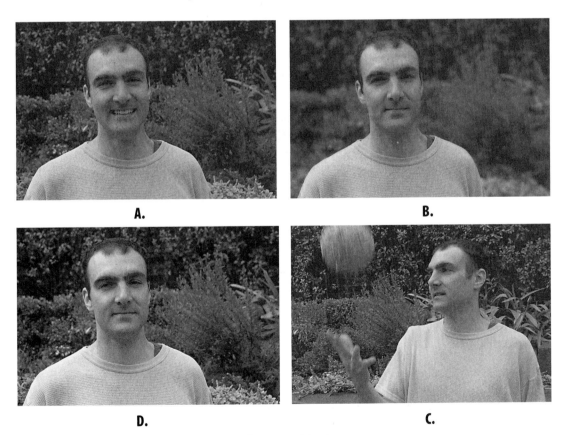

FIGURE 4.5   Same subject, different exposure, different resulting images.

enough light, your image will be underexposed. If you underexpose an image too far, you will have an image that is completely black. Finding the right exposure is a complex process involving light meters and a lot of theory. We'll discuss exposure in more detail in Chapter 7, "Shooting," and Chapter 8, "Manual Exposure."

Your camera has two controls that enable you to change the amount of light that strikes the camera's CCD. You can change the size of the aperture in your camera's lens, and you can control the length of time that the camera's shutter stays open.

The aperture in your camera is usually an *iris* composed of thin, sliding, interlocking metal plates. As you close the iris down to a smaller aperture, it stops more light from passing through to the CCD. The size of the aperture is measured in *stops* or *f-stops*. The higher the f-stop rating, the more light your aperture is stopping. For example, a lens set on f8 has a smaller aperture than a lens set on f4 (Figure 4.6).

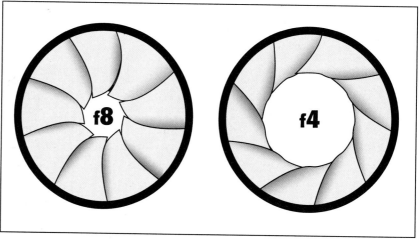

FIGURE 4.6   The iris on the left is stopping more light than the iris on the right; consequently, it has a higher f-stop value.

 F-STOP DEFINED

In case you're wondering where those f-numbers come from, f-stop values are simply the ratio of the focal length of the lens to the diameter of the opening in the aperture.

Your second tool for controlling exposure is shutter speed. Shutter speeds are simply measurements of how long a shutter is open.

Shutter speeds can vary from as fast as 1/16,000th of a second to several seconds or minutes. Obviously, a longer shutter speed exposes your camera's CCD to more light, so a shutter speed of 1/30th of a second allows more light to reach the CCD than an exposure of 1/1000th of a second does.

Reciprocity

Modern digital and film cameras offer a vast selection of aperture and shutter speed settings. For the sake of example, let's assume for a minute that you're using a more "conventional," all-manual film camera. Traditionally, each aperture setting on a lens stopped twice as much light as the previous setting. Therefore, a lens typically had a range of f-stop settings that went something like f2, f2.8, f4, f5.6, f8, f11, f16. (The presence of fractional numbers has to do with the fact that apertures are circular, and halving the area of a circle involves some fractional numbers.)

Like apertures, shutter speeds typically double with each setting. Therefore, a list of possible shutter speeds on a camera will often progress as follows: 1/500th, 1/250th, 1/125th, 1/60th, 1/30th, 1/15th, 1/8th, 1/4th, 1/2, 1, 2, 4, 8, and so on (all times are in seconds).

Because aperture size and shutter speed always increases by 2, it's easy to calculate different, equivalent exposures. For example, let's say you are shooting a picture of a very fast-moving race car, and your light meter has told you that the "correct" exposure for the image is f16 at 1/60th of a second. (That is, your light meter says you should set your aperture to f16 and your shutter speed to 1/60th.) However, because your subject is moving so fast, you have decided that you want to use a higher shutter speed to guarantee that your subject won't be blurry.

If you increase your shutter speed to the next setting—1/125th—the shutter will only be open for half as long and the amount of light hitting the CCD will be cut in half. If your light meter was correct, then your new setting will result in an image that is underexposed. To correct this, you simply open your aperture from f16 to f8. Your aperture is now twice as wide, which lets in twice as much light, and compensates for the fact that the shutter is only open half as long. This relationship between apertures and shutter speeds is called *reciprocity* because of the reciprocal relationship between the two values.

Reciprocity is a very powerful function because it means that many different shutter speed/aperture combinations all yield the same exposure. In Chapter 7, you'll see how different shutter speeds or apertures affect your final image. Because of reciprocity, you can select the settings that are appropriate for your creative goals.

Digital cameras and many new film cameras expand on this traditional approach by allowing aperture settings that progress in one-half or one-third of a stop. Moreover, with the electronic, computer-controlled shutters on modern cameras, you can have odd shutter speeds; for example, 1/252nd. We'll cover the uses and implications of these new settings in Chapter 7.

Lens Speed

Another way to understand a lens is to think of it as a device for gathering light onto the camera's focal plane. Depending on its quality, one lens might take longer to gather the same amount of light as another lens. Simply put, it's going to take more time for the same amount of light to shine through a lens made of murky glass than it will to shine through very clear glass.

The speed of a lens is measured in terms of its widest aperture. Therefore, a lens that can be opened to f2 is a faster lens than a lens that can only be opened to f4. A lens that can be opened to f2 has better glass and more refined engineering than a lens that can be opened to f4, and is therefore capable of gathering more light in the same amount of time as an f4 lens. Faster lenses enable you to shoot in less light and provide a greater range of apertures, and therefore more creative freedom. A faster lens is also more difficult to build and, therefore, more expensive.

Zoom lenses usually have different speeds at different focal lengths. That is, at full telephoto, your lens might have a maximum aperture of f5.6 while at full wide, it might have a faster aperture of f4. Engineering a lens in this way allows lens designers to reduce the size of the front element of the lens, making for a physically lighter, smaller lens.

ISO, Or "Try to Be More Sensitive"

Different types of films have different sensitivities to light as measured by their *ISO* rating (ASA is another measure of film speed, but most photographers now use the more common ISO system). The higher the ISO rating, the more sensitive the film is to light. Because it is more sensitive, a film with a higher ISO rating doesn't need as long an exposure to make an image. Consequently, films with high ISO ratings are often referred to as "faster" films. Because faster films need less light to make an image, they facilitate shooting in low-light situations, and offer the ability to shoot in bright daylight with faster shutter speeds and smaller apertures.

The downside to a faster film is that it produces images with far more grain. Although grain can be stylish and attractive, it can also be problematic if you want to enlarge your image, or blow up just a part of it.

The sensitivity of CCDs is also measured and rated using the ISO system. As with film, a CCD with a higher ISO rating produces images with more noise. Because the ISO rating on your digital camera can be changed on a shot-by-shot basis (unlike film, where ISO is fixed for the whole roll), ISO is a third factor that you can control when choosing an exposure.

CONFUSED BY "SPEED"

The word speed comes up a lot when speaking of photography, but it can be used to describe three different things: how quickly the shutter opens and closes, the maximum aperture of a lens, and how sensitive a piece of film or image sensor is. As you become more comfortable with these concepts, you should have no trouble determining which meaning is being used at any given time.

MOSTLY THE SAME

For the most part, all of the terms and topics we discussed here apply directly to digital cameras. However, because of differences between film and CCDs and because of features made possible by new digital technology, some of the systems and functions we discussed in this chapter work a little differently in the digital world.

In the next chapter, you will build on the basics you learned here by taking a look at the features and capabilities of the modern digital camera. In the process, you will learn how to choose the camera that's right for your needs. In Chapters 7 and 8, you'll learn more about using your camera's exposure controls.

CHOOSING A DIGITAL CAMERA

In This Chapter

- Basic Anatomy
- CCDs, Resolution, Image Size, and Compression
- Cameras
- Lenses
- Viewfinders
- Exposure Control
- Shooting Modes
- Camera Performance
- Flash
- Playback Options
- Storage and Input/Output
- What's in the Box?
- Special Features
- Compare for Yourself

A good camera doesn't guarantee that you'll take good pictures, but it certainly does help. However, buying a digital camera is a bit more complex than buying a film camera because, in addition to all of the usual camera concerns such as optics, features, durability, and comfort, you also have to worry about the camera's imaging quality. With a film camera, that's left up to the film. In this chapter, you'll learn about all the little details that must be considered when you are choosing and buying a digital camera.

Over the last few years, digital camera manufacturers have been migrating their higher-end technology down to their lower-priced cameras, meaning that you can get a much more feature-rich camera for far less money today than you could when the first edition of this book was published.

Digital cameras currently run the gamut from inexpensive ($100) low-resolution cameras, to very expensive ($45,000) digital backs for medium and large-format cameras. Most of the technical details discussed here apply to the entire camera spectrum. For our purposes, however, we will be focusing our discussion on the $200 to $5,000 range. In this market, you can find any number of cameras that produce excellent images—and image quality should always be your primary concern when selecting a camera. Choosing the camera that's right for you involves balancing the features you want with your particular image aesthetic.

BASIC ANATOMY

Just as all film cameras have certain things in common—shutter button, film advance, aperture controls—digital cameras all share some basic external anatomy. Although there are variations in implementation, the anatomical characteristics shown in Figure 5.1 are typical of most of the digital cameras you'll see, no matter what their cost or body design.

In the rest of this chapter, we will discuss all of the issues and features that you need to consider when shopping for a digital camera, in addition to providing tips and guidelines for evaluating each feature. To begin, we'll look at the very guts of the camera, and weigh the merits of different image sensors.

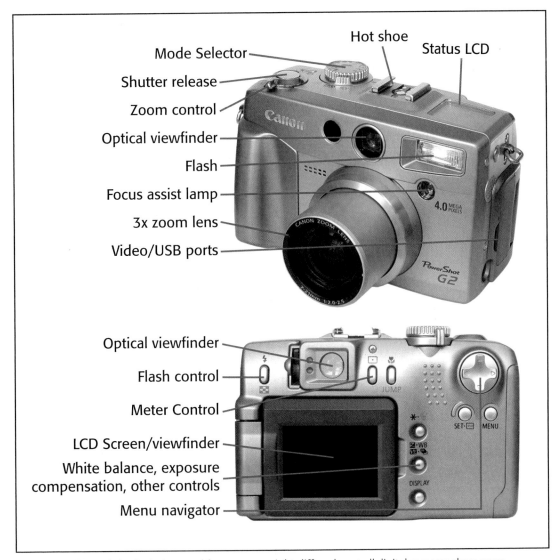

FIGURE 5.1   Although body designs and feature sets might differ, almost all digital cameras share some variation of the feature set shown here.

CCDs, Resolution, Image Size, and Compression

There are many digital cameras out there, but you can quickly winnow the field by determining how much resolution you need for the type of output you'll be creating (desktop printer, Web, commercial press, etc.). In general, cameras fall into groupings based on the resolution of their *CCD*. Therefore, you'll typically find cameras categorized as sub-megapixel, 2-megapixel, 3-, 4-, or even 5-megapixel (at the time of this writing, a few vendors still make 1-megapixel cameras). Each category denotes a CCD resolution—the higher the pixel count, the greater the resolution.

Obviously, more pixels mean more resolution, which means more detail, which should mean a better picture. However, it doesn't always work this way. The *quality* of the pixels being captured is every bit as important as the *number* of pixels being captured, so resolution alone is not a measure of a camera's quality. Consequently, it's important not to get caught up in the "resolution wars" that many vendors wage with each other. As you'll see, more resolution is not necessarily better.

Resolution can be a tricky number because most vendors will make their resolution claims based on the total number of pixels on the camera's CCD when, in fact, the camera doesn't use all of those pixels! For example, Nikon claims that their Coolpix 990 delivers a resolution of 3.34 megapixels. The CCD in the camera *does* contain 3.34 million pixels, but the maximum image resolution that the 990 can actually deliver is 2048 × 1536 pixels, or 3.1 megapixels (Figure 5.2). Where did the other 240,000 pixels go? Some are masked away to deliver the image proportions that Nikon wanted, while others are needed by the camera for internal functions such as determining black levels. Therefore, if you're a resolution stickler, be sure to check the number of pixels being used, or the *effective pixel count*.

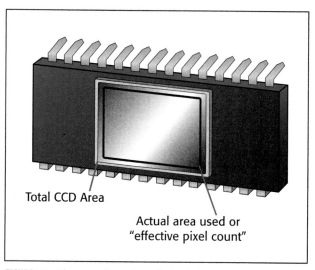

FIGURE 5.2   The actual number of pixels that a CCD uses is often smaller than the total number of pixels it provides.

Resolution Categories

As mentioned earlier, CCDs can be very small—as small as 1/4". Should you be concerned about the physical size of the CCD if it packs the resolution you want? In many cases, yes, because it is ideally better to have a physically larger CCD. Building a lens that can focus onto a very small area can be difficult, so lens quality becomes *more* important when the CCD is very small.

As explained in Chapter 3, "How a Digital Camera Works" the surface of a CCD is divided into a grid of pixels. On a larger CCD, each pixel is physically larger than those of a smaller CCD. Larger pixels are capable of collecting more light, which means they are usually more color-accurate than smaller pixels are. In addition, on a smaller CCD, where the pixels are packed closer together, there's a greater chance of electron spillage and blooming (see Chapter 3), which can appear as weird color artifacts in your images. Finally, larger pixels result in a better signal-to-noise ratio, resulting in clearer images.

These are just some of the reasons that raw pixel count is not necessarily a measure of a camera's imaging quality. The Nikon D1, for example, has a CCD that is roughly eight times the size of the CCD found in a Nikon Coolpix 995. Although the D1's sensor has a lower resolution than the 995 does, the D1's pixels are 2.5 times the size of those found on the 995's CCD. This results in a CCD with higher sensitivity, and a much better signal-to-noise ratio than the small CCDs you'll find in less expensive cameras.

Unfortunately, CCDs are very difficult to make, so it's more cost effective for a manufacturer to create physically smaller chips. The Nikon D1's large (23.7 × 15.6mm) CCD is one of the reasons that the D1 body sells for $5,000. If you're in the sub-$1,000 price range, then you're probably not going to have many options when it comes to CCD size.

Here's what you can expect from each resolution class.

Sub-Megapixel Cameras

For as little as $100, you can find a digital camera that offers a resolution somewhere between 640 × 480 pixels and 800 × 600 pixels. These cameras can provide enough resolution for the Web, video, or computer display, but it's important to realize that they don't provide enough resolution for quality print work. In addition, their inferior optics and image processing often yield poor results.

Single-Megapixel Cameras

At the time of this writing only a few manufacturers still sell single-megapixel cameras. However, these cameras are very inexpensive—usually less than $150. Single-megapixel cameras typically offer resolutions around 1280 × 960 pixels—enough resolution to print a decent quality 4 × 6" print on a desktop inkjet printer. However, if you want to enlarge the print, or enlarge an area of it, you might find that a single megapixel doesn't provide enough information. Many single-megapixel cameras, such as the Canon PowerShot A100, provide a good assortment of features such as *exposure compensation* and adjustable ISOs (Figure 5.3).

FIGURE 5.3   Single-megapixel cameras typically follow the design and features of 35mm point-and-shoot cameras.

These cameras are the entry point for the digital photographer who wants to shoot images for printing, but doesn't want to spend too much money.

2-Megapixel Cameras

With resolutions around 1600 × 1200 pixels, the typical 2-megapixel camera (Figure 5.4) can output a high quality 4" × 6" print on a desktop printer, and can do an okay job printing up to 8" × 10". If you have commercial printing needs—such as advertisements or brochures—you can often get away with a high-quality 2-megapixel camera for print sizes up to 6" × 8".

FIGURE 5.4   Digital cameras, like these 2-megapixel models, come in a variety of designs ranging from simple point-and-shoots to unique LCD-only designs to more full-featured cameras with manual controls and through-the-lens (TTL) viewfinders.

3-Megapixel Cameras

For those of you who can't wait to print out big 8" × 10" digital glossies on your desktop printer, you'll want at least a 3-megapixel model (Figure 5.5). Offering resolutions around 2048 × 1536 pixels, these cameras can provide quality suitable for most commercial printing needs.

FIGURE 5.5   In the 3-megapixel category, you can choose from point-and-shoot, or higher-end prosumer cameras like this Olympus C3040.

Be warned, however; starting with 2- and 3-megapixel resolution, you will likely run into the dreaded "purple fringe" problem. This mysterious artifact (shown in Figure 8.30) occurs when you shoot high contrast areas (usually images shot into bright light, such as skies) using a wide-angle lens. Most often, purple fringing occurs in landscape shots, as these types of images usually contain a broad contrast range and are typically shot with the lens at a wide angle.

Purple fringing is caused by one pixel on a CCD "filling up" with too much light and overflowing into the surrounding pixels. This effect, called *blooming*, is much more prevalent on cameras with smaller CCDs, where the pixels are smaller and packed closely together. Purple fringing is often referred to as *chromatic aberration*. However, true chromatic aberration, which is caused by the inability of the lens to equally focus all wavelengths of light, typically shows up as red or green fringing. Some cameras are better able to handle blooming, thanks to more sophisticated on-board image processing.

Although the problem only occurs occasionally (and can be easily avoided as we'll see in Chapter 8, "Manual Exposure"), purple fringing can be annoying and can corrupt otherwise okay images. The easiest way to test a camera for purple fringing is to shoot at wide angles into a back-lit situation such as a window, or through some trees. You probably won't be able to see the fringing on the camera's LCD, so you'll need to take the images home and examine them in your photo editing software.

4 and 5 Megapixels

At the time of this writing, it's possible to buy consumer digital cameras with resolutions up to a whopping *six* megapixels! While six megapixels is still somewhat rare, four and five megapixels are becoming the norm for the high end of the consumer market. With four or five megapixels, you can easily get a high-quality 8" × 10" image from a typical desktop photo-printer and can push to higher print sizes without significant loss of quality. Even if you don't want to print that large, the extra resolution can be very useful if you want to enlarge *part* of an image to a printable size (Figure 5.6).

You can also get better detail with 4- and 5-megapixel cameras (assuming the lens on the camera is good enough to resolve fine detail). On the downside, 4 and 5-megapixel cameras typically use the same CCD sizes as 2 and 3-megapixel cameras do, which means that their pixels are very small. As discussed previously, smaller pixel sizes can lead to certain problems, so it's important to look for specific types of artifacts when evaluating 4- and 5-megapixel cameras. We'll discuss these concerns in more detail later in this chapter.

FIGURE 5.6   4- and 5-megapixel cameras such as the Olympus Camedia D40 and the Minolta Dimage 7 can yield very large printed images. The extra resolution also lets you blow up parts of an image.

 HOW MUCH BIGGER IS THAT EXTRA MEGAPIXEL?

If you're considering spending the extra money for a camera with higher resolution, it's worth doing a little math. A 50% increase in the number of pixels in a camera adds only 22.5% more print area. This is the difference between an 8" × 10" print and a 10" × 12" print. Therefore, the extra resolution won't give you substantially bigger prints. However, if your camera and optics are good enough, it can give you better detail (Figure 5.7).

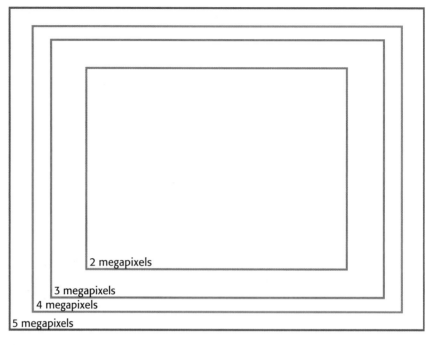

■ 1600 x 1200 (2.1 megapixels)
■ 2048 x 1536 (3.14 megapixels)
■ 2272 x 1704 (3.8 megapixels)
■ 2560 x 1920 (4.92 megapixels)

FIGURE 5.7   Before you decide that you need a particular resolution, it's important to realize that the difference between one resolution and another is not always as large as it might seem. You might find that you don't need to spend the extra money on extra pixels.

BLOWING UP YOUR IMAGES

With modern imaging software, you don't have to settle for the resolution provided by your camera. Through interpolation (also called *resampling*), you can use your image editing software to enlarge your pictures. Therefore, when we say that a typical 3-megapixel camera can print an 8" × 10" picture, we mean that it can do so without any post-processing. You can, of course, print much larger than this by blowing up your images.

However, you can only enlarge a picture so far before you begin to see interpolation artifacts (Figure 5.8). Obviously, the more resolution you have to start with, the better the results. Therefore, if you want to be able to print your images bigger than 8" × 10", you should definitely go with a 3-megapixel (or better) camera.

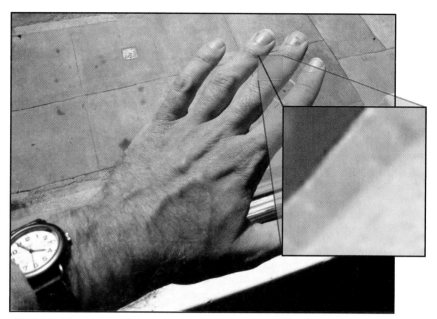

FIGURE 5.8   If you interpolate an image up too far, you will begin to see stair-stepping artifacts, posterization of tones, and loss of detail and sharpness.

6 Megapixels and Up

At 6-megapixel resolution, you find yourself in the digital *single lens reflex* (SLR) category (Figure 5.9). These are digital cameras based on traditional SLR film camera bodies. In addition to supporting interchangeable lenses, and more sophisticated light meters and controls, these cameras provide the feel and durability that professional photographers (and serious amateurs) are used to. In addition, they provide superior image quality, usually providing better color rendition with substantially less noise than lower-priced cameras.

If you have the cash, you don't have to settle for a mere 6-million pixels. With super-high resolutions of 8 or 10 megapixels, digital camera backs offer digital alternatives to photographers who already have a medium- or large-format camera body. These options are typically very expensive ($10,000 to $25,000), and most photographers rent rather than buy such hardware.

BUY SOME MEDIA BEFORE SHOPPING

Because a camera's LCD screen is too small to accurately judge a camera's performance, consider buying your own media card. You can then take the card to your local camera store, use it in a few different cameras, and then examine the results at home. When you finally buy a camera, you can always re-use the card.

FIGURE 5.9 Digital SLRs such as this Canon EOS D60 provide the ultimate in photographic control. In addition to their support for interchangeable lenses, digital SLRs offer the performance and features that professional photographers demand. Moreover, because their image sensors are usually larger than what you'll find in a prosumer camera, SLRs deliver higher image quality.

Image Resolution and Compression

Almost all digital cameras offer a choice of resolutions when shooting. In addition to the camera's maximum resolution, most cameras offer lower-res options that allow you to fit more images onto the camera's storage card. Although you might have spent the extra money for a 4- or 5-megapixel camera, you might not always need to shoot at full resolution. For example, if you need to shoot images for the Web (and you're *sure* you'll never want to print them), your storage will go a lot farther if you shoot at *VGA* or *XGA* resolution (that is, 640 × 480 pixels or 800 × 600 pixels, respectively) than if you shoot at the camera's full resolution.

For maximum flexibility, you want to be sure that you choose a camera that provides a range of switchable resolutions. Most cameras offer at least full-resolution, an intermediate resolution, and two Web-quality low resolutions (usually VGA and XGA).

PUT YOUR MONEY WHERE YOUR STORAGE GOES

Nowadays, digital camera storage is so cheap that there's really no reason not to always shoot at the highest resolution your camera provides. In other words, instead of trying to conserve space on your storage card, just buy some additional cards. By shooting at full res, you'll have the option to enlarge parts of your images, and if you decide later that you want to print your images, you'll have the resolution you need to get a good print.

ABANDON HOPE, YE WHO INTERPOLATE HERE

Some cameras offer special interpolation modes that produce higher resolutions than the pixel count that their CCDs actually provide. These cameras achieve their results by shooting an image, and then performing an upsample, or interpolation, to produce an image of higher resolution. Unfortunately, these modes sometimes produce images with nasty interpolation artifacts. If you want a bigger image than what your camera can provide, it's much better to shoot the cleanest, highest-quality image that your camera can manage, and then sample it up later in an image editor. You'll have more control, will get better results, and your camera's storage will go farther.

Image Compression

Compression can save a tremendous amount of storage space, but it can also adversely affect image quality. Ideally, your camera will offer a range of compression settings, from a high-quality JPEG compression to a really squeezed, low-quality JPEG compression. JPEG compressors that deliver 3:1 or 4:1 compression ratios are considered high quality. Lower-quality JPEG compression typically provides ratios of 10:1 or 20:1.

If image quality is your highest concern, and storage is of little consequence, then you'll want to get a camera that can also store an uncompressed image, usually a TIFF file. While these files are typically huge (9 or more megabytes on a 3-megapixel camera), they won't suffer from any compression artifacts.

For the most part, on many digital cameras, the best-quality JPEG settings are so good that they're indistinguishable from uncompressed TIFF images. Nevertheless, certain shooting conditions leave your images especially susceptible to JPEG artifacts. Areas of complex contrast, such as foliage and leaves, as well as areas of broad flat color, such as skies, are often prone to bad artifacting. Having an uncompressed option can be a life-saver if you find yourself shooting under these circumstances.

Finally, when you evaluate a camera's resolution and compression options, pay particular attention to the camera's interface to these features. If you think you will be changing resolutions often, then you'll want to be sure these options are easy to get to, rather than buried beneath a ton of menus.

Today, more and more cameras are offering an option to store *raw data*. Remember that your camera works by taking the data from the pixels on the CCD (which is usually 8, 10, or 12 bits of data per pixel) and interpolating it up to a full 24 bits per pixel before compressing it and storing it on your camera's storage card. In raw mode, the camera stores the *original* information that came directly off the CCD. Raw data has several advantages over normal processed data. Because raw data has not been interpolated (you do the interpolation later, using your computer), it's usually significantly smaller than a full, uncompressed TIFF file. For example, a 2048 × 1536 pixel image at 10 bits per pixel comes out to around 3.9MB, while a 2048 × 1536 pixel image at 24 bits per pixel comes out to 9.4MB. Some cameras use a *lossless* compressor on raw data to further reduce its size.

JPEG files always store 8 bits of color data per pixel. Therefore, if your camera normally shoots 10 or 12 bits per pixel, then the camera will be throwing out some color data during the JPEG conversion. With raw files, you usually have the option of converting the image into a 16-bit format that can be used with many editing programs. For this reason, you can often get better dynamic range out of a raw image than a JPEG image.

It's also important to note that because the raw data hasn't been JPEG compressed, it won't suffer from compression artifacts. Finally, raw images are stored *before* the camera performs any internal processing such as color balancing, contrast adjustment, white balance, sharpening, or noise reduction. This frees you to control these processes *after* you've taken the shot, using software provided with the camera. (Figure 5.10)

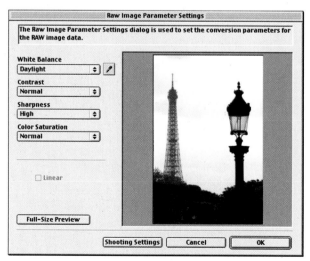

FIGURE 5.10   If your camera provides a Raw data mode, you can use special software to change parameters such as white balance, sharpening, and contrast after you've shot your image.

Aspect Ratio

The ratio of an image's length to its width is called the *aspect ratio*. Most digital cameras use the same 4:3 aspect ratio that your computer screen and television use, while some higher-end cameras use the 3:2 aspect ratio of 35mm film (Figure 5.11).

FIGURE 5.11   Most digital cameras use the same 4:3 aspect ratio as your computer monitor. Other cameras offer the 3:2 aspect ratio of 35mm film.

Some cameras, such as the Nikon Coolpix 990, offer a choice of either aspect ratio (Figure 5.12). However, it's important to note that when you shoot in 3:2 mode, you're simply shooting a cropped version of the

FIGURE 5.12   Some cameras offer a choice of aspect ratios. Usually, the wider choice is nothing more than a cropped version of the normal 4:3 aspect ratio. Better to shoot full-screen and do the cropping yourself later.

camera's native 4:3 ratio. Therefore, when you shoot 3:2, you're shooting lower-resolution images. It's often better to simply shoot 4:3 and crop the image yourself later. If you prefer a particular aspect ratio, you'll want to make sure to pick a camera that can shoot with those dimensions.

CAMERA DESIGN

Like any tool, a camera will be of dubious value if it is poorly designed and difficult to use. After you assess your image quality and resolution needs, it's time to start thinking about the camera design that is right for you.

With 150 years of photographic practice behind them, photographers are used to thinking and working in a particular way. However, with the elimination of film—and all of the film-handling mechanics that a film camera requires—it's possible to make a digital camera that provides a body design and features that film photographers of 10 years ago would never have dreamed of. Consequently, camera makers find themselves trying to balance the old against the new. Sometimes the balance works, and sometimes it doesn't.

When you are considering a camera's design, you will be evaluating size, comfort, and features. However, camera selection also involves trying to find a camera that facilitates your style of shooting. For example, if you're a film photographer, you might be used to SLR viewfinders and so will want a digital SLR. If you're used to the ground glass of a medium format viewfinder, though, you might be biased toward a camera with a good LCD viewfinder. Perhaps you're a sports or nature photographer who needs to be able to shoot at a moment's notice. If so, you'll want to choose a camera that doesn't require a lengthy *boot time* and offers a good burst mode and a long lens. Or, maybe you take lots of candid "people" shots, which will be facilitated by a "split-body" camera that allows for unobtrusive shooting.

Finally, the design of your camera's body influences how easily and quickly you can get to the camera's controls and settings. Therefore, you want a camera whose design makes sense to you and allows you to "feel" your way around without having to take your eye off of your subject.

Point-and-Shoot Cameras

Many vendors are making digital cameras that follow the design of their 35mm or APS point-and-shoot cameras. Looking little different than their film counterparts, these cameras offer the convenience and familiarity of the point-and-shoot film camera you might already have, and often offer advanced features such as *spot meters* and *macro* functions (Figure 5.13).

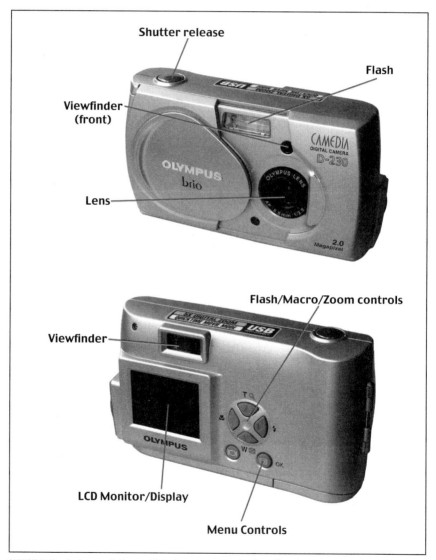

FIGURE 5.13 Point-and-shoot digital cameras typically offer the same designs and controls as point-and-shoot film cameras.

Point-and-shoot digital cameras range in price from $200 to $600 and typically sport decent optics and a bare-bones feature set. At the time of this writing, point-and-shoot digital cameras have a maximum resolution of 4 megapixels.

The advantage of point-and-shoot cameras is that they're easy to use; familiarity makes for quick learning. Point-and-shoot cameras can also be made very small (Canon's S200 Digital Elph, for example, is the length and width of a credit card), making it simple to carry them anywhere. The downside to these models is that they often lack the features that a serious photographer might want, and their optics are not always as good as those found in a more expensive camera.

Prosumer

The more serious photographer will demand more control and better optics than what the typical point-and-shoot camera offers. Although "prosumer" is a loathsome buzzword, it really is the best description of the $500 to $2,000 digital cameras that offer advanced features, manual

---

A FEW WORDS ABOUT VIEWFINDERS

The *viewfinder* on a camera is the window you look through to frame your shot. Because viewfinders can vary greatly in quality—and because they are such an important part of your shooting process—it's important to carefully consider your camera's viewfinder. Digital cameras typically provide two types of viewfinders.

Most point-and-shoot and prosumer digital cameras use the same type of rangefinder viewfinders found on point-and-shoot film cameras. Vendors typically refer to the rangefinder as the camera's *optical viewfinder*, to distinguish it from the LCD viewfinder that is also usually provided. Because the camera uses separate lenses for the optical viewfinder and for imaging (Figure 5.14, page 72), you will be unable to see the effects of filters and lens extensions when you use an optical viewfinder. In addition, this two-lens arrangement can create *parallax* troubles when you shoot close-up or *macro photography*.

The main drawback to most rangefinder cameras is the generally poor quality of the optical viewfinders provided.

Most digital cameras also allow you to use their LCD screens as a viewfinder, affording you a very different way of shooting.

We'll discuss viewfinders in more detail later in this chapter.

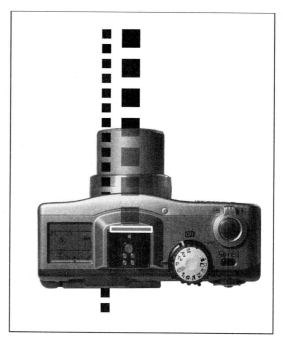

FIGURE 5.14 In a rangefinder camera, the light passing through the camera's lens falls onto the focal plane. The viewfinder uses a completely different light path, meaning that what you're seeing in your viewfinder is not exactly what's landing on the CCD.

control, and high-quality lenses (Figure 5.15). Affordably priced, some of these cameras offer a level of quality that's suitable for some professional work.

Prosumer cameras currently offer resolutions from 1.5 to 6 megapixels and a vast assortment of features ranging from full manual control of shutter speed and aperture to support for add-on lens extensions. Prosumer camera body designs are incredibly varied, running the gamut from larger point-and-shoot style bodies to unusual split-body designs that house the lens and CCD in a swiveling compartment that is kept separate from the camera's LCD screen and controls (Figure 5.16, page 74). Such designs can feel very strange to a photographer used to a traditional SLR, but don't rush to discount them. Many of the new, unorthodox designs offer a number of shooting advantages, as we'll see later.

Prosumer SLR

Some manufacturers offer prosumer SLR cameras. In an SLR, the viewfinder you look through to frame your shot uses the same lens that

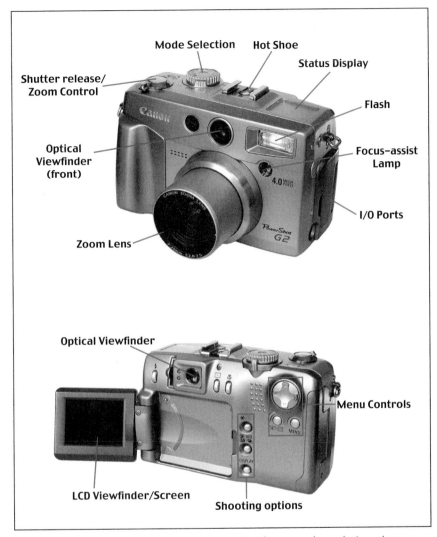

FIGURE 5.15   At the more-expensive, "prosumer" end, cameras have designs that are similar to normal point-and-shoot models, but offer many more options such as advanced metering and white balance control.

your camera uses to make its exposure (Figure 5.17). Consequently, you can be sure that what you're seeing through the lens is what's going onto the CCD. This approach has several advantages over rangefinder cameras. Because they look directly through the lens, SLR viewfinders present a much higher-quality view than a rangefinder, which looks through separate, low-quality optics. The result is a viewfinder that is usually brighter

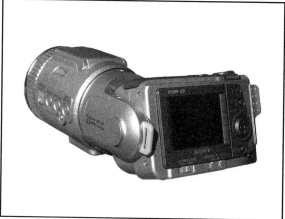

FIGURE 5.16   Because they don't have to handle film, digital cameras can have very unusual designs, like the split body of this Sony f505v. Its swiveling LCD viewfinder means that you can frame shots from many different angles.

and offers more clarity than a rangefinder does. In addition, an SLR viewfinder allows you to see the effects of any filters that you might have placed over the lens. Moreover, when you shoot macro photos, you won't have to worry about the parallax problem found in rangefinder cameras. SLR viewfinders also include status displays that show exposure information and other camera settings. Because you can see your image and all of your settings in the same viewfinder, you're more free to concentrate on your image.

Most SLRs use a mirror placed in front of the shutter to bounce light up toward the optical viewfinder. When you press the shutter button, the

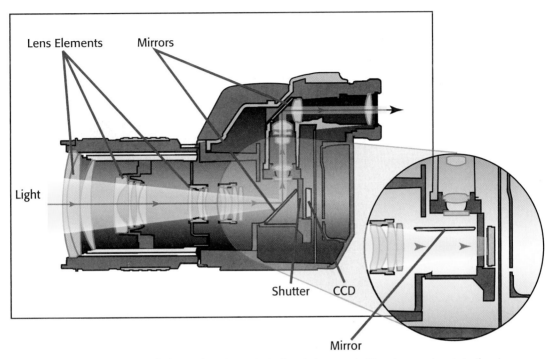

FIGURE 5.17   In an SLR camera, light passing through the lens is bounced off a mirror and up into the view-finder. This TTL light path ensures that you are seeing the same thing the camera sees. When you press the shutter release, the mirror is flipped up so that the light can pass on to the CCD.

mirror is raised out of the way, the shutter is opened, and the CCD is exposed. The movement of the mirror is what causes your viewfinder to black out when you press the shutter release (with the mirror pulled up, your viewfinder is no longer being fed the light that's coming through the lens). Because digital SLRs have a mirror—and, usually, a mechanical rather than electronic shutter—they deliver all of the same visual and audible feedback that a film camera does. In other words, when you press the button, you hear a discernible click, and your viewfinder goes dark for a moment. For an experienced film photographer, this can be much more comfortable and familiar than the simple electronic beeps that most rangefinder cameras use to indicate that they have fired.

However, because the light in an SLR is being fed up to the optical viewfinder, you cannot use a digital camera's LCD screen as a viewfinder. As long as the mirror is down, there's simply no light reaching the CCD. (The Olympus E10 and E20 cameras get around this problem by using a *beam-splitter* rather than a pivoting mirror to feed light to the viewfinder.) SLR cameras are usually more expensive than rangefinder cameras simply because it's more complicated to build a through-the-lens viewfinder.

Some SLRs now offer electronic viewfinders. Although they look and feel like a normal SLR, when you look through the viewfinder you see a tiny LCD screen—like the viewfinder on a video camera. These viewfinders are not as clear as an optical SLR viewfinder, but they typically offer full status displays.

Prosumer SLR models currently run the gamut from $750 to $2,000.

LCD-Only Cameras

Eschewing optical viewfinders altogether, LCD-only cameras assume that you would only ever want to use an LCD viewfinder (Figure 5.18). Available in a range of resolutions, and packing vast arrays of features, these cameras often offer the most radical departures in camera design.

FIGURE 5.18   Some cameras provide an LCD screen as their only viewfinder, such as the Nikon Coolpix 2500 shown here with its lens and LCD screen pointed in the same direction. This ability to swivel the lens makes the Coolpix 2500 ideal for self-portraits and for shooting at odd angles.

On the downside, LCD screens tend to devour batteries, making LCD-only cameras great battery hogs. If most of your photography takes you into the wilderness, foreign countries, or other situations where battery charging is difficult or impossible, then an LCD-only camera might not be practical. Moreover, without an optical viewfinder, you might find shooting in bright daylight to be difficult or impossible with these cameras, as direct sunlight can wash out the LCD screen, making it too hard to see images. Similarly, shooting in very dark situations can be difficult, as the image on the CCD might not be contrasty enough to show image detail, making it difficult to frame your shot. Finally, many photographers simply never get used to the process of holding a camera at odd angles, or a few inches from the eye.

Professional SLR

There are a number of cameras aimed at the higher-end, advanced amateur/professional market. Most of these cameras are built around traditional 35mm film camera bodies, and start at around $2,000 for a body. At the time of this writing, the cheapest of these high-end SLRs are Olympus' $1,500 4-megapixel E10, which is a true SLR but lacks interchangeable lenses, and Canon's $2,000 EOS D60, a 6-megapixel SLR body that supports Canon's excellent EOS-series lenses.

In addition to superior image quality and the ability to use high-end, professional lenses, these advanced SLRs typically offer other features that the professional photographer needs to have: high frame rates (3 to 5 frames per second), sturdy body, multiple focus zones, and advanced exposure control. Professional SLRs are also usually much faster than their prosumer counterparts. By accelerating everything from image processing to menu navigation, these cameras are always ready to shoot, and are definitely the only viable option for the experienced professional.

"HOW ABOUT USING MY DIGITAL VIDEO CAMERA?"

Your digital video (DV) camera probably has a "still" or "picture" mode of some kind. These modes usually record a still image over seven seconds of videotape, or, alternately, record it to a removable flash card. For the user who needs both stills and video, this might seem like an ideal solution.

However, video cameras typically shoot still images that are far inferior to even an inexpensive digital still camera. First, video has a much lower resolution (usually 768 × 540) than a good still camera does. Second, the images are usually interlaced, meaning that they are composed of two alternating, interwoven images (unless your camera has a progressive scan mode). In addition, if the image is being stored on tape, the image will be compressed using DV compression. Third, a video camera is designed and optimized to produce images for the NTSC or PAL color gamut, color spaces that are more limited than what a digital still camera can produce. Fourth, DV cameras use rectangular pixels so you might have to correct all of your images to compensate for the change to the square pixels of your computer monitor. Finally, if your camera stores images on tape, you'll face a workflow hassle when you're ready to pull out your images. All in all, it's best to use a video camera for video. Buy a still camera for your still images, unless you're going for a somewhat degraded, video look.

Body Design and Construction

Modern cameras can be made out of any number of materials, from metal to carbon fiber to aluminum to plastic (Figure 5.19). Obviously, sturdier materials are more durable (and usually feel better in terms of finish and heft), but even a predominantly plastic body can hold up well.

FIGURE 5.19   Although small, Canon's S200 Digital Elph is a very sturdy, all-metal camera.

When you are assessing a camera, try to get a feel for the quality of its build. If you lightly squeeze it, does it creak or does it feel solid? A creaky camera might just get creakier—and possibly more fragile—as its screws and joints loosen. If the camera has a split body, or other unusual design, try to get an idea of the durability of the swiveling mechanism. Will it hold up to normal use, or might it wear out?

Digital cameras can often have strange designs, so make sure that your camera sports a finish and moldings that make it comfortable to hold on to and difficult to drop. Finger moldings and rubberized components can make an otherwise odd shape comfortable to hold.

Doors and port covers can be especially fragile components. Check the battery compartment door and media card door for durability and easy access (Figure 5.20). You'll be using these mechanisms a *lot*, so make sure they can stand up to repeated use. In addition, make sure that you can get to them in a hurry if you need to, even when the camera is mounted on a tripod. Rubber or plastic port covers (such as what might go over a battery charging port or a USB port) are often the flimsiest part of a camera. Try to get a feeling for the weaknesses of these covers. Although you won't be able to improve them, they might at least last a bit longer if you are aware of how easily they can be broken off.

FIGURE 5.20 Pay attention to the doors and covers that a camera uses for its media, batteries, and ports. You'll be opening and closing these a lot, so make sure they're sturdy and durable.

Heft is often a concern for more serious photographers. A heavier camera, although a bit of a pain to lug around, is usually easier to shoot with, as extra weight makes for a more stable shot. If you're used to a film camera with a good deal of weight, you might want to look for the same thing in a digital camera.

Finally, try to get an idea as to how much of the camera's body and internal chassis are made of metal. As we'll see in Chapter 9, "Special Shooting," heat can greatly degrade image quality, and components such as LCD screens and large capacity memory cards can produce a lot of heat. Metal substructures and chassis can serve to dissipate heat that might otherwise affect image quality.

Status LCDs

Not to be confused with your camera's full-color viewfinder/playback LCD, is the small status LCD that might be present on the top of the camera. Most modern digital cameras have such a screen for displaying current camera settings and number of shots remaining.

Some cameras skip these displays and assume that you'll simply get this information from the viewfinder LCD. However, if you're in bright sunlight or if your batteries are running low, you might not want to activate your main LCD just to find out if your flash is turned on. Moreover, having a permanent display of camera status makes for faster, more convenient shooting.

Figure 5.21 shows a status LCD from an Olympus C2500, an example of a status display that provides a good amount of information.

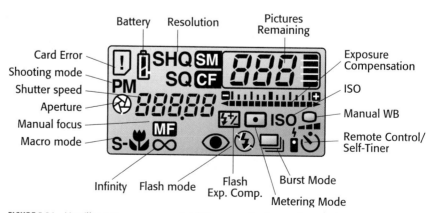

FIGURE 5.21   You'll want your camera's LCD status display to show at least as many options as this display from an Olympus C2500.

Tripod Mount

This might seem like a superfluous item to bring up for discussion (rather like considering what bag you'll choose to carry your camera in), but a poor tripod mount can really ruin your entire day. Any experienced photographer will tell you that there is a difference between a good tripod mount and a bad one. Here's what makes for a good tripod mount:

- **Metal construction.** A tripod mount is a simple screw socket recessed into the bottom of the camera. (Some tripod mounts also include additional stabilizing holes.) If the screw socket is made out of plastic, it can be very easy to strip out the screw threads by forcing the camera in at the wrong angle. Even if you're always very careful, fragile plastic threads can wear out with repeated use. Look for a metal screw mount.
- **Positioned along the lens axis.** Ideally, you want a tripod mount that is positioned so that the camera will pan (rotate) around the axis of its focal plane (Figure 5.22). Such a tripod is required for shooting panoramas.

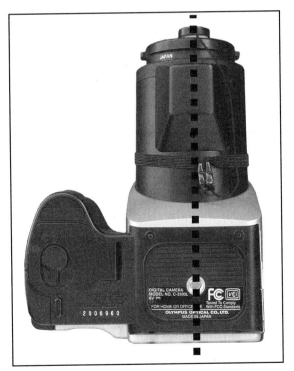

FIGURE 5.22   Ideally, you want a tripod mount that lies on the same axis as the lens.

- **Positioned so you can remove the batteries and media.** Once you put a camera on a tripod for a shoot, you don't want to have to dismount it to change batteries or storage media. Make sure the battery and media doors are unblocked when the camera is tripod-mounted.

How to Choose

In the end, it will most likely be a camera's image quality that wins you over. However, after you've test-driven a few different models, you might find yourself willing to compromise a little bit on quality for the sake of a more comfortable camera.

LENSES

Your camera's lens is where the whole imaging process starts. (Actually, your light source is where the whole imaging process starts, but let's forget about that for the moment.) If you have an inferior lens that can't do a good job of focusing light onto the camera's focal plane, then the quality of the camera's CCD and internal processing software won't really matter.

The bad news for digital camera owners is that, because CCDs are so small, the lens on a digital camera has to be of very high quality to effectively focus light onto the small imaging area. The good news is that it's much easier to correct aberrations in small-diameter lenses—which is what most digital cameras have. Consequently, many digital cameras—even inexpensive ones—have *very* good lenses. Often, the lens on a point-and-shoot digital camera is far superior to the lens on a point-and-shoot film camera, meaning that you'll usually get *better* results from a low-end digital camera than from a low-end film camera.

If you're an experienced photographer who is used to using a 35mm SLR camera with a range of interchangeable lenses, you'll probably be disappointed to find that your options are more limited in the digital camera realm. At the time of this writing, you cannot get a digital camera with interchangeable lenses for less than $2,000. Consequently, unless you have a lot of money to spend, you'll be looking at cameras with fixed (that is, nonremovable) zoom lenses.

As with other features, you should do a little lens testing before you commit to buying a particular camera. The easiest way to test a lens is to shoot some images with it and look for aberrations and image quality troubles. There are a number of different types of lens aberrations ranging from *astigmatism* to *comas,* but in a modern, high-quality lens, there are only a few types of aberrations that you need to worry about. When you look for aberrations or image quality issues, be sure to test the lens throughout its zoom range. If the camera offers manual control of aperture, you'll want to shoot a few more test shots using the biggest and smallest apertures for the lens. When evaluating a lens, consider the following:

- First, check for general focus and sharpness. How does the lens render fine detail? Does it focus equally from the middle to the edges and corners of the image?
- Chromatic aberrations occur when the camera cannot equally focus all wavelengths of light. Look for slightly blurred or smeared color or red or green fringes around brightly lit objects.
- *Vignetting* is a darkening of the image around the edges, and usually occurs at the extremes of the camera's zoom range. Look for changes in brightness across the image and throughout the zoom range.
- Barrel and pincushion distortion (Figure 5.23) are spatial distortions of your image that work similar to a fun-house mirror. *Barrel distortion*

FIGURE 5.23 Although it's slight, this image has a bit of barrel distortion, a slight outward bowing of lines near the edge of the frame. In this image, it is especially noticeable along the edges of the garage door. Barrel distortion is usually only visible at the widest angle of a lens.

causes a straight vertical line to be bowed outward toward the edges of the frame, while *pincushion distortion* causes a straight vertical line to be bowed inward toward the middle of the frame. These distortions are more prevalent at the wide angles of your zoom lens and will definitely occur if you attach a telephoto, wide-angle, or *fisheye* attachment to your lens.

- The contrast produced by a lens might vary when you are using smaller apertures. Try shooting some high-contrast areas using the widest and narrowest apertures of the lens.

- Wider-angle lenses are more prone to lens flares (Figure 5.24). Zoom the lens to its widest angle and shoot some tests into bright light sources (but never point a camera directly at the sun!) to test for flares.

FIGURE 5.24 This lens flare is an example of one of the types of flares that can occur as light bounces around inside the lens. Better lenses are less prone to flaring.

- Lens quality can also affect color reproduction. If you find that a camera tends to shoot images that are a little "warm" or "cold," the trouble might be in the lens.

It is impossible to eliminate all aberrations in a lens. Your goal in testing a lens is to determine what kind of troubles it has, how bad those troubles are, if you think they will affect the type of shooting that you tend to do, and if you can work around them. For example, all aberrations except for distortions can be reduced by stopping down the lens, and many kinds of distortion can be eliminated using special software.

When you are looking at cameras, you'll often see specifications that describe a lens as being *aspherical*. This simply means that the lens is not a perfectly round hemisphere, but has some nonspherical elements in it that are designed to eliminate certain aberrations. You might also see that a lens has some type of *coating* on it that usually serves to reduce reflections and flares.

Zoom Ranges and Focal Lengths

If you have much experience shooting 35mm film, then you probably have a good understanding of the field of view and magnification provided by lenses with particular focal lengths. For example, you're probably used to the idea of a 28mm lens being wide-angle and a 200mm lens being telephoto.

A CCD is much smaller than a piece of 35mm film, and the distance between the lens and the focal plane is usually much shorter. Consequently, the focal length of a lens on a digital camera doesn't yield the same field of view as the same focal length on a 35mm camera. Fortunately, most digital camera vendors are diligent about publishing *35mm equivalencies* when they list focal lengths for their cameras. These equivalencies provide a standard reference point when you compare the lenses of cameras with radically different lens sizes and body designs. For example, the Olympus C2100 Ultra Zoom has a zoom lens with focal lengths that range from 7 to 70mm. In 35mm equivalencies, though, this equates to 38 to 380mm. Often, vendors will publish a *focal length multiplier*, which makes it easy to figure out equivalent focal lengths. For example, the C2100 has a multiplier of roughly 5.4 ($70 \times 5.4 = 378$).

For the photographer who's used to working with super-wide 18 or 28mm lenses, 38mm might not seem very wide. Unfortunately, making a high-quality wide-angle lens of the typically small diameter found on a digital camera is very difficult. Consequently, if you're holding out for a camera with a really wide-angle lens, know that you might have to wait a while. Fortunately, several manufacturers and third-party vendors offer wide-angle and fisheye attachments that clip or screw onto the front of the lens. Although not as high quality as a dedicated lens, these attachments do provide a workable solution. Similarly, users longing for a powerful telephoto lens can usually find telephoto extenders and adapters for select cameras.

Unfortunately, digital camera makers have adopted a convention started by the camcorder industry wherein zoom lenses are measured using a multiplication factor, rather than by focal range. For example, you'll see lenses labeled as "3x" zooms. The problem with this convention is that it doesn't tell you anything about where that 3x range begins and ends. A little research will usually yield the focal length range in both millimeters and 35mm equivalencies.

Finally, some lower-end cameras have a fixed focal length, fixed focus lens. Such lenses usually have a wide field of view and a very small aperture, ensuring that everything in the image will be in focus. The advantage to such cameras is that they're easy to use—you don't really even need to look through the viewfinder—and they are usually inexpensive. The downside is that they offer very limited creative control.

"I WANT MY INTERCHANGEABLE LENSES!"

It can be difficult for the experienced 35mm photographer to get used to the idea of being stuck with a camera that has only a fixed lens. Yes, this is a limitation—you won't be able to upgrade to higher-quality lenses or use lenses you might already have. In addition, the fixed lenses on most digital cameras don't allow for very shallow depth of field. However, despite these caveats, things aren't nearly as bad as they seem.

As discussed previously, the zoom lenses on most respectable digital cameras (even ones as cheap as $500) are very good. In fact, depending on how much money you've spent on your 35mm lenses, the lens on a digital camera might be better than what you're used to, thanks to the engineering advantages of making small lenses.

Digital cameras that do have interchangeable lenses usually also have image sensors that are a little smaller than a piece of 35mm film. Consequently, because your image area is smaller, you'll need higher-quality (thus "more expensive") lenses than what you would need if you were shooting film. In other words, the lenses you already have might suffer some when they are attached to a digital SLR. Moreover, because of the smaller imaging size, the focal lengths of all lenses will be subject to a focal length multiplier. For example, you have to multiply the focal length of lenses attached to the Canon D60 by 1.6 to determine their 35mm equivalency. All your existing lenses will become more telephoto. On the upside, digital SLRs tend to gather most of their image from the center of a lens, eliminating any vignetting or distortion that might plague the edges of the lens.

Finally, you might not actually want a detachable lens on a digital camera. Because CCDs are smaller than 35mm film, they are much more susceptible to dust and dirt. By taking the lens off the camera, you expose the CCD to dust particles that can appear in your final image as dark smudges, black marks, or rings. Typically, dust particles are only visible at small apertures, but if you've just spent $5,000 on a Nikon D1, having to avoid small apertures is not an enticing thought.

Because CCDs are charged with electricity, they can develop a static field that makes them attract even more dust. Some theorize that because CMOS chips don't require such a powerful charge, cameras that are CMOS-based are less dust-prone. Only time will tell.

Although you might think "big deal, I'll just be careful when I change lenses," be warned that many users claim that it is impossible to keep dust off the CCD. In addition, because vendors do not recommend using compressed air inside the camera, cleaning the CCD can be very difficult.

If you've been waiting around for less expensive digital cameras with interchangeable lenses, you might have to wait quite a while. If you're on a budget, it's worth taking a serious look at the quality of the fixed zoom lenses that are already available.

Lens Features

Different camera vendors take different approaches to lens design, and it's worth considering a few lens-related points when you evaluate a camera:

- **Does the lens have threads?** A *threaded lens* allows you to add filters, which can be essential for achieving certain types of effects. Some cameras require a special adapter for attaching threaded components. If you're considering such a camera, be sure to add in the cost of the extra adapter and try to determine how easy it is to attach and remove the adapter. In addition, find out if you have to remove your attachments before you can remove the adapter, as these actions will make the camera a bit more difficult to use.

- **Are there lens extensions and attachments available?** The lenses on some prosumer cameras can be fitted with special lens attachments that make the lens more telephoto, more wide angle, or even fisheye (Figure 5.25). If the lens on a camera doesn't offer the focal lengths you want, see if any manufacturer or third-party attachments are available.

- **Does the lens extend and retract?** For the sake of miniaturization, some vendors make lenses that extend and retract when the

FIGURE 5.25 Some cameras support special telephoto, wide-angle, or fisheye lens attachments.

camera is powered on. Although this is most prevalent in tiny point-and-shoot cameras, a number of prosumer cameras, such as the Olympus C4040 and the Canon G2, use extending lenses. Although such lenses allow for a smaller camera, they also make for longer boot and shutdown times, and a little bit of battery drain. Some require you to remove any filters or lens attachments before you shut down.

- **Does the lens come with a lens cap?** Believe it or not, some vendors still don't provide lens caps with their cameras. The theory goes that digital camera lenses are so small that any scratches or abrasions will be tiny enough that the lens will simply focus past them. Although this might be true, the idea of scratching the lens on a $1,000 camera is enough to make most people cringe. If the camera doesn't include a lens cap, make sure you can get a third-party cap that will fit.

- **If the camera has a zoom lens, is its zoom control proportional?** A *proportional zoom control* varies zoom speed depending on how far you push the zoom lens. In other words, if you push the zoom control just a little way "in," the lens zooms in slowly. If you press it a long way "in," the lens zooms in quickly. Proportional zoom controls make it easier to make fine adjustments and to quickly get the lens zoomed to the area you're looking for.

Digital Zoom

Loosely related to lenses are the *digital zooms* provided by most cameras. Evaluating a digital zoom feature is a very simple two-step process:

Step 1: Turn off the digital zoom feature.
Step 2: Don't ever turn it on again.

That's it! You're done and can now go on to consider other features.

The fact is that most digital zoom features do a terrible job of acting like a zoom lens. Obviously, the camera cannot digitally increase its focal length, so these features work by cropping the image to a smaller area, and then scaling that area up to the full size of the frame. The problem with most digital zooms is that they use bad interpolation algorithms when they scale up, so they tend to produce jagged, blocky images. Consequently, rather than using a digital zoom, it's much better to shoot the image with your camera's maximum optical zoom, and then crop and enlarge it yourself using Photoshop. This will provide a better form of interpolation.

There are three occasions when digital zoom might be useful:

- If you don't have any image editing software that is capable of cropping and upsampling.
- If you don't want to magnify the JPEG artifacts in your image. Because the camera enlarges your image *before* compressing, digital zooms don't worsen any JPEG artifacts. Enlarging in an image editor will.
- If you're shooting at one of the camera's lower resolutions. Most of the time, when you shoot at a lower resolution, the camera simply shoots at full res and then downsamples. Because there's more resolution to start with, using a digital zoom on a lower-res image often produces fine results.

If you must use a digital zoom feature, you ideally want to have one that offers good interpolation and provides a continuous range of zooming rather than fixed zoom ratios.

Focus

Most point-and-shoot cameras and all prosumer cameras offer autofocus lenses. From the user's perspective, these features all work the same. Using the camera's viewfinder, you place the focusing target (usually the middle of the viewfinder) on the object in your scene that you want to have in focus. When you press the shutter release button halfway, the camera will measure the distance to that object and *lock the focus*; pressing the rest of the way will take the picture. (If your camera has a fixed-focus lens, you can skip this section.)

We'll discuss all of the concerns and practices of using an autofocus system in Chapter 7, "Shooting." When you choose a camera, though, there are a few simple things to look for:

- **Passive versus active autofocus.** Autofocus systems that use a *passive* TTL system determine focus by looking through the lens. *Active autofocus* mechanisms employ a separate sensor outside the lens to measure distance; focus is then set accordingly. *Passive autofocus* systems are usually more accurate and have the advantage of working with lens extensions and attachments.

- **Focus assist lamp.** The downside to most passive TTL autofocus mechanisms is that they don't work very well (or at all) in low-contrast situations. A *focus assist lamp* (sometimes called an *autofocus assist lamp*) (Figure 5.26) is a white or red light that the camera automati-

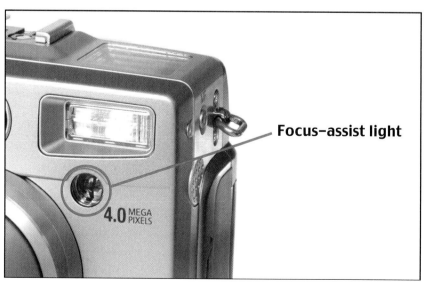

Focus–assist light

FIGURE 5.26   A focus assist light shines a white or red light into low-contrast scenes to help the camera's autofocus mechanism.

cally shines into your scene when there isn't enough contrast to lock focus. Look for a focus assist lamp that can be deactivated for more distinct shooting.

- **Number of autofocus steps.** With more autofocus steps, there are more locations that a lens can set itself to in order to get focused. However, as we'll see in Chapter 7, this doesn't necessarily mean that the camera will do a better job of focusing.

Continuous Autofocus

Some cameras offer a *continuous autofocus* that constantly refocuses as you move the camera around. The advantage to this mechanism is that when you're finally ready to shoot, the camera might already be in focus. If you're considering a camera with a continuous autofocus feature, make sure it's possible to disable the feature because you might need to occasionally turn it off to save your battery.

Manual Focus

Manual focus can be a boon for times when your camera's autofocus mechanism can't lock focus, or when you want to force the camera to focus on something in particular. Unfortunately, because of their designs, most digital cameras don't have an old-fashioned, lens-mounted manual focus ring. Instead, most cameras use a special menu option that requires you to dial in the distance to your subject, or use buttons on your camera to manually focus the lens. Although these controls are okay, the lack of high-quality viewfinders on most cameras can make manual focusing difficult.

At the very least, try to get a camera that has a manual infinity focus lock. This will allow you to lock the focus on infinity, which can be a real time and battery saver when you know you'll only be shooting objects that are far away.

Only recently—with the release of Olympus' E10—has a camera with a real, manual focus ring (with distance markings) become available for less than $2,000. Hopefully, more vendors will follow Olympus' lead.

Shutters and Irises

Your camera's shutter and iris controls allow you to change your camera's exposure to control the depth of field, contrast, and color saturation in your image. While film cameras have mechanical irises and shutters—actual metal, cloth, or plastic mechanisms that open and close—digital cameras often use different methods, such as electronic shutters, for exposing the CCD. Rather than having a mechanism that opens and closes in front of the CCD, a camera with an electronic shutter simply turns its CCD on and off for the appropriate length of time. One shutter mechanism is not necessarily better than another, as long as the camera offers the shutter speed control that you need to take the kind of shots you want.

All digital cameras offer an *automatic exposure* feature, which will automatically calculate the appropriate shutter speed and aperture at the time you take a picture. Some cameras, though, also offer manual controls for shutter speed and aperture. When you are assessing a camera's manual overrides, make sure that the camera offers a good range of shutter speeds—ideally ranging from a few seconds to at least 1/500th of a second. It's also nice to have a *bulb mode,* which makes the camera leave the shutter open for as long as you hold down the shutter release button.

As in a film camera, the aperture in a digital camera is controlled by an iris, an interlocking set of metal blades whose opening can expand or contract to make a bigger or smaller aperture. Many digital cameras, however, only have two apertures, usually f2.8 and f5.6 or f8 and f11. These cameras make up for their lack of aperture options by varying shutter speed. While this configuration doesn't limit the conditions under which you can shoot, it does possibly hobble your creative possibilities. Ideally, you want a camera with more aperture options.

Some cameras, such as the Canon G1 and G2, use their iris as a shutter, simply snapping it open and closed to make an exposure. The downside to this scheme is that at higher shutter speeds, the camera might require you to use smaller apertures—f8 on the Canon G1—since a wider aperture would take too long to close and would prevent the camera from achieving the desired shutter speed. Again, if you want maximum creative flexibility, this type of mechanism might be too limiting.

VIEWFINDERS

One of the most important features on a camera is the viewfinder. Most point-and-shoot and rangefinder cameras provide both an optical viewfinder—that is, a glass or plastic viewfinder like you'd find on a typical film camera—and an LCD screen that can be used as a viewfinder. LCD-only cameras have, obviously, only an LCD viewfinder, while SLR cameras typically have only an optical viewfinder. There are advantages to each type of viewfinder, and trying to choose just one can be difficult.

LCD Viewfinders

One of the great advantages of a digital camera, of course, is the built-in LCD screen that can be used to review your images as soon as you've taken them. Most cameras also let you use their LCDs as a viewfinder, displaying a real-time, continuously updated image of what the camera is pointed at.

LCD viewfinders have a number of advantages over optical viewfinders. Because the image on the LCD is coming directly off the camera's CCD, you get to see a very close approximation of your final image. It's not an exact image because your camera will do some processing (color correction, sharpening, noise reduction, etc.) of the image data before saving. If you're using any lens filters, or lens attachments, though, you'll be able to see their effects on the LCD.

The downside to LCD viewfinders is that images in them can be difficult, if not impossible, to see in direct sunlight. Also troublesome is that LCD screens are very battery-hungry. Most digital cameras use a *thin film transistor* (TFT) LCD screen. When you evaluate a camera's LCD viewfinder, consider the following:

- **How big is the LCD?** Simply put, when it comes to an LCD viewfinder, bigger is better. Most LCDs range between 1.5 and 2 inches (measured diagonally).
- **How bright is the LCD?** Brighter is better because it will make the screen easier to read in direct sunlight. Also find out if the camera offers a brightness control.
- **How good is the refresh rate?** The frequency with which the camera updates its LCD viewfinder is referred to as the *refresh rate*. A camera with a low refresh rate will deliver a stuttery image in the viewfinder. A low refresh rate can also cause smeared color artifacts and lower resolution. Simply put: An LCD with a slow refresh rate can make it difficult to see and frame the shot you want.
- **How does the LCD viewfinder perform in low light?** If you plan on doing a lot of night shooting, you'll probably need a camera with both an LCD and an optical viewfinder, as there's a good chance that images in your LCD screen will simply appear black in low-light situations.
- **How good is the coverage on the LCD?** Most LCD viewfinders show an image that is 95% to 98% of the image that will actually be shot. Any less than this should be considered a liability.
- **Does the LCD have an anti-reflective coating?** These can make a big difference when you are shooting in bright sunlight, as they'll greatly cut down on glare on the LCD.

- **Does the LCD offer a brightness control?** Many cameras now feature LCD screens with adjustable brightness. Although a brighter screen uses more power, it can be easier to see in direct sunlight.

You'll also want to consider the physical design of the LCD. Most cameras simply mount their LCD screens on the back of the camera. Some models, though, such as the Canon G2 and the Nikon Coolpix 5000, mount the LCD on a swiveling panel that can be flipped out, away from the camera. The LCD can be quickly and easily rotated to just about any viewing angle, and then safely stored against the camera's body (Figure 5.27). This design is very similar in flexibility to a swiveling design such as the Nikon Coolpix 995. The swiveling viewfinders of these cameras make it possible to shoot self-portraits, over-the-head shots, and low angles without having to twist, crouch, or crawl on your stomach. For these reasons, swiveling LCDs are ideal for *macro photography*.

FIGURE 5.27   The LCD screen on the Canon G2 can tilt and swivel into many positions, making it easier to shoot with the camera at different angles.

 VIEWFINDER HOODS

Although the quality of LCD viewfinders has greatly improved, it can still be difficult to see them in bright sunlight. Special hoods that fit over the LCD screen, such as the Hoodman, offer a simple, portable solution for reducing glare in direct sunlight.

Optical Viewfinders

Most point-and-shoot and rangefinder cameras include some type of optical viewfinder. Unfortunately, most vendors don't put much effort into their optical viewfinders, so you won't have a lot of options when you shop around. When you are testing an optical viewfinder, check for simple issues such as clarity and distortion. Does the viewfinder provide an image that is clear and easy to see? Most cameras also include one or two status lights within their optical viewfinders—one to tell you that the camera has focused, and another to tell you that the flash is ready. Make sure that these lights are easy to see within the viewfinder and that they are visible in bright daylight.

You'll also want to be sure that the viewfinder provides some type of focusing target such as *crosshairs*, and if you'll be doing a lot of macro photography, then you'll probably want some parallax guides (Figure 5.28).

FIGURE 5.28 When you shoot at close range, what you see through a rangefinder's viewfinder is not what your camera will actually shoot. Parallax guides give you an indication of where the real edges of the image are. The image on the left shows the view through the viewfinder, while the image on the right shows the resulting picture. Notice that the parallax lines allow us to correctly frame the left side of the image, even though we can't see the right side (because we're too close to our subject). If a camera's viewfinder is above the lens rather than next to it, the camera will exhibit parallax shift vertically rather than horizontally.

Unfortunately, the rather cheap optical viewfinders on most cameras don't provide very good coverage. That is, they don't show you the same field of view that the camera's lens is seeing. On average, an optical viewfinder will display about 85% of the final image, although some can go as low as 65% or 70% (Figure 5.29). By comparison, LCD viewfinders and the viewfinders in high-quality SLRs deliver about 95% coverage.

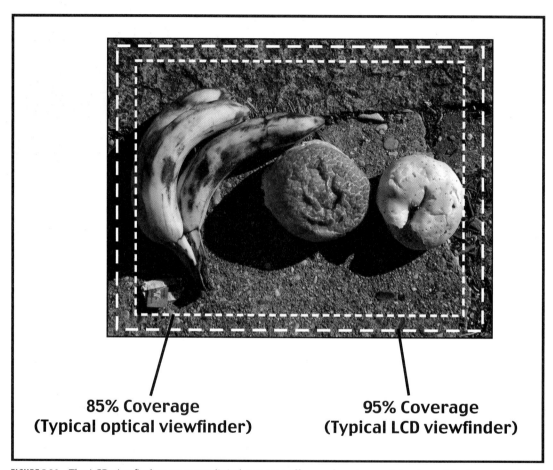

**85% Coverage
(Typical optical viewfinder)**   **95% Coverage
(Typical LCD viewfinder)**

FIGURE 5.29   The LCD viewfinders on most digital cameras offer an almost complete view of the image that will be captured. The optical viewfinders on most point-and-shoot and prosumer cameras offer much lower coverage.

Because these lower-quality viewfinders show a smaller-than-actual-size image, you don't have to worry about accidentally cropping something out of your frame, but you will have to crop your image later. Moreover, since you have limited resolution in your camera, optical viewfinders can be frustrating in that they don't allow you to make the best use of all of the pixels at your disposal.

Finally, if you wear glasses, look for a *diopter* adjustment next to the optical viewfinder (Figure 5.30). This is a small wheel that allows you to adjust the optical viewfinder to keep it in focus.

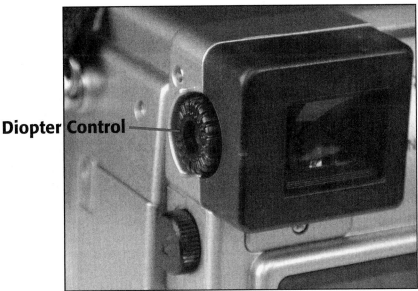

Diopter Control

FIGURE 5.30 A diopter wheel lets you adjust your optical viewfinder to compensate for your own vision.

Electronic TTL Viewfinder

Just to complicate things even further, some vendors are now including optical viewfinders that aren't really optical. Rather, they use a tiny LCD screen just like you'd find in the viewfinder on a video camera. Sometimes called *electronic TTL viewfinders*, these mechanisms have the advantage of showing you the exact same thing that you'd see on a larger LCD viewfinder. Therefore, in addition to better coverage than you'd get from a typical optical viewfinder, you also get the status and menu displays that you'd see on a large LCD viewfinder. Because you look at them through an eyepiece, they're easily visible in bright daylight, and offer the feel of an SLR viewfinder. However, their grainy displays make it difficult to see small detail and nearly impossible to manually focus. Although better than the optical viewfinders found on most digital cameras, they're no substitute for a true, high-quality, optical TTL viewfinder.

SLR Viewfinders

As you saw earlier, the advantage to an SLR viewfinder is that, while a rangefinder uses separate lenses for framing and shooting, an SLR lets you look through the same lens that is being used to shoot the actual image. For this reason, SLR viewfinders are sometimes referred to as TTL viewfinders.

Another advantage of the TTL approach is that you end up with an optical viewfinder that shows an accurate view of what the final image will look like. In addition to providing better coverage (sometimes as high as 95%) than a rangefinder does, SLR viewfinders let you see your image through any filters or lens attachments you might have installed. SLR viewfinders also feel very familiar if you've spent a lot of time with a film-based SLR because they provide the same visual and audible feedback.

SLR viewfinders are most prevalent in the $1,500 and up range of cameras, where you find digital cameras based on professional film-camera bodies.

When you are assessing the quality of an SLR viewfinder, you want to examine the same image and optical qualities that you would look for in any other type of viewfinder. In addition, pay attention to the readouts and displays that are present. Ideally, you want a viewfinder that displays all of the camera's salient settings (Figure 5.31). After all, when you're framing a shot, you don't want to have to move your eye from the viewfinder to find out whether your flash is turned on. Figure 5.31 shows items you should see in a viewfinder display.

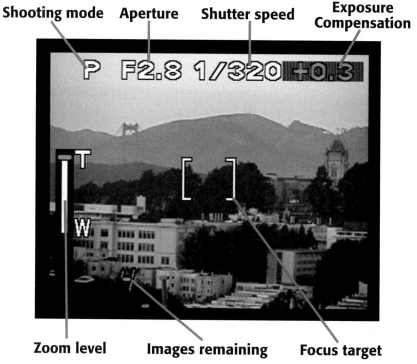

FIGURE 5.31   Ideally, you want the viewfinder of an SLR to display all of the camera's exposure settings. This image shows the viewfinder from an Olympus C2100 Ultrazoom.

THE FRAME-UP

The type of viewfinder you choose will have a substantial impact on your photographic experience. If you're used to a traditional SLR, then you're probably accustomed to holding the camera up to your eye, blocking out the rest of the world, and concentrating on your image. Consequently, using an LCD viewfinder—where you typically hold the camera away from your eye—might take some getting used to. However, if you're a long-time user of medium format cameras that provide ground glass viewfinders on the top of the camera, then an LCD screen might feel very familiar.

These are two very different approaches to framing an image, and it's important to consider how you like to work. Ideally, it would be nice to have both high-quality optical and LCD viewfinders. Unfortunately, we have yet to see a camera that delivers both of these options for less than $1,500.

EXPOSURE CONTROL

At the simplest level, *exposure*—that combination of shutter speed, aperture size, and your ISO setting—controls whether an image will be bright or dark. These parameters also let you control everything from which parts of the image are in focus, to how saturated the colors are, and how much detail is present. Because exposure controls determine how much control you will have over your final image, it is essential to take a good look at them before you buy.

White Balance

White balance is not actually part of the exposure process. However, because it's a parameter that you'll want to consider right before you shoot, we're going to discuss it alongside the exposure controls. The sooner you get into the habit of remembering white balance, the better off you'll be.

White balancing is the process of calibrating your camera so that it can correctly interpret colors under the type of light in which you're shooting. We'll discuss white balance in great detail in Chapter 7. When you are assessing a camera, though, there are some simple things you'll want to consider:

- In addition to an automatic white balance control, find out if the camera offers separate settings for daylight, fluorescent, and tungsten. Some systems provide white balance presets that are measured in degrees Kelvin (5500°K, for example). This is fine as long as you know which *color temperatures* relate to which kinds of light.
- For maximum flexibility, you'll want a manual white balance control that lets you set white balance for your particular situation by focusing the white balance system onto a white object. Make sure these controls are easy to get to, as you'll be using them often.
- Does the camera use a TTL white balance system, or an external white balance sensor? Ideally, you want a TTL white balance system for better accuracy.

Finally, you'll want to take a look at the quality of the camera's white balance. Take some sample pictures using the appropriate white balance settings and check for odd color casts. Chapter 7 will give you a better idea of what to expect when white balance goes wrong.

Metering

Whether you're shooting on full automatic, or calculating your exposures by hand, if you don't have a decent light meter you'll end up with the wrong exposure. The modern light meter is an incredibly sophisticated device, and many camera vendors have not scrimped on adding high-caliber, state-of-the-art metering systems to their digital cameras.

Arguing which company's metering software is better is a discussion far too technical for this book. Fortunately, metering systems from companies such as Nikon, Olympus, and Canon come with years of refinements and redesigns. However, you'll probably find that metering systems from different companies have different characteristics and tendencies. Some might consistently meter shadows well, while others might excel at mid-tones or highlights. The good news is that a meter's tendencies will usually be consistent, meaning that over time you will come to learn how your meter will handle specific situations.

Most higher-quality cameras include a selection of different metering modes. These typically break down into variations of the following categories:

- **Matrix (sometimes called multi-segment).** A *multi-segment (matrix) metering* system divides the imaging area into a grid, or matrix, and meters the light coming from each cell. These readings are then analyzed and averaged to calculate the ideal exposure for the shot.

- **Center-weighted metering.** A variation of matrix metering, *center-weighted metering* also divides the image area into a grid, but lends more "weight" to the readings from the middle of the image.
- **Spot metering.** A *spot meter* reads only a single area in your image, usually the center. Spot meters allow you to do everything from simple backlight compensations to complex *zone system* metering.

As with white balance sensors, you want a camera that uses TTL metering rather than a meter that's external to the lens. With an external meter, your camera will not be able to accurately account for any filters or lens attachments that you might be using.

There is no one "right" metering system. Fortunately, most cameras include some mix of the three systems described previously. To test them, try shooting in complex lighting situations (dark foreground with a bright background and vice versa; darkly shadowed areas; and areas with lots of bright highlights) and see how the camera chooses to meter. Does it preserve shadows? Does it blow out highlights? Most important, does it do these things consistently? Before testing a metering system, it would be a good idea to read the metering and exposure sections in Chapter 7.

Exposure Compensation

To quickly sum up: Exposure compensation controls let you force the camera to over- or underexpose by a certain number of stops (or fractions of stops) without having to worry about actual apertures and shutter speeds. Tell the camera to underexpose by half a stop and it will find a way to do it. These controls are powerful and will often be the only exposure controls you'll need to use.

When you are evaluating a camera, take a quick look to see how these controls are implemented. You'll be using them a lot, so make sure they're easy to use. Second, check that they allow for at least two stops of adjustment in both directions. Most controls let you adjust in 1/3-stop increments.

ISO Control

One of the great advantages of a film camera over a digital camera is that you can change your recording medium (the film). Although ripping out your digital camera's CCD and replacing it with a more sensitive chip is hardly practical, many cameras do offer an option to change the "speed" or sensitivity of their CCD using the same ISO measure that film photographers use.

Most digital cameras have a standard ISO rating somewhere between 80 and 110. These cameras have a light sensitivity that is roughly equivalent to film rated at 100 ISO. Some digital cameras allow you to increase their ISO rating, typically offering a choice of 100, 200, or 400. The Canon G2 offers a slower ISO 50 speed, while some higher-end cameras can go as high as 1600 ISO! These faster, more sensitive modes allow you to shoot in lower light without using a flash (which is ideal for concerts or other situations where a flash is inappropriate) and allow you to use faster shutter speeds and smaller apertures in bright daylight. However, just as faster film produces grainier images, higher ISO settings in a digital camera produce images with a lot more noise.

The ideal camera is one that provides an automatic ISO mechanism (that is, it automatically selects a faster ISO when there is not enough light) and allows manual selection of ISO. Be sure to look at images shot with different ISOs to get a sense of how noisy the camera becomes at higher speeds.

Exposure Locks and Panoramas

Panoramic shooting is a great way to capture broad vistas without having to spring for a fancy wide-angle adapter. Although you might have experimented with shooting panoramas with your film camera, your digital camera is a much better tool for creating collaged (panoramic) images, thanks to powerful stitching software that you can use to process your images.

We'll discuss panoramic shooting in more detail in Chapter 9. When you buy a camera, it's worth trying to get one that has a *panoramic* or *exposure lock* mode. Exposure lock simply means that, after you take the first image, the camera locks its exposure and shoots the rest of your panoramic series using those same settings to ensure even exposure across the entire image.

Some cameras offer a special *stitch assist* mode that provides visual cues to ease panoramic shooting. These modes often work with special software that can automatically stitch an image as it's transferred to your computer. Although such automation is nice, it's not required for high-quality panoramic shooting.

Exposure lock can also be handy in normal shooting situations when you want to spot meter off one part of an image and then reframe your shot. Although you can do this on most cameras by pressing the shutter button, they will lock focus as well as exposure. A dedicated exposure lock lets you independently control exposure and focus.

Preset Exposure Modes

A number of cameras include special preset exposure modes designed for shooting under specific conditions. These modes don't do any type of magic processing or anything; they simply favor—or lock the camera into—particular apertures and shutter speeds that are appropriate to certain situations. Most cameras with this feature include variations on the following modes:

- **Landscape.** Cancels the flash, locks focus on infinity, and typically uses as small an aperture as possible for maximum depth of field.
- **Portrait.** Favors wider apertures to produce a more blurred background.
- **Pan-focus.** Intended for times when you need really fast shooting. Focal length is locked on full wide; focus is locked on infinity. This essentially turns your camera into a speedy, fixed-focus camera.
- **Fast shutter.** (Sometimes called "sports.") Forces a large aperture to facilitate a fast shutter speed.
- **Night.** (Sometimes called "slow sync.") Uses slow shutter speeds for dimly lit scenes and typically fires the flash to provide some foreground illumination. Many cameras let you choose whether to fire the flash at the beginning or end of the exposure.

If you're already used to thinking in terms of appropriate aperture and shutter, then you'll probably just use your camera's manual functions to achieve the exposure effects you need. If your camera doesn't have manual controls, though, preset exposure modes might be the only manual choices you'll have.

Sharpness and Saturation Controls

Many digital cameras now include adjustable levels of sharpness and saturation. Technically, these have nothing to do with exposure. Rather, they are settings that control the post-processing that your camera performs before storing the image. The idea of "too much" sharpening might seem strange at first, but as we'll see later, it is possible to oversharpen an image. Similarly, the default settings on some cameras yield images that can be oversaturated. Sharpness and saturation controls let you tailor your camera to your personal tastes, and to the needs of particular shooting situations (Figure 5.32).

FIGURE 5.32 If your camera supports different contrast, brightness, and/or saturation settings, you can dramatically change the camera's color qualities. Shown here are settings from a Nikon Coolpix 5000. All photos were shot using full-automatic mode. The only difference was the change in settings noted beneath each image.

SHOOTING MODES

In the old days (circa 20 years ago) of film cameras, you had to pay a lot of extra money to get a camera that offered completely automatic operation. Now, every digital camera offers complete automation, and you have to pay a lot of money for a camera that offers any manual controls.

Priority Modes

Since it's a given fact that a digital camera will have a fully automatic mode, you'll want to spend a little time investigating a camera's other shooting modes. For maximum creative control, you'll want to have at least one of the following shooting modes in addition to the camera's automatic mode:

- **Aperture priority.** *Aperture priority mode* lets you select the aperture you want to use, leaving the selection of an appropriate shutter speed up to the camera. When you are looking at a camera's aperture priority mode, pay particular attention to the range of f-stops available. You want an aperture priority control that will let you pick any of the camera's possible apertures.
- **Shutter priority.** *Shutter priority mode* is just the opposite of aperture priority mode. Pick a shutter speed and the camera will automatically select the right aperture.
- **Manual.** In true *manual mode*, you get to set both the aperture and shutter speed, giving you full control over the camera's exposure. When you are checking out the manual mode on a camera, be sure that the controls for both aperture and shutter speed are easy to use and convenient. You don't want to miss a shot because you couldn't figure out how to change the camera's aperture, or because it took too long to set the shutter speed. In addition, make sure the camera displays some type of meter reading while you're changing your settings; otherwise, it will be impossible to know if you're over- or underexposing.

Fortunately, most higher-end prosumer cameras, and all higher-end professional cameras, offer all four shooting modes, so you probably won't have to skimp on these features. Just make sure the controls are implemented to your liking.

Image Buffering

As you'll recall from Chapter 3, after a digital camera exposes its CCD, the image data is passed to a special on-board computer for processing. After it is interpolated for color, white balanced, sharpened, and de-noised (among other things), the data is compressed and then stored on the camera's storage device. All this processing can take a lot of time, which means that your camera can be too busy to take any more pictures. Slower digital cameras can require 5 to 10 seconds between shots to allow the processor time to do its job.

Fortunately, most higher-end cameras now include special memory buffers (and sometimes separate processors) to handle the processing of an image, which frees up the camera to shoot again immediately. When you evaluate a camera, make sure that the *image buffer* can hold at least five or six full-resolution shots. Odds are that you won't be shooting more than that in quick succession, but if you are, you'll need to use a special "continuous" shooting mode.

Continuous Shooting

Most higher-end prosumer cameras offer special modes for shooting a rapid series of images. With speeds varying from a single frame to 2.5 to 3 frames per second, these features are ideal for shooting sports, fast-moving objects, or any subject where you want to record a simple motion.

Referred to as *burst, continuous,* or *drive mode,* continuous shooting modes usually work just like an autowinder on a film camera. Just press the shutter button, hold it down, and the camera will shoot as quickly as it can (Figure 5.33).

Note that some cameras can only achieve their full burst speed when they are shooting at a lower resolution. If you want full print quality from your burst images, make sure that your camera's continuous mode supports the full resolution of your camera. Note, too, that some cameras can only shoot up to a certain number of shots before they have to stop and flush the series of images out to storage. Be sure to investigate the maximum number of burst shots that can be taken at once.

CONTINUOUS FLASH SHOTS

Most cameras can't use a flash when shooting in continuous mode, as there isn't enough time for the flash to recharge. At the time of this writing, one camera, the Canon G2, can manage a frame per second in continuous mode while it is firing the flash. If you have a job that needs continuous flash shots, this might be the camera for you.

Movie Mode

Many digital cameras offer the ability to shoot little QuickTime movies. And when we say little, we mean little—both in area (320 × 240 pixels) and duration (usually a maximum of 20 to 40 seconds).

Most movie modes work the same way: you simply press the shutter button and the camera begins recording; press it again and recording

FIGURE 5.33 If your camera has a drive mode, you can shoot a sequence of shots in rapid succession. Not all cameras support burst shooting at full resolution.

stops. With resolutions limited to 320 × 240 pixels, such movies are really only good for Web posting or just playing around.

Because movies—even 320 × 240 movies—quickly generate a lot of data, your camera can't shoot, compress, and store a movie on-the-fly. Therefore, most digital cameras record video by storing the video frames in the camera's internal memory buffer (the one that buffers full-resolution images to increase shooting speed). When the buffer is full, the movie is dumped to the camera's storage card. Consequently, the length of individual movies is determined by the size of the camera's internal buffer, not the size of the camera's storage media.

Note that it can take a while to flush the buffer out to the card—sometimes 30 or 40 seconds—so you can't just keep hitting the button after each movie to immediately start another one.

When you are assessing a camera's movie mode, your main concerns are the maximum duration of an individual movie and whether the camera can record sound. Although these movie modes can be fun, they greedily consume storage and produce low-resolution, short movies. The fact is, if your video needs are at all serious, you'll need to buy a video camera.

Black and White

Many digital cameras offer special black-and-white modes for shooting grayscale images. Because you can use your image editing program to convert a color image to grayscale, and because a black-and-white image takes the same amount of storage space as a color image does, you might wonder why you would want to shoot in black and white? After all, isn't it better to shoot in color and have the *option* of black and white later?

The advantage of a dedicated black-and-white mode is that the camera skips the color interpolation process that it would normally go through. In other words, instead of having to make up a bunch of data (as we saw in Chapter 3), a black-and-white image can use the full, un-interpolated resolution of your camera's CCD.

A black-and-white mode is essential if you want to perform zone system black-and-white photography using your digital camera. We'll discuss black-and-white photography and color to black-and-white conversion in more detail in Chapter 9.

Self-Timers and Remote Controls

At some point, you've probably owned a film camera that had a self-timer on it. You know, you set the timer and then run as fast as you can to try to get in the shot and look natural in the five seconds or so that you have before the camera fires. Most digital cameras have the same type of feature.

Some cameras also offer a wireless remote control that provides zoom and shutter controls (Figure 5.34). These remotes not only facilitate self-portraits, but also serve as a shutter release for long-exposure images. If remote operation is important to you, consider the following:

- What's the range of the remote? Make sure it's long enough for your typical remote shooting jobs.

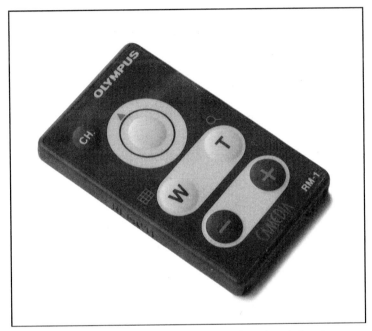

FIGURE 5.34 A wireless remote control lets you shoot hands-free, just as you would with a cable release on a film camera.

- Ideally, you'll want to have an infrared sensor on both the front and back of your camera.
- If you will be using your camera to run slide shows (through its video out port), you'll want remote playback control and shooting control.

CAMERA PERFORMANCE

Great image quality doesn't do you any good if your camera is too slow to get the shots you need. Because a digital camera must do so much calculating and processing to create an image, it's easy for it to get bogged down in ways that film cameras can't. You'll *definitely* want to consider the speed and performance of a camera before you buy one. In addition to the speed of the menuing system, be sure to consider and measure the following:

- **Boot time.** How long does it take the camera to boot up? Ideally, you'll want a camera that doesn't need more than three or four seconds of preparation from the time you switch it on—any more than this, and you might miss a shot. Check to see if the camera offers a low-power sleep mode, and test how long it takes the camera to wake up. Leaving your camera in sleep mode will help ensure that it's always ready to shoot, although sleep mode can drain your batteries. One of the downsides to cameras with an extensible lens is that they take a while to boot up because they have to take the time to extend the lens. In addition, you might not feel comfortable walking around with the camera in sleep mode, as the lens will still be extended. However, if you shut the camera down to retract the lens, you'll be forced to wait through a boot cycle when you're ready to shoot again.

- **Prefocus time.** When you press your camera's shutter release halfway down, the camera will perform all of its autofocusing as well as its metering and white balancing (we'll discuss this *prefocusing* step more in Chapter 7). When you test a camera, try to get a sense of how quickly it can perform these prefocusing steps.

- **Shutter lag.** Some digital cameras still have a noticeable lag between the time you press the shutter release and the time the camera actually takes a picture, even if you've already prefocused. If the *shutter lag* is long enough, you might miss that moment you were trying to capture. This is probably the most important performance characteristic to assess before you buy.

- **Recycling.** Be sure to check how long it takes the camera to *recycle* itself after you take a shot. Ideally, you'll want to be able to shoot again immediately. Most modern cameras can recycle right away by storing the previous image in a memory buffer. When the buffer is full, you'll have to wait for it to flush out to the storage card. Be sure to test the camera's performance both before and after the buffer has filled.

FLASH

No matter what level of camera you are considering, most units will have a built-in flash. Obviously, bigger cameras will have a larger, more powerful flash unit, but even small cameras can offer good flash hardware.

Flash photography is one of the most difficult things for any camera to handle, and digital cameras are no exception. Consequently, it's important to carefully evaluate a camera's flash system before you buy.

There are a few simple issues to clarify up front:

- **What is the range of the flash?** Because of their small size, most built-in flashes only have a range of around 10 to 15 feet. Although this is fine for most snapshot situations, for more serious work you'll need additional lighting.

- **Does the flash have a hot shoe or external flash sync connection?** For maximum flash flexibility and control, you want a *hot shoe* for connecting an external flash (Figure 5.35). These standard connections are usually designed to work with specific flash units made by the manufacturer. Make sure that the camera offers TTL metering with the hot shoe. If the camera doesn't have an actual hot shoe (or is too small to have one), then look for a connection for an *external flash sync*. This will allow you to connect an external flash (again, usually a specific model) to the camera using a small cable. You'll probably need to buy some type of bracket to hold the flash.

FIGURE 5.35   For serious flash work, you'll want a camera with a hot shoe or external flash sync connector.

- **Where is the internal flash positioned?** Ideally, you want a flash that is as far from the lens as possible. If the flash is too close to the lens, the camera will be more susceptible to the red-eye effect. We'll discuss this in more detail in Chapter 13, "Essential Imaging Tactics."
- **What flash modes does the camera offer?** Look for a camera that offers a completely automatic mode—wherein the camera decides when to use the flash—a *force flash* or *fill flash* mode, which allows you to force the flash to fire to provide a slight fill light, and a *red-eye reduction* mode, which reduces the chance of red eye in your image by first firing a short flash to close down the irises in the eyes of your subject. Many cameras also offer a *slow sync* mode that lets you

combine flash photography with long shutter speeds to create cool motion blur effects. Be sure that the camera lets you specify whether the flash fires at the beginning or end of the exposure. And, of course, you want the ability to turn the flash off altogether.

- **Does the camera offer control over flash intensity?** Many cameras let you control how strong the flash will be by specifying more or less power, usually measured in f-stops, or fractions of a stop. Given the difficulty that many cameras have with flash metering, this manual override can be essential to getting good flash photos.

In addition to the physical specifications of the camera's flash, you'll also want to assess how well the camera meters and white balances when you use the flash. The best test of a flash's performance is to shoot pictures of people's faces indoors under a slight mix of lighting. The human eye is well-tuned to flesh tones, so pictures of faces make a good test of how well a flash system is reproducing color.

Look at the overall exposure of your image. A poor flash system will overexpose the highlights, resulting in bright white smears instead of smoothly gradated highlights. Skin tones will often go pale or wash out when they are shot with a less-capable flash system. A flash that is too bright will also cast harsh shadows across and behind your subject.

Look at the overall color tone of the image. Is there a color cast of some kind? If you're in a room with strong lights (usually incandescent, or tungsten, lights), your camera might choose to favor those lights when it white balances, resulting in an image with slightly blue highlights. If your image ends up with a slight yellow cast to its highlights, then it probably favored the on-board flash when it was white balancing.

If your camera has a special manual white balance setting for use with a flash, be sure to switch to that setting and try a few shots. You might get better results.

PLAYBACK OPTIONS

You'll be spending a lot of time reviewing images using your camera's playback options, especially when you're in the field. Consequently, it's worth taking a little time to explore a camera's playback features. Are they easy to use? How quickly can you switch from record to playback mode?

In addition to general usability, look for the following features:

- **A *thumbnail* view that lets you view multiple images on-screen at once.** This can greatly speed navigation of a large media card (Figure 5.36).

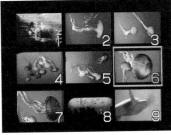 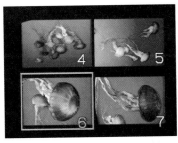 

FIGURE 5.36 A thumbnail view lets you quickly see the contents of your media card. Some cameras also allow you to zoom in to an image, making it easier to check focus and depth of field.

- **Zoom features that let you zoom in on an image and pan around.** A good zoom feature can be a great way of ensuring that a shot was in focus. Most cameras include a number of preset zoom levels (2x, 4x, etc.) as well as the ability to zoom out to view multiple thumbnails. For panning about an image, a smooth pan is much better than a camera that restricts you to looking at specific "quadrants" of an image.
- **Easy deleting and locking features are a must.** In other words, you need a simple, quick interface for deleting single or multiple images. When you have to free up space on a card, you don't want to miss a shot because your camera's interface is too complex.

Some cameras also offer features that automatically rotate the image so that it's upright, whether you shot it vertically or horizontally. This is clever technology, but rotating your camera usually isn't too hard. Other cameras feature printing commands that let you print to special printers designed to work with your camera. Such features can turn your digital camera into a "Polaroid" camera, but for serious work, you'll want more image editing and printing control.

Finally, as you'll see in Chapter 8, *histograms* (computer-generated graphs of the distribution of tones in an image) can be a great exposure calculation aid. Many cameras can display a histogram of an image that you've already shot (Figure 5.37).

This is a valuable feature if you plan on using any manual exposure features.

STORAGE AND INPUT/OUTPUT

A digital camera isn't much good if you can't get your pictures out of it. Fortunately, most cameras come equipped with a number of interfaces for moving your pictures to another device.

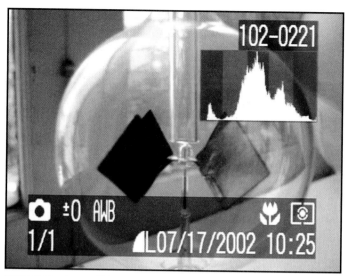

FIGURE 5.37   As you'll learn in Chapter 8, having a camera that can display a histogram is an invaluable aid for using your camera's manual exposure features.

Transferring and Viewing Images

Early generations of cameras typically sported serial ports. These were usually implemented using a simple mini-plug and a special cable that attached to the standard serial port on your computer. As *RS-232* and *RS-432 ports* have been replaced by *USB* and *FireWire* ports, most vendors have been diligent about updating their camera designs.

Today, almost all cameras come equipped with a USB connector of some kind, along with a cable to connect the camera's USB port to the standard USB port on your computer. USB is a good interface that makes for reasonably quick transfer of images. Some cameras also provide remote camera control through the USB port. If you need a computer-operated camera (either for time-lapse, or other automated operations), then be sure that your camera's software supports remote operation.

Transfer Software

Your camera will come bundled with software for transferring images to and from your camera. Some units come with a simple *TWAIN driver* that can be used from within your editing package, while others offer stand-alone applications that allow for *media cataloging,* simple editing, and printing. Many computer operating systems (such as Apple's OS X) offer automatic image transfer. With these systems, any time you plug a camera into your computer, the OS automatically transfers all of the images in the camera to your hard drive.

Because transferring via cable can take a while (and drain your camera batteries in the process) and because you'll usually want more editing power than what is provided by most bundled software, you don't need to worry too much about the capabilities of a camera's software.

Nevertheless, here are some things that make for a stand-out camera application:

- Drag-and-drop transfer of images to and from the camera.
- Automatic panoramic stitching (this is not usually included in the main application itself, but in some bundled software).

Of course, if your camera supports a raw data format, you'll want software that allows you to manipulate the raw data.

EPSON SOFTWARE

One of the great things about Epson cameras is that their bundled software interfaces smoothly with Epson's excellent color printers. Therefore, you can simply click a button in their software and your computer will immediately grab the images off your Epson camera (via USB) and print them on your Epson printer.

Video Input/Output

Most cameras provide a special video output that lets you connect your camera to a television to view your images. Although televisions don't provide nearly enough *dynamic range* to view your images in all their glory, they do seem to be everywhere, providing a convenient way to review images when you are traveling. A video connection can also provide a convenient way to present a slide show of images, and most cameras offer some type of automatic slide-show feature that allows you to step through all of the images on your camera.

Because not all countries use the same video standard, make sure you get a camera that supports the appropriate standard. Most cameras come in either NTSC or PAL versions.

Storage

Film is a very clever invention because it can both capture and store an image. A CCD, on the other hand, can only capture an image.

Consequently, once your camera is done *sampling* and processing an image, it needs a place to put it.

Today, most cameras use some form of *flash memory* card. These are small wafer-like cards that house a type of RAM that doesn't require a constant stream of power (that is, it is *nonvolatile*). Therefore, after your camera has recorded an image, you can shut off the power without worrying about what has been stored on the memory card.

Flash memory cards (or just "flash cards") are a great solution to the digital camera storage problem. They're small, they can hold huge amounts of data (up to 384MB in some cases), and they can be easily swapped with other cards, just like a roll of film.

Currently, there are three major competing flash memory standards. Each has its strengths and weaknesses, but the different technologies are so close in price and performance that you won't need to base your buying decision on a camera's storage device.

CompactFlash

Developed by SanDisk, *CompactFlash* cards are small rigid plastic cards with a row of socket holes that protect the contacts of the cards (Figure 5.38). CompactFlash cards are very durable and currently come in capacities up to 1GB. Inserting a CompactFlash card is very simple because the card can only fit in a CompactFlash slot in the correct way.

Although CompactFlash cards are very durable, they are thin enough that you don't have to apply much pressure to snap one in two. Nevertheless, normal use (including the occasional drop) seems to have no effect on the cards. In addition, many vendors offer lifetime guarantees.

One advantage that CompactFlash cards have over some technologies (such as SmartMedia) is that the controller (the circuitry that the camera uses to interface with the card) is built into the card itself. This means that camera vendors don't have to do anything different with their cameras when a higher-capacity card becomes available—newer cards will always work in older cameras.

Some vendors tout their cards as being faster than other vendors' cards and, in tests, this can be proven to be true. However, in everyday use, you might not be able to feel a difference between one type of card and another. They all seem much faster than using film, and much slower than the instantaneous times that we'd all love to see from our computers.

CompactFlash cards come in two sizes:

- Type I CompactFlash cards are the standard-size cards used in most cameras. Note that Lexar (a company made up of former SanDisk en-

FIGURE 5.38 CompactFlash cards provide high capacities and better compatibility than other formats do.

gineers) manufactures a variation of the Type I card that includes a USB port. If your camera only has a serial port, using a Lexar Smart-Media card can provide you with USB access to your camera's images.

- Type II CompactFlash cards are twice as thick as Type I cards, meaning that they can hold twice as much memory. Currently, the most successful use of the Type II format is IBM's series of Type II-sized *MicroDrive*s, tiny hard drives with capacities up to 1GB. Seemingly the ideal storage solution, there are some MicroDrive caveats to be aware of. Because they use a physical mechanism—a tiny little hard drive— they are, in theory, more prone to data loss than a solid-state memory card. MicroDrives also tend to produce a lot of heat. Consequently, in addition to having a Type II CompactFlash slot, a camera needs to be designed to manage the extra heat produced by a Micro-Drive. MicroDrives also use more battery power than flash memory cards do. Because of their high capacities, MicroDrives present something of an "all your eggs in one basket" risk—should your Micro-Drive crash, you'll lose a *lot* of images. On the plus side, all that space is great for long shoots.

Most CompactFlash vendors label their cards with some type of speed claim—16x, 24x, and so forth. Unfortunately, vendors have never agreed on what, exactly, 1x is, so it's difficult to say what these speed claims really equate to. Also note that read and write times are often more dependent on the camera than on the storage card, so a particular card might be speedier or slower in one device than it will be in another.

SIZE DOES MATTER

Although vendors usually measure their flash cards in terms of megabytes, many vendors define a megabyte as being 1,000,000 bytes. Your computer, on the other hand, defines a megabyte as being 1,048,576 bytes. Therefore, when you stick a flash card in your computer, it might display a slightly smaller capacity than what you were expecting.

SmartMedia

Even thinner than a CompactFlash card, *SmartMedia cards* are barely thicker than a piece of paper. Between their size and their exposed plane of electrical contacts, SmartMedia cards feel very fragile. However, in regular use, they don't seem to be any less durable than a CompactFlash card.

The main downside to SmartMedia technology is that the controller circuitry is not included in the card; it must be built into the camera. Consequently, if a company comes up with some breakthrough that allows for twice as much storage on a SmartMedia card, you won't be able to use those new cards in your older camera. Many vendors provide upgrades to their SmartMedia-based cameras, but these require sending your camera back to the factory to have it altered, a time-consuming process that most people are hesitant to do.

SmartMedia currently has a much lower maximum capacity than CompactFlash (at the time of this writing, SmartMedia has a maximum of 128MB), although their prices are very competitive.

SmartMedia cards (Figure 5.39) come in two variations: 3.3v and 5v cards. The variants are not interchangeable, and you can tell which is which by looking at the corners of your card. It is possible to incorrectly insert a card, but this doesn't seem to damage the card or camera.

Memory Stick

A proprietary format developed by Sony for use in their digital cameras, camcorders, and MP3 players, the *Memory Stick* is a small, rectangular

FIGURE 5.39   SmartMedia cards are small and surprisingly sturdy.

flash card with shielded contacts on one end. No better or worse than any of the other formats, the main drawback to Memory Sticks is that the technology is completely controlled by Sony. (Just think "Beta video-tape" and you'll understand why this is a problem.) Consequently, without third-party development, Memory Stick capacities lag behind other technologies and are often pricier.

PC Cards

Larger cameras such as large format digital backs and some older SLR bodies use PC Card (also known as PCMCIA) flash memory. These cards are the size of the standard Type I PC Card that you might use in your laptop computer and are typically more expensive than the smaller format flash cards, simply because they're not as popular. Increasingly, vendors are switching to the smaller formats for all their cameras.

Floppy Disks

Sony's Mavica cameras are well known for their ability to store images on standard 3.5″ 1.2MB floppy disks. Given that the average JPEG compressed 3-megapixel image takes up around 800K, the only way to fit images on floppy disks is to severely compress them and use a low-resolution CCD. Consequently, these cameras usually produce poor images. Floppy drives are also somewhat power hungry and slow.

3" CDs

As of this writing, one or two vendors have announced cameras that record images onto a tiny, 3" CD writer built into the back of the camera. On the positive side, a 3" CD can hold up to 150MB and, in theory, could be very inexpensive in quantity. On the downside, the big drives make for big cameras, and it remains to be seen if this technology will catch on. Moreover, you can't delete images from CDs as you can from flash media, making them far less flexible than electronic storage.

Does Any of This Matter?

Although there are people who will make arguments for one format over another, there's really not much difference. They are all equally reliable, equally speedy, and (mostly) equivalently priced. CompactFlash is the most popular of the three and, consequently, might have the greatest longevity.

How Much Do You Need?

How much storage you need depends largely on your shooting conditions, how many pictures you typically take, how big your camera's images are, and what level of compression you're using. Obviously, if you're shooting in a computer-equipped studio, then storage is less of a concern as you can dump your pictures to disk as you shoot. Similarly, if you're in the field with your laptop, you'll be able to clear your camera's storage as it fills. However, if you're planning a three-month trip through the Amazon (or even a three-hour trip to the zoo, and you tend to be shutter-happy), then storage might be a bit of a concern.

If you're like most people, when you shoot film you probably take 36 exposures and get back three or four shots that you like—maybe. Digital cameras are no different. For every 40 or so images that you shoot, you'll maybe want to keep a third of them. However, with a digital camera, you don't have to wait until you've shot all 40 before you decide which ones you want to keep. Rather, you can delete the bad pictures as soon as you've taken them. Consequently, digital camera storage goes a little farther than an equivalent number of film exposures because you'll be more selective along the way.

Unfortunately, experience is the only way to find out what your storage needs are. It's safe to assume that on a typical 2- or 3-megapixel camera, a 32MB card will get you two dozen high-quality images. Start with this estimate and try to get an idea for what this translates into in terms of "keeper" images. Then, make sure you have an appropriate amount of storage before embarking on an important shoot.

Media Tips

There are a few things you should know about removable media. Obviously, these cards are fragile, so treat them with care. A good potential storage case for your cards is an empty Altoids box. It's just the right size and will keep your cards protected. Here are other issues to consider:

- The number of images a card can hold depends on the resolution and compression settings that you're currently shooting with. These vary greatly from camera to camera, so you'll need to consult the camera's manual to find these statistics.
- The bigger the card's capacity, the more power it takes to keep it running. Consequently, in theory, smaller cards use less battery. Although it's difficult to tell if this has any bearing in the real world, switching to a smaller capacity card when your batteries run low might garner you a few extra shots.
- Larger-capacity cards generate more heat. If you're using a tiny camera—such as the Canon S200 Digital Elph—which tends to get hot simply because of its design, it might be worth sticking to smaller-capacity cards. As you'll see later, excess heat can make your images noisier.
- If something goes wrong with a larger-capacity card, you'll lose more images than you would if you had been using a smaller-capacity card. Therefore, it might be worth buying a number of smaller cards instead of one big one.
- X-rays don't seem to matter, so feel free to take your camera with you to the airport, dentist, or thoracic surgeon.

MEDIA DRIVES

The best way to get images transferred to your computer is through a drive that supports the same media that your camera uses. These USB devices work just like any other drive on your computer. Insert your media card into the drive and it will show up on your desktop. You can then copy files to and from the card. Priced anywhere between $40 and $100, these drives are the fastest and easiest way to transfer images to your computer, and they don't require you to drain your camera batteries (Figure 6.6).

If you have a laptop computer with a PC Card slot, then you might consider getting a PC card adapter for your camera's media. These are special PC cards into which you insert your camera's media. Put the card into your laptop's PC slot and it will appear on your desktop like any other drive (Figure 6.2).

WHAT'S IN THE BOX?

When you buy a camera, you'll want to consider everything you're getting for your money, so take some time to assess what else is bundled with your camera (Figure 5.40).

Camera (with strap)   Manuals
Software   Cables (video & USB)
Battery charger and set of batteries   Media Card

FIGURE 5.40   Ideally, you want a camera package that includes these components.

Don't expect to get a huge media card with your camera. Most vendors ship 8MB cards with their 1- and 2-megapixel cameras, and 16MB cards with their 3-megapixel cameras. If these seem small, that's because they are. Unfortunately, because of the economies of scale, adding a bigger card would usually raise the price of the camera by more than it would cost you to buy a bigger card on your own. Therefore, you should plan to buy some additional media along with your camera.

In addition, don't count on getting rechargeable batteries. As with media, most manufacturers can't compete with third-party offerings, so they skip the rechargeable batteries to keep the camera's price down.

Batteries

What with the CCD, the LCD screen, the media drive, the flash, and the motorized zoom lens, the typical digital camera demands a *lot* of power. Because most cameras can really tear through batteries, power management is an important concern, particularly if you'll be shooting in the field for extended periods.

Digital cameras offer two battery options: a proprietary, (custom) battery, or support for batteries of standard size (usually AA size).

- **Proprietary batteries.** Canon and Sony consistently use special *proprietary (custom) battery packs* in their cameras. The advantage to these is that they usually include special controllers that can provide very accurate charge estimates (Sony InfoLithium batteries are particularly accurate in their estimation of remaining charge) and special power-saving operations. They also tend to last a long time. On the downside, custom batteries require custom chargers, so if your battery dies in the field, you can't just run down to the corner store and buy another.
- **Standard-size rechargeable batteries.** Offering the same battery technology as a proprietary battery, standard-size rechargeable batteries offer the advantage of universality. As better battery technology comes along (as long as it comes along in the same size), you can drop these batteries into your camera. Standard-size rechargeables are much cheaper than proprietary designs, are readily available, and in a pinch can always be replaced by normal alkaline batteries (Figure 5.41).

In addition to sizes, there are a number of different battery technologies available.

- **Alkaline batteries.** Alkaline batteries are really not good for much when it comes to a digital camera. In some cases, you'll be hard-pressed to get half a dozen shots out of a set of alkalines before they

FIGURE 5.41   Rechargeable batteries come in special proprietary formats, or standard AA sizes.

are too weak to be used. Digital cameras have very specific power requirements, and as soon as a set of alkalines drops below those levels, the camera will register them as dead. You can usually continue to use them for a while in a lower-power device such as a Walkman. In general, use alkalines only when you absolutely have to. The cost, waste, and environmental impact just isn't worth it.

- **NiCAD (Nickel Cadmium) batteries.** *NiCAD batteries* were, until recently, the most popular rechargeable technology. NiCADs don't deliver a lot of power, though, and they need to be drained completely before you recharge them or they will develop a "memory" that will prevent them from being completely recharged.

- **NiMH (Nickel-Metal-Hydride) batteries.** *NiMH batteries* are relatively inexpensive (usually $25 to $30 for a set of four, plus another $35 or $40 for a charger), powerful, quick to recharge, and lack a memory. In addition, NiMH batteries are more environmentally friendly than either NiCADs or Alkalines. NiMH batteries are the ideal choice for the digital camera owner. In fact, buy a few sets—one for your camera, an extra set to go in your pocket, and a set to go in your recharger.

- **L-Ion (Lithium Ion) batteries.** *L-Ion batteries* are also a good choice, although not as prevalent, and they are sometimes more expensive. You can often find chargers that will charge both NiMH and L-Ion batteries.
- **Lithium batteries.** Lithium batteries are not rechargeable, but offer a lot of power for a long time. Roughly the shape of two AA-size batteries stuck together, you'll need to be sure your camera can use Lithium batteries. Although strong and long lasting, they're still disposable, and are usually rather pricey.

When you shop for a recharger, you might want to consider the strength of the charger. Some chargers can recharge faster than others, although they will all take several hours. In general, any recharger will probably serve you just fine. We'll discuss battery use, management, and performance in more detail in Chapter 7.

SOLAR RECHARGER

If you want to take your digital camera camping, hiking, or boating, then you might consider buying a solar-powered battery charge. A solar recharger is able to recharge a set of four AA-size batteries in 12 hours of direct sunlight exposure and can solve most of your power requirements when you're literally "in the field."

SPECIAL FEATURES

On top of the many features we just discussed, many vendors pack their cameras with special, unique features that can be a boon or a burden to the digital photographer. With their on-board computers and automatic functions, digital cameras can perform many tricks that film cameras can't. Listed next are some unique features that you might encounter in your camera shopping. Some of these features are great; others are rather silly.

- **Time-lapse.** A scant few cameras offer a time-lapse feature that lets you program the camera to automatically shoot a picture at a predefined interval. A good time-lapse feature will let you specify an interval ranging from a few seconds to a few days. For documenting slow processes, creating animations, or producing high-quality time-lapse video, a time-lapse feature is essential.
- **Remote computer control.** Some cameras include software that lets you control your camera from your computer via the same serial or USB link that the camera uses to download images. If you need to take pictures in harsh, industrial conditions, or want to leave your camera unattended, this feature might be the answer.

- **Auto-bracketing.** As we'll see in Chapter 8, *bracketing* is the process of shooting the same image with slightly different exposure settings to help ensure that you get a good shot. Many cameras now feature an *auto-bracketing* feature that will automatically shoot four or five images with slightly different exposures each time you press the shutter release.

- **Voice annotation.** Although the ability to record and store small voice annotations (comments) with each image is not a tremendously useful feature, some applications—real estate photography, for example—can benefit from it. However, if you're trying to take images with as much quality as your camera can muster, then you won't really want to use up extra storage on voice recording.

- **Best-shot selection.** Some of Nikon's digital cameras include a unique "best-shot selector" that automatically shoots a series of images when you press the shutter button, analyzes them to determine which one is best, saves that one, and throws out the rest. This feature is best used in tricky macro situations where it can be difficult to hold the camera steady enough to get a clear shot. (Best-shot selection seems to work by simply selecting the largest file as the best. Since the sharpest image will compress the least, the file with the largest size is most likely the sharpest.)

- **In-camera effects.** Many cameras offer special effects features that can automatically *solarize*, tint, or turn your images into negatives. These are, of course, all tasks that can be performed in your computer with a great deal more control. It's almost always better to skip these features and shoot the cleanest, best-looking image you can.

- **Noise reduction.** Some cameras include special noise reduction modes that kick in automatically during longer exposures. Such schemes can often greatly improve the quality of low-light shots.

- **Pixel mapping.** It is possible for a pixel on your CCD to die or "get stuck." Some cameras now feature *pixel mapping* features that will cause the camera to analyze its CCD and map out any dead pixels. The camera will then interpolate the missing pixels when it produces the final image.

- **User sets.** User sets allow you to define different combinations of features that can be quickly accessed by simply changing feature sets. For example, you might define a particular configuration for indoor flash photography, and another for outdoor manual exposures.

COMPARE FOR YOURSELF

Included on the companion CD-ROM is a set of comparison images from a number of cameras ranging from inexpensive point-and-shoots to professional SLRs. These images were all shot at roughly the same time of day over the course of a week. Although not a stringent laboratory comparison, they should give you an idea of the range of quality differences that are available from camera to camera (Figure 5.42).

Kodak DX4900   **Nikon Coolpix 885**   **Olympus E20**

FIGURE 5.42 Included on the companion CD-ROM is a collection of comparison shots from over a dozen different digital cameras. Each image was shot on full auto, at roughly the same time of day, within a few weeks of each other. Although not a definitive sample of the capabilities of each camera, the comparison is a good way to see how different an image can appear from camera to camera, and is a good opportunity to practice your image evaluation skills.

Even if you're not interested in any of these particular cameras, comparing all of these images will give you some practice in evaluating image quality, and prepare you for the variations in images that you're likely to see once you start shopping for a camera.

WHAT SHOULD I BUY?

As you've seen, choosing a digital camera involves balancing and compromising on a number of different features and technical considerations. In the end, though, there are baseline features that you should absolutely demand from a camera. If you want the simplest buying advice possible, then you'll want to pick a camera that provides the following:

- Satisfactory (or better) image quality. Always defer to image quality as the ultimate arbiter of camera value, because when the shooting's over (no matter how easy or difficult it was), if you don't have a decent image, then you've wasted your time.
- Controls and body design that you find comfortable and will facilitate the way you like to shoot. This includes not only the shape and feel of the camera, but the quality and coverage of the unit's viewfinder(s) and the focal length of the lens (in other words, does the lens provide the wide angles or telephoto qualities you want), the right type of storage and connectivity, and support for any external flash units you might want to use.
- Resolution that's appropriate for your intended output medium. Although it's simple to follow the "more is better" approach when choosing a resolution, this isn't always the case. If you're not sure about the resolution needs of your intended output medium, see Chapter 15, "Output."
- Exposure compensation controls that are easy to access.
- For maximum creative flexibility, look for manual exposure and priority modes.
- Manual white balance control is a must for ensuring color quality.
- Adjustable ISOs guarantee that you'll be able to shoot under different lighting conditions.
- At the very least, your camera should have two metering modes: a matrix metering mode and a spot meter.

Obviously, your needs might go far beyond this, but these items will help to ensure that you can get the shots you want.

6

BUILDING A WORKSTATION

In This Chapter

- Choosing an Operating System
- Building Your System
- Software
- Accessories

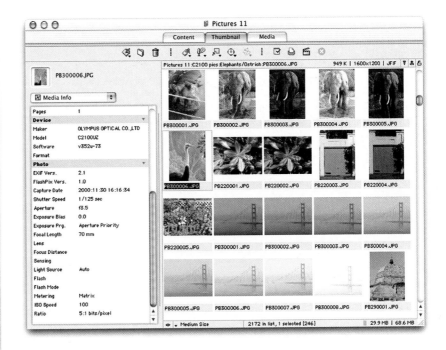

Ask any experienced film photographer and he or she will tell you that shooting the picture is only half the work of taking a photograph. The other half occurs in the darkroom where you exercise precise control of developing and printing techniques to achieve the results you imagined when you were shooting. Digital photography is no different—but, of course, there's no darkroom involved. While film photographers rely on rooms full of enlargers, plumbing, and photographic chemicals, you need nothing more than a decent computer, a lot of storage, some image processing software, and a printer.

In this chapter, you'll learn the issues and questions that you need to resolve when you construct a workstation for processing your digital images. Although we discuss computer hardware and image editing software in this chapter, printers and other output devices will be covered separately in Chapter 15, "Output."

Your first step in assembling a workstation is one you might have already taken: select an operating system.

CHOOSING AN OPERATING SYSTEM

If you're interested in digital photography, you probably already own a computer and so have already chosen an operating system (OS). If you haven't, or if you're thinking of upgrading, or if you simply don't like your operating system, then it's time to make a choice. Since the OS you choose will affect all your other buying decisions, it's the first issue to consider.

As far as digital photography is concerned, OS choice is really a matter of preference. Whether you choose the Mac or Windows, you'll get pretty much the same capability and spend about the same amount of money. The main differences between them are in their interfaces, but a discussion of the strengths and weakness of each system is far beyond the scope of this book. Rather, this chapter will simply cover the issues that are relevant to digital photographers.

Macintosh

The Macintosh is where mainstream digital image editing began. Photoshop and its first competitors were originally written for the Mac OS between 1988 and 1990, providing Apple and its developers with 10 years of tweaking and refining. As a result, the Mac OS has a slight advantage over Windows when it comes to photography. Apple's *color matching software*, ColorSync, is several years ahead of its Windows competition, and is supported by a huge range of vendors, from software developers to scanner and printer manufacturers. However, it takes a little work to use color matching software. If you don't really think you'll bother with the necessary practices (see Chapter 10, "Preparing Your Images for Editing"), then ColorSync doesn't really matter.

On the hardware side, Apple's thorough integration of FireWire and USB into all of their latest hardware makes for systems—both desktop and laptop—that are well prepared for connecting to digital cameras. In addition, all Macs include built-in video hardware that allows for *Video LUT animation*—a feature that greatly eases many image editing tasks (see the section *Monitors* later in this chapter).

Apple's OS X offers another advantage in the form of Aqua, Apple's new user interface. Built into Aqua is a new display technology called Quartz. Based on Adobe's *PDF* technology, Quartz provides incredibly sophisticated compositing technology at the OS level. As such, Quartz offers the promise of new compositing applications and improved printing workflow.

Windows

The main advantage of Windows over the Mac OS is that it is ubiquitous. Consequently, you probably won't ever have trouble finding a service bureau that can handle your Windows-based files. Similarly, repair shops and new equipment are often easier to find and less expensive because the Windows realm is more competitive.

The main disadvantage to a Windows-based computer is that it is more difficult to maintain. With more complicated hardware and software setups, you might spend a lot more time fidgeting with your computer than working with your images.

For the type of work covered in this book, your only real concern is the capability to run a capable image editing program, so either the Mac or Windows should work just fine for your digital darkroom forays.

BUILDING YOUR SYSTEM

Once you've chosen an OS, you're ready to select a computer. Your hardware concerns are mostly the same no matter which OS you use. When you select a computer, you'll want to pay particular attention to:

- RAM
- Processor speed
- Storage

- Monitors
- Input/output options

Of course, you'll probably be using your computer for more than just processing images, so if you have other concerns (perhaps you'll also be using it for editing video, making music, checking e-mail), then you'll need to factor in the particular requirements of those tasks as well.

RAM

Although a fast processor is essential for good image editing performance, of greater concern is the amount of random access memory (RAM) in your computer. High-resolution digital photos can be very memory hungry, and if you start performing complex effects, your memory needs will go even higher. As such, the amount of RAM installed in your computer will have a huge effect on image editing performance.

Adobe recommends a RAM size equal to two to three times the size of your typical image. Although your image might only be 4MB, by the time you've added three or four more layers, your image's RAM requirements will have quadrupled. Things get even more complicated when you factor in the RAM requirements of Photoshop's History palette or if you plan to use filters that need to load your entire image into RAM. For maximum performance, you'll want a RAM level closer to 20 times the size of your image. In addition, remember that your OS and other applications will also need some memory, so don't base your RAM needs on Photoshop alone.

In the end, if you're on a budget, you might want to consider paying for a slightly slower, less-expensive processor and putting the money you save into more RAM (Figure 6.1).

Processor Speed

These days, even the slowest processors are fast enough for most Photoshop work. If you're in a high-pressure production environment where you need to crank out images in a hurry, then it's worth investing a little more for a faster CPU. For most work, however, you can get by with a fairly average (by today's standards) processor.

Many people think that a higher clock rate means an inherently faster processor. Consequently, when they see 700MHz, they immediately assume that the processor must be faster than a 500MHz unit. If the processors in question are the same type of processor, then that assumption is correct. However, a 500MHz G4 will perform much faster than a

Memory efficiency gauge

FIGURE 6.1 Photoshop provides RAM displays that make it easy to determine if your computer would benefit from more RAM.

500MHz Pentium III, so, it's important to look at more than just the clock speed of a chip when you assess processor speed. Unfortunately, many computer salespeople simply push higher clock speeds because it's the easiest way to make a sale. Do a little research before you buy.

In the end, if you're having trouble deciding between a 500MHz and 750MHz processor, go for the 500MHz computer and spend the extra money on RAM. More RAM will make a bigger difference to your image editing application than an extra 200MHz of processor speed will.

Storage

The bad news is that digital images can take up a lot of space. The good news is that hard disk storage is really cheap. Simply put, the more storage you have, the better. Bear in mind that you'll need space for your OS, your image editing applications, and any other software you plan on using, and that's all *before* you've shot any pictures. A 20 to 30GB will keep you editing for a long time. You will also want to consider how easy it is to expand your computer's storage for future use.

For Mac users, storage expansion will take the form of external FireWire drives or internal IDE drives (as long as you're using a tower machine that has internal drive bays). For Windows users, extra storage will usually be in the form of inexpensive IDE drives. SCSI drives are also possible for both platforms; however, these drives are more expensive, and most digital photography tasks don't require the extra speed that SCSI can provide.

You'll also want some type of storage for backing up and for transporting images to service bureaus. Recordable CDs offer the best price per megabyte. Zip and Jaz drives are speedy and re-writable, but are too expensive for long-term storage. Ideally, it's nice to have both, but if you have to choose just one, go with a recordable CD. Blank CDs are cheap, everyone has a CD reader, and the CDs have a long shelf life.

CD-R OR CD-RW

Some recordable CD drives can also create re-writeable discs using special, more expensive re-writeable media. CD-RWs are great for storing copies of work in progress. Backing up in-progress works to a re-usable CD-RW while you're working and then to a normal CD when you're finished is a great way to prevent the confusion of having multiple versions of a work-in-progress.

Monitors

You're going to be spending a lot of time staring at your computer screen so it's important to choose wisely when you select that screen. In addition to the usual questions of brightness, sharpness, and contrast, as a digital photographer you should be particularly choosy about color reproduction. How picky you should be depends largely on the final destination of your photos.

If you're shooting for the Web, color fidelity is less of a concern because there is no *color calibration* system for the Web. That is, even though you might have the color perfect on your screen, there's no telling what it will look like on someone else's monitor. Therefore, simply choose a monitor that looks good to you and is comfortable to use.

If print is your final destination, then get ready to spend some additional money. For serious print work (that is, commercial press-ready print work), you're going to want a high-quality monitor that can be hardware calibrated. (We'll discuss hardware calibration more in Chapter 10.) Typically, a print-quality monitor is going to start at $800 or $900 and go up from there.

Of course, you'll need a video card to feed a signal to your monitor. If your computer doesn't already have a video card, then you'll want to consider the following when you shop:

- **What resolutions does it support?** For most image editing work, you want to be sure you're using a video card that supports 1024 × 768 pixels. Because of the palette-heavy interfaces of most image editing programs, a screen with a resolution less than 1024 × 786 can feel uncomfortably cramped. Higher resolution is fine, but it takes a good monitor to display a very high-resolution image with no visible distortion.

- **What color depth does it support?** Or, how much *video RAM (VRAM)* does it have? The number of colors that a video card can simultaneously display is known as its *color depth*. Color depth is also referred to as *bit depth* because more bits per pixel means more simultaneous colors. The amount of video RAM installed on the card determines both the color depth and resolution that the card can display. Make sure that your card can support millions of colors (or *24-bit color*) at your desired resolution.

- **Does it provide any acceleration?** Some video cards include special co-processors for accelerating both two-dimensional (2D) and three-dimensional (3D) performance. 2D acceleration means that scrolling and screen redrawing will be much faster, while 3D acceleration will greatly improve your computer's performance when you're working in a 3D modeling and animation package.

- **Can it perform video LUT animation?** A look-up table, or LUT, is the full index of colors that a monitor can display. By changing the contents of the LUT, it's possible to immediately change the contents of the screen. Animating the LUT is a quick and easy way for a program to show changes on-screen. If your video card supports *video LUT animation*, then many color correction and editing tasks in Photoshop will be much easier because the program will be able to manipulate the LUT to display color corrections in real time.

When you shop for a monitor, you'll want to try to assess the monitor's image quality. First, look for overall color quality and sharpness. Check the edges of the screen for any convergence troubles (slight red, green, or blue fringing around pixels) and for distortion problems—slight bulging or pinching of the image. In addition, you'll need to consider these issues:

- **Size.** The physical area of your screen is largely a subjective choice. Do you prefer squinting at a smaller image on a 15" monitor, or bathing in the radiation of a 22" monitor? Whatever size fits your ocular preference and desktop space is the size that's right for you.

- **Frequency.** The refresh rate—the frequency with which a monitor's screen is redrawn—is measured in hertz (Hz). The higher the number, the more frequently the screen refreshes. The more frequent the refresh, the less flicker a screen will have. Ideally, you want a screen that supports multiple frequencies and different resolutions. Higher frequency is better.

- **Curvature.** The front of a monitor usually has a slight curve to it. If you're willing to pay more money, you can get a monitor with less curve, or even one that's totally flat. Less curve means less distortion at the edges of your image.

LCD Monitors

If desk space is a concern, or if you're not thrilled about the potential health effects of sitting in front of a cathode ray tube (CRT), then an LCD monitor might be a good choice for you. Just a few years ago, there was no point in even considering an LCD for serious photography work, because the image quality simply wasn't good enough. LCD technology has greatly improved, however, and an LCD monitor is now a viable option for the serious digital photographer and image editor.

However, be warned that LCD monitors often don't offer *contrast ratios* that are as good as what you'll find on a CRT. Lighter shades, for example, will often appear completely white on an LCD, making it difficult to judge the true color balance of an image. As with any monitor, over time you'll probably come to understand how the image you see on your LCD screen will actually look when it is printed. In the meantime, expect to do a lot of printing and adjusting and reprinting to get the colors and contrast ratios that you're looking for.

When you use an LCD screen, be aware that the brightness and contrast of most screens change depending on your viewing angle. If you're using a big enough screen, you can be tricked into thinking that the edge of the screen is darker than it really is. When you consider an LCD, try moving from side to side, and up and down in front of the screen to see how the brightness and contrast varies over the surface of the image (yes, people will look at you funny, but given the price of the typical LCD monitor, it will be worth the humiliation).

WHAT ABOUT A LAPTOP?

The ideal computer choice for a digital photographer is a good, high-powered laptop. Because it is portable, a laptop computer allows you to edit, retouch, and print your images anywhere, and makes for a great mass storage device for those extended digital photography expeditions.

For the most part, choosing a laptop computer involves all of the same processor, RAM, and storage considerations as choosing a desktop. Although there are currently no Mac or Windows laptops available that offer all the computer power that you can find in a desktop, you should have no trouble finding a laptop that delivers all the performance you'll need for digital photography.

In addition to the performance concerns discussed previously, you'll want to look for the following:

- **A very good screen.** An LCD is never as good as an expensive monitor, but there are plenty of laptops that offer very good screens suitable for image editing. As with a desktop monitor, look for a resolution of 1024 × 768, and check the screen for general image quality and sharpness.
- **A video out port.** The ideal laptop setup is to use your laptop LCD screen in the field, and a high-quality monitor when you're back home. At the very least, a video out port will allow you to take your computer to a service bureau and connect to a monitor there for final proofing. Using a two-monitor system can also make your virtual workspace more comfortable. You can, for example, keep all of your image editor's tool palettes on your laptop's LCD screen and your image on your CRT.
- **USB, FireWire, or serial ports.** Be sure to get a computer that provides the type of port that your camera uses. Currently, most cameras connect through a USB port, but some higher-end cameras use FireWire, while most older cameras use a normal serial connection.
- **A PC Card slot.** A PC Card slot provides a simple, quick way to transfer images to your computer. Using an adapter like the one shown in Figure 6.2, you can simply insert the media from your camera directly into your laptop. The media will show up on your desktop just as a floppy disk or CD would. You can then drag and drop files from the card to your computer's hard drive. PC Card adapters are currently available for CompactFlash, SmartMedia, and Memory Sticks.

Finally, you'll want to consider size and weight when you shop for a laptop. Remember that you're already going to be carrying a bag of camera gear, so you don't want to weigh yourself down even more with a computer that's too heavy.

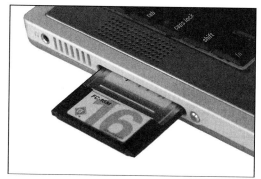

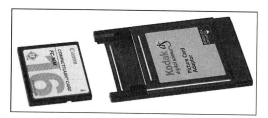

FIGURE 6.2 With a PC Card adapter, you can insert your camera's media directly into your laptop.

SOFTWARE

When it comes to editing, correcting, manipulating, and adjusting your digital images, you'll probably spend most of your time in a single image editing application. However, there might be times when you also move your images into special programs designed for panoramic stitching, animation, video production, or compression.

Image Editing Applications

In case you haven't noticed already, this book was written by a Photoshop devotee. Yes, there are other good image editing applications out there, and yes, some of them have features that Photoshop needs. In the end, though, the combination of features, interface, third-party and user support, and Photoshop's excellent color fidelity and printer support make it difficult to recommend anything else.

Beginning users might find Photoshop very complicated because it is a complex, powerful program. However, with just a little bit of explanation, even novice users can quickly learn the Photoshop basics. In this book, all examples and tutorials are Photoshop-based, and a demonstration version is included on the companion CD-ROM.

ON THE CD

Photoshop Elements is a less expensive, stripped-down version of Photoshop that probably offers all of the functionality that most users will ever need. If you don't expect to do any commercial printing of your photos, then you probably don't need the extra four-color support and additional modes of the full-blown Photoshop package. Elements is a great way to get into Photoshop. If you need more power later, you can always upgrade to the full version, which shares most of Elements' interface.

If, for some reason, you decide to use something other than Photoshop, make sure it has the following features.

Levels and Curves Controls

There's no better, easier way to adjust contrast, color, and saturation than with Levels and Curves controls. Although your program's interface might vary somewhat, make sure that its Levels and Curves features include the controls and adjustments that are highlighted in Figures 6.3A and 6.3B.

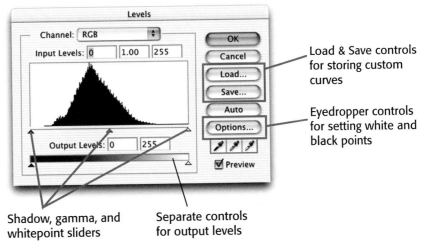

Load & Save controls for storing custom curves

Eyedropper controls for setting white and black points

Shadow, gamma, and whitepoint sliders

Separate controls for output levels

A.

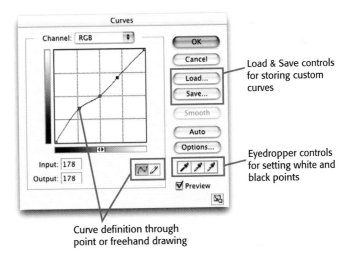

Load & Save controls for storing custom curves

Eyedropper controls for setting white and black points

Curve definition through point or freehand drawing

B.

FIGURE 6.3 If you're not going to use Photoshop for your image editing tasks, be sure that the program you choose offers Levels and Curves dialog boxes similar to the ones shown here. You will learn more about shadow, gamma, and white point later in this book.

An Eyedropper Tool with an Information Readout

For more refined image analysis, it's essential to have an Eyedropper tool and some type of Information window or palette. With these tools, you can find out exactly what the color values are in a particular part of an image. Such information can be very handy when you make tone and color adjustments.

Good Paintbrush and Clone Tools

For retouching, you have to have a good set of paintbrushes. Make sure your program supports pressure-sensitive tablets for more natural-looking brush strokes. A *Clone* (sometimes called Rubber Stamp) tool is absolutely essential for everything from erasing artifacts to touching up images. Although nowadays this shouldn't be too much of a concern, make sure that your program's paint brushes are anti-*aliased* (that is, they have soft edges).

Access to Individual Color Channels

You'll perform a lot of corrections and adjustments by working on specific color channels (Figure 6.4). Make sure your image editor lets you view and edit specific color channels directly.

Support for Multiple Color Spaces

Although your camera and desktop printer both operate in RGB color space, you might need other color spaces for specific tasks. Commercial printers usually require documents to be in CMYK color, while some corrections and adjustments are easier to perform in L*A*B color. If you do a lot of black-and-white work, you'll probably want the capability to make *duotones, tritones,* and *quadtones.*

Support for Photoshop Plug-Ins

You can expand and extend Photoshop's features through the use of special *plug-ins,* small bits of code that can be added to Photoshop. Photoshop plug-ins (sometimes referred to as *filters*) allow you to do everything from blurring an image to adding 3D objects. Many digital cameras interface with your computer through a Photoshop *Acquire Plug-in,* a special piece of software that lets Photoshop communicate with your camera through a serial, USB, or FireWire cable. If your camera requires the use of such a

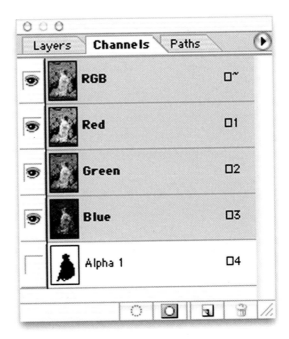

FIGURE 6.4   The image editor you choose should have
support for editing and viewing individual color channels.

plug-in, then you'll definitely need an image editor that supports Photoshop's plug-in format.

Unsharp Mask, Blur, and Noise Filters

You'll use these three basic filters for many everyday editing chores, so make sure your application provides some equivalent.

File Format Support

TIFF, JPEG, GIF, BMP, and ideally Photoshop are the bare minimum file formats that your application should support. Obviously, if your job requires specific file formats, you'll want to be sure your application supports those as well.

The tutorials and examples included in this book use all of the features discussed here. Even if your program of choice provides different approaches to these features, you should be able to follow along with the tutorials and examples.

ADOBE PHOTOSHOP ELEMENTS

One of the most important software developments since the last edition of this book is Adobe's release of Photoshop Elements, a scaled-down more affordable version of Adobe's full-blown Photoshop package. Elements scores over Photoshop's previous low-end package, PhotoDeluxe, in that it offers a Photoshop-like interface, editing tools, and far more editing power. What's more, with a street price of less than $100, Elements makes it possible to get most of the Photoshop power that you need at a very affordable price (Figure 6.5).

So, what do you not get for $100? Most of the features missing from Elements are higher-end features that you might not need anyway. For example, Elements lacks the capability to work with CMYK images—the type of images you need to create if you're going to prepare images for professional offset printing. Elements also lacks the capability to edit and view individual *color channels*. As you'll see later, this can important, as channel editing is a necessary feature for creating certain types of effects. Finally, Elements does not include some of Photoshop 7's more advanced editing tools such as the Healing Brush.

However, you might be surprised to hear that Elements provides some features that are *not* found in the full, pro-level Photoshop. Elements includes a built-in panorama stitcher, and a number of automated editing tools, such as a red-eye removal tool and "recipes" that can automatically take care of common image problems.

In general, Elements is probably enough power for most of your image processing needs. Whether it's right for you should become more apparent as you learn more about the techniques and theories presented in Chapters 10 through15. Most of the editing operations included in this book can be performed using Elements.

Panoramic Software

In Chapter 9, "Special Shooting," we'll discuss panoramic shooting, the process of shooting a series of image "tiles" that can be *stitched* together to create a seamless panorama. If your camera didn't ship with stitching software, you'll need to buy some.

FIGURE 6.5 Photoshop Elements offers a good deal of Photoshop's power, but at a far more affordable price.

Wavelet Compression

Using new *wavelet compression* technologies, products such as AltaMira's Genuine Fractals PrintPro do an extraordinary job of both losslessly compressing your image and enlarging it to huge dimensions with little or no artifacting. If you want to blow your images up to larger sizes, Genuine Fractals, a set of Photoshop Import and Export plug-ins, is the only way to go.

How big can you enlarge images? In November of 2000, Nikon took a photograph from a Coolpix 990 and used Genuine Fractals to blow it up to 65 × 43 feet (that's right, *feet!).* The resulting six-story image was printed on vinyl and hung on the side of a building in New York City's Times Square.

Image Cataloging Software

One of the great things about a digital camera is that you can shoot and shoot and shoot. Unfortunately, one result of all this shooting is that you'll end up with a drive filled with zillions of files, each with a vague name like P000394.jpg. An image cataloging program not only provides a way of keeping your images organized, sortable, and searchable, it can also provide a quick and easy way of viewing a disk full of images at the end of the day. Think of it as a giant digital light table. Although there are a number of applications out there, iView is one of the best (Figure 6.6). Offering good speed, powerful features, and decent networking, it's a good choice for the typical digital photographer, and a demo version is included on the companion CD-ROM.

ON THE CD

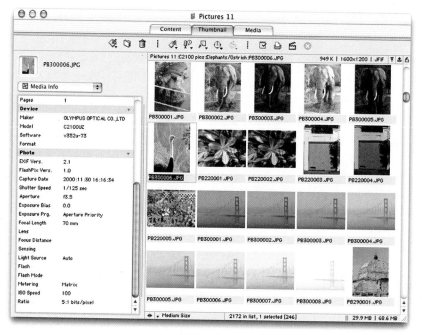

FIGURE 6.6   An image cataloging program such as iView Multimedia is a must-have for managing the huge number of images that you can quickly produce with a digital camera.

File Recovery Software

Alas, there might come a time when you accidentally erase an image, or an entire card of images, without realizing that you haven't backed them up to your computer. Fortunately, there are a number of excellent file recovery programs that can often recover your images intact, as long as you haven't already recorded new images onto the card.

Although you might already own file recovery software such as Norton Utilities, it's important to note that such programs usually can't recognize removable media such as CompactFlash and SmartMedia cards. Fortunately, a number of vendors have written software specifically designed for recovering data from these types of media.

PhotoRescue is one such program. Available for Mac and Windows, a demo version is included on the companion CD-ROM. Although the program is well designed and very effective, you will, hopefully, never need to use it.

ON THE CD

ACCESSORIES

Finally, one or two accessory items can make your life with your digital camera easier, the main one being a media drive that supports the type of media used by your camera (Figure 6.7). These drives typically connect through your computer's USB or FireWire port. Insert your camera's media into the drive's slot, just as you would insert a floppy into a floppy drive, and it will appear on your desktop as another volume, allowing you to drag and drop images onto your computer's hard drive.

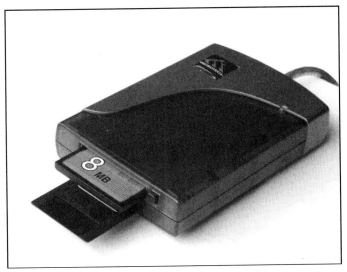

FIGURE 6.7   A CompactFlash or SmartMedia drive provides a simple, quick way to get your images into your computer. In addition to saving time, you'll save camera battery power.

If your camera uses a USB cable to connect to your computer, and if you already have a number of USB devices installed, then you might need to get a *USB hub*. Offering multiple USB ports, USB hubs make it possible to connect several USB devices simultaneously.

Finally, you will, of course, want a printer of some kind. Printing is a huge topic, however, and Chapter 15 is devoted entirely to choosing and using any number of different types of printers.

READY! AIM!

If you read and considered the last two chapters, and made all of the relevant purchases, then you have everything you need to start shooting! The next section of the book (Chapters 7 through 9) deals exclusively with shooting and, for the most part, won't involve your computer very much. Don't worry, though, you'll get plenty of mouse time when you start working with Photoshop in Chapter 10.

7

SHOOTING

In This Chapter

- Initial Camera Settings
- Framing and Focusing
- Metering
- Automatic Exposure
- Simple Flash Photography
- Power and Storage Management

Supposedly, when she was shooting, famed photographer Margaret Bourke-White used to simply set her camera on 1/100th of a second and then shoot the same image over and over using every aperture that her camera could manage. This, combined with her gift for composition, ensured that at least one of her images would come out the way she envisioned.

If you're like most people, you probably find yourself shooting whole rolls of film hoping that one or two of the images will be "keepers." Unfortunately, no camera technology can guarantee that you'll always shoot great images, but there are a number of things you can do to improve your chances of getting images you like, and digital cameras offer a number of creative advantages that make it easier to take good shots.

Because you don't have to concern yourself with film and processing, digital cameras make it very easy to use Bourke-White's approach to photography. A much better philosophy, though, is to spend some time learning how to intelligently use the tools and features found on your camera.

Although there is plenty of room for artistry in the photographic process, when it finally comes down to pressing that shutter button, you have to make a *lot* of simple mechanical decisions, ranging from lens choice to exposure options. As discussed earlier, this book is going to leave the discussion of photographic artistry to the photographic artists. Composition, perception, and other more "artistic" topics are well covered in any number of books, and a list of recommendations is included in Appendix A, "Suggested Reading."

Once you have a vision of how you want a particular image to look, you need to know how to use the controls and settings on your camera to achieve that vision. In this chapter, you'll learn about the framing controls and automatic exposure options that your camera provides. In the next chapter, we'll delve more deeply into the complex processes of light metering and selecting an exposure.

INITIAL CAMERA SETTINGS

Before you start to shoot a picture, you'll need to configure your camera based on your current shooting conditions, and on the type of output you want. For example, you'll need to set the camera's resolution and compression settings differently if your images will be used on the Web rather than print. Preparing your camera to shoot begins with selecting a shooting mode.

Choosing a Mode

Most likely, your digital camera has a number of shooting modes that dictate what exposure decisions will be made by the camera, and what decisions will be left up to you. Your first task when you approach a shot, therefore, is to choose the appropriate shooting mode. Often, shooting on full automatic will be all you need to do (and don't worry, shooting on automatic doesn't mean you're a wimpy photographer). In other cases, you might have a lighting situation that's just tricky enough, or a compositional vision that's just unusual enough that you need to put the camera into a mode that will provide you with the appropriate manual overrides. Every photographic situation is unique, of course, but there are some general guidelines you can follow to determine when you should use each shooting mode. As you learn more about digital photography, and your camera in general, you'll get a better idea of which mode to choose.

Full Automatic

Most automatic modes take care of everything. They select a white balance, ISO, shutter speed, and aperture, and choose whether to use the flash. Most automatic modes also let you select a metering mode, if your camera offers a choice. Some automatic modes will let you override white balance and ISO settings, while others require you to switch to a special Program mode if you want to change these settings. For the most part, the automatic mode on your camera will do a good job in just about any situation. If you're in a hurry to catch a fleeting action, this might be your best bet. Or, if you're simply tired of thinking about your camera all the time, and just want to take a picture, go with automatic mode.

Shutter Priority and Aperture Priority Modes

Automatic modes can yield excellent results, but they tend to take pictures that are "correct." That is, everything in the scene will be in focus, well-lit, and sharp. There will be times, however, when you'll want to shoot an image "incorrectly." Perhaps you want to use a slow shutter speed to make a fast-moving object look blurry, for example. Or maybe you want to try to render some parts of your image out of focus to bring attention to other parts.

Shutter priority mode lets you select the shutter speed you'd like to use. The camera then selects an aperture that can be used with that shutter speed to create a proper exposure. Shutter priority is ideal for times when you have to freeze motion, such as capturing action at a sporting event, because it lets you force the camera to shoot with a particular (fast) shutter speed. Similarly, there might be other times when you want to ensure that a speeding object looks blurry in your final image. By forcing the camera to use a slow shutter, you'll get a more dynamic image.

Aperture priority mode works the same way, but allows you to select an aperture, and leaves the choice of shutter speed up to the camera. Aperture priority modes give you control over the *depth of field* in your image, allowing you to control how much of the image is in focus (Figure 7.1).

FIGURE 7.1   By changing the camera's aperture, we can control the depth of field in an image. Note the difference in background in these two images. The upper image has a much deeper depth of field, resulting in a sharply focused background, while the lower image has a shallow depth of field, resulting in a blurry, softly focused background.

Most shutter and aperture priority modes also yield control of ISO and white balance. In Chapter 8, "Manual Exposure," you'll learn much more about how to use these modes.

Manual Mode

As you would expect, full manual mode gives you control of everything. Although this might seem like the ultimate "power user" mode, you might find that you often only need control of one exposure parameter or the other, and so you will use a priority mode. However, full manual mode is a must for maximum creative freedom and for handling difficult lighting situations.

Special Shooting Modes

Some cameras offer special shooting modes for specific situations. In these modes, certain features are preset. For example, Landscape modes typically fix the focus on infinity and select the smallest possible aperture to ensure maximum focus and depth of field. Sometimes, these special modes are the only way to gain access to certain features such as slow-sync flash (which we'll discuss later). Before you use any of these modes, however, check the camera's documentation and be sure that you understand *all* of the settings that might be affected.

As you learn more about the decisions you'll make when you shoot, choosing a mode will become more obvious. Because this book won't cover how to use the controls of specific cameras, it's important for you to spend some time learning how the various modes on your camera work.

Image Size and Compression

Your camera probably allows you to select from a number of different size and compression settings, so before you shoot, you want to be sure that you've chosen settings that are right for the type of output that you want, and that make the best use of your available storage space.

Image size is simply the dimensions, in pixels, of the image the camera will create. A 3-megapixel camera, for example, typically offers a maximum resolution of roughly 2048 × 1536 pixels, along with options for shooting in XGA resolution (1024 × 768 pixels) and VGA resolution (640 × 480 pixels). Some cameras offer additional resolutions, such as the Coolpix 995's 2048 × 1360 pixels, an image size that's a slightly lower resolution than the camera's highest setting but offers the same 3:2 aspect ratio as 35mm film.

Which size is the "correct" size depends on how you will be outputting your images. If your images are destined for the Web, you might be able to get away with 640 × 480 resolution. The correct image size for print depends on the type of printer to which you'll be outputting, as well as the final print size of your image. We'll discuss these issues in detail in Chapter 10, "Preparing Your Images for Editing," and Chapter 15, "Output."

In general, it's best to shoot at the highest resolution that your camera provides. This will yield the greatest image detail and best print quality, and provide you with the most flexibility when you output. Although you might be shooting images that are destined for the Web, shooting at full resolution gives you the option to repurpose your images at a later date.

Higher resolutions also make it possible to enlarge sections of an image, allowing you to blow up a single element in a picture, or to crop and enlarge an image to create a new framing.

When it comes to compression, it's best to always shoot with the lowest level (highest quality), particularly if you're shooting images that don't fare well under JPEG compression (see Chapter 3, "How a Digital Camera Works"). JPEG artifacts are difficult, if not impossible, to remove later, so it's best to avoid them altogether.

Obviously, choosing the largest image size with the lowest compression setting means you won't be able to fit as many images onto your storage medium. If you run short on storage when you're in the field, you might want to switch to different image size and compression settings. If your destination is the Web, then you can afford to lower the camera's resolution (and hope that you never want to print any of your images). On the other hand, if your final destination is print, you'll want to keep your resolution the same, but increase your compression (and hope that the artifacting isn't too bad).

MONEY CAN BUY PHOTOGRAPHIC HAPPINESS

Storage is one of those few problems that you can easily solve by spending additional money. If you want to be sure that you can always shoot at the highest quality that your camera allows, you'll need to invest in more storage.

Most cameras will remember the last resolution and compression settings you used, even after the camera has been shut off. If your camera doesn't remember its settings, and if it doesn't default to the settings you'd like, then you'll need to get into the habit of configuring these settings every time you turn on your camera.

White Balance

Once you've set resolution and compression, it's time to start thinking about white balance.

Different types of lights shine at different temperatures, or colors. Direct sunlight, for example, has a color temperature of 5500°K (light is always measured in degrees Kelvin), while fluorescent lights have a color temperature of 4500°K. One of the amazing characteristics of your eyes is that they can adjust automatically to all of these different temperatures, and can even understand mixed temperatures—sunlight shining through a window into a fluorescent-lit room, for example.

Film and digital cameras are not so sophisticated. To accurately record color, film has to be specially formulated for the type of light in which you are shooting. There is "daylight" film that is formulated for recording color in daylight, or "tungsten" film that is capable of accurately recording color under tungsten lighting. Use either film in the wrong kind of light, and your colors will be off (using daylight film indoors will produce images that are very gold or reddish, while using tungsten film outdoors will produce images with a bluish cast).

CCDs have the same trouble. Fortunately, though, a digital camera's understanding of color is entirely dependent on how the data coming off the CCD is processed by the camera's internal computer. Therefore, by telling the camera what type of light you're shooting in, you can make sure that the camera interprets its color data correctly.

White balancing is the process of getting a camera to accurately represent white. Because white light contains every other color (remember Maxwell's experiment), if a camera can accurately reproduce white, then it can accurately render all other colors. Figure 7.2 shows the same scene shot several times, each with a different white balance setting.

Setting White Balance

Every time you take your camera into a new lighting situation, you need to consider how to best white balance it for the available light. Proper white balance is essential to getting accurate color, and it's a step that has no equivalent in the film world. Consequently, even if you're an experienced film photographer, *you must learn to start thinking about white balance!* All cameras have an automatic white balance feature and, depending on the quality of your camera, this might be all you need to use to get accurate white balance. The simplest automatic white balance mechanisms look for the brightest point in your shot, assume that that point is white, and then balance accordingly. More sophisticated automatic white bal-

Auto White Balance   **Daylight Balance**

Cloudy White Balance   **Fluorescent Balance**

FIGURE 7.2 While film photographers need to select a film that is balanced for the type of light in which they'll be shooting, digital photographers need to make certain that their cameras are properly white balanced for the current light. Use the wrong white balance setting, and your images will have strange color casts that can be difficult to remove.

ancers perform a complex analysis of many different areas in your image. Both mechanisms are surprisingly effective, but sometimes you have to second-guess them.

Let's say, for example, that you're shooting a marching band on a dreary, foggy day, and the brightest thing in the scene is the gold sheen of a tuba. Your camera could very well assume that the bright gold tuba was white, and throw off the color balance of your entire image. As another example, let's say you're shooting the Irish golf team at a well-watered golf course on St. Patrick's Day. Because the dominant color in the scene would be green, the camera could easily get confused about how to balance for white. Auto white balance works best outdoors in bright sunlight. Even a few clouds can confuse an auto white balance mechanism, though, and shift the colors in your image toward blue.

Fortunately, any high-quality camera will offer preset configurations for different lighting conditions. For example, most cameras offer preset modes for Daylight, Tungsten, Fluorescent, and possibly a Cloudy or Overcast setting. (Tungsten is sometimes called "Incandescent" or "Indoors.") Because there are two different temperatures of fluorescent lights—"cool white" and "warm white"—some cameras offer separate settings for each fluorescent color.

Other cameras will actually specify manual white balance settings in degrees Kelvin. Be sure you understand which setting corresponds to which type of light (Figure 7.3).

White Balance in K°		
3000°K	–	**White Tungsten**
3700°K	–	**Yellow Tungsten**
4000°K	–	**Fluorescent**
4500°K	–	**Fluorescent**
5500°K	–	**Sunlight**
6500°K	–	**Cloudy**
7500°K	–	**Shade**

FIGURE 7.3   Some cameras use manual white balance controls that are measured in degrees Kelvin. If your camera simply presents a list of temperatures, here are the types of lights to which those temperatures correspond.

These white balance presets are usually more accurate than automatic white balance in the situations for which they're designed. However, you can't always be sure that your lighting situation is exactly the color temperature that your camera's preset is expecting. For example, partial cloud cover might change the daylight temperature in your scene just enough that your camera's Daylight preset will no longer be accurate. Some cameras offer white balance "fine tuning" that allows you to alter a preset white balance to be warmer or cooler.

For the absolute best results under any lighting situation—and especially under mixed lighting—you'll want to use your camera's manual white balance. To use a manual white balance control, hold a white object—such as a piece of paper—in front of the camera, and then press the camera's manual white balance button. The camera will calculate a white balance based on the light in your scene.

MEASURE THE RIGHT LIGHT WITH THE RIGHT WHITE

When you manually white balance, be sure to hold your white card in the light that is hitting your subject. This is particularly critical in a studio situation where your camera might be sitting in very different light from your subject.

In addition, don't use a super bright white paper like you might use in your inkjet printer. A normal piece of 20-lb copier paper is just the right level of white for a good white balance and can be easily glued onto the back of your gray card.

When you first get your camera, it's worth taking some test pictures to learn more about your camera's white balance peculiarities. You might, for example, learn that your camera's automatic white balance does a much better job outside than it does indoors. You'll probably also get a feel for the accuracy of your camera's white balance presets.

You should also dig through your camera's manual to determine if your camera has a *TTL* white balance system, or a white balance sensor that sits outside the camera's lens. External sensors can sometimes pick up color casts from objects that are outside the picture. A bright red car sitting just outside the frame of your image might be all it takes to throw the camera's white balance off. Some experimentation will help you understand how sensitive your camera's external white balance sensor is.

Bad White Balance

Many people assume that they can simply use their image editor to correct images with bad white balance. This is true, but it can take a lot of work to correct a bad white balance. The color shifts that occur from incorrect white balance don't affect all of the colors in an image equally. For example, the highlights in an image might be shifted more than the shadows. Consequently, you won't be able to do a simple "remove a certain amount of blue from the image" type of correction. Moreover, by the time you're done correcting the white balance, you might have used up enough of your image's dynamic range that further color corrections and adjustments will be difficult. In the end, it's best to shoot with the most accurate white balance that your camera can manage.

WHITE BALANCE AND RAW MODE

If your camera offers a Raw mode, you can choose to set the white balance of your image later. Although Raw images take up more space and can be a bit of a hassle to work with, if you aren't sure of a correct white balance setting for a particular lighting situation, and if you don't have a white object that you can use for a man-

ual white balance, then shoot in Raw mode and adjust the white balance of the image later.

White Balance and Interchangeable Lenses

If you have a digital SLR with interchangeable lenses, be aware that your camera's white balance presets might work better with some lenses than with others. Different lenses have different color qualities—some are warmer or cooler than others. Your camera's white balance presets, unfortunately, might not be calibrated correctly for the color qualities of some of your lenses. Only experimentation can tell you whether a particular lens works properly with, say, the daylight white balance on your camera. If you find that it doesn't (e.g., perhaps Daylight white balance always produces images that are too warm when it is used with a particular lens), then you'll need to use auto or full manual white balance when you shoot with that lens.

BE CAREFUL WITH THOSE FILTERS

Fitting your lens with a filter or lens attachment can alter your camera's automatic or preset white balances because they can shift the color of the light passing through your lens. You'll usually want to use manual white balance when attaching anything to your lens.

Metering

You're going to be reading a lot about metering, both later in this chapter and in Chapter 8. For now, simply be aware that your camera has different metering choices. It probably defaults to some form of matrix metering, which will be the best option for most shooting situations. However, like other settings, your camera might remember its meter setting even after you've turned it off. Therefore, it's a good idea to get in the habit of making a quick check that your meter is set to the appropriate mode before you shoot.

Sharpness, Saturation, or Contrast

Many cameras offer different levels of sharpness, color saturation, contrast, or all three. Only you can decide which settings suit your taste, so you'll need to try a lot of test shots with these different settings. Be aware, however, that as you increase sharpness, you will also increase contrast. Your goal when you configure these settings is to allow the camera to capture the most dynamic range and detail possible. If you set contrast or sharpness too high, you might lose color information that you need later (you'll learn more about these issues in Chapter 11, "Correcting Tone and Color").

For example, consider the images in Figure 7.4.

FIGURE 7.4   Some cameras allow you to change the amount of in-camera sharpening they perform. These images have been shrunk to fit on this page, a process that tends to sharpen images. Check out the full-res versions on the companion CD-ROM for a better look at the sharpness differences.

ISOs

As you saw in Chapter 4, "Basic Photography: A Quick Primer," a digital camera's sensitivity to light is measured using the same ISO scale used by film cameras. As ISO rating increases, the camera becomes more light sensitive, and a more light-sensitive camera offers different creative possibilities. In addition to allowing you to shoot using less light, a higher ISO rating allows you to shoot in bright light, but with smaller apertures and higher shutter speeds.

In Chapter 3, you saw that when data is dumped from the camera's CCD, it is passed through an amplifier and then to an analog-to-digital converter. By increasing the amount of amplification between the CCD and the analog-to-digital converter, a camera becomes more sensitive to light (Figure 3.1). Simply put, your camera's ISO settings do nothing more than amplify the signal coming from the CCD.

Although the most common ISO speeds are 100, 200, and 400, higher-end models can go as high as 1600 ISO, while cameras such as the Canon G2 offer a super slow ISO 50.

There is a price to pay for this increased sensitivity, though. As you amplify the CCD's signal, you also increase any noise that the CCD has picked up. Consequently, higher-ISO images tend to be fairly noisy (Figure 7.5, page 161).

Some cameras handle this extra noise better than others, producing low-contrast noise that almost looks like the increased grain that you'd find in a high-speed film. Higher-end cameras often don't show a noticeable increase in noise until around ISO 800. Other cameras, though, produce increased noise that is quite ugly (Figure 7.6, page 163).

In Chapter 13, "Essential Imaging Tactics," we'll look at some methods for trying to remove noise from your images.

Cameras with very low ISOs, like the ISO 50 found on the Canon G2, produce images with very little noise. However, shooting at ISO 50 is only practical in bright sunlight.

KEEP AN EYE ON YOUR ISO

Most cameras remember your last ISO setting, even after you've turned the camera off. Therefore, if you spent a long night shooting at ISO 400, don't forget to check your ISO setting the next day, before you go out shooting in bright daylight. Although your camera will be able to shoot in daylight at ISO 400, your images might be overexposed; they will certainly be noisier than at a slower speed, and your depth of field will be deeper.

ISO 100

ISO 400

FIGURE 7.5   Although using higher ISOs affords greater shooting flexibility, it also increases the amount of noise in your image.

ON THE CD

FIGURE 7.6   All noise is bad, but some noise is worse than others. When shooting at a high ISO, the Canon G1 produces very speckly noise with bright color artifacts, as seen in this image. Check out the color image on the companion CD-ROM.

FRAMING AND FOCUSING

After you configure your camera settings as described in the last section, you're ready to start framing and focusing your shot. As we said at the beginning of this chapter, composition and other areas of photographic "artistry" are beyond the scope of this book. However, there are a number of technical concerns that will immediately improve the composition of your images, no matter what your artistic or journalistic intent might be.

Focal Length

The great thing about a zoom lens is that it provides great flexibility when you frame a shot. Without changing your position, you can quickly zoom into a subject to get a tighter view and a different framing. However, it's essential that you pay attention to the other characteristics of your image that change when you zoom in and out.

It's easy to think of your zoom lens as a big magnifying glass and, to a degree, it is. As you zoom in, your subject appears larger and larger. This is why digital camera manufacturers label their lenses with a magnification factor—2x, 3x, and so forth. However, a few other things happen to your image when you zoom.

As you go to a longer focal length (zoom in), your field of view gets narrower. The human eye has a field of view of about 50 to 55°. This is considered a "normal" field of view, and any lens that produces a 50 to 55° viewing angle is said to be a "normal lens."

More important, though, is to pay attention to the way a lens magnifies different parts of your image and how it compresses depth overall as you zoom in and out.

Consider the images in Figure 7.7.

Both of these images were shot from the same location. The only thing that changed between shots was the focal length of the lens. In addition to the framing and the size of the subject, notice how the background appears much farther away in the wide-angle image. In general, the wide-angle image has a much greater sense of depth. Now look at the two images in Figure 7.8, page 166.

In these two images, the subject remained in the same place, but the photographer moved farther away and used a different focal length to keep the images identically framed. Notice how much closer the tables and chairs look in the second image. As the photographer moved back and zoomed in, the depth in the image became compressed, resulting in the background elements appearing closer.

As you can see, both field of view and the sense of depth in an image are functions of the position of your camera and the focal length that you choose to use. When you shoot with a wide-angle lens, objects that are closer to the lens get magnified more than objects that are farther away, while a telephoto lens magnifies near and far images equally. Because all

FIGURE 7.7   In these two images, neither the photographer nor the subject moved. In the first image, a longer (telephoto) focal length was used, while in the second image, a very wide (shorter) focal length was used. In addition to the different framings, notice how much farther away the background trees appear in the second image. Though you might be tempted to simply use your zoom lens to frame your shot a particular way, it's important to consider how different focal lengths affect the appearance of your background, and choose your shooting position accordingly.

objects, no matter how far away they are, are magnified equally, a telephoto lens compresses the depth in your scene.

At some point, you've probably looked at a photograph of yourself and thought "that doesn't really look like me." One reason for the poor result might be that the photographer used a wide-angle lens. Shooting a

FIGURE 7.8   Although these two images are framed the same, notice how different the backgrounds are. In the left-hand image, the camera was positioned close to the subject and zoomed out, while in the right-hand image, the camera was pulled back and zoomed in. Note how much closer the background chairs appear in the telephoto (right-hand) image. The sense of depth in the scene is more compressed as the lens goes more telephoto. Note too that the road seems steeper in the left-hand image. In general, the entire sense of space differs in the two images, even though the subject didn't move.

portrait with a wide-angle lens can be problematic because some parts of your subject's face are closer to the lens than others. Consequently, those parts will be magnified more than the parts that are farther away. Check out the pictures in Figure 7.9. The image on the left was shot with a slightly telephoto lens and really does look like the actual person. The image on the right is not such a good likeness. The nose is too big, and the ears have been rendered too small. In addition, the distance between the nose and ears—the depth of the picture—is too long. (Of course, although the picture on the right is less literally correct, it might be a better expression of the person's true character.)

Typically, portrait photographers use a slightly telephoto lens. Some even use special "portrait" lenses that have some spherical aberration designed into the lens. These aberrations tend to soften the detail in the image to improve skin tones.

Your choice of focal length—and the corresponding position of your camera—will have a lot to do with the sense of space and depth in your image. As you saw in Figure 7.9, the difference in results when you shoot

FIGURE 7.9   A change in focal length can make a huge difference in the appearance of your subject. The image on the left was shot with a long (telephoto) focal length. Next, we zoomed out and moved closer to our subject to produce the oddly distorted image on the right. (As in the previous example, note how the telephoto lens has compressed the depth in the scene. The clock over the man's shoulder appears much closer in the left-hand image.)

at close proximity with a wide-angle lens and when you shoot from far away with a telephoto lens can be quite dramatic. Therefore, just because you can zoom in to the framing that you want for a particular shot doesn't mean that it's the right choice for the shot. Your subject might be better served by repositioning the camera, and choosing a different focal length.

Geometric Distortion

It's important to pay attention to any potential distortion cause by inferior optics in your lens. Most zoom lenses exhibit some form of barrel or pincushion distortion when the lenses are zoomed to either of their extremes. These distortions will show up as curves and warps around the edges and corners of your image (you can see an example in Figure 5.23).

When you find yourself at the limits of your zoom range, check the edges of your image to see if there's any distortion. If there is, and you can live with it, then by all means take the shot. If it bothers you, then you might need to reposition your camera and select a new focal length. If the distortion isn't too bad, you might be able to remove it with your image editing software, as we'll see in Chapter 10.

ONE WAY TO AVOID EMBARRASSMENT

If you're using a rangefinder *camera with an* optical viewfinder, *note that, because you aren't looking through the camera's imaging lens, it is actually possible to shoot with the lens cap on! Some cameras are smart enough to warn you, and others will let you blithely go along shooting black frames. Be sure to double-check!*

CUTTING DOWN ON LENS FLARES

Figure 5.24 shows the type of flaring that can occur with some lenses. Typically, lenses with wider diameters are more prone to flaring. There are several ways to eliminate flares, the easiest being to simply hold your hand above the lens (or put a sunshade on your lens) to block the flare-causing light. Circular polarizers will also help reduce flare, although at the expense of f-stops.

Focusing

Although your digital camera invariably has an automatic focus, it doesn't mean that you don't have to give some thought to focusing. One downside to the typical digital camera is that it can be difficult to tell whether the autofocus mechanism has really worked. LCD screens are usually too small to be an accurate gauge of focus, while most optical viewfinders are just plain terrible. Consequently, it's a good idea to understand some of the workings of your camera's autofocus system so that you can learn when you might be facing a troublesome focusing situation.

Using Autofocus

No matter what type of system your camera uses for determining focus, the process of focusing the camera is probably the same: you frame your shot and press the shutter button down halfway. The camera will calculate and lock focus (as well as exposure and auto white balance) and then beep, or show a light to indicate that it's ready. Pressing the button the rest of the way will take the picture using the focus, exposure, and white balance settings that the camera has calculated.

Although this system is simple to use, photographers who are new to autofocus cameras can be quickly frustrated by what seems to be an extreme lag between the time they push the button and the time the camera actually takes the picture. This *shutter lag* is usually because the photographer is simply pressing the button down all the way to take the picture, rather than pressing the button down halfway and giving the camera a chance to prefocus. By pressing the button all the way down, you're asking the camera to focus, calculate exposure, and figure out white balance all in the instant that you want to take the picture. *Neglecting to prefocus is the biggest mistake that beginning autofocus photographers make, and it's one that can lead to a great deal of frustrating, missed photos. Get in the habit of prefocusing!*

Although this prefocusing step might sound like an inconvenience, it's really no more trouble than what you'd have to do with a manually focused camera, except that instead of focusing manually, the camera is focusing for you.

SHUTTER LAG EVEN WITH PREFOCUSING

Some older cameras (and, unfortunately, a few newer ones) have a bit of a shutter lag even if you've already pressed the shutter release halfway down to go through the prefocusing step. Unfortunately, there's really nothing you can do to work around this problem except to learn how long the lag is so that you can try to anticipate when you need to press the shutter to capture the action you want.

Your camera might also have a continuous autofocus mechanism, which automatically focuses every time you move or zoom the camera. With continuous autofocus, your camera stands a much better chance of being ready to shoot at any time. However, it can also drain your battery and sometimes be distracting, as you will constantly hear the lens working. If your camera has a speedy autofocus, you might find little advantage to a continuous mechanism.

Some higher-end cameras such as the Nikon D1 and the Canon D60 also feature a *focus tracking* or *servo tracking* feature that can automatically track a moving object and keep it in focus for as long as you hold the shutter button halfway down. For sports photography, this feature can help to ensure that you're always ready to get the shot.

Most digital cameras employ one of two different autofocus mechanisms, each with its own strengths and weaknesses.

Active Autofocus

Although less popular than it used to be, some lower-end cameras still provide *active autofocus* mechanisms because they're typically the cheapest system to implement. An active autofocus mechanism works by using an infrared beam to measure the distance to your subject; your camera then sets the focus accordingly. It's called an "active" system because the camera is actively emitting a signal in an effort to measure distance.

The easiest way to tell if your camera uses an active system is to look at the technical specifications included in your camera's manual. You can also simply search the front of the camera for anything that looks like an infrared emitter (it will look something like the little window on the front of a TV remote control).

Although active infrared autofocus mechanisms work fairly well, they have a number of limitations.

- You must have a clear line of sight between you and your subject. Bars in a zoo, fence posts, or other obstructions can keep the camera from accurately measuring distance.
- Because the infrared beam is not originating from the lens, the camera might not correctly calculate focus if you're using any type of lens attachment such as a wide-angle or telephoto adapter. Consequently, most cameras with active autofocus mechanisms don't provide for such attachments.
- If you're standing close to another strong infrared source—such as a very hot campfire, or a birthday cake covered with candles—then the heat from that source can confuse the camera's autofocus mechanism.
- On the positive side, active autofocus systems work just fine in the dark.

Passive Autofocus

Most higher-end prosumer cameras use a *passive autofocus* system, sometimes called a *contrast detection* system. You should be able to find out what type of system your camera uses by simply looking at the specifications table in your camera's manual. For example, the Olympus C2100 specifies its autofocus system as a *"TTL* contrast detection autofocus."

As you might have guessed, contrast-detecting autofocus systems work by focusing the lens until the image has as much contrast as possible. The idea is that a low-contrast image is a blurry image. Therefore, by increasing contrast, the camera increases sharpness. The top image in Figure 7.10 shows an out-of-focus image. Look at the individual pixels up close and you'll see that there is very little change from one pixel to the next. That is, the pixels have little contrast between them. In the lower image in Figure 7.10, a sharp image, you can see that individual pixels have a more dramatic change in contrast from pixel to pixel.

FIGURE 7.10 If you look closely at the pixels in the upper, blurry image, you'll see that there is very little change in tone from one to the next. That is, there is very little contrast between them. In the lower image, there is a big contrast change from pixel to pixel. This is why searching for high contrast is a good way to detect focus.

When you press the shutter release halfway, a passive autofocus camera takes an initial reading of the contrast in your shot. It then focuses the lens closer and checks the contrast again. If contrast has increased, the camera continues focusing inward until the contrast decreases. With a decrease in focus, the camera knows that it has gone too far and can step back to the correct focus. Obviously, many variables can affect this process, such as the camera's ability to detect contrast, the precision with which it can move its lens, and the speed at which it can go through the entire procedure. Theoretically, a camera with more autofocus steps can achieve a more precise focus position and, therefore, achieve better focus. However, digital cameras typically have *very* deep depths of field, so tiny changes in focus usually aren't that important. Moreover, most of the steps in an autofocus system are centered around very close (macro) ranges where they tend to be needed, and where depth of field offers less compensation.

Contrast detection is largely a function of the available light in your scene. If the area in which you're pointing your camera is too dark, or is uniformly colored, your camera won't be able to detect any contrast and will be unable to determine focus. Today, most cameras include an automatic *focus assist lamp* (also known as an *autofocus assist lamp*) that simply shines a light onto your scene if the camera can't detect focus. By lighting up the scene, your camera's autofocus mechanism can simply "see" better. Some cameras use a normal white light focus assist lamp, while others use a less intrusive red lamp.

A passive autofocus mechanism has many advantages:

- Because they look through the camera's lens, passive autofocus systems work with any filters or lens attachments that you might be using.
- Because they're simply analyzing what the camera is seeing, they can work through windows, water, or other transparent materials.
- They have no distance limitation, although your camera's autofocus assist lamp will have some type of limiting distance.
- Unlike non-TTL active systems, you can be sure that a passive system is focusing on something that's actually in the camera's field of view.

On the downside, passive systems do require light in your scene and a subject that has enough detail to produce contrast. However, these limitations are minor and, as you'll see later, you can usually work around them using one of several techniques.

AUTOFOCUS AND WIDE-ANGLE LENSES

If you're using a digital SLR with interchangeable lenses, be aware that very wide-angle lenses (14 to 18mm) can confuse autofocus mechanisms. For example, although the camera's autofocus might think that it's focused at infinity, it might actually be focused much closer. When you use such lenses, you might get much better results by focusing manually.

Focus Spots

Obviously, you want your autofocusing system to focus on the subject of your image, not something else in the scene. Therefore, your camera has a *focusing zone* or *spot* that determines which part of the image will be analyzed for focus. Most cameras simply use a small area in the middle of the frame as the focus target. Sometimes this area is marked with crosshairs or a box.

However, if your subject isn't in the middle of the frame, then there's a good chance that your camera is going to focus on the background of your image, leaving the foreground soft or outright blurry. You can get around this problem by taking advantage of the fact that when you press your camera's shutter button down halfway, the camera calculates focus and then locks it until you either let go or take the picture.

Therefore, if you want to focus on something on the right side of the frame, you can simply point the camera's focusing target (usually the middle of the frame) at that object, press your shutter button halfway, hold it down, *and then reframe your shot* to your desired framing. When you press the button the rest of the way, the camera will take the picture using the focus that it initially calculated. Figure 7.11 shows an example.

FIGURE 7.11 To keep the camera from focusing on the sky, the camera's focusing target was pointed at the lamp post and the shutter release was pressed halfway down to lock focus. The image was reframed, and the picture was shot with the correct focus.

Be aware, though, that there are some potential pitfalls to this technique.

In addition to calculating focus, when you do a half-press of your shutter button, your camera also calculates exposure and white balance (if you're using automatic white balance). If the lighting in your frame is substantially different after you reframe from it was when you locked focus, your camera's exposure could be off (as you'll see in the next chapter, you can sometimes use this exposure change to your advantage).

As we explained earlier, automatic white balance mechanisms can be confused when presented with a preponderance of similar colors. When you perform your initial focus, make sure there are no fields of color that might confuse your camera's white balance. For example, if your subject is standing against a dull gray wall when you lock focus, and then you reframe so that only a bit of that wall is showing, your white balance could be inaccurate.

Camera manufacturers have come up with two solutions for these problems. The first is a separate *exposure lock* button that allows you to lock your camera's exposure and focus independently (Figure 7.12). Different exposure lock features work in different ways, but most allow you to do something like this: frame your shot; measure and lock the exposure; move your camera and lock focus on your subject; and then return to your final framing with everything ready to go. As we'll see later, exposure lock is also necessary for taking good panoramic shots.

Other cameras include multiple focus zones, usually three, but sometimes as many as seven. A camera with multiple focus spots analyzes several different points in your image to try to determine where your subject

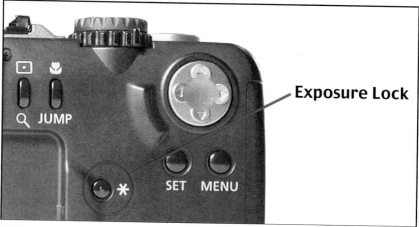

FIGURE 7.12   The exposure lock button on the Canon G1 allows you to lock focus and exposure independently of each other.

might be. Once it has decided, it analyzes the focus spot closest to that subject to calculate focus.

Multiple autofocus spots (Figure 7.13) allow you to frame your image as you like without having to worry about your subject being in the middle of the frame. However, it's important to pay attention to where the camera is focusing, as it will often pick the wrong subject. Consequently, some cameras let you manually select a focus point to ensure that your autofocus mechanism analyzes the right area. Most cameras with multi-spot autofocus mechanisms also allow you to put the camera into a single, *center-spot focusing* mode (sometimes called *spot focus*), which forces the camera to behave like a normal single-spot autofocus camera.

FIGURE 7.13   Multiple focus zones let you choose where the camera's autofocus mechanism will look when it determines focus. Shown here is the viewfinder from a Nikon Coolpix 990.

If your camera uses a TTL contrast detection focusing system, the center focusing spot (no matter how many focus zones the camera has) is usually a *dual-axis zone*. That is, it examines contrast along both a horizontal and vertical axis. If the camera has multiple focus spots, there's a good chance that the other zones are *single-axis zones,* which only measure contrast (and therefore, focus) along a horizontal axis. For locking focus on horizontal subjects, such as horizons, a single-axis zone can be problematic. For these situations, you might want to force the camera to use its center, dual-axis zone.

If there's any one rule to using an autofocus camera—whether a single-spot, or multi-spot focusing system—it's simply to pay attention. Don't just assume that the camera will be able to calculate everything accurately. If your camera has a single-spot focusing system that sometimes requires you to lock focus and reframe, be sure to look for any potential metering and white balance troubles before you shoot. If your camera has a multi-spot focusing system, then be certain that it has chosen the correct subject and focusing zone.

What to Do if Your Autofocus Won't Lock Focus

If you're using a contrast detection autofocus system, there will be times when it won't be able to lock focus. Shooting in low light is especially problematic, as there might not be enough contrast in your scene for the camera to detect focus. Hopefully, the camera has an automatic focus assist lamp that will activate to light the scene. If the focus assist lamp lights up and the camera still can't focus, try moving the camera slightly. You might illuminate something that has enough contrast for the camera to be able to focus. Be careful that the camera doesn't focus on something at the wrong distance.

Autofocus mechanisms can even get confused in bright daylight if your camera is pointed at something with low contrast. In Figure 7.14, you can see that the middle of the frame is filled with an object that is a solid color (the lamp). In this case, the lamp had so little contrast that the camera's contrast-detecting autofocus system was unable to focus. By tilting the camera up so that its focusing target sits on top of a more contrasty subject at the same distance, the autofocus mechanism can find and lock focus, as shown in the image on the left. After locking focus, we tilted the camera back down to our desired framing, as shown in the image on the right.

ADVANCED AUTOFOCUS MECHANISMS

If you have a higher-end digital SLR such as the Nikon D1, your camera probably uses a more advanced form of autofocus called *phase difference* or *phase detection*. Phase detection autofocus is a TTL metering system that uses a complex arrangement of prisms and two tiny CCD arrays that are placed next to the focal plane. Both CCDs see the same part of the image, but one CCD looks through the left edge of the lens while the other looks through the right edge.

When the lens is focused too close, the image in the left-looking CCD will be slightly to the left of the right-looking CCD. When the lens is focused too far, the opposite occurs. By analyzing the two images and determining the difference in shift between them, the camera can calculate which way to move the lens, and how far it needs to go.

As with other autofocus systems, the quality of a phase difference system depends on its ability to quickly and accurately control the lens motor, as well as its ability to detect what area needs to be in focus.

Phase difference systems are incredibly accurate and generally very speedy. In addition, many of these systems are capable of focusing in near darkness. On the downside, some phase difference autofocus mechanisms become less reliable at apertures below f5.6. As the aperture gets smaller, the CCDs lose their line of sight out of the lens and the mechanism can become confused. In general, though, these systems, whether single- or multi-spot, are by far the most accurate, quickest autofocus mechanisms available.

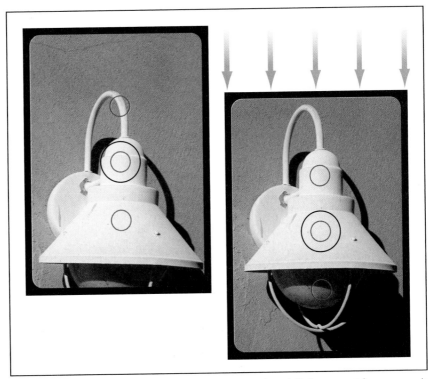

FIGURE 7.14   Because this white lamp is a solid color, there's little contrast for a camera's contrast-detecting autofocus mechanism to detect. To get the camera to lock focus, you must frame the shot at a point where there is some contrast, lock focus, and then reframe (be sure you lock on a point that's the same distance away as is your subject).

Manual Focus

Your camera's autofocus system is probably all the focusing control you'll ever need. However, if you run into a situation where your camera can't autofocus, and you can't work around it, or if you have a particularly "creative" shot that you want to compose, you might need to resort to your camera's manual focus. (This is all assuming you're using a prosumer-type camera that lacks interchangeable lenses with focus rings. If you're using a professional-level SLR, you'll probably be regularly switching between automatic and manual focus.)

Unfortunately, manual focus features on non-SLR digital cameras leave a *lot* to be desired. Between poorly designed controls and viewfinders that lack focusing aids, getting an accurate manual focus out of your camera can be difficult. A few years ago, most digital cameras simply offered you a choice of distances. Consequently, in addition to having to try to estimate the distance to your subject, you had to hope that the camera provided a preset focus distance that was close to what you needed.

Many digital cameras still work this way, but a number of vendors now include a more robust control that lets you smoothly move throughout the focus range of your camera. However, determining when you've achieved focus will be difficult, as neither your camera's LCD screen or optical viewfinder might be good enough to let you see focus.

Fortunately, digital cameras typically use very small apertures and, as we'll see, small apertures create such deep depth of field that you often don't have to worry about your focus being dead on. You can further improve your chances of getting good focus by using your camera's manual controls to set as small an aperture as possible when you're using manual focus.

Even if your camera doesn't have a full manual focus control, it probably has a preset control for locking focus at infinity. This can be a handy feature for landscape photography or other times when your subject is far away. Lock your camera camera's focus at infinity and it perform faster (since it won't be trying to autofocus) and your batteries might last a little longer (since the camera won't be moving the lens around).

METERING

When you press your camera's shutter release, you expose the camera's CCD to light. By adjusting the camera's shutter speed and aperture size, you can control how much light will reach the CCD, but how do you know how much is enough? By using your camera's light meter.

At the simplest level, a light meter helps ensure that your pictures are not too bright or too dark, so that you can actually see the subjects in your image. With a little thought and planning, your light meter—and the associated exposure controls—becomes the most powerful creative tool on your camera. In this section, you'll learn the basics of metering, and look at what exposure options you have when you shoot with your camera in automatic mode. Manual controls and advanced exposure topics will be covered in Chapter 8.

What Your Light Meter Tells You

To really know how to get the most from your camera's built-in light meter, it's almost as important to understand what it *cannot* do as it is to understand what it *can* do. The light meter on a typical point-and-shoot, prosumer, or even most higher-end cameras, cannot tell you anything about the colors in your scene, how much contrast there is, or how to preserve all of the detail that's present. In other words, your light meter doesn't tell you (or your camera) the *best* exposure for the scene you are shooting. Rather, your light meter simply tells you an *adequate* exposure for the scene you are shooting—one that will not grossly over- or under-expose your image. In many cases, you will take your meter's adequate reading as a starting point, and build from there into the best exposure.

Your light meter does only one thing: measure the *luminance* of the light reflected by your subject. Whether it measures the luminance of the entire scene or just a part of it depends on the type of meter you are using.

Figure 7.15 shows a grid with an equal number of black and white squares. If you were to measure this grid with a light meter, you would find that it is reflecting 18% of the light that is striking it. (Yes, it might seem like it should be reflecting 50% of the light, but it's not.) The luminance of most scenes averages out to be the same as this grid—that is, most scenes in the real world reflect 18% of the light that strikes them. Since this is only a measure of luminance (not color), you can also think of this 18% reflectance as a shade of gray. This particular gray shade is known to photographers as *18% gray* or *middle gray.*

The most important thing to know about your camera's light meter is that *it always assumes that it is pointed at something that is 18% gray.* In other words, your light meter calculates an exposure recommendation that will accurately reproduce middle gray under the current lighting. Because a typical scene reflects 18% of the light that hits it, this assumption is usually fairly accurate. Obviously, if the lighting in your scene suddenly changes, the readings will no longer be accurate (even if the scene is still reflecting 18% of that light), and you'll have to re-meter.

FIGURE 7.15   Although each of these squares is black or white, the entire field of squares meters as 18%, or middle gray.

However, because your scene might not be exactly 18% gray, to get the best results from your light meter, you'll want to meter off of something that is middle gray, such as an 18% gray card. Readily available at any photo supply store, you can simply place this card in your scene and use it as the subject for your metering.

As explained earlier, the assumptions made by your camera's light meter should yield an adequately exposed image, neither too dark nor too light. Of course, many of the objects in your scene will be brighter or darker than middle gray. Look at the penguin in Figure 7.16. Notice that in the first shot, his black feathers are not completely black nor are his white feathers completely white. As expected, the camera's light meter assumed that it was pointed at something gray, and so calculated a meter reading to accurately reproduce that gray. Consequently, the black and white parts of the image came out looking somewhat gray.

The second image was overexposed by one stop. Notice that now his white feathers really do look white, although they have lost some detail. The black feathers, though, are now even grayer. The third image was intentionally underexposed by one stop. Now the black feathers are truly black, although the whites have been dulled. In Chapter 8, you'll learn

FIGURE 7.16   When left to its own devices, your camera will assume that this penguin is gray and will meter incorrectly for both his white and black feathers. With some overexposure, we can restore the white to his feathers, or we can underexpose to darken up his black feathers.

how to adjust an image to restore the white values, and achieve a penguin with dark blacks and white whites.

As you can see, by choosing to over- or underexpose, you can restore the blacks and whites in your image to true black and white, resulting in an image that is more contrasty and appealing than the dull grays produced by your camera's default metering.

Colors have a luminance—or tone—just as black-and-white images do and, therefore, need the same type of compensation for accurate reproduction. For example, look at Figure 7.17. The left-hand image was shot with the camera's recommended metering, while the right-hand image was underexposed by half a stop because the orange color of the car was a bit darker than 18% gray. Simply put: By overexposing your images, your colors will become lighter, while underexposing will make your colors darker. Such adjustments allow you to either restore the right color to the objects in your scene, or intentionally boost or decrease the saturation of objects within your scene.

As stated earlier, your camera's light meter generates exposure settings that create an adequate picture. In general, your camera's meter will yield images with good color and proper exposure throughout the shadows and highlights. However, because of your light meter's assumptions, your picture might come out looking a little flat, as darker or lighter

FIGURE 7.17 Through careful choice of exposure when shooting, you can capture images with better color saturation.

tones will all be rendered as middle tones. With some simple exposure adjustments you can turn these images from adequate to exceptional, yielding images with improved color accuracy, contrast, and saturation (or tonal accuracy and contrast if you're shooting black and white).

The Right Meter for the Job

Your camera probably offers a choice of different metering modes. These are usually selected from a button on the camera's body, or from a menu within the camera's menuing system. To shoot a well-exposed image, you need to choose a metering mode that's right for your scene.

Matrix Metering

A *matrix meter* (sometimes called a *multi-segment* meter) divides your image into a grid and takes a separate meter reading for each cell in the grid. These cells are then analyzed to determine an exposure setting.

Matrix metering is the best choice for most situations and is certainly the best option when you're simply trying to get a quick shot using your camera's automatic features. However, some situations are particularly difficult for a matrix metering system. Learning to identify such situations will make it easier to understand when you should switch to a different metering mode.

In general, if you are facing a scene that has both bright highlights and dark shadows, there's a good chance your meter will get confused. Different meters respond to these types of situations in different ways, and only experience with your camera will help you predict how your meter might respond to the lighting situation shown in Figure 7.18.

Your main concern when you use a matrix meter is to understand how it will preserve shadow and highlight areas. Try to find some locations that have both bright highlights and dark shadows, and spend some time experimenting with your camera's capability to preserve shadow information. Then, try to determine how far you can overexpose before you blow out bright areas such as skies. This information will inform the exposure adjustment decisions you'll be making later.

Shooting the same scene with two different cameras can produce very different results, as you can see in Figure 7.18. This street scene presents a difficult lighting situation, as the street-level details are dark and shadowy, while up at the top of the buildings things are bright and sunny. Notice how the Nikon chose a metering that revealed lots of street-level detail, while the Olympus chose to provide more extreme contrast between the daylight and shadowy areas. Neither is "right" or "wrong," but they are different.

Center-Weighted Metering

A variation of matrix metering, *center-weight metering* also divides your image into a grid of cells. But when analyzing the readings, a

FIGURE 7.18 The left image was shot with a Nikon Coolpix 990, while the right-hand image was shot with an Olympus C-2500. Both cameras were set for matrix metering and were on full automatic. Notice how differently they chose to meter.

center-weighted metering system gives preference to the cells in the middle of the image. Typically, the middle 80% of the cells are considered more important than the outlying regions. Center-weighted metering is designed for those times when your subject is in the middle of your frame, and your background contains bright lights, dark shadows, or other extreme lighting situations that might throw off the metering in the center of your image.

Spot Metering

A *spot meter* measures only a small area of your image, usually the center. The metering from this area is the only information used to calculate an exposure. The most common use for a spot meter is for dealing with extremely backlit situations—a person standing in front of a window, for example—that would normally cause your camera to underexpose your foreground. Spot meters can also be handy with dark backgrounds, such as the one shown in Figure 7.19. In the upper image, the background is

FIGURE 7.19 Switching from the matrix meter to the spot meter made it possible to reveal more detail in the shadowy background area, albeit at the cost of overexposed highlights.

deeply shadowed and has lost detail. By activating the camera's spot meter and metering off of the shadowy background, the camera produces an image with much better shadow detail. Unfortunately, some foreground detail and color saturation was washed out in the process.

Spot meters are also used for complex *zone system* metering, as we'll see in the next chapter. However, such metering usually requires a spot meter with a very small—1° or so—metering circle. The spot meters in most cameras use a much bigger sample area. To get an idea of how big your camera's spot is, try shooting a series of images like the one shown in Figure 7.19, but from greater and greater distances. Eventually, your spot will be larger than your subject, and your metering will fail. At this point, you can get a rough idea of the size of your camera's metering spot.

Automatic Exposure

If you're shooting using your camera's automatic mode, it will automatically meter and select an exposure whenever you press the shutter release halfway. As you saw earlier, the camera's meter makes a number of assumptions about the contents of your scene, the main one being that your scene has an average reflectance of 18%. This is great for most scenes, but if you point your camera into a bright white, highly reflective field of snow, then your meter will be dead wrong, because rather than telling you the correct exposure for bright snow, it will tell you the correct exposure for middle gray. Your white snow will then come out gray.

When you shoot a scene that's brighter or darker than middle gray, you need to correct for your meter's assumption by over- or underexposing your shot. In the old days, if you were using a manual film camera, you would over- or underexpose by adjusting your camera's aperture and shutter speed controls. If you're using your digital camera in its automatic mode, or if your digital camera doesn't have manual shutter speed and aperture controls, you'll have to use other tricks to force a change in exposure.

Fortunately, almost all digital cameras these days offer exposure compensation features—simple controls that let you easily over- or underexpose by up to two stops, usually in 1/2-stop increments. If you think your scene needs to be overexposed by a stop, simply press the + exposure button twice (assuming your exposure compensation increments in half stops). Exposure compensation controls are the quickest and easiest way (and, on some cameras, the only way) to make exposure adjustments.

When you shoot in automatic mode, most cameras will opt for a high shutter speed to help ensure a sharp image—slower speeds can result in a blurry image if you're not holding the camera steady. When you use exposure compensation, most cameras try to achieve the requested change in exposure by changing shutter speed. When this isn't possible, either because the camera's shutter can't go any faster, or because slowing the shutter speed would risk blurring the image, then the camera will make changes to aperture. Sometimes, the camera will make slight changes to both shutter speed and aperture. Fortunately, these changes are usually minor enough that you won't see any change in the camera's ability to freeze motion, or in the image's depth of field.

CONTROLLING EXPOSURE WITH YOUR LIGHT METER

Using the built-in light meter, you can force an over- or underexposure by pointing the camera at something darker or lighter. Meter off a darker subject and your camera will overexpose. Meter off a lighter subject, and you'll get an underexposure (Figure 7.20). However, because your camera will probably lock focus at the same time as exposure, you'll need to be certain that you are metering off something that is at the same distance as the image you would like to have in focus, or use your camera's exposure lock feature (if it has one).

Automatic metering and exposure compensation can be summed up very simply:

- If your scene contains bright objects, your meter will underexpose, and the bright objects in your scene will appear gray. Correct this by using your exposure compensation controls to overexpose.
- Conversely, if your scene contains dark elements, your meter will overexpose, and the darker objects in your scene will appear gray. Correct this by using your exposure compensation controls to underexpose.

Exposure compensation controls are powerful tools, and you will continue to use them even after you've learned some of the more advanced techniques that will be covered in the next chapter. Get comfortable with your camera's exposure compensation controls, learn how to use them quickly, and begin learning how to recognize how much compensation is necessary for different situations. Because there are no hard-and-fast rules for over- or underexposing, you have to go out and practice!

FIGURE 7.20   The left image was exposed using the camera's default metering, and although it is the more striking image, it does lack detail in the shadowy areas. By tilting the camera down, we were able to force the camera to meter off of the shadow areas instead of the sky, resulting in the image on the right. Although the sky is overexposed in the right-hand image, the shadow areas on the ground possess more detail. In Chapter 8, you'll learn how to expose separate images and then merge them together to create a final, well-exposed composite image.

Simple Flash Photography

Using your camera's built-in flash is pretty simple: just turn it on and let the camera worry about when and how much to fire it. Using your camera's built-in flash *well* is a bit more difficult. Unfortunately, the small flash units provided by most cameras are low powered and, because they are usually positioned so close to the camera's lens, they don't often produce very flattering light. However, your camera's built-in flash does have its uses, and with a little know-how you can get it to yield good results.

Flash Modes

Most digital cameras provide several different flash modes. If you're shooting in a fully automatic mode, then your camera is probably using its automatic flash mode, which tries to determine, on-the-fly, whether the flash is needed. If the camera decides the flash is needed, it fires it for the appropriate time. In addition to this mode, your camera probably provides the following:

- **Fill.** This mode uses the flash to fill in shadows. It is typically used for back-lit situations, or other instances where you're shooting in bright light, but your subject is in shadow. Usually, the camera uses a lower-power flash setting so as not to overexpose the shadows in your image.
- **Force flash.** Force flash mode simply forces your camera's flash to fire, whether or not the camera's light meter thinks a flash is necessary. Not all cameras have both fill and force flash modes. If your camera lacks a fill mode, you can use the force flash mode, although the resulting image might be somewhat overexposed, as the camera will fire the flash at full intensity.
- **Red-eye reduction.** The "red-eye" effect (Figure 7.21) occurs when the light from your flash bounces off the retinas of your subject's eyes as they look into the lens. The red color is simply the illumination of

FIGURE 7.21   Red eye is prevalent in small cameras because of the position of the flash. Fortunately, correcting the problem is fairly simple using tools found in most image editors.

the blood vessels in the back of their eyes. If the flash on your camera is placed very close to the lens, there's a much better chance of getting red-eye, because it's easier for the light to bounce straight back into the lens. Red-eye reduction modes work by firing a flash, or the camera's autofocus assist lamp, to close the subject's irises. When you use these modes, be sure to inform your subjects that there will be two flashes. Otherwise, they might move or close their eyes after the first firing. Whether you're shooting with or without a red-eye reduction flash, moving slightly to one side before you shoot can prevent your subjects from looking directly into the camera's lens. You can also try turning on all the lights in the room in an attempt to narrow everyone's pupils.

OL' BLUE, ER, RED EYES...

Generally, people with lighter-colored eyes are more susceptible to red-eye in photographs than people with darker-colored eyes. Probably the worst red-eye situation is shooting a blue-eyed person in a dark room. When you shoot lighter-eyed people, it's a good idea to take the time to review your images on your camera's LCD. If your camera has a zoom feature in its playback mode, zoom in and check out the eyes. You might find you need to re-shoot.

- **Cancel.** This simply deactivates the flash. This isn't exactly a mode, but it is an important feature for times when you're shooting in an area where a flash is not appropriate or when you want to handle low light in a different way.

Spend some time using the different flash modes on your camera to learn their characteristics. In particular, determine if the flash consistently over- or underexposes, and if it tends to produce odd color casts. If so, you might want to adjust its settings as described in this section.

When you shoot a picture using your flash, many things happen in a very short amount of time. First, the camera opens its shutter and begins exposing the image sensor according to the settings defined by you, or your camera's light meter. Then, the camera turns on the lamp in its flash unit. With the lamp on, the camera begins measuring the flash illumination that is bouncing off the subject and returning to the camera. In this way, the camera can meter the light of the flash while it's flashing. When it has decided that the flash has cast enough illumination, it shuts off the flash, finishes the exposure, and closes the shutter.

After the flash is done firing, any leftover charge is saved for the next firing. Consequently, your flash's recycle time can vary depending on how much it had to fire. In other words, you'll get faster recycle times when you use your flash in brighter light, since the flash won't have to fire for as long and, hence, won't have to recharge as much.

One problem with on-board flashes is that they're really not positioned to provide very flattering light. Our eyes are used to a strong overhead light source, so placing a light source directly in front of a subject usually produces a somewhat weird lighting perspective. In addition, a poor flash exposure can result in harsh lighting with overblown highlights and hard-edged black shadows if the flash fired too much, or an underexposed image if the flash fired too little (Figure 7.22),

FIGURE 7.22   At times, you might find that your camera's on-board flash creates harshly lit scenes with blown-out highlights.

Fortunately, many cameras now offer flash power adjustment controls that let you increase or decrease the power of the flash by one or two stops in either direction. After a test shot, you might find that your camera's flash is too strong. Dialing down the power by a stop or so might be enough to produce a much better exposure (Figure 7.23, page 190).

Remember that your camera's flash has a limited range, usually no more than 10 to 15 feet. Consequently, as your focal length increases, your flash's effectiveness decreases. That is, if you zoom in on an object 20 feet away, don't expect your flash to do a great job of illuminating it. Increasing the flash power by a couple of stops might improve your flash performance at these distances.

FIGURE 7.23   After dialing a −3 flash exposure compensation, our slightly overexposed image becomes much more pleasantly lit.

Flash White Balance

You don't usually use your flash in a room that is completely dark because there are usually other lights on, creating a complex mixed-lighting situation that requires a special white balance.

Some cameras have a separate white balance setting for flash that can often correct color cast problems, but on most cameras, automatic white balance will yield the best results. In fact, on most cameras, using anything *but* automatic will yield bad results.

To get an idea of your how your camera white balances when you use the flash, take some test flash pictures indoors under normal incandescent (tungsten) lighting using the camera's automatic white balance. If the images come out with a slightly blue cast, or if the highlights are blue, then the camera's white balance chose to favor the room's tungsten lighting. If the images come out a little yellow, or have yellow highlights, then the camera white balanced in favor of the flash.

There's little you can do about these color casts. Sometimes dialing down the flash's power will reduce the effect, or you can try to filter your flash. If you find blue highlights in your flash pictures, buy some yellow filter material at your camera store and tape a piece of it over your flash. This will balance your flash for tungsten, making it better match the indoor lighting (which your camera is white balancing for anyway).

Fill Flash

Don't get trapped into thinking that your flash is only for shooting at night or indoors. Your camera's fill flash mode is a great tool for shooting better pictures in bright sunlight.

When you shoot into backlit situations, you usually have two choices. You can spot-meter off your foreground subject, which will cause the background to overexpose and wash out completely. Alternatively, you can matrix meter, which will properly expose the background, but leave your foreground subject dark and underexposed. A third solution is to activate your camera's fill flash. This will throw enough light on your foreground that the camera will properly expose both the foreground and background (Figure 7.24).

Fill flash is also great for subjects wearing hats, or for subjects that are shaded by overhanging foreground objects. Usually, the bright outdoor light will be so strong that your flash will provide a rather soft fill light, with none of the harsh shadows you might see indoors or in lower light.

FIGURE 7.24   Your camera's flash is not just for shooting in dark, low-light situations. Even in bright sunlight, you might sometimes need to use your camera's flash to compensate for a very bright background or, in the case of this photo, for a shadow-producing hat.

POWER AND STORAGE MANAGEMENT

Film cameras do have one marked advantage over digital cameras: they don't *have* to have batteries. With an all-manual film camera, all you need is film (as long as you don't want a light meter), making it simple to go on long photographic excursions without carrying batteries, battery chargers, and laptop computers.

Digital cameras are not so efficient. For a simple day's shooting, you probably won't have to worry too much about batteries and storage when you use your digital camera, unless you're very shutter happy or have a tiny storage card. For long trips, though, you'll want to make some effort to conserve and maximize both batteries and storage.

Feel the Power

The easiest way to allay your power fears is simply to buy lots of batteries. If your camera uses a custom, proprietary battery, then buy an extra. If your camera didn't ship with an external charger (that is, you have to recharge batteries in the camera), then you'll probably want to spring for a charger as well. If your camera uses AA-size batteries, then pick up two sets of NiMH rechargeables and a charger.

NiMH batteries don't usually reach their full level of performance until they've been charged a couple of times, so make sure to give them good strong charges the first few times you recharge them. Unlike *NiCad* batteries, you don't have to drain NiMH batteries before you charge them because they have no "memory effect," so after the second recharging, feel free to "top them off" before you go shooting. Be aware, though, that NiMH batteries will lose their charge over time, whether they're in or out of your camera. A month on the shelf is often enough for them to drain completely, so if you haven't used your batteries in a while, be sure to give them a good charge. In addition, once they're fully charged, take them out of the charger. Leaving the batteries in the charger, constantly recharging, can shorten their life.

Obviously, when you travel abroad, you'll need to buy the appropriate adapters and converters to power your charger, as well as any other equipment you might choose to bring along.

Even with a spare set of batteries, it's still a good idea to get in the habit of shooting with an eye toward battery conservation. The two systems on your camera that use the most power are the LCD screen and the flash. If your camera only has an LCD viewfinder (or if you prefer using the LCD viewfinder), then you might want to conserve power by limiting the amount of time you spend reviewing images on the LCD screen.

Your camera probably has a sleep mode that causes it to switch to a low-power setting if you don't use it for a while. Try to get a feel for how long it takes the camera to wake up. You might need to wait an extra 2 to 5 seconds if your camera has gone into its sleep mode. Most cameras doze off if you don't use them for 30 seconds. This is fine for everyday, snapshot shooting, but it can be a real bother if you're shooting portraits or other studio work that requires a long setup. For these occasions, you might want to change the sleep time to its maximum (15 to 30 minutes). If you know you're going to be away from the camera for a bit, turn off the LCD screen to conserve power.

Over time, you'll get a better idea of how many pictures you can expect to get from a set of batteries. However, there will still be times when your batteries will wane before you're done shooting. For these instances, you might want to employ some of the following battery-saving measures:

- Switch off your camera's LCD and use the optical viewfinder. If your camera doesn't have an optical viewfinder, then turn the LCD off whenever you're not framing a shot. In addition, if your camera's LCD provides a backlight that can be turned off, turn it off!

- Some cameras include a "review" setting that lets you specify how long an image will be displayed on the LCD after you shoot. Turn this review off, or at least lower it to its smallest value.
- Try to avoid flash pictures. If you have to shoot in low light, switch to a higher ISO, or try long exposures from a tripod.
- Switch to a smaller storage card. Higher-capacity cards consume more power, so a smaller card can sometimes let you coax one or two more pictures out of your batteries. If you use an IBM MicroDrive, try switching to a flash memory card, as they use less power.
- Turning your camera off and on often uses more power than simply letting it sleep (turning it off and on usually causes the camera to zoom the lens a lot). Unless you know it will be a while until your next shot, simply let your camera sleep.
- If you know that your pictures will all be shot at the same distance (infinity, for example), lock the camera's focus on infinity. Keeping the camera from autofocusing will save a tiny bit of power.
- If you need to transfer pictures to a computer in the field, don't use your camera's cable connection. Use a media drive or PC card adapter instead.

Finally, be aware that cold temperatures will noticeably shorten battery life. If you're shooting outside in below freezing temperatures, your batteries will probably die quickly. You can often squeeze a little more power out of them by taking them out of the camera and warming them up inside your pocket. This might sound hard to believe, but it's true. A few minutes inside your coat can often get you an additional dozen pictures. Don't put the whole camera in your pocket, as this will most likely fog up your lens (see the cold weather tips in Chapter 9, "Special Shooting"). Lithium batteries (not to be confused with L-Ion rechargeables) often stand up much better to cold weather than do NiMH or alkaline batteries.

Media Baron

Earlier in this chapter, you read about some image size/compression strategies for saving media. Although these practices can make your storage go farther, the ideal solution is simply to buy more media cards. The price of media cards continues to drop, but if you tend to shoot *lots* of images, or if you're planning an extended trip, consider some of these storage alternatives.

Laptop Computers

For longer trips, consider taking a laptop computer. In addition to giving you a place to store images, you'll have a complete darkroom with you. With a laptop and your favorite image editing application, you can assess right away whether your day's shooting was successful, and determine if you need to go re-shoot something. Be sure to bring all necessary power, media adapters (or drives), and cables.

Digital Wallet

If you don't feel like lugging your laptop computer around, consider a device like the Minds@Work *Digital Wallet* (Figure 7.25). Measuring roughly the same size as a paperback book, the Digital Wallet is nothing more than a hard drive with a media slot in the side. Stick a PC Card, Compact Flash, SmartMedia Card, or Memory Stick into the slot, and the Digital Wallet will copy the card's contents to its drive. You can then put the card back into your camera, erase it, and start shooting again. Once you're back home, you can connect the Digital Wallet's USB port to your computer and copy your images to your workstation.

FIGURE 7.25   The Digital Wallet provides 6GB of portable, battery-powered storage. With the right adapter, you can simply insert your camera's media card and dump your images into the Digital Wallet, freeing your card for more shooting.

Zip Disks, Cables, and PC Adapters

Finally, you can simply carry around some Zip disks and all of your camera's connectivity options. Then, you only need to find a service bureau, Internet café, or a friend with a computer to transfer your camera's images to your Zip disks. Obviously, your service bureau or friend will need a Zip drive and the appropriate port, and you'll need to bring your camera's transfer software.

 HEDGE YOUR BETS BY OFFLOADING

Even if you have a very large storage card—one that can hold all the pictures you might conceivably need to shoot—it's still a good idea to offload some images from time to time. Media cards can crash, so backing up to another form of media is a good way to ensure that you won't lose all of your images in the event of a storage crash. If you have the space, consider making more than one backup.

And That's Just the Beginning!

The automatic modes on many digital cameras can do an extraordinary job of metering, white balancing, and shooting. Even the best photographic algorithms can be fooled, however, and none of them really know how to do anything but take "correct" pictures. For tricky lighting situations, or for times when you want to break the rules, you're going to have to take control of your camera—and that's the subject of the next chapter.

MANUAL EXPOSURE

In This Chapter

- Motion Control

- Depth of Field

- Shutter Speed and Depth of Field

- Tonal Control

- Adjusting Exposure

- Exposure Practice

- Of Brackets and Histograms

- Exposing to Avoid Purple Fringing

As you've probably already discovered, your digital camera's automatic shooting features can—and usually do—produce great pictures. Some of today's sophisticated matrix metering systems go far beyond simple light metering and offer a level of sophistication that's roughly akin to having an experienced photographer with a spot meter standing by your side.

However, like all automated systems, the light meters in your camera have to make certain assumptions, and most meters assume that you want to take a "correct" photograph. That is, most cameras will produce images with good tone and contrast and with the subject clearly in focus. There will be times, however, when you might disagree with your camera about what the subject of your image is. Or, perhaps you have different ideas about focus, contrast, or tone.

In these instances, you need to throw your camera into manual override and start making some exposure decisions on your own. Manual exposure controls allow you to create images that are very different from what your camera's automatic features might deem "correct." They also allow you to shoot higher-quality images by affording you more control of the color and contrast that your camera will produce.

Your exposure choice determines more than just how bright or dark your image will be. By changing your camera's exposure, you can alter four characteristics of an image:

- Motion control
- Depth of field
- Tonality
- Detail

Selecting the proper exposure involves balancing these choices against what your camera is capable of under your current lighting. To get the most out of this chapter, you'll need to have an understanding of the reciprocity concepts discussed in Chapter 4, "Basic Photography: A Quick Primer," and the basic metering theory introduced in Chapter 7, "Shooting."

Motion Control

Controlling motion in your image—that is, controlling how much your camera freezes motion as opposed to letting it blur—is a very intuitive process. Simply set your shutter speed higher to freeze motion, lower to let things blur. Once you dip below 1/30th of a second, you'll need a tripod to hold the camera steady; otherwise, camera shake will introduce unwanted blur into your image (Figure 8.1).

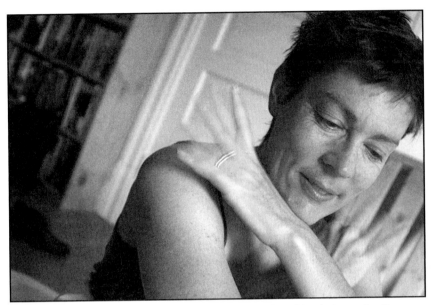

FIGURE 8.1   A slow shutter speed was used to capture the subject's drumming fingers. Because she was sitting still, no other blur was introduced.

Slow shutter speeds are also handy for shooting in very low light. By leaving the shutter open for several seconds, or even minutes, your camera's image sensor can gather enough light to create an image. However, be warned that at longer shutter speeds, your image will get noisier and noisier (Figure 8.2). The sensors in most consumer digital cameras are designed for exposures of less than one second. In addition to producing noisier images, at longer shutter speeds, many of the individual pixels in the camera's sensor might begin to behave strangely, sometimes getting "stuck" so that they appear bright white.

Some cameras employ special noise reduction schemes when you shoot at speeds longer than one second. Most of these schemes employ some form of *dark frame subtraction,* a noise reduction process you can perform yourself using your image editing application. To perform a dark frame subtraction, you need two images: your long-exposure image, and a second image shot with the same exposure settings as your first image, *but with your camera's lens cap on.*

Because the exposure is the same, the pixels in the camera's CCD have time to malfunction in exactly the same way they did in the first image. However, because the lens cap was on, the black frame is essentially a photograph of only the stuck, noisy pixels from the first image. In Photoshop, you can subtract the black frame from the image frame.

FIGURE 8.2 During long exposures, your images will get noisier and noisier.

Chapter 13, "Essential Imaging Tactics," covers the details of performing dark frame subtraction.

The amount of noise in an image is strongly affected by the temperature of the camera's image sensor, so be sure to shoot your dark frame right away to ensure that both images are shot with the camera at the same temperature. A difference of even one or two degrees will result in enough change in noise that the technique won't work.

Because long-exposure images are usually noisier, when shooting such images it's best to use a slower ISO speed, so as to not introduce any extra noise (remember, higher ISO speeds produce noisier images). However, for really long exposure times, you might want to switch to a higher ISO to cut the exposure time.

SHOOTING OUTSIDE AT NIGHT? COOL YOUR CAMERA BEFORE YOU SHOOT

The noise that a digital camera produces is directly related to the temperature of the camera's image sensor. For every 6 to 8°C increase in the temperature of the CCD, noise will double! Therefore, if you know you're going to be shooting long exposures outside, take your camera out 20 to 30 minutes early and let it cool down to the outside temperature. As the camera cools, you should see a marked decrease in noise. Do not try to cool your camera down by putting it in the refrigerator or putting it on ice! Cooling it too quickly can cause damaging condensation to form inside the camera.

Despite the excellent low-light capabilities of most digital cameras, it will often be too dark to shoot anything but a long-exposure image. If you find yourself in such a circumstance, look for a way to steady your camera, and try shooting some longer exposures, such as the one in Figure 8.3.

FIGURE 8.3   There wasn't enough light in this dark venue to get a good shot of this trumpet player, but that didn't mean that, with the help of a slow shutter speed, there wasn't an interesting picture.

If you don't have a tripod handy, try leaning against something, or setting the camera down on a sturdy object. If you must shoot with the camera handheld, switch on the camera's LCD viewfinder, put the camera's neck strap (if it has one) around your neck, and pull the camera taut. You might find that the strap offers a good amount of support. Remember to squeeze the shutter gently to prevent shake, and *don't* hold your breath when you shoot. Holding your breath usually causes your body to tense up, resulting in more shake. Instead, shoot while gently exhaling, or take long inhales and exhales and shoot in the slight pause that occurs between them.

USING LONGER SHUTTER SPEED IN BRIGHT LIGHT

When you shoot in daylight, choosing a slower ISO will allow you to use longer, motion-blurring shutter speeds (since the CCD will be less sensitive to light, it will be able to withstand longer exposure). If you want to be sure that you're able to freeze an action, switch to a higher ISO (but, as is always the case when you shoot high ISO, be aware that your images might be noisier).

DEPTH OF FIELD

Depth of field is the measure of how deep the focused area of your image will be. In an image with deep depth of field, everything will be in focus. A more shallow depth of field will yield blurry backgrounds or foregrounds.

It is important to understand that the depth of field in an image is centered on the area on which you are focusing. In other words, if you currently have a depth of field that is about 10 feet deep, that doesn't mean that things farther than 10 feet from your lens will be out of focus. Rather, it means that things *within 10 feet of the point on which you are focusing* will be in focus.

Figure 8.4 shows the same image shot with varying depths of field.

Depth of field is a function of two parameters: aperture size and focal length. *Smaller apertures and shorter focal lengths yield deeper depths of field.* Therefore, for the greatest depth of field you'll want to choose a high f-stop and zoom *out* as far as possible.

In the first image in Figure 8.4, a small aperture and mèdium focal length were used. For the second shot, the camera was positioned farther from the subject and zoomed in to increase the focal length, and a very large aperture was selected. Notice that, as discussed earlier, the longer focal length resulted in an image with compressed depth—the trees in the lower image appear closer. However, because the background is out of focus, this change in depth is not too noticeable. Balancing depth of field against focal length is one of the considerations you'll have to weigh when you shoot.

DEPTH OF FIELD AND FIELD OF VIEW

The rule that a lens with a long focal length produces a shorter depth of field than a lens with a short focal length assumes that both lenses are positioned to produce the same field of view.

FIGURE 8.4   In the second image, our depth of field is much shallower than in the first image. To vary the depth of field, we moved farther away from our subject, zoomed in, and used a smaller aperture.

If you have some experience with 35mm or larger formats, it is important to realize that, because of the tiny focal lengths found on most digital cameras (which are inherent to the small designs of most models), digital camera depth of field is much deeper than you might be used to. On a typical digital camera, the depth of field produced by an f5.6 aperture works out to be more like the depth of field produced by an f16 aperture on a 35mm camera. This is great news for users who want really deep depths of field. However, photographers who are used to being able to separate foregrounds from backgrounds using very shallow depths of field might be frustrated.

As with any camera, to get shallow depth of field from a digital camera, you'll first need to use the widest aperture possible. If your camera has an aperture or manual mode, open the iris as far as you can (this might be limited by the light in your scene). If your camera lacks these types of manual overrides, then you might be out of luck. Next, zoom in to your camera's full telephoto setting, and position the camera as far from your subject as possible. (Note that, depending on the framing that you want, this might not be very far). See Figure 8.5. If you're using a digital SLR with interchangeable lenses, you'll have an easier time achieving very shallow depths of field. Although the sensor in a digital SLR is still smaller than a piece of 35mm film, the longer focal lengths provided by an SLR's larger lenses make for shorter depths of field. In Chapter 14, "Special Effects," we'll look at some ways of simulating depth of field in Photoshop.

FIGURE 8.5   Most digital cameras are not capable of capturing very shallow depth of field. While this is great for maintaining sharp focus, you might be frustrated if you want to intentionally blur out the background. The slight blurring of the background in this image is about the most you can expect from a small digital camera. This image was shot using a Nikon Coolpix 990.

DEPTH OF FIELD AND FOCAL LENGTH MULTIPLIERS

If you're using a digital SLR with interchangeable lenses, your camera probably has a focal length multiplier (see Chapter 5, "Choosing a Digital Camera"). Note that depth of field is not impacted by this multiplier.

No matter what type of camera you have, it can be difficult to achieve shallow depth of field in bright daylight. Unless your camera provides very fast shutter speeds, you might be unable to completely open your aperture in very bright light. *Neutral density filters* are special filters that screw on to the end of your lens and serve to cut down the amount of light entering your lens, without altering the light's color. By cutting down the light, you might find that you have some extra flexibility, exposure-wise.

Neutral density filters are usually rated using an ND scale, where .1ND equals 1/3rd of a stop. Therefore, a .3ND filter will reduce the incoming light by one full stop. Neutral density filters can be stacked on top of one another to selectively add or subtract more stops. However, even the best filters are not optically perfect, so it's better to use as few as possible to reduce the chance of introducing optical aberrations into your lens system. In other words, if you want a 1-stop filter, use a single .3ND filter instead of three .1ND filters.

Here's a great neutral density filtering trick. Let's say you want to photograph a building on a busy street corner at noon, but you don't want to include any of the people who are pouring into and out of the building. Stack up a few neutral density filters until you have an 8- to 10-stop filter. This will increase your exposure time to 10 or 15 minutes, meaning that anything that's not stationary for at least that long won't be included in the shot. Obviously, you'll need a camera that provides a manual shutter speed control and allows for such long exposures. When the exposure is finished, you'll have an image of just the building.

SHUTTER SPEED AND DEPTH OF FIELD

Because of the reciprocal nature of apertures and shutter speeds (again, see Chapter 4), you can trade depth of field for more motion stopping power. That is, you can go to a wider aperture (less depth of field) so as to use a higher shutter speed (more motion stopping). Conversely, you can switch to a slower shutter speed (less motion stopping) to use a smaller aperture (more depth of field).

These are the types of trade-offs and considerations that you need to consider when you choose an aperture. Because there can be many different aperture/shutter combinations that will work for a given lighting situation, understanding the effects of different combinations will allow you more creative freedom.

NEARSIGHTED?

If you are nearsighted enough to need glasses, try this quick little depth of field experiment. Take off your glasses and curl up your index finger against your thumb. You should be able to curl your finger tight enough to create a tiny little hole in the curve of your index finger. If you look through the hole without your glasses, you will probably find that everything is in focus. This hole is a very tiny aperture and, therefore, provides very deep depth of field. Deep enough, in fact, that it can correct your vision. On the downside, it doesn't let a lot of light through so, unless you're in bright daylight, you might not be able to see anything well enough to determine if it's in focus. The next time you're confused about how aperture relates to depth of field, remember this test.

STAYING SHARP

Today's high-resolution digital cameras are capable of delivering very sharp images with lots of fine detail. The biggest contributing factor to the sharpness of your image is the quality of your lens. However, even if you have an extraordinary lens, it's still easy to shoot blurry images. To ensure maximum sharpness in your images, there are some additional steps you can take.

- **Use a low ISO.** At higher ISOs, extra noise will obscure the sharpness of your image.
- **Use a tripod.** Although you learned earlier that shutter speeds of less than 1/30 of a second are difficult to shoot without a tripod, your images will tend to be sharper if you *always* use a tripod, even when shooting at faster shutter speeds. No matter what shutter speed you're using, even a little motion can impact the sharpness of your images.
- **Use a remote control or self timer.** As long as your camera is on a tripod, you might as well get your potentially shaky hands completely off it by using a remote control, or the camera's built-in self-timer.
- **Don't use an aperture at the extreme end of your camera's range.** Stopping your lens down all the way can introduce diffraction effects that can affect image sharpness. Similarly, the sharpness of most lenses suffers when the aperture is set to full wide. Sharpness-wise, most lenses perform best with an aperture 2 to 3 stops below full wide.

- **Use an image stabilized lens.** If you're shooting with a higher-end camera that supports interchangeable lenses, spend the extra money for image stabilized lenses and use the stabilization even when tripod-mounted.

Although these rules are true for all cameras, they're not going to be as effective on lower-resolution models (where there simply aren't enough pixels to render extremely sharp images) or on cameras with cheaper lenses.

TONAL CONTROL

In addition to motion control and depth of field, the exposure you choose determines how much contrast your image will have, how saturated its colors will be, and how much detail you'll be able to see. As you saw in the last chapter, your light meter generates exposure settings that render the tones in your image as middle gray. By over- or underexposing, you can boost those gray shades to white or black. In the case of color images, your light meter generates exposure settings that render the colors in your image as mid-toned colors. With a change in exposure, you can boost the saturation in the image to produce darker or lighter colors, and stronger contrast.

Figure 8.6 shows two images, both shot with a Canon G1. In the first image, the camera's default metering was used, while the second image was intentionally underexposed. Notice that, in addition to a more pronounced contrast, the underexposed image has deeper, more saturated colors.

To capture the best tonality and saturation—and to improve your options when you correct and adjust an image—you want to expose your image to capture the widest contrast range that you can manage. That is, you want good solid blacks, nice white whites, and everything in between. The trick is to not over- or underexpose too far.

As you underexpose an image, shadow areas get darker. If you underexpose too far, those areas will turn to solid black. Once your shadows become solid black, you will be unable to adjust those areas to restore detail, because there simply won't be any detail there. Similarly, if you overexpose an image too far, its highlight areas will blow out to solid white, and will lose all of their subtle light-toned details (Figure 8.7, page 211).

FIGURE 8.6   Through careful choice of exposure when shooting, you can capture images with better color saturation. The image on the right was intentionally underexposed by 1/3 of a stop to increase color saturation and contrast in the image.

However, good photographs contain more than just black blacks and white whites. Because most of the image in a good photo occurs in the tones *between* black and white, you want to ensure that your image contains a wide tonal range. If you expose for a wide tonal range, you'll have a broad range of middle tones between those black and white extremes (that is, the image will have a lot of contrast), which will allow you to control detail across the image.

Film photographers often follow the maxim that you should "expose for shadows and print for highlights." In other words, when you shoot, you should underexpose to preserve shadow details, but then adjust your printing exposure to brighten the shadows back up and return the highlights to white. This rule often holds for digital photography, but with a slight twist: you should expose your image to preserve detail in the shadows, with the idea that you'll restore the whites in the image using image editing software.

FIGURE 8.7   If you overexpose an image too far, you'll lose detail in the bright midtones and highlight areas, as colors wash out to complete white. Similarly, if an image is underexposed too far, it will lose shadow detail, as those areas darken to complete black.

Unfortunately, there are often times when you must make a choice as to which details you want to preserve. In situations of extreme contrast (Figure 8.8), if you expose for shadows by opening your aperture wider and choosing a slower shutter speed, you might end up underexposing the sky so far that it loses all detail. Conversely, if you try to expose in favor of the sky, you might lose all of your shadow detail. In these instances, you sometimes simply have to choose to sacrifice detail in one area to preserve detail in another.

FIGURE 8.8   This canyon presented a difficult contrast situation. Because it was dark at the canyon floor, the camera's meter overexposed the sky resulting in the image on the left. However, if we exposed for the sky, the canyon bottom was plunged into darkness.

There are some ways around this problem. *Gradient neutral density filters* work just like a normal neutral density filter—that is, they cut down on the light coming into the lens—but they are graduated so that they have more of an effect at the top or bottom of the frame. These allow you to reduce the amount of contrast between the highlight and shadow areas of your image, allowing you to get a more even exposure.

Possibly the easiest option is simply to shoot two identical images, one exposed for shadows and the other for highlights. You can then use your image editing software to composite these two images (Figure 8.9). You'll usually need a tripod for such shots, although it is possible to get good results shooting handheld, if you're careful. In Chapter 14, you'll learn how to composite images shot with different exposures.

FIGURE 8.9   Through some simple compositing, we sandwiched the two images shown in Figure 8.9 to create a final image with good overall contrast.

The examples shown in the previous figures are extreme contrast situations. Most of the time, exposing for shadows is a good guideline, although your final exposure choice will also be affected by your depth of field concerns, the exposure compensation concerns discussed in Chapter 7, and some additional factors discussed here.

Different films respond differently, of course, but most photographers always underexpose slide film by about half a stop when they shoot in typical outdoor lighting situations. When they shoot indoors under controlled lighting situations, slide photographers typically expose "normally" so as not to oversaturate skin tones.

Why should you be concerned about quaint, old-fashioned, analog technologies such as slide film? Because, for the most part, the sensors in digital cameras behave just like Kodachrome slide film. Therefore, if you have some experience shooting 35mm slide film, you can keep doing what you've always done, although the workflow in the digital world is a little different and, as you'll see in a minute, your digital camera provides some extra tools to help you calculate exposure.

The downside to both color slide film and the typical digital camera is that neither has very much color *latitude,* so there is very little margin for error. If you underexpose too far, you'll lose both shadow detail and highlights.

TREAT YOUR DIGITAL CAMERA AS SLIDE FILM

On most digital cameras, you can simply set your exposure compensation control to –3 and leave it there. This little compensation will help increase the saturation in most of your images. Obviously, if you're shooting in low light, or shooting bright images that need to be overexposed, then you'll need to change your exposure. For most bright lighting situations, though, you can stick to this simple adjustment.

Don't Know Much about Histograms

A *histogram* is a simple graph of the distribution of all of the tones in your image. Histograms can be easily created by most image editing applications and are a great way to understand exposure.

Look at Figure 8.10 and its accompanying histogram.

Grayscale images can contain up to 256 shades of gray ranging from solid black to solid white. A histogram, like the one shown in Figure 8.10, is simply a bar chart showing how much of each shade of gray is present in the image, with each vertical line representing one shade. Black is at the far left and white is at the far right.

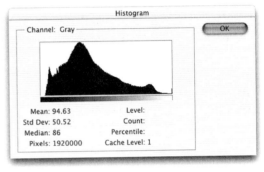

FIGURE 8.10 With a histogram, you can analyze your images to determine which type of tonal corrections they might need.

From the histogram, you can see that the image in Figure 8.10 is fairly well exposed. It has a good range of tones from black to light gray, which means it has a lot of contrast. Most of the tones are distributed toward the lower end because of the dark grays and shadows in the background. However, even though the background is dark, there is still a good range of middle gray tones and lighter tones from the gray of the baby flamingo.

Notice that the shadow areas do not *clip*. That is, they curve down to nothing by the time the graph reaches the left side. These means that the shadowy details in the image have not gone to solid black. In fact, there is very little solid black in the image at all. This is an indication that there's plenty of detail in the shadow areas. Also notice that there are a large number of tones overall, an indication that the image has a good dynamic range and, therefore, a lot of editing potential. Although the brighter areas are a little weak, we can correct for this in our image editor.

Now, look at Figure 8.11.

You can probably tell by looking at Figure 8.11 that the image is underexposed, but the histogram still provides some interesting information.

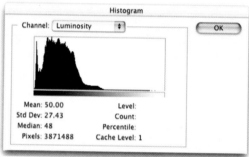

FIGURE 8.11   An underexposed image has a very characteristic histogram.

As you can see, there is no white in this image at all (nor any light or medium gray), and at the lower end there is a preponderance of solid black. Notice that the shadow areas don't curve down to black as they do in Figure 8.10. Rather, they are "clipped" off the edge of the histogram. In a well-exposed image, the shadow areas would be spread over a large number of darker tones, with only a little solid black. If you look in the shadow areas of the image, you'll see that they look completely black, rather than having any variation or range in their dark tones. In other words, the shadows have lost detail.

In a grayscale image, a histogram is literally a graph of the gray tones in an image. As you saw in Chapter 7, colors have a tone that roughly corresponds to the tonal qualities of a shade of gray. When you take a histogram of a color image, such as the one in Figure 8.11, the resulting graph shows a composite of the red, green, and blue channels in the image. The practical upshot is a graph that is still a very accurate gauge of the contrast and tonal information in your image.

An image that is overexposed will exhibit a similar histogram, but weighted on the other end, with tones grouped in the white areas, and with clipped highlights (Figure 8.12).

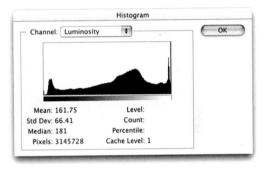

FIGURE 8.12 In an overexposed image, the tones are weighted to the right of the histogram. In this image, you can see that the highlights are clipped—they get cut off by the right side of the histogram.

Now look at Figure 8.13.

This image was shot using the camera's suggested exposure, and the result is an image that lacks punch. The image is very flat, and has little contrast. A quick look at the histogram shows why. All of the tones are grouped in the middle of the graph—they don't cover a broad range—and there are no white or black tones at all.

Just as careful processing and printing is essential to producing good photographic prints, your digital images sometimes need some special adjustments to take advantage of the tonal information that your camera

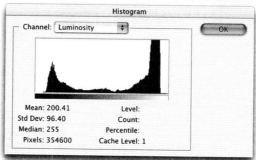

FIGURE 8.13 In a low-contrast image, the tones will be in the center of the histogram. Notice the lack of dark black or light gray tones.

captures. In Chapter 13, you'll see how you can use the tools in your image editing application to adjust and correct an image, so that a low-contrast image like the one in Figure 8.13 can be turned into something more like the image shown in Figure 8.14.

Many digital cameras can show you a histogram of any image you've taken. Figure 8.15 shows a histogram display from a Nikon Coolpix 990. In addition to displaying the histogram, the thumbnail display flashes any areas that have clipped highlights. If you think you're shooting in a diffi-

FIGURE 8.14   After a simple tonal correction, the image in Figure 8.13 appears punchier and more contrasty.

cult lighting situation, shoot a test shot and then take a quick look at the image's histogram. If you see clipped highlights or shadows, you'll need to try a different exposure and shoot again.

In addition to the RGB composite histograms shown in these examples, most image editing applications can also produce separate histograms for each color channel, or a histogram of just the brightness (luminosity) in an image. As we'll see later, these can be useful for identifying some types of problems. For general exposure analysis, though, the normal RGB composite histogram is fine.

Details, Details

Earlier, you learned that some autofocus mechanisms work by detecting contrast within an image. The fact that more contrast means sharper focus—and therefore, more detail—is an important concept to remember when you choose an exposure for an image.

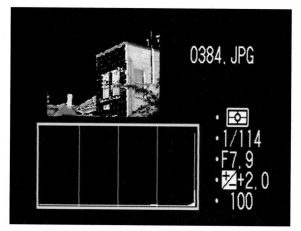

FIGURE 8.15 The Nikon Coolpix 990 can display a histogram of any image you've shot. Notice that the image thumbnail also indicates areas where the highlights have been overexposed, or "clipped."

Figure 8.16 shows the same image shot with a range of exposures. Notice how the level of detail and sense of texture changes from exposure to exposure.

As you learned earlier, when an image is underexposed, the shadow areas lose detail because they go down to solid black. Similarly, when an image is overexposed, the highlight areas wash out to complete white, reducing contrast in the highlight areas. Fine texture and detail is often defined by the small highlight and shadow areas on the texture's surface. Consequently, you'll want to expose to reveal these highlights and shadows. In general, to preserve texture, you'll want to capture as broad a tonal range as you can.

LOWER YOUR CAMERA'S SHARPENING

Sometimes, in high-contrast situations, you can get better tonal range by setting your camera's contrast or sharpening setting to low (assuming your camera has a contrast or sharpening setting). As you've seen, an image with more sharpness has greater contrast between individual pixels. This can sometimes mean less tonal range, because more pixels are represented by high-contrast shades than by a broad range of tones. All cameras are different, of course, so do some experimenting with your camera's sharpness controls. Take some test shots with identical exposure settings, but different sharpness settings, and examine the resulting histograms to learn how each setting affects tonal range.

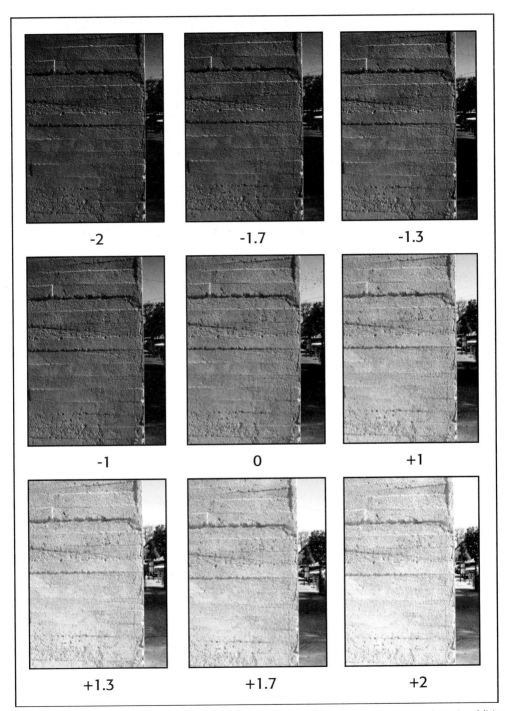

FIGURE 8.16   This heavily textured wall was shot with a variety of exposure-compensation settings. In addition to looking brighter or darker, notice how the level of detail and texture changes with different exposure settings.

To sum up, in addition to depth of field and motion control, your goal when you choose an exposure is to pick settings that will produce the broadest tonal range, while preserving shadow and highlight detail. When you use a digital camera in most situations, it's safe to assume that if you protect your shadow areas when you shoot, you can always save the highlights later in editing.

ADJUSTING EXPOSURE

As you've seen, there are many creative options to weigh, and choices to make when you choose an exposure for an image. For example, you might know that you want a shallow depth of field, so you will select a long focal length and wide aperture. However, perhaps your images include many dark-colored objects that you feel need to be underexposed. At this point, you would probably choose to adopt a shorter shutter speed—rather than a smaller aperture—to preserve your shallow depth of field. Of course, if there are some fast-moving objects in your scene that you were hoping to blur, then you'll have to consider just how much you can slow down your shutter speed. All of these different factors must be weighed and balanced.

Once you've made your decisions, you can begin to use your camera's controls to adjust your exposure accordingly. Fortunately, even if you have a less expensive camera, you probably have enough controls to make some simple adjustments.

In this section, we'll cover all of the ways that you can adjust exposure on your digital camera. Which adjustments to make will depend on your image, of course, and which controls to use to make your adjustment will depend on which exposure characteristics you want to change, and those you want to preserve.

Exposure Compensation

Nowadays, even if they don't include priority or manual exposure modes, most digital cameras provide exposure compensation controls. Whether you access them through buttons on the camera or through the camera's menuing system, exposure compensation controls give you a quick, easy, and very effective way to adjust the exposure that your camera's light meter has chosen. What's nice about exposure compensation tools is that they let you calculate exposure in terms of over- or underexposing, without worrying about how to achieve those changes in exposure. In other words, you can simply think "I want to overexpose by one stop" instead of thinking along the lines of "I want to overexpose by one stop but in this mode I don't have control of aperture so I'll have to change the shutter speed; I'm currently at 1/250th so overexposing by one stop would be 1/125th" (Figure 8.17).

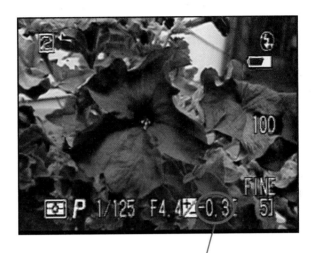

Exposure Compensation Display

FIGURE 8.17   Most cameras simply indicate exposure compensation with a numeric readout of the current amount of compensation (in this case, –3 stops).

The downside to exposure compensation is that you have no control over *how* the camera achieves its new exposure. In other words, if you tell it to overexpose by two stops, you don't know if this overexposure will come through changes in aperture or shutter speed. Consequently, you can't predict if the compensation will change your image's depth of field (through aperture change) or motion control (through shutter speed change). Because of the tiny focal lengths of the average digital camera, a change of a stop won't make much—if any—difference in depth of field. However, if you're shooting in low light—low enough that an extra stop could push you into a slow shutter speed—then you might want to carefully review your images after shooting to make sure they're sharp.

If you throw your camera into automatic mode and watch its exposure choices (assuming your camera displays its selected shutter speed and aperture) while you change exposure compensation settings, you will probably think that there's no seeming logic to whether it adjusts aperture size or shutter speed. Typically, a camera will adjust shutter speed first and only adjust aperture if a change in shutter speed would result in a blurry image. If your camera only has two or three apertures, then adjusting shutter speed might be its only choice.

Priority and Manual Modes

If you're an old-school photographer who isn't used to a camera with exposure compensation controls (or if you're simply not interested in using exposure compensation controls), you will probably select a priority mode when you want to adjust your exposure. With priority modes, you'll have complete control over how your exposure adjustments are being achieved (Figure 8.18).

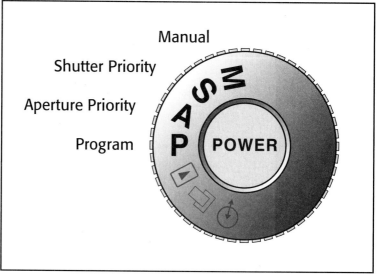

FIGURE 8.18   Most cameras offer a simple dial or switch for changing the camera from full automatic mode to a priority, or completely manual mode.

Typically, you'll select shutter priority when you want to control motion, and aperture priority when you want to control depth of field. You can select either aperture or shutter if you want to change tone and saturation, texture, or detail. Alternatively, you can combine a priority mode with your camera's exposure compensation controls. For example, you might use a shutter priority mode to ensure the motion control that you want, but then use exposure compensation controls to intentionally over- or underexpose.

Using a priority mode is very simple: just select the aperture or shutter speed that's appropriate for what you're trying to achieve, and let the camera calculate the other value. Most cameras will warn you when they think you've chosen an exposure combination that will result in over- or underexposure. Don't worry, the camera will still shoot the picture; it's just trying to tell you that your settings don't conform to its idea of a good picture. Check your manual for details on how your camera indicates a bad exposure combination.

Full manual modes give you control of both aperture and shutter speed and offer more flexibility than any other shooting mode. However, because some digital cameras have cumbersome manual controls, you might find it easier to simply use a priority mode.

Automatic Reciprocity

Many cameras allow you to automatically cycle through reciprocal apertures after the camera has metered (Figure 8.19). Many of the Nikon Coolpix cameras, for example, provide a simple wheel that, when turned in automatic mode, cycles through all the other aperture and shutter speed combinations that yield the same exposure. In this way, you can quickly choose an equivalent exposure with a shutter speed or aperture that is more to your taste. Note that, because these are reciprocal exposure settings, they will still yield the same middle gray exposure as the camera's initial setting. If you want to over- or underexpose, you'll have to perform those adjustments separately. An automatic reciprocity feature combined with the camera's exposure compensation controls usually provides all of the manual control you'll ever need, since you can usually achieve any exposure you want using these simple adjustments.

ISO Control

When you put a roll of film in a film camera, you're stuck with that film's ISO rating for the entire roll. That is not always true with a digital camera. If your camera has an adjustable ISO feature, you can change the ISO for each picture you take. Higher ISOs mean you can take pictures in less light, but you can also look at ISO adjustments as an additional exposure control.

ISO 200 is twice as sensitive to light as ISO 100 is. Moreover, as you might expect, ISO 400 is twice as sensitive as ISO 200 and four times as sensitive as ISO 100. As you learned in Chapter 4, every doubling of light is measured as a stop. Therefore, when you change from ISO 100 to 200, it's as if you've opened your camera's aperture one more stop, or cut your shutter speed in half. This extra stop can often be what you need to save a shot.

1/60th @ f. 19   1/125th @ f. 13

1/60th @ f.19
Adjusted

1/250th @ f. 5.3   1/500th @ f. 6.7

FIGURE 8.19 These images were all shot with reciprocal exposure settings. That is, all of these exposures are equivalent, they simply yield different characteristics.

For example, let's say you're shooting at dusk at ISO 100 and you have your camera's aperture open pretty wide to reduce depth of field. Unfortunately, with your current aperture, your meter has recommended a shutter speed of 1/15th of a second, too slow to be shooting with your camera handheld. Although you left your tripod at home, you don't have to compromise your depth of field choice. Just increase your ISO to 200 to pick up an extra stop, allowing you to set your shutter to 1/30th.

Or, maybe you're shooting a football game on a somewhat cloudy day and, even with your aperture open all the way, the fastest shutter speed your meter recommends is 1/60th. Crank the ISO up to 200 or 400 and you can shoot as fast as 1/250th for plenty of action-stopping power.

Of course, as you increase ISO rating, you'll be increasing the amount of noise in your image. Different cameras produce different amounts and qualities of noise so you'll want to experiment with your camera to determine if you can accept the noise it produces at higher ISOs.

TINY ISO CHANGES

Some cameras that only have a few apertures will make tiny changes to ISO sensitivity to create additional stops, usually without introducing too much noise.

Just as there is a reciprocal relationship between aperture and shutter speed, when you start manipulating ISO you must think of reciprocity between all three factors. As you increase ISO, you might need to close your aperture or increase your shutter speed.

Exposure Practice

Over the last few chapters, you've read a lot of theory and ideas about how exposure works. Now it's time to actually go out and practice some of it by doing some shooting. However, for your practice to do you much good, you need to take the time to annotate your images. You won't learn much about which exposure calculations work if you can't remember what the exposures were when you get home and look at your images.

For each picture you take, you'll want to record all of the camera's exposure settings—shutter speed, aperture, ISO setting—as well as your white balance setting. If you tend to change compression settings while you shoot (to save storage space, for example), then you might want to note this as well, as knowing the compression settings for an image might provide a clue to any annoying artifacts or contrast changes. In addition, if you've made any changes to the camera's sharpening, contrast, or saturation settings, you'll want to take note of those.

You can either choose to make these notations the old-fashioned way (that is, write them down), or you can see if your camera will remember them for you. Most digital cameras record a number of parameters when an image is stored to disk. Figure 8.20 shows the information screen from a Nikon Coolpix 5000.

This information is stored using a standard format called *Exchangeable Image File* (EXIF) that was created by the Japan Electronic Industry Development Association in 1995. If your digital camera is EXIF compatible (and most are), then all of its files are EXIF files, whether they use JPEG or TIFF compression.

FIGURE 8.20   The Nikon Coolpix 990 stores several screenfulls of information and parameters about each shot. This data is stored with the file and can be read using special software.

The great thing about EXIF files is that their image data can be read by any program, even if that program isn't specifically EXIF compatible. The EXIF data is simply stored in the header information of the file, so any application that can read JPEG or TIFF files can still read an EXIF-compatible file.

If your image editing or cataloging apps don't allow you to look at an image's EXIF data (Figure 8.21), you'll need to find an application that does.

EXIF is great because it means that you don't have to take time away from your shooting to record settings. On the other hand, you do have to use special software to read the settings. If you're a photographer who's already used to making exposure notes, then you might find that writing them down by hand is still the way to go. Many people find that taking the time to write the information by hand also serves to help them remember and understand their choices. If your camera offers a voice annotation feature, you can simply dictate the exposure settings to your camera. This will, of course, consume valuable image space, so use this feature carefully.

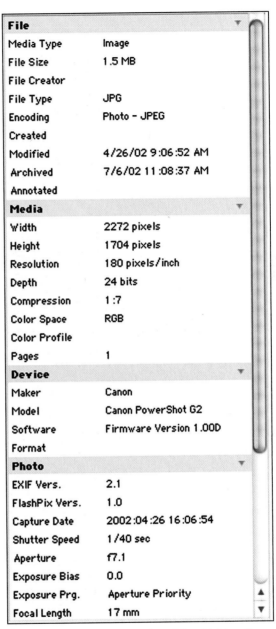

File	▼
Media Type	Image
File Size	1.5 MB
File Creator	
File Type	JPG
Encoding	Photo - JPEG
Created	
Modified	4/26/02 9:06:52 AM
Archived	7/6/02 11:08:37 AM
Annotated	
Media	▼
Width	2272 pixels
Height	1704 pixels
Resolution	180 pixels/inch
Depth	24 bits
Compression	1:7
Color Space	RGB
Color Profile	
Pages	1
Device	▼
Maker	Canon
Model	Canon PowerShot G2
Software	Firmware Version 1.00D
Format	
Photo	▼
EXIF Vers.	2.1
FlashPix Vers.	1.0
Capture Date	2002:04:26 16:06:54
Shutter Speed	1/40 sec
Aperture	f7.1
Exposure Bias	0.0
Exposure Prg.	Aperture Priority
Focal Length	17 mm

ON THE CD

FIGURE 8.21   The EXIF display from iView Multimedia, a shareware image cataloger included on the companion CD-ROM.

In this section, you'll be led through the exposure decisions required to take several photographs.

An Intentional Underexposure

The good news is that there is no "right" or "wrong" way to take a picture. There might be "better" or "worse" ways, but the only thing that makes an image right, or correct, is whether the image serves to reveal what you saw in the scene that you were photographing.

You could argue that an image is "right" if it looks like the subject that was being photographed, but the question of what something *actually* looks like is subjective. True, you could get a color meter and a luminance meter and carefully measure everything in a scene to determine what it looks like. However, even if you managed to perfectly reproduce that color and luminance, you still wouldn't necessarily have a good picture.

You also wouldn't necessarily have an image that matched what you *saw*. Remember that your eyes have very different sensitivities than your camera does. You might often have to force the camera to see things the way your eyes do.

For example, look at Figure 8.22.

FIGURE 8.22   This street scene was shot with the camera's default metering and is, consequently, a little "flat" in tone, lacking contrast and good saturation.

This matrix-metered exposure is probably fairly close to what this street scene actually looked like. The sun was low and there were some dark shadows, but they weren't too dark. Because of a slight haze in the air, there were no strong white highlights. In general, it was a fairly medium-toned scene, and the medium-oriented light meter in the camera did a good job of recording those tones.

When looking at the scene in person, however, there was a marked perception of a dark swath being cut through a lighter area. This was a purely geometric/tonal perception that can be reduced to a very simple illustration as seen in Figure 8.23.

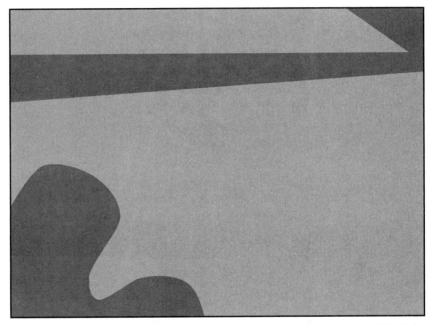

FIGURE 8.23   While actually standing at the scene of this photograph, one couldn't help perceiving large shapes of dark and light.

To capture this idea, it was essential to reveal the contrast between the dark street and the brighter houses. The human eye is far more sensitive to luminance and contrast than is the sensor in a digital camera. This, and the fact that the camera's light meter assumes that the scene is 18% gray, means that it was necessary to underexpose the image to plunge the street into deeper shadow.

Dialing −.3 into the camera's exposure compensation control created just enough underexposure to render the image the way it was envisioned without compromising either shadow or highlight detail (Figure 8.24). (By the way, a second image was also shot using an exposure compensation of −.7, just in case −.3 wasn't enough, but the second image was too dark.)

FIGURE 8.24 With a simple underexposure, the shadows were plunged into darkness, and the desired contrast was created.

Another Underexposure

While I was out walking one afternoon, I looked up to see Sutro Tower—a large radio antenna that sits in the middle of San Francisco—casting shadows into a light haze that had moved in (Figure 8.25). It was obvious that an underexposure was necessary to ensure preservation of the subtle, dark shadows that the tower was causing. Unfortunately, it was very windy, so a fast shutter speed was necessary to freeze the motion of the trees.

The camera, a Canon EOS D30, was switched to shutter priority to allow for manual selection of a fast, tree-freezing shutter speed, and the camera's exposure compensation controls were dialed to a −.3 exposure compensation to darken the shadows and increase the saturation of the hazy sky. After shooting the image, a quick check of the camera's information screen showed that the exposure compensation had not altered the desired shutter speed. (The camera's LCD was too small to check the focus visually—slight motion blurs would not appear. By checking

FIGURE 8.25   One afternoon, Sutro Tower in San Francisco was throwing impressive shadows into the afternoon haze. To ensure that the camera would capture the subtle shadings, shutter priority with a fast shutter speed was used.

the shutter speed, however, we were able to ensure that the trees were frozen.)

Manual Override

The rooftop greenhouse shown in Figure 8.26 presented a few exposure concerns. First, there was the bright white panel on the roof of the greenhouse, which definitely needed to be overexposed, ideally without ruining the nice dark shadows of the foreground roof. Second, because of the position of the camera, a shorter focal length was required. Therefore, to preserve a shallow depth of field and set the greenhouse apart from the background, it was necessary to use a wide aperture.

FIGURE 8.26   This image presented a few exposure problems that were easily corrected for, while we were shooting.

Finally, there was the overall tone of the image. The misty background and white sides of the greenhouse presented a situation with many subtle gray shades. To smoothly render the subtle striations of the mist-shrouded hillside and to preserve the deep yellow of the greenhouse windows (which would lose saturation from the aforementioned overexposure), it was essential to capture as much tonal range as possible.

The light meter read f5.6 at 1/250th of a second. To overexpose by a half stop, the camera's manual controls were used to increase the aperture to f4. After we shot the image, we consulted the camera's histogram (Figure 8.27). As you can see, neither shadows or highlights are clipped,

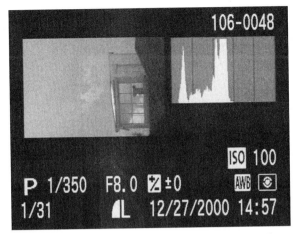

FIGURE 8.27   Checking the camera's histogram after taking the shot shows that both highlights and shadows are okay, and that there's a fair amount of dynamic range.

and the image has a fairly wide tonal range. An additional shot was taken at normal exposure. The histogram in Figure 8.28 shows that without the overexposure, the camera captured a much lower range of tones.

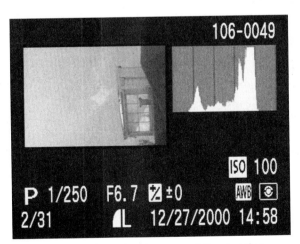

FIGURE 8.28   Checking the histogram of the shot that didn't have our exposure adjustment shows that, indeed, overexposing produced more dynamic range.

OF BRACKETS AND HISTOGRAMS

As you can see from the previous examples, a number of decisions go into choosing an exposure. The good news is that you don't necessarily have to be right about your choice, because you can always shoot multiple shots, each with a different exposure, just as Margaret Bourke-White did. *Bracketing* is the process of shooting one or two extra exposures above and below your target exposure to provide yourself with a margin of error in your exposure calculation. If you've made a somewhat accurate, educated guess about exposure, one of your bracketed images will most likely be good, even if your original guess was off. Bracketing is a tried-and-true practice of film photographers, but it's much easier with a digital camera.

With digital bracketing you don't have to worry about the waste and expense of shooting extra film. Sure, storage might be a concern, but after bracketing, you can quickly check your images on your camera's LCD and throw out the images that are obviously wrong. Therefore, if you've bracketed two shots on each side (resulting in five pictures) and two of the pictures are obviously bad, you can simply delete them.

Many digital cameras offer *auto-bracketing* features, which let the camera take care of bracketing for you. On the Canon EOS D60, for example, you can dial in a bracketing range (Figure 8.29). Then, when you press the shutter, the camera will automatically shoot three exposures, one at your chosen exposure, one stopped down a stop, and a third overexposed by one stop. (The D60 also lets you change the bracketing interval.)

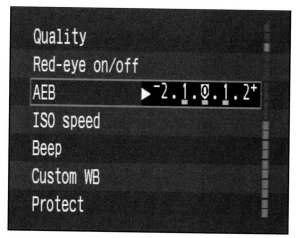

FIGURE 8.29 If your camera has an auto-bracketing feature, you can set it to automatically shoot a series of bracketed exposures.

Even if you don't have an auto-bracketing feature, your camera's exposure compensation controls make it simple to quickly bracket your shots. If your camera's compensation controls are located externally (rather than buried within a menu), learn to change them without moving the camera. This will allow you to shoot, make a quick compensation, and then shoot another shot right away. It's best to always perform your brackets in the same order to prevent confusion. Most auto-bracketing features start with the desired exposure, then shoot one interval under, then one interval over, then the next interval under, the next over, and so on.

Whether you bracket your shots or not, if your camera provides a histogram, *get into the habit of using it!* After you've bracketed a series of shots, for example, you can quickly go through them, identify the ones that have badly clipped highlights or shadows, and throw them out.

Even if you're not bracketing, if you're facing a difficult shot—or one where you want to ensure that you've captured a wide tonal range (as in the greenhouse example in Figures 8.7 and 8.8)—then shoot a couple of shots and compare their histograms. Similarly, if you're unsure whether an image needs to be over- or underexposed, taking a quick test shot and examining its histogram will probably provide you with an answer.

If the meaning and use of the histogram is a bit confusing for you now, don't worry; it will become more clear when you start correcting some images in Chapter 11, "Correcting Tone and Color."

EXPOSING TO AVOID PURPLE FRINGING

As discussed in Chapters 2 and 5, cameras with resolutions above 2 megapixels suffer from a unique digital artifact known as the "purple fringe." Purple fringing is a calculation artifact caused by *sensor blooming*, and occurs in cameras with these higher resolutions because their pixels are packed so closely together. You can see an example of purple fringing in Figure 8.30.

Fortunately, the conditions that produce this artifact are fairly easy to predict, so if your camera has a tendency to fringe, you can often keep things under control with some simple exposure adjustments.

Purple fringing usually occurs when you shoot into a high-contrast situation using your camera's full wide angle (or close to it). For these reasons, landscape shots usually suffer the most from purple fringing. Skies often create troublesome contrast situations, and landscapes typically prompt you to use a wide angle. Trees are also particularly bad subjects when it comes to purple fringing. Because they typically have a bright sky behind them, and because they include so many difficult small details, you'll often find that shots taken from beneath a tree or through

FIGURE 8.30   Some 2- and 3-megapixel digital cameras suffer from a type of color aberration that causes purple fringing along areas of high contrast in an image.

a tree (for example, on a horizon) will have bad purple fringing around the small foliage details.

If you find yourself in such a situation, and you know that your camera is subject to this problem (not all cameras will be), try the following:

- Zoom in to a longer focal length. In fact, shooting several images at different focal lengths might be best.
- If you can't get a framing you like without shooting at full wide, try closing down your camera's aperture. You will, of course, have to adjust your shutter speed appropriately. Be careful if you make this adjustment using your camera's exposure compensation controls, as they won't necessarily compensate with an aperture adjustment. It's better to use your camera's manual controls (or automatic reciprocity control, if your camera has one).
- Some cameras seem to only exhibit purple fringing in the edges of their photographs. If this seems to be true of your camera, then try to frame the image so that particularly troublesome subject matter

(trees, bright shapes, fine details) are away from the edge of the frame.

Obviously, no matter how careful you are, you won't always be able to avoid these purple fringing artifacts. As you might expect, there are some ways to remove these problems using your image editing program. It's much easier, though, to simply avoid the problem in the first place. You'll learn some purple fringe removal techniques in Chapter 13.

TAKING CONTROL

The good news about the concepts and techniques described in this chapter is that you probably won't have to rely on them very often. The fact is, modern digital camera meters and pre-programmed modes are *very* good. Nevertheless, if you're serious about photography, there will be times when taking control will be the only way to get the shot you envision. After working through this chapter, you should be comfortable with the concepts of manual exposure and should understand how your camera meters. Most important, you should know how to use and read a histogram, as we'll be relying heavily on histograms later in the book.

SPECIAL SHOOTING

In This Chapter

- Macro Photography
- Black-and-White Photography
- Shooting Panoramas
- Shooting for the Web
- Shooting for Video
- Using Filters
- Shooting in Extreme Conditions

At the end of the Apollo 11 moon landing, Neil Armstrong and Buzz Aldrin blasted off from the moon in their tiny lunar module, aiming for a rendezvous with crewmate Michael Collins in the orbiting *Columbia* service module. As the tiny speck of a spaceship rose up from the moon, ground controllers recorded Collins saying "I got the earth coming up behind you—it's fantastic!" Back on earth, after the rocks and spacesuits and Hasselblad cameras were all unloaded, and the film was developed, Armstrong and Aldrin were able to see what Collins had been so excited about: a photograph of the earth rising above the moon, with the lunar lander flying close by in the foreground. In other words, a single picture encompassing all of humanity except for one man: Mike Collins, the photographer.

Like all of the astronauts, in addition to having the "right stuff," Collins had to have a comfortable knowledge of basic photographic principles. A quarter of a million miles from earth, he still had to worry about f-stops, shutter speeds, and film stocks in addition to worrying about asphyxiation, burning up on re-entry, and drowning in the ocean.

Hopefully, you won't ever have to face such photographic concerns. However, it is important to realize that certain types of photography require special equipment, techniques, and preparation. In the case of lunar photography, you would need a massive government-funded space program in addition to your digital camera and a decent computer. Web photography, on the other hand, requires a camera with appropriate resolution, and a good understanding of how your images will be sized and compressed for delivery.

In this chapter, you'll learn about all types of special shooting considerations, ranging from shooting in black and white to shooting in extreme weather.

MACRO PHOTOGRAPHY

Although the term *macro photography* would seem to describe a process of photographing very large objects, it's actually just the opposite. With your digital camera's macro photography feature, you can take high-quality images of extremely small things.

Digital cameras are particularly well suited to macro photography. Their generally excellent optics make for sharp, clear images, while their low light sensitivity means you can get them into small spaces to capture up-close images. Finally, the macro features of some cameras allow for amazingly close shots—as close as 2 cm in some cases! A 35mm film camera would normally require a very expensive, specialized macro lens for such photography, and often need a lot of extra lighting (Figure 9.1).

Nevertheless, when you shoot macro with your digital camera, there are some things to remember.

FIGURE 9.1   Your digital camera's macro feature lets you take close-up photos that would require a very expensive lens if you were shooting with a film camera.

Finding the Optimal Macro Focal Length

After you've put your camera into macro mode, the camera's zoom control will still function. However, your macro feature might have been designed to work with a very specific range of focal lengths. Although you'll be able to shoot at any focal length, focal distances in the camera's macro "sweet spot" will produce superior images. In fact, some cameras can't automatically focus in macro mode unless they are set within a particular focal range. Most cameras indicate when you are within the optimal macro focal length through a display on the camera's LCD.

Check your camera's manual for details, and remember to zoom the camera to the appropriate focal length before shooting.

Macro Focusing

Your camera's autofocus mechanism should work normally when you shoot in macro mode. However, be aware that at very close distances, even slight, subtle changes in camera position can ruin your focus.

Macro photography is usually a low-light situation, mostly because the camera itself will block much of the light in your scene. Because of the low light levels, your camera will tend to use a slower shutter speed. Therefore, to get the best results when you focus at macro distances, use a tripod. This will ensure that the camera remains steady in the event of a slow shutter speed and will also prevent you from accidentally making slight movements after the camera has already focused.

If you don't have a tripod, consider activating your camera's continuous autofocus feature, if it has one. This will help keep the image in focus even if you accidentally jiggle the camera.

It's usually easier to hold the camera steady if you *don't* try to press the camera's zoom buttons. Instead of using the camera's zoom controls to frame your shot, simply move the camera in and out. At macro distances, you won't have to move it very far to get a reframing.

The best rule of thumb is simply to work quickly. Get the image framed, prefocus, and then shoot right away. Finally, just to be safe, shoot a few frames. If your first is out of focus, perhaps the second or third will be okay. If your camera has a drive mode (also known as *burst mode* or *continuous mode*) that is capable of shooting at the resolution you want, consider turning it on. If you're facing a difficult macro shot, shooting a burst of images will improve your chances of getting a good image.

Some Nikon cameras include a unique "Best Shot Selection" feature that is ideal for macro photography. This feature shoots a burst of images and tries to identify the one that is in sharpest focus. The others are automatically discarded.

Poor Depth of Field

Be warned that, when you are in macro mode, your camera will have a *very* shallow depth of field. Although this can create very nice effects and excellent isolation of your subject, if your subject is large enough, you might have trouble keeping all of it in focus.

Consider the image in Figure 9.2.

The depth of field in this image is so shallow that the lily's petals are out of focus. In fact, the depth of field is short enough that this image might have been better served by switching out of macro mode, pulling the camera back, zooming in, and shooting the image normally. Another

FIGURE 9.2   This calla lily was shot with the macro feature of a Nikon Coolpix 990. Although this is not a particularly large flower, it is deep enough that the image has a depth of field problem. The flower's stamen is in focus, but the edges of its petals are blurry.

option would have been to autofocus on the petals and re-frame the shot. However, the stamen in the center of the flower would then be out of focus.

If you're shooting a flat subject, depth of field won't be a problem, of course. If you're shooting something that's even a few inches deep, though, you need to start thinking about which parts will be in focus. Judging depth of field on your camera's LCD can be very difficult, as the screen is simply too small to reveal which parts of your subject are in focus. Sometimes you can use your camera's playback zoom feature to examine different parts of your image up close. Even with a 4x magnification, however, you still probably won't be able to determine focus. If you're concerned about depth of field, your best option is to protect yourself by shooting multiple shots with a number of different focal lengths— including some non-macro shots. You should also take some shots with your autofocus locked on to different parts of the subject.

If you're shooting a flat subject, try to keep the camera parallel to the plane of your subject. Any tilt will introduce extra depth into your image.

Those areas of depth might be rendered blurry by your camera's shallow depth of field.

PLAY TO YOUR WEAKNESSES

When shooting in macro mode, any lens distortions that your camera might be prone to will be more pronounced. If you know that your lens has particular weaknesses such as barrel or pincushion distortion, pay close attention to them when taking macro shots and try to choose a focal length that will avoid them.

BLACK-AND-WHITE PHOTOGRAPHY

Some digital cameras offer special black-and-white modes for shooting grayscale images. Why would you want to shoot in black and white? After all, you can always convert your color images to grayscale using your image editing program (you'll learn more about this in Chapter 14, "Special Effects"), so why not shoot color and have the option for either color or grayscale?

All of the aforementioned is true, yet there are some advantages to using your camera's black-and-white feature. First, because a black-and-white mode doesn't require your camera to interpolate up to 24-bit color, you can—theoretically—get better detail than when you shoot in color. Since your camera can ignore its color filters and simply treat each pixel as a true pixel, your images might be sharper than when you shoot in color.

In practice, as shown in Figure 9.3, you might find little difference between shooting in a black-and-white mode, and shooting in color and then converting to black and white. Because black-and-white images take up the same amount of space as color images, there is no storage advantage to a black-and-white mode. If you find there is no difference with your camera, go ahead and shoot color to preserve your options.

The main advantage to shooting in black and white is that you can immediately review your image as a black-and-white image. If you have trouble visualizing a scene in black and white, this immediate grayscale review can be very helpful.

The Zone System

Serious black-and-white film photographers often employ a system of special exposure calculation techniques called the *zone system*. Formalized by Ansel Adams, Minor White, and Edward Weston, the zone system can provide a very accurate way of determining the exposure that will cap-

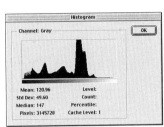

Converted from color image by
changing the color mode to
Grayscale in Photoshop.

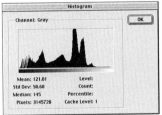

Shot using the Coolpix 990's
Black and White function.

FIGURE 9.3   As you can see, there is often little differences between an image shot in black-and-white mode and an image shot in color and converted to grayscale later. If you have trouble visualizing in grayscale, though, the immediate feedback can be invaluable.

ture the greatest tonal range, and preserve the details that you need to make a good print.

In the zone system, the tonal range is divided into 11 zones, each separated by one complete stop. Middle gray (18% gray, that is) is equivalent to zone V (Figure 9.4).

Whether you shoot black and white or color, film or digital—and whether you choose to master the zone system or not—there are some good things to learn about these 11 zones, because each zone has different characteristics (Figure 9.5).

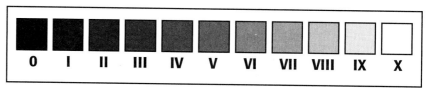

FIGURE 9.4   Serious black-and-white photographers often use the zone system to calculate exposure. In the zone system, the tonal range is divided into 11 different zones, each separated by one stop.

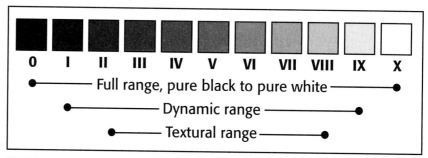

FIGURE 9.5   To get the best dynamic range and the most texture, it's important to realize that only certain zones hold useful imaging information.

In other words, any tones in your final image that fall in zones 0, I, IX, or X will not hold any texture. Any tones in your final image that fall in zones 0 or X will be beyond the usable dynamic range of the typical printing process. Zone X tones, for example, will simply be bare photographic paper, and the problem with bare photographic paper is that you can't change or control its color if you need to.

One of the trickiest things about the zone system is learning to identify which zone corresponds to the real-world object that you are trying to photograph. It can be difficult to recognize an object's tonal value by eye, particularly if it's something colored! Figure 9.6 provides some simple examples to show you how objects in the real world fit into the zone system (or, how the zone system represents objects in the real world).

To use the zone system, you must have a spot meter with a very tight—1 to 3°—focus. If your camera doesn't have such a tightly focused built-in spot meter, you'll need to invest in a separate meter. As with any light meter, your spot meter will assume that it is pointing at something that is 18% gray (zone V). By carefully spot metering different parts of an image—bright highlights, dark shadows, or areas whose texture you want to preserve—and then determining which zone those tones correspond to, you can calculate exactly how much to over- or underexpose.

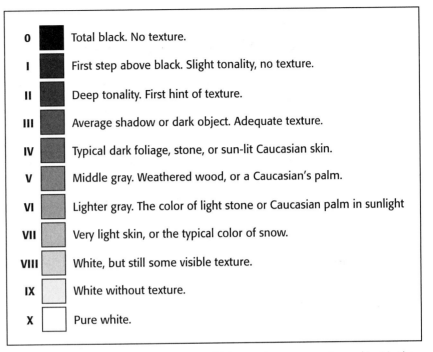

0		Total black. No texture.
I		First step above black. Slight tonality, no texture.
II		Deep tonality. First hint of texture.
III		Average shadow or dark object. Adequate texture.
IV		Typical dark foliage, stone, or sun-lit Caucasian skin.
V		Middle gray. Weathered wood, or a Caucasian's palm.
VI		Lighter gray. The color of light stone or Caucasian palm in sunlight
VII		Very light skin, or the typical color of snow.
VIII		White, but still some visible texture.
IX		White without texture.
X		Pure white.

FIGURE 9.6   It can be difficult to recognize which zone best represents an object in the real world. Here are some examples to help you get started.

For example, let's say you want to meter photograph a very dark stone, a tone that is typically considered to be in zone III. Your meter will, of course, return exposure settings to properly expose that stone *as a zone V tone*. Because the stone really belongs in zone III (and remember that each zone represents a one-stop change in exposure), then you know to underexpose by two stops to preserve the stone's color and tone.

You can further improve your black-and-white photography by using red or orange lens filters that serve to increase contrast. You'll learn more about filters later in this chapter.

Infrared Photography

Infrared light is not visible to the human eye. However, special infrared-sensitive films can be used to capture infrared light, allowing you to see objects in a completely new way. Skies and foliage are particularly well suited to infrared photography, as leafy greens will appear white and skies will be rendered with much more contrast. Digital infrared photography is possible with any digital camera, although some cameras will produce far better results than others (Figure 9.7).

FIGURE 9.7 With an infrared filter, you can capture just the near-infrared spectrum of light. In infrared, vegetation appears bright green while skies turn very dark.

All digital cameras have an infrared filter in front of their image sensor. Most CCDs and CMOS sensors are too sensitive to the infrared range, and if the incoming light is not filtered for infrared (IR), images can take on strong color casts.

Despite these filters, though, some infrared does get passed through to the camera's sensor, allowing you to use your digital camera for infrared photography. Unfortunately, there's no hard-and-fast rule for how strong a camera's IR filter is—the only way to find out is to experiment. You can get a rough idea of a camera's infrared sensitivity with the help of the infrared remote control from a TV, VCR, or stereo. Just point the remote at the camera's lens, press and hold a button on the remote, and take a picture. If the camera can see the light of the remote (Figure 9.8), then you'll know that the sensor is picking up some IR. The brighter the light, the better your camera will be for infrared shooting.

To shoot infrared images, you'll need to put some infrared filters on your camera's lens (the *Filters* section at the end of this chapter has a lot of general information on filters and how to mount them). There are a number of filters available for infrared photography, but the most popular are the Kodak Wratten 89b, 87, and 87C filters. Hoya makes two filters, the R72 and RM72, which are equivalent to the Kodak 89B. B+W also make Wratten equivalents, the 092 and 093.

The right filter is partly a matter of taste, as different filters will yield different levels of contrast. Depending on your camera's infrared sensitivity, you'll either need a brighter or darker filter. Unfortunately, experimentation is the only way to determine the right infrared filter for your camera.

Because they are so dark, you can expect infrared filters to cut 4 to 10 stops from the available light! That means you'll be using very long exposures even in bright daylight. Obviously, a tripod is essential for infrared photography. To pick up some extra stops (and reduce lengthy exposure times), you can set your camera to a higher ISO, but this will make your images noisier. Typically, Wratten 87 exposures in bright daylight at ISO 200 start at around five seconds. Because the filter can confuse your camera's light meter, you might have to do a little experimenting to find the right exposure.

When they shoot film, infrared photographers often have to worry about the infrared filter causing a focus shift that can result in the camera focusing beyond its focal plane. Fortunately, the deep depths of field of a typical consumer digital camera greatly reduce the chances of focus troubles. Just to be safe, though, you might as well lock your camera on infinity when you shoot landscapes, and if you seem to be having focusing troubles, put your camera in manual mode and decrease the aperture to increase depth of field.

You don't have to have a black-and-white mode on your camera to shoot infrared images. When you shoot color through an infrared filter, most images will appear in brick red and cyan tones, rather like a duotone. You can easily convert these to grayscale later.

FIGURE 9.8   You can get a pretty good idea of the infrared capabilities of your camera by taking a picture of a remote control's infrared emitter. Note that, in the second image, the remote's emitter is "lit up" with infrared light.

Because of the bright light required, you'll typically only shoot infrared outdoors. Any incandescent objects—glowing coals, molten metal—will emit a lot of infrared radiation. The thermal radiation produced by the human body, however, is way beyond the sensitivity of the near-infrared capabilities provided by your camera.

SHOOTING PANORAMAS

At one time or another, you might have tried to capture a wide vista or panoramic scene by shooting a series of overlapping images like the ones in Figure 9.9.

FIGURE 9.9   These two images were shot separately with the idea that they would be stitched into a panorama. Panoramic images can be stitched together from any number of overlapping images.

Although this can be a very nice, stylized way to represent a very wide-angle view, it's obviously not a very *accurate* image. The seams don't join together properly, some elements are repeated from one image to the next, and each frame has its own perspective—notice how all the lines in each image recede to separate vanishing points.

If you want a panorama that looks like a single image, you can use your computer to correct the aforementioned problems and produce an image like the one in Figure 9.10.

Panoramic software can take a series of overlapping images and stitch them together to create a single image. Besides hiding the seams of an image, panoramic software corrects the perspective of each image by essentially mapping the images onto a giant virtual cylinder (Figure 9.11). The curvature of the imaginary cylinder corrects the perspective troubles in your image.

In addition to printing out wide panoramic prints of your images, you can also deliver your panoramas as *virtual reality* (VR) movies that present a window onto your panoramic scene, and allow the user to "navigate" the scene by pivoting and tilting their view (Figure 9.12).

You'll learn all about stitching in Chapter 14, but getting a good-looking panorama begins with your shoot.

FIGURE 9.10   The finished, stitched, and color-corrected panorama.

FIGURE 9.11   Your panoramic software performs complex cylindrical distortions of your images to correct the perspective in each frame.

FIGURE 9.12   If you store your images as VR movies, users can use special viewing software to pan and tilt around your scene. With more advanced authoring tools, you can build fully navigable VR environments.

Preparing Your Camera

To shoot a panorama, you need a wide-angle lens. Although you can use a telephoto lens, you'll have to shoot more images to get the same coverage. Moreover, telephoto lenses tend to compress depth a little too much. The deep sense of space that a wide-angle lens produces is much more appropriate to the proportions of the wide field of view that you'll capture with a panorama.

The good news is that the wide angle on your digital camera's zoom lens is probably wide enough to take good panoramas. For even better results, consider purchasing a wide-angle attachment, if the camera supports such an option. With a wider angle, you'll shoot fewer images, which means fewer potential stitching errors.

There are two ways to shoot panoramas: the correct way, which involves a lot of special equipment but produces very precise, accurate images for stitching; and the sloppy way, which is prone to error but can still produce fine results.

Whether you choose to be precise or sloppy, one of your main concerns when you shoot a panorama is to ensure that you are properly rotating the camera between shots. If you're going for extreme precision, then you'll want to identify the camera's *nodal point*, the optical center of the camera's lens (Figure 9.13). If your camera's nodal point is not marked, you can still get perfectly good panoramas. Just pay attention to the center of rotation when shooting. You'll want to rotate the camera's body around a point that is in line with its lens.

Several manufacturers make special tripod heads for shooting panoramic images. These heads include special movable brackets that allow you to precisely position the camera so that its nodal point sits directly above the tripod's axis of rotation (Figure 9.14).

Note that if you're shooting landscapes, such concern for nodal point rotation is not as crucial. However, a custom panoramic head can still

Nodal Point Marker

FIGURE 9.13 Some cameras, such as this Canon EDS D-30, mark their nodal points with a special indicator. If you're really picky about accurate panoramic shooting, this marker will help you ensure that you are rotating the camera about its nodal point.

FIGURE 9.14 This panoramic tripod head properly positions your camera for extremely accurate panorama shooting.

help because most feature special stops that allow you to accurately rotate the camera into the position required for each shot of your panorama. Such heads typically sell for $100 to $300 (depending on the size of the camera they must support) and are worth the money if you do a lot of panoramas.

For most uses, though, you can simply use your normal tripod, or even shoot with the camera handheld. If your camera's tripod mount is positioned so that the camera can be panned around the axis of its lens, you're in luck: you can simply pan your tripod to frame each shot. If your tripod mount is off-axis, as shown in Figure 9.15, then you might be better off shooting with the camera handheld.

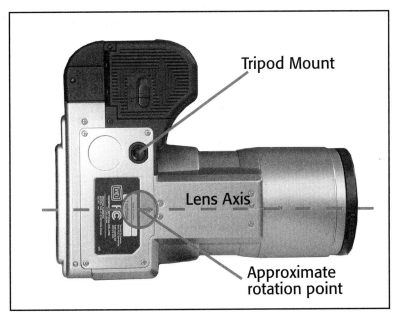

FIGURE 9.15   If your camera's tripod mount is off-axis from the rotational center of the lens, you'll have a hard time shooting panoramas from a tripod.

OFF-AXIS TRIPOD MOUNT ADAPTERS

If the tripod mount on your camera is off-axis, you might be able to correct it with a special bracket. Some vendors make brackets that mount onto your camera's tripod mount and provide a new *tripod mount in a better location. Check out www.completedigitalphotography.com/tripodmounts for more details.*

When you shoot with the camera handheld, remember to pivot the *camera* and not your head or body. Your eyes are a few inches in front of the center of rotation of your neck, and your camera's lens will be even further removed from your neck or body's rotation, meaning that you'll actually be rotating around a point several inches *behind* the camera. Therefore, between shots, rotate the *camera* properly and then—if necessary—reposition your body behind the camera's new position. Although this sounds complicated, with a little practice it's not too difficult. Your main concern when you rotate the camera is to keep its bottom parallel to the ground. If you tilt the camera in addition to rotating it, you'll run into some problems when you are stitching.

When you pivot the camera, remember that your images must *overlap,* not sit adjacent to each other. Most stitching software recommends a 15% to 30% overlap between images. Many cameras feature panoramic assist modes that offer on-screen cues as to how much you need to overlap (Figure 9.16). If your camera has such a feature, it's definitely worth using. A little experience with your stitching program will give you a better idea of how images need to overlap.

Panoramic Exposure

Because you will be pointing your camera in many different directions as you shoot a panorama, it's important to plan your exposure ahead of time. Your goal is to have an even exposure across all of the images in your panorama to prevent *banding*—bright strips of incorrect exposure that will appear along the seams of your stitched image (refer to Figure 9.16).

FIGURE 9.16   The original shots in this panorama were not evenly exposed. After stitching, color differences and banding are visible in the final panorama, particularly in the sky.

If your camera has some type of panoramic assist mode, it will, in addition to indicating overlap guidelines, lock the camera's exposure after the first image. Although this exposure might not be appropriate to every image in the panorama—that is, some areas might be under- or overexposed—it will at least provide a consistent exposure across the final image.

If your camera doesn't have an assist mode, but does provide an exposure lock control, then you can simply lock the exposure yourself. If you're using your camera's automatic exposure mode, try to meter off of an area that will produce an exposure appropriate to the entire panorama—in other words, when you lock exposure, make sure the camera isn't pointed at something brighter or darker than most of the image.

Landscapes pose particular exposure problems because some frame of the panorama might include the sun (unless the sun is completely behind you). Landscapes can also be tricky because the sky can often cause an underexposure of your ground elements. Be sure to use a metering mode or exposure compensation that will correct for this.

If your camera has manual controls, you can plan your panoramic exposure with more care. Before you shoot, take meter readings from each frame of your panorama, and try to come up with a compromise that will serve the entire image. If your camera has a long enough focal length that depth of field is a concern, then use your manual controls to ensure a deep depth of field.

Shoot with Care

When you shoot around people, animals, or other moving objects, pay attention to where you position the seams of your image. A person who is present in one image and gone in the next might turn partially transparent if he or she falls on a seam in the final panorama (Figure 9.17).

FIGURE 9.17   When shooting a panorama, be certain that moving images do not fall on a seam, or you'll end up with weird, split objects in your final panorama.

If the objects in your panorama are moving in a particular direction, then shoot in the opposite direction. That is, if a person is walking across your scene from right to left, then shoot your images from left to right. This is assuming that you don't *want* to see multiple copies of the person across your panoramic field of view. If you *do*, then by all means, shoot from right to left and ensure that the person is in the middle of each shot when you shoot (Figure 9.18).

FIGURE 9.18 Because we were shooting our panorama images from left to right, we inadvertently shot the Jeep twice. Consequently, when stitched, there are too identical Jeeps in the shot.

Of course, many times it's fine to violate all of these rules. Figure 9.19 shows an example of a technically incorrect panorama.

FIGURE 9.19 Technically, this panorama has many mistakes: uneven exposure, bad seams, weird perspective, not to mention the noise. Nevertheless, despite its technical flaws, it's still a good image. The photographic edge was added in Photoshop.

Finally, learn to think of the panoramic process as a complex—but free—super-wide angle lens. Don't just use panoramas for capturing wide vistas; use them for any occasion where you'd like to have a wide-angle, or fisheye lens (Figure 9.20).

FIGURE 9.20   Panoramas aren't just for landscapes. Think about shooting them any time you would normally opt for a really wide-angle—or even fisheye—lens.

SPECIAL PANORAMA ATTACHMENTS

If you regularly need to shoot panoramic images, you might want to invest in a special, single-shot panoramic attachment. Products such as the Kaidan 360 One VR adapter and the SunPak SurroundPhoto adapter allow you to shoot full 360° panoramic images with a single shot from your digital camera!

Both devices attach to the front of the camera through the use of a special adapter ring. At the time of this writing, adapters are only available for the Coolpix 990/995 (Figure 9.21).

These contraptions work by positioning a slightly hemispherically shaped mirror in front of the lens. When the camera—with the device—is pointed straight up, the hemispherical mirror shoots a full 360° image. Unfortunately, the image is somewhat strange (Figure 9.22).

Using special "de-warping" software included with the device, you can process the image to produce a normal panoramic image (Figure 9.23), As with any other 360° panorama, these files can be used to create a Quick-Time VR movie in addition to simple panoramic images.

If you have a Coolpix, there's no easier, better way to create a 360° panorama. Hopefully, both companies will release adapters for other cameras. The only downside to these devices is that they are very large. The Kaidan 360 One VR, for example, is about the size of a very large mayonnaise jar. Not the type of thing you want to travel with, but a great solution if you shoot panoramas for a living.

SHOOTING FOR THE WEB

Shooting with the highest resolution and quality that your camera affords will allow you to use your images for anything from print to video to the Web. However, there might be times when you know that your images will be used only for the Web. In these instances, there are a few Web-specific settings to consider.

THINK TWICE BEFORE SHOOTING LO-RES!

As you might have already guessed, this author thinks that it's best to always shoot at the highest quality possible. Although the extra resolution might be overkill for your intended output, the extra resolution will afford you more editing and cropping power, and allow for printing if you later find a reason to repurpose your images. Storage is cheap these days, so why not hedge your bets against future need, and shoot all of your images as if you intended to print them?

FIGURE 9.21   The 360One VR panoramic attachment lets you capture full 360° panoramas with a single shot! Using a special paraboloid mirror and custom software, this type of lens attachment is a must-have for users who need to shoot lots of panoramic images and movies.

Image Size and Quality

If you plan to shoot only for the Web, you might as well switch your camera to a lower resolution to save space. Resolution will be discussed in more detail in Chapter 15, "Output," but for now it's safe to say that XGA resolution (1024 × 768) will probably be all that you'll ever need for Web images. Note that if you plan on blowing up part of your image—for example, if you can't get near enough to your subject to get a really good close-up shot—then you might want to shoot at higher resolution, to provide more data for enlarging.

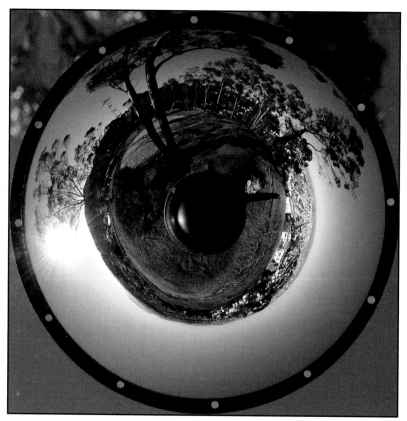

FIGURE 9.22 Single-shot panoramic devices like the 360 One produce an image that looks like this. A parabolic mirror reflects an entire 360° perspective into the lens of your digital camera.

FIGURE 9.23 Special dewarping software is used to turn the spherical image shown in Figure 9.22 into this full panoramic image. To see the resulting QuickTime VR movie, check out *www.completedigitalphotography.com/vrsample.*

Every time you save an image using JPEG compression, you lose some image quality. Hopefully, it's an imperceptible loss of quality, but you never know. Assuming your camera is saving in JPEG format, then your images have already been compressed once before they even leave your camera. Consequently, you want to be careful about compressing them again. You'll most likely make some edits to your image—color or tonal corrections, cropping and resizing—and then save the image out as a JPEG file for Web posting, which means it will get compressed again and lose more data. Therefore, it's best to shoot at the compression level that provides the best level of quality. Since you're going to lose some more data later, you might as well start with the highest quality you can manage. In Chapter 10, "Preparing Your Images for Editing," you'll learn more about moving and re-saving your images.

Consider the Legibility of the Image

Most pictures on the Web are small. To help improve the legibility of the image at small sizes, you'll want to strive for clean compositions with good lighting. Consider shooting with shallow depth of field (if your camera can manage it) to provide good separation of foreground and background.

Finally, a Use for That Digital Zoom!

If you're shooting at a lower resolution, it might be okay to go ahead and use your camera's digital zoom. Many digital zoom features work by simply taking a smaller area of the image and interpolating it up to full resolution. However, since you'll typically be shooting at lower resolution—XGA or VGA resolution— the camera won't necessarily have to enlarge its digitally zoomed crop. The result: no image degradation when you digitally zoom—up to a point.

On the Coolpix 990, for example, you can digitally zoom up to 2x at XGA resolution with no degradation. At VGA resolution, you can go up to 3.2x.

If you'll be shooting a lot of Web-resolution images, it's worth experimenting with your digital zoom to learn how and when it degrades your image.

SHOOTING FOR VIDEO

If your still images are destined for video, then you're in luck, because even a single-megapixel camera produces far more resolution than you need for video. For most video formats, you can get away with shooting at 640 × 480 (VGA) resolution. High Definition footage will require higher, XGA resolution.

When you shoot for video, it's important to remember that the quality of the image will be greatly reduced by the time it hits a video screen. Small details, fine lines, and very bright colors will not render properly on video. In particular, avoid bright reds and magentas, as these can have a tendency to smear. If capturing a small detail is important, then go for a close-up.

It's also imperative to be aware that there are *action-safe* and *title-safe* areas in a video image. Anything outside of these areas might be cropped by the viewer's monitor or television. Most video editing programs provide guides that show the boundaries of these areas. Ask your video producer to provide you with a reference for these areas (Figure 9.24).

FIGURE 9.24   If you're shooting images for video, be aware of the action- and title-safe areas. Any important action should be kept within the outer square, while titles should be kept within the inner square.

USING FILTERS

When you edit and correct your images, you'll often use a lot of filters, small bits of programming code that can add functionality to your image editing program. There's another type of filter, however, the kind that screws onto the end of your lens and modifies the light passing into your camera. Filters can be used for everything from creating special effects to correcting image problems, but before you can start using a filter, you have to figure out how to get it onto your camera.

First, check the lens on your camera for lens threads; if it isn't threaded, you won't be able to attach any filters. The filter size for your lens is probably written on the end of the lens (Figure 9.25). If not, check your manual.

FIGURE 9.25   If your lens has threads, you can find out what size filters you need by looking for a thread-size marking on the end of your lens. The lens shown here needs 49mm filters.

When you buy filters, be sure to get filters that have the same thread size as your lens. Most filters will also have lens threads, which will allow you to stack filters.

Other filters might not be available in the right size for your lens and so might require the use of a *step-up ring,* a simple adapter that screws onto the front of your lens and provides a bigger (or sometimes smaller) set of threads for accepting filters with different thread sizes (Figure 9.26). Be careful with step-up rings, though—if they're too big, they might block your camera's metering sensors, flash, or optical viewfinder.

Lens filters are completely flat, meaning that they don't add any magnification power to your lens. Although optically they are simpler than a lens, you still want to be careful about your choice of filter. There

FIGURE 9.26 Many cameras, such as this Olympus C2500, require a step-up ring or adapter to use lens attachments or filters. When using a lens attachment such as this telephoto adapter, you usually need to set a special menu option to let the camera know that the attachment is being used. This setting alters the focus and metering functions of the camera.

is a difference between a $100 ultraviolet filter and a $35 ultraviolet filter. Just as an element in your lens can introduce aberrations, a poorly made filter can introduce flares and color shifts. Although it can be tempting to go for the less expensive filter, spend a little time researching the more costly competition. You might find that there is a big difference in image quality.

Types of Filters

In Chapter 8, "Manual Exposure," you read about neutral density filters, noncolored filters that you can use to cut out a few stops' worth of light to increase your exposure options. In addition, earlier in this chapter you read about infrared filters that can be used to photograph objects in infrared light. There are many other types of filters—too many to cover here. However, if there is a group of "essential" filters, it would probably include the following:

- **Polarizers.** *Polarizers* only allow light that is polarized in a particular direction to pass through your lens. The practical upshot is that polarizers can completely remove distracting reflections from water, glass, or other shiny surfaces. To use a polarizer, you simply attach it to the end of your lens and rotate it until the reflections are gone (if you're not using an SLR, then you'll need to watch your camera's LCD viewfinder, as the optical viewfinder won't show the effect of the filter). Polarizers can also be used to increase the contrast in skies and clouds (Figure 9.27).
- **Ultraviolet filters.** Ultraviolet filters are used to cut down on haze and other atmospheric conditions that can sometimes result in color shifts in your image.
- **Contrast filters.** You can increase contrast and saturation in your images by using simple colored *contrast filters*. Yellow filters will typically darken skies and shadows, and yellow-green and red filters will increase such contrast even further. Conversely, blue filters will lighten skies and darken green foliage and trees.
- **Effects filters.** There are any number of *effects filters*, ranging from filters that will render bright lights as starbursts to filters that will soften, or haze, an image. Major filter manufacturers such as Tiffen, B+W, and Hoya publish complete, detailed catalogs of all their filter options.

If your camera does not have a TTL light meter, you're going to have to do some manual compensating when you use a filter. Since the metered light is not passing through the filter, the meter will lead you to overexpose. Most filters will have a documented *filter factor*, which will inform you of the exposure compensation (in stops) required when you use that filter.

Similarly, if your camera does not use a TTL white balance system, your white balance might not be properly adjusted for the filter's effect. The only way to find out for sure is to do a little experimenting.

Obviously, if your camera is not an SLR, you won't see the effects of the filter when you look through the camera's optical viewfinder. Switch to the camera's LCD.

FIGURE 9.27   These images show the difference in shooting with and without a circular polarizing filter. In the upper images, you can see how a polarizer lets you control the color and contrast of skies and clouds, while the lower images show how you can use a polarizer to eliminate reflections. No post-processing was applied to any of these images.

BEWARE OF ULTRAVIOLET FILTERS

It's fairly common practice to mount an ultraviolet filter on your lens and leave it there to protect your lens from bumps and scratches. Be aware, however, that an ultraviolet filter can affect the white balance presets on your camera. You might find, for example, that your daylight white balance preset becomes too warm, as the camera will be expecting more ultraviolet light to be coming through the lens. If this seems to be true of your camera, either remove the filter when you use this setting, or use automatic white balance or a manual white balance when you shoot with the filter in bright sunlight. If your camera does not have a TTL white balance system, you might have difficulty getting good white balance when shooting with filters.

Cheap Filters

Gels are thin pieces of plastic that are usually placed in front of lights to create colored lighting effects. Available at any theatrical lighting supply store, and at many photography stores, gels can also be used as inexpensive filters. Simply hold the gel in front of your lens and fire away.

On the downside, gels are not as optically pure as a fine piece of glass, and holding them in front of your lens can introduce even more aberrations, as any buckles, folds, or reflections in the gel will introduce distortion into your image. You'll also need to be wary of fingerprints on the gel material. To avoid such troubles, you can always try sandwiching gel material between two ultraviolet filters and mount the whole contraption onto your lens.

Lens Extensions

Some cameras support screw-on lens extensions that attach to your camera's filter threads to create a more telephoto or wide-angle lens (Figure 9.26). As with filters, these extensions might require a step-up ring. Also note that some cameras require you to choose special settings—usually accessed a menu option—when using a lens extension. If you don't let the camera know that an extension is attached, its focus and metering operations can become confused.

Spend some time experimenting with your camera's extensions to determine their idiosyncrasies. For example, some lenses might have bad barrel or pincushion distortion or vignetting problems.

Finally, if the extension or step-up ring is very large, it might obscure the camera's optical viewfinder or, more importantly, the onboard flash.

If the extension protrudes too far in front of the flash, it will cast a shadow when you take the shot. Usually, the only solution is to use an external flash.

SHOOTING IN EXTREME CONDITIONS

One great advantage of film cameras over digital cameras is that they can be incredibly simple machines and, thus, very durable. Since all of the imaging and storage technology in a film camera is contained in the film, the camera itself can be little more than a box. This is not true with a digital camera, which requires batteries, silicon chips, LCD screens, and many more potentially fragile components.

When you shoot in extreme heat or cold, or in very wet or dusty situations, you need to take a number of precautions to ensure that you don't damage your camera. Obviously, as with any mechanical apparatus, dirt, dust, sand, water, and extreme temperatures are definite hazards.

Dirt, Dust, and Sand and Digital Cameras

Be particularly cautious about dirt, dust, and sand because, even if it doesn't get inside the camera, a single grain of sand can be abrasive enough to scratch your lens. With their deep depths of field, minor lens scratches are usually nothing to worry about, but why take chances?

Water and Digital Cameras

Digital cameras and water definitely do not mix. Although a few sprinkles are nothing to worry about, you absolutely do *not* want to submerge your camera. The rule of thumb for manual film cameras has always been: if it falls in the water, grab the camera and put it in a bucket of that same water. Keeping a film camera submerged will prevent rust until you can get the bucket and camera to a repair person who can take it apart, clean it, and dry it.

Unfortunately, this doesn't apply to today's electronics-laden digital cameras (or even to modern film cameras). If your camera goes in the drink, fish it out immediately and do everything you can to get it dry. Immediately remove the battery and media card; open all port covers, lids, and flaps, and wipe off any water you can see, no matter how small. Set the camera in a warm place and do *not* turn it on until you're sure the camera has had time to dry off, both inside and out.

If you know you're going to be using your camera in potentially wet situations (kayaking, canoeing, taking your convertible to the car wash), consider buying a *drybag*—a sealable, waterproof bag that will keep your camera dry even if it gets submerged.

If you absolutely have to shoot in the rain, try sticking your camera in a Ziploc® bag. You'll still be able to access the controls, and you can always cut a hole for the lens (Figure 9.28).

FIGURE 9.28   If you're shooting in light rain, consider using a Ziploc® bag to protect your camera. Be warned, though, that your camera is very sensitive to cold and damp.

The Camera That Came in from the Cold

Shooting in cold weather presents a number of problems for the digital photographer. First, there are the LCDs on your camera. Remember that the "L" in LCD stands for liquid. As temperatures drop, your LCD will become far less "L," and the last thing you want is for it to turn into a solid crystal display. Although the LCD won't necessarily be damaged by cold weather, it might prove to be unusable.

Other, smaller, electronic components might actually be damaged if you try to use them in cold weather. Extreme cold might cause small electronic components to expand or contract enough that using them will cause them to break. Your camera's documentation should list a range of operating temperatures and, although you *might* be able to push these an extra 20° on the cold end, it's safe to say that such use won't be covered by your warranty.

Even if you're shooting within your camera's proscribed operating temperatures, be very careful when you move the camera from cold temperatures to warm. Walking into a heated house from a day of shooting in the snow can cause potentially damaging condensation to form inside the camera. If you know you're going to be shooting in cold weather, take a Ziploc® bag with you. Before you go into a warm building, put the camera in the bag and zip it up. Once inside, give it 20 or 30 minutes to warm up to room temperature before you let it out of the bag. If you don't have a bag, then be sure not to turn it on until any condensation has had time to evaporate.

If the temperature is cold enough to freeze your camera, then it's probably cold enough that you'll be wearing gloves. Because gloves tend to reduce your manual dexterity, be absolutely certain your camera has a neck or wrist strap and that it's securely attached to some part of your body.

In addition, if you're shooting in icy, slippery conditions where you might be prone to falling, then definitely attach a UV filter to the end of your lens. This will add an extra level of scratch and shatter protection that might save your lens in the event of a fall.

As discussed in Chapter 7, "Shooting," batteries can be greatly affected by cold weather. Take a look at the cold-weather battery tips in Chapter 7 in the section *Power and Storage Management*.

Hot Weather and Digital Cameras

Hot weather can also affect your camera and, again, the first thing to go will be the LCD screen. If you turn on your camera and your LCD appears black, then it's safe to say that your LCD has overheated—they're not very reliable above 32°C (90°F). Turn your camera off and try to get it somewhere where it can cool down. If you must shoot in high temperatures, consider keeping your camera in some type of dry cooler (an ice chest with some blue ice) until you're ready to shoot.

If you haven't exceeded the camera's recommended operating temperature, but your LCD has overheated and isn't working, it's probably safe to keep shooting using the camera's optical viewfinder (if it has one). Turn off the picture review function since your LCD won't be visible anyway.

ASTRO-PHOTOGRAPHY

Although you might not have the massive space program necessary to shoot like the Apollo astronauts, there's no reason you can't photograph the same subject matter. Because of its extreme sensitivity to light, your digital camera is an ideal camera for photographing astronomical objects through a telescope (Figure 9.29). In fact, many astronomers are finding that even cheap $100 Web cameras produce good astro photos.

In addition to providing you with a way to record your astronomical observations, your digital camera can help you capture images of subjects that you normally can't see, and it can let you see those objects in color. Your eye has to gather a lot of light to discern the color of an object, and it simply cannot gather light fast enough to see the color of objects millions of miles (or light years) away. Because your digital camera can sit and gather light for a long time, it can help you see the color of objects that would appear black and white if you simply looked at them through a telescope.

Some quick astro-photography tips include the following:

- Obviously, you'll have to buy a lens mount that will allow you to attach your camera to your telescope. There are many such mounts and adapters; check with your telescope dealer or camera manufacturer for details. You might need a number of different step-up rings and adapters depending on the type of camera and telescope you have.
- Your camera will need to have a manual mode that allows for shutter and aperture control and provides for long exposures (greater than 30 seconds). Open your aperture all the way. Your light meter will be useless for this type of photography, so you'll be doing everything manually.
- To prevent vibration, you'll want to use a remote control or self-timer to fire your camera's shutter release.
- If you're using a digital SLR with removable lenses, consider using a very fast prime lens rather than a zoom lens. Because zooms are usually slower than primes and not quite as sharp, a prime lens will yield better resolution when you shoot point light sources such as stars. In addition, if your camera has a mirror lock-up feature, use it, as this will further reduce camera vibration when you shoot.
- Ideally, you'll want a camera that has a long-exposure noise reduction feature. If your camera doesn't have such a feature, you'll want

to perform a manual dark frame subtraction, as explained in Chapter 13, "Essential Imaging Tactics."

- As your camera gets warmer, the noise in your images will increase. Let your camera cool down outside before you start shooting. As your camera cools, its propensity for noise will decrease. Some astrophotographers even modify their cameras with special cooling units (Figure 9.29).

FIGURE 9.29 These four images show what can be done with a 2-megapixel Olympus 2020 digital camera and a good telescope. The lunar photos on the left were shot by Greg Konkel. The photos of Saturn and the Whirlpool galaxy were shot by Gary Honis using a custom-modified, air-cooled Olympus camera. For a detailed description of their techniques—as well as many more excellent pictures—check out www.completedigitalphotography.com/astro.

HALFWAY THERE

Like a film camera, to get the best prints from your digital camera you'll need to manipulate your image to turn its tonal information into the image you originally envisioned. That process begins by making some preparations on your computer. In Chapter 10, you will learn how to transfer your images to your computer and how to configure your image editing software.

10

PREPARING YOUR IMAGES FOR EDITING

In This Chapter

- Moving Pictures: How to Transfer and Organize Your Images
- Preparing Your Image Editor
- Preparing Your Image
- Cropping and Resizing an Image

In the rest of this book, you will learn about what happens after you've finished shooting. From color correcting to editing to printing, the following chapters will cover the processes that have traditionally happened in the darkroom, but now happen inside your computer.

Although your image editing application is capable of amazing photographic feats, it's also capable of producing really terrible images. To get the best results—and to get them in a predictable, reproducible manner—you need to make some preparations to both your images and to your computer. In this chapter, you will learn how to configure your system to get the best results from the processes you'll learn in the rest of the book.

Before you can begin editing, though, you need to move your images into your computer.

MOVING PICTURES: HOW TO TRANSFER AND ORGANIZE YOUR IMAGES

No matter how serious you are about your photography, there has probably been some time in your life when you've gone on vacation, shot a bunch of pictures, brought your film back home, and then never had it developed. For some reason—jet lag, going back to work —you just never got around to taking the film down to the lab, and so the film sits in a drawer where it will remain for years until your children eventually inherit it, develop it, and have no idea what they're looking at.

This problem is even more pronounced in the digital world. Because you don't have to worry about wasting film, you'll probably find yourself shooting many more pictures than you would with a film camera. In no time at all, you can have hundreds of images on your hard drive, each with a vague name like DSC00453.JPG that offers no idea of what the image is.

With just a little effort, and some special software, you can save yourself (or your descendents) from one day facing a 30GB drive full of unlabeled images.

Make the Transfer

As discussed earlier in this book, there are a number of ways that you can transfer images from your camera to your computer. Your camera probably includes a serial port of some kind, either RS-432 or USB, or possibly even a FireWire port. Using the special cable and software included with your camera, you can transfer your pictures to your computer.

This is usually the least convenient and most time-consuming method of transferring digital images. Depending on the size and number of your images and the speed of your connection, transferring a single image can take anywhere from a few seconds to several minutes. In addition, using your camera's cable connection will drain your camera's batteries

A speedier option is to use a media drive or CompactFlash adapter like those discussed in Chapter 5, "Choosing a Digital Camera." With these devices, your media card will appear on your desktop just like any other disk or drive. You can then quickly drag and drop files to your hard drive.

If you must transfer your images through a cable, your main concern will be to not recompress your images before saving them. For example, some transfer programs give you the option to download an image to your hard drive, or to open it up on-screen. Be warned that if you open the image on-screen, the only save options available might be to resave the image as a JPEG file, introducing more JPEG compression and, therefore, a loss in quality. Some programs will allow you to save in a non-*lossy* format such as TIFF, but these files will be much larger than JPEG files.

Not all programs work this way, but if yours does, you might want to consider downloading all of the images to your hard drive first, and then looking at them later. Remember, avoiding repeated JPEG compression is one of your primary image editing workflow concerns.

No matter how you move your images, it's essential to stay organized and to keep your images labeled. If your camera's image transfer software includes a *light table* or *image cataloging* function, you can quickly generate a page of thumbnails showing the contents of an entire media card.

ON THE CD

If your camera's included software doesn't include such a function, or if you'd like more power, consider using a third-party media cataloging application such as iView Multimedia, Thumber, or Extensis Portfolio. Demos and evaluation copies of several media catalogers are included on the companion CD-ROM.

Organize Your Digital Media

Although everyone will have different ideas about organization and workflow, here are a few tips and suggestions for managing your digital media.

- Get a cataloging program that allows you to rename or move files. Being able to rename a file from within your cataloger is easier than having to switch back to your operating system's File Manager.
- Start by grouping images into folders, by subject. If you're in a hurry, don't worry about naming every file, just quickly sort by subject. You can always label individual files later.

- If you have a series of bracketed images, label each file with the appropriate exposure; this is the easiest way to keep track of how each image was exposed (Figure 10.1). You can look up the settings using your camera's information display, or by using an EXIF- compatible application.

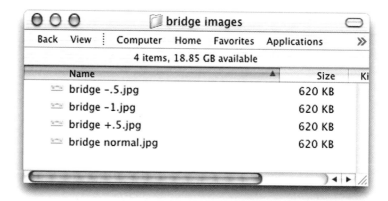

FIGURE 10.1   If you have a group of bracketed images, change their filenames to reflect the degree of exposure adjustment in each image. This will make it easier to keep track of which image is which.

- Similarly, sort panoramic images into folders. Whether you stitch them right away or not, it's a good idea to keep related images together.
- Lock valuable images before editing. Because most images are stored as JPEG files, you want to be sure that you don't accidentally save them again as a JPEG file and introduce more compression. Locking your original file gives you the equivalent of a digital negative. You can then save new copies as you make edits. If you're storing images on a removable medium such as a Zip disk, lock the entire disk after you've moved your files.
- Most likely, your image cataloging software won't be able to display images stored in a Raw data format. Cameras that offer Raw data support usually save separate, small, JPEG thumbnails for viewing. When you transfer images, be sure to copy both the thumbnail files and the Raw files, as you'll need these for cataloging and sorting.

Once you settle on a system of organization, use it! Although it might seem strange to devote several pages to this one topic, it's very easy to become overwhelmed by the number of images that your camera will produce in a heavy day of shooting. With a well-designed system of organization, you can quickly keep image glut under control.

PREPARING YOUR IMAGE EDITOR

Before you can get started editing, you'll need to make sure that your image editing software is configured to accurately display colors. Color management and calibration is a complex subject, and how far you should delve into it depends largely on your printing and output needs. Most likely, no matter what software or printer you're using, you're going to need to spend a little time trying to manage the display and output of color.

In this section, you'll learn how to configure the color management tools in Adobe Photoshop 7 to more accurately represent colors on your monitor and printer. (Note that these techniques also work for Photoshop 6, although there might be some subtle differences. While the methods discussed herein are specific to Photoshop, much of the theory applies to any application, and should be helpful no matter what application you ultimately decide to use. Even if Photoshop is not your image editor of choice, it's worth installing the Photoshop 7 demo from the companion CD-ROM to follow the instructions in this text more easily.

ON THE CD

A Little More Color Theory

As you saw in Chapter 3, "How a Digital Camera Works," light mixes together in an additive process so that as colors are added together they appear more and more white. Ink, on the other hand, mixes in a subtractive manner. That is, as colors are mixed they appear darker. While the primary colors of light—the fundamental colors from which all other colors can be made—are red, green, and blue, the primary colors of ink are cyan, magenta, and yellow (Figure 10.2).

This difference in the way color can be created is what makes accurate printing of your images so difficult. Each time you print, your computer has to figure out how to take your image—which it represents as a combination of red, green, and blue light—and convert it into a mix of cyan, magenta, and yellow ink.

SPECIAL K

As you might already know, color printing uses four colors: cyan, magenta, yellow, and black. Black is not a primary color, of course, but black ink is added to the mix

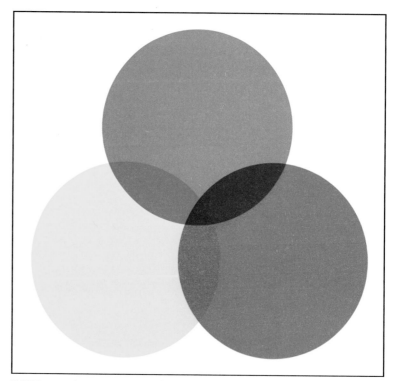

FIGURE 10.2 The primary colors of ink: cyan, magenta, and yellow. These colors differ from the primary colors of light—red, green, and blue—that your camera uses to create images. This difference is one of the things that makes accurate printing so complicated.

because it is impossible to create perfectly pure ink pigments. Therefore, although the theory says that if you mix cyan, magenta, and yellow together you will eventually get black, the truth is you'll just get very dark brown because of impurities in your color pigments. Adding a little black ink is the only way to get true black. This is why four-color printing is called CMYK.

As if converting colors between these two different color spaces wasn't difficult enough, accurate color reproduction is further complicated by the fact that not every monitor or TV is the same. If you've ever looked at a wall of TVs in an appliance store, you've seen that an image can vary greatly even between identical models. There are a number of reasons why, ranging from differences in color adjustments on each set, to differences in age, to differences in manufacturing. Computer monitors vary in the same way, which is why a digital image or Web page on your monitor might look completely different on someone else's monitor.

Printers have their own collection trouble. Each manufacturer might take a different approach to reproducing colors, while different brands of ink and types of paper have their own unique color qualities. Further complicating matters is the fact that printers often use completely different approaches to reproducing color. Some printers use four colors, some add two extra colors to reproduce lighter tones, some use ink, some use solid wax, and so on.

So, how in the world will you manage and account for all of these variables? Fortunately, if you properly configure your software, you won't have to.

Color Management Systems

There are a number of ways that you can try to calibrate your monitor with your printer (or another monitor if you will be moving your images to different computers). Some people simply print a sample from their printer and then fool around with their monitor controls until the color on-screen matches the print. This is just about the worst way to approach color management because, in addition to being wildly inaccurate, your monitor adjustments won't necessarily be appropriate for all colors.

Another approach is to print an image using your preferred printer and paper, and then look at what's wrong with the print and adjust the color in your image accordingly. This works okay (and even in the best of circumstances, you'll always have to output test prints and make adjustments), and over time you'll probably begin to better understand the idiosyncrasies of your monitor and printer. However, you'll have to do a lot of printing to get good results, and if you ever change monitors or printers, everything you will have learned about what looks right on-screen will be wrong.

The best approach to color management, therefore, is to use a *color management system* or *CMS*. A CMS is a set of software components that work together to compensate for the differences in your monitor, printer, and scanner, so that your images appear as accurately as possible on your display.

Using a CMS is pretty simple, but it does require a little time to gather the appropriate data and configure your software properly. With this small investment of time, though, you'll have a much better chance of reproducing your images correctly.

Color Management Workflow

A color management system works by adjusting the *display* of the colors in your image file (also referred to as your document in this text) so that they appear correct on the particular monitor you are using. Note that the color values of the pixels in your document are not being changed. Instead, the colors are being adjusted on the way to your monitor or printer. To make these adjustments, your color management system needs to know some details about the color characteristics of your monitor, your printer, and the device that produced your image. With Photoshop 6 or later, and a properly configured color management system, you can make your monitor do a fairly accurate job of simulating a particular printer, allowing you to perform on-screen proofing, sometimes called *soft proofing*.

To perform these color manipulations, your CMS needs to have accurate *device profiles*. Also referred to as *ICC profiles* or simply *profiles*, these small files describe certain color characteristics of each device in your color management workflow. Obviously, for your CMS to work properly, you'll need accurate device profiles.

In Chapter 3 you learned about color models—the different approaches to representing color in an image. Different color models have different *gamuts*, or ranges of colors that they are capable of representing. For example, a CMYK offset printing process has a very particular gamut of colors that it can reproduce. If any of the colors in your image fall outside the color gamut of the press, they won't print properly. Part of the job of your color management system is to properly adjust colors between different gamuts.

Photoshop 7 performs most of its color calculations and manipulations in an RGB color space. Although you can choose to convert to another color space—*CMYK* or *L*A*B*, for example—for most digital photography and desktop printing applications you'll stick with RGB. However, there are many different RGB color spaces, and each has a different gamut. For example, Microsoft and Hewlett-Packard defined the *sRGB* color space, a rather small RGB color space that attempts to reflect the color gamut of the average color monitor. Adobe, meanwhile, created the Adobe 1998 color space, a slightly larger color space that is more appropriate for typical desktop and offset printing jobs.

To ease its color management chores, Photoshop asks you to select a default RGB color space that it will use for its color management calculations. Adobe provides several options, and you can even add more if you want. In general, though, you simply want to choose a space that is large enough to support the colors produced by your camera. Photoshop also adds an extra wrinkle to the normal color management process: it attaches a profile to your image. This profile contains information about the RGB space used by the image.

Once you've selected a color space and installed your device profiles, Photoshop—with help from your *color matching engine*—can start managing color. By examining the profile from your camera (if you have a camera profile) and the profile attached to your document, the CMS has a much better idea of what the colors in your image are supposed to be. By examining the profile for your monitor, it can figure out how to represent your colors on-screen, while your printer profile will provide the information necessary for your CMS to more accurately print those original colors.

What's more, if you take your image to another monitor and printer, it should look exactly the same on those devices as it did on yours—assuming those new devices have accurate profiles.

It's important to realize, however, that although a CMS can do a very good job of accurately displaying colors, it still can't exactly represent printed output on your screen—or vice versa. Color created by a self-illuminated computer monitor is going to be inherently brighter and simply have a different quality than color ink on paper.

In the next section, you'll learn how to configure your color management system.

Configuring Your Color Management System

There are a number of different color management systems, but the most popular are ColorSync, which comes built into the Macintosh operating system, and Windows' Integrated Color Management, which comes built into Windows. One of the nice things about color management in Photoshop 7 is that, from the Color Settings dialog box, you can choose to use any CMS, and Photoshop even includes a built-in CMS of its own. Although extreme color fanatics will argue the merits of one CMS over another, it's safe to say that for almost any application, the CMS that's built into your operating system—or Photoshop's built-in color manager—will be all that you'll ever need.

Your most important CMS-related concern is to configure your CMS settings properly by specifying which profiles you want to use for your monitor and printer (and, ideally, your camera, although you probably won't be able to find a camera profile) and tweaking a few settings. Most of your CMS configuration will happen inside Photoshop, but before you head there, you need to select a profile for your monitor.

If you're a Macintosh user using an Apple-brand monitor, then your operating system probably shipped with an appropriate profile. If you're a Mac or Windows user using a third-party monitor, check your vendor's

Web site to see if they offer a profile for your CMS. If they don't, you can build one yourself as described next.

WHAT A COLOR LOOKS LIKE VERSUS WHAT IT IS MADE OF

Unfortunately, although CMYK or RGB color spaces can represent many colors, they don't describe what a color actually looks like; rather, they simply describe what a color is made of. In other words, a set of RGB values is nothing more than a recipe for displaying a certain color. In theory, this might seem like a great idea. In practice, though, it doesn't really work very well because there's no guarantee that your chosen monitor or printer has the right ingredients to properly make your color recipe.

For example, if your computer says that a particular pixel is supposed to be 50% red, 30% green, and 70% blue, but the red gun in your monitor is no longer the nice pure red that it once was, then what gets displayed might be closer to 40% red, 50% green, and 75% blue.

Fortunately, in 1976 CIE, the Commission Internationale de l'Éclairage (the International Commission on Illumination) came up with the Lab color model (actually, Lab is a modification of a color model created by CIE in 1931). Rather than describing how a color is made, Lab describes what a color looks like. Because Lab has nothing to do with any actual color reproduction method (such as the red, green, and blue electron guns used by your monitor, or the four different inks used by a printer), it is referred to as a *device-independent color space*.

A CMS works by using the profile of your camera or scanner to convert your image into a device-independent color space such as Lab. In other words, your camera's profile helps the CMS understand what the colors in your image are supposed to be, and Lab mode provides a reference space for modeling those colors.

Specifying a Monitor Profile on a Macintosh

If you're using Macintosh operating system 8.6 or later, then ColorSync, Apple's color management system, is probably already installed on your computer. If you don't see a ColorSync control panel in your Control Panel folder, then you need to install ColorSync from your original operating system disk. ColorSync ships with pre-defined profiles for most of the monitors that Apple makes, including iMacs and PowerBooks. If you're using a third-party monitor, you should check with your vendor to see if they offer ColorSync profiles.

If you don't have a profile for your monitor, you can always create one. Special hardware calibrators—such as the $400 OptiCal system from ColorVision—can be used to measure the characteristics of your display and create a monitor profile. Alternatively, you can build a profile by eye using Apple's Monitor Calibration Assistant software as shown in Figure 10.3.

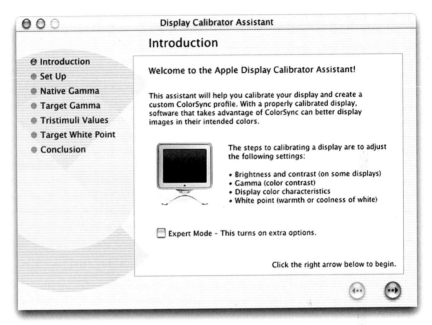

FIGURE 10.3   Apple's Monitor Calibration Assistant provides a way to build a monitor profile by eye. Although less accurate than a hardware-calibrated profile, it's better than nothing.

Although it is not as precise as a hardware calibrator, Apple's calibrate-by-eye approach is still much better than not using a profile. Even if you have a pre-defined profile for your monitor, you might want to build a new profile from scratch. If your monitor is old, it might have changed enough from its original design specifications that the pre-defined profile no longer matches. To use the Monitor Calibration Assistant, simply follow the on-screen instructions.

Once you've found or created and installed a monitor profile, you use the Displays control panel (or Monitors control panel if using Mac OS 8 or 9) to select the appropriate profile from the list of available options (the Monitor Calibration Assistant will do these two steps for you).

That's it. Your monitor profile is now configured and you're ready to move on to the settings in Photoshop's Color Settings dialog box.

Specifying a Monitor Profile in Windows

Before you can specify a monitor profile in Windows, you'll need a profile. Windows ships with only one default profile—which is unlikely to be the perfect match for your monitor—so it's better to try to build your own. You'll get the most accurate profile by using a hardware calibrator of some kind. You can also build a reasonable profile using the Adobe Gamma Control Panel (Figure 10.4). Simply follow the instructions on-screen to build a profile by eye.

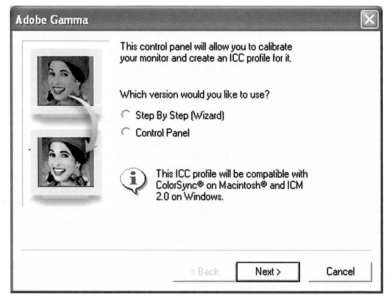

FIGURE 10.4 The Adobe Gamma control panel walks you through the process of creating a monitor profile by eye.

Monitor profiles in Windows 98 and 98 Second Edition need to be stored in the Windows/System/Color folder, while monitor profiles for Windows 2000 and Millennium Edition (ME) need to be stored in the Windows/System32/Spool/ Drivers/Color folder.

Once you've placed your profile in the right folder, you need to attach it to your monitor. Open the Display control panel and click on the Settings tab. Click the Advanced button at the bottom of the window and then click on the Color Management tab (Figure 10.5). From this screen, you can simply click the Add button to choose a profile.

As on the Macintosh, the rest of your color management settings will be defined from within Photoshop.

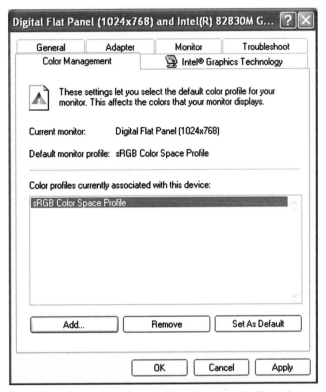

FIGURE 10.5 Once you've installed your monitor profile in the proper folder, you can use the Display control panel to define it as your current profile.

MONITOR CALIBRATION TIPS

Before you calibrate your monitor, whether by eye or with a hardware calibrator, let the monitor warm up for half an hour or so. This will give it time to get up to its usual operating temperature. For best results, turn the lights in the room down and block any reflections or glare that might be striking the monitor.

Set your desktop background or pattern to a neutral gray (when you do any precise color manipulation or editing, you should set your desktop to gray to keep your eyes from getting confused). If you want to get really picky, then it's a good idea to move any large, bright-colored objects out of your field of view. In general, you want your working space to be neutrally colored.

Photoshop 7's Color Settings Dialog Box

Figure 10.6 shows the Photoshop 7 Color Settings dialog box. Although it might look a bit complex, you really only need to make one or two adjustments if you're printing to a desktop printer. If you have more complex, offset printing jobs, then you'll need to delve into your Photoshop manual to learn more about CMYK settings.

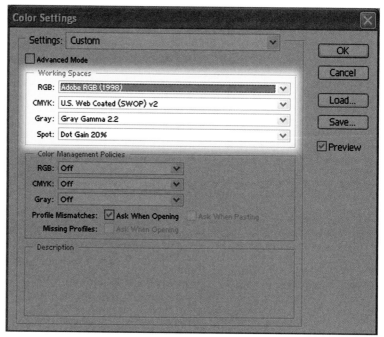

FIGURE 10.6 You define the color spaces you want to use for different types of editing using the Working Spaces section of the Color Settings dialog box.

Your first choice is to configure your working spaces. A color space is just a mathematical model of a particular range of colors. As such, you can simply tell your computer to use one model or another. When you work in a particular color space, you won't be allowed to pick colors outside of that space, and when you perform corrections and other color-altering operations, your colors will be kept "legal." That is, they won't ever extend beyond the colors of that space.

The Working Spaces section of Photoshop's Color Settings dialog box lets you specify the color spaces you want to use for different types of editing. Therefore, you can select a particular color gamut for all of your RGB editing, another for all of your CMYK editing, and others for your grayscale editing or spot color work (Figure 10.7). Because digital cameras and desktop color printers are RGB devices, you only need to worry about choosing an RGB color space.

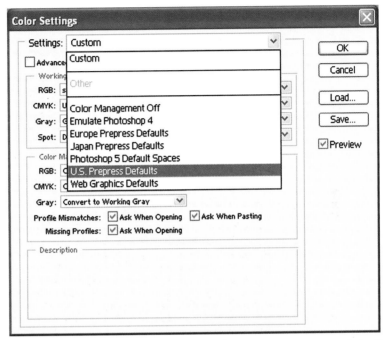

FIGURE 10.7 Photoshop 7 includes several color management presets that will automatically configure your color settings for specific printing situations.

"I THOUGHT MY PRINTER USED CMYK INKS?"

Although your desktop printer uses CMYK inks (or, in the case of a six-color inkjet photo printer, CMYK with extra C and extra M), the driver software for the printer expects to receive RGB data. The driver takes care of making the appropriate conversion to a CMYK color space. Therefore, from your computer's point of view, your color printer is an RGB device.

Photoshop provides four different RGB spaces that differ slightly in the size of their gamuts. For most uses, the Adobe RGB (1998) space is probably the most appropriate. It's bigger than the sRGB space and has a wide enough gamut to handle all of the colors a digital camera can produce.

If your work is ultimately destined for output to a CMYK offset printing process, then you'll need to choose a CMYK space. For most uses, the best CMYK choice is to choose one of the Prepress Default presets from the Settings pop-up menu in the Color Settings dialog box (refer to Figure 10.7). Before getting too far into your work, though, you should consult with your printing service bureau to learn more about the color gamut of their particular press.

Photoshop tags your documents with the working space that you define in the Color Settings dialog box. These tags are part of the document's profile, and any new documents that you create will automatically be tagged with this working space profile. Later in this chapter, you'll see how these tags are used to proof your documents on-screen. First, though, you need to learn a little bit about profile management.

Making Policy

Because not everyone will choose to use the same color space, Photoshop allows you to set policies that govern how to handle documents that are tagged with a different color space than your chosen working space. For example, let's say you've chosen to use Adobe RGB (1998) as your default working space, and a friend who does a lot of Web design gives you a Photoshop document. Most likely, your friend will have selected sRGB as his default working space, and his document will be tagged as such. Photoshop will handle the document in different ways depending on how you've set your color management policies.

With version 7's default policy options, any time you open a document that has been tagged with a color space that is different from your default working space, Photoshop will present the message box shown in Figure 10.8.

Simply put, Photoshop doesn't know what to do with the discrepancy between the document's color space and your stated color space preference. Therefore, it lets you choose to use the attached (embedded) document profile, change the profile to your working space, or discard the profile completely. In Figure 10.9, the discrepancy has occurred because the document's attached sRGB profile doesn't match the AdobeRGB working space defined in your Color Settings dialog box.

You could choose to use the document's profile, but your printed results might not be as good as they would be if you converted the document to your chosen RGB space. It's better to go ahead and re-tag the document with your working space. Be aware, however, that you might want to warn the owner of this document that you've changed the working space, if you have to return the document to him.

The Color Settings dialog box lets you specify how mismatches in profiles should be handled. The bottom of the Color Settings dialog box

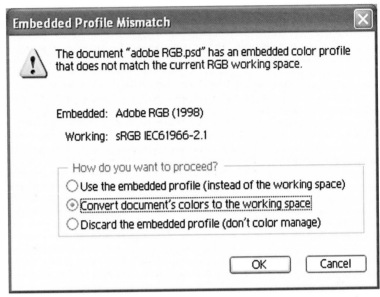

FIGURE 10.8   If a document's profile doesn't match your default color working space, Photoshop lets you change to a new profile upon opening.

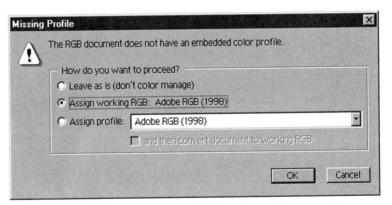

FIGURE 10.9   If a document has no profile, Photoshop will let you assign one upon opening.

provides detailed descriptions of each setting, and it's worth spending some time learning about the different policies. In general, though, Photoshop's default settings are the best for general use.

Finally, if you open a document that doesn't have a profile attached, Photoshop will present the message box shown in Figure 10.9 (unless you've specified different behavior in the Color Settings dialog).

At this point, you can choose to not attach a profile, meaning that Photoshop will perform no color management functions, or you can attach your default working space, or another profile of your choice. In most cases, you'll probably want to attach your default color space. Photoshop presents similar documents if there is a profile mismatch when you paste something from one document into another.

When you change the profile of a document, Photoshop converts the document's colors into the new color space. Thanks to your color management system, this is a nearly lossless process, but there is—technically—a little loss of data when this occurs. Although you probably won't ever notice this loss, it's best not to go wantonly converting your images from space to space.

TROUBLE MOVING IMAGES INTO OTHER APPLICATIONS

If you're using Photoshop's color management features, you might find that an image looks different in Photoshop than in another application. This is because Photoshop is "correcting" the color before it hits your monitor. This can create problems if you're trying to pick or edit colors to match color elements in another application—for example, a page-layout or Web design package. To prevent this, you can choose to not tag an image with a profile when you first open the image, or you can select Color Management Off from the Settings pop-up menu in the Color Settings dialog box.

"Aaaarrrgh! This Is Too Confusing!"

You can choose to ignore color management altogether. Although there's no way to completely disable Photoshop's color management, choosing Color Management Off from the Settings pop-up menu at the top of the Color Settings dialog box will select some good, all-purpose color spaces, and will disable Photoshop's color management policies. However, if you open a document with a profile that's different from your chosen working space, Photoshop will still present you with the Embedded Profile Mismatch message box shown in Figure 10.9. When this happens, choose the "Use the embedded profile" option. This will prevent color conversions and will leave the document's profile intact so that, if you return the document to its original owner, it will still behave as expected.

CHANGES FROM PHOTOSHOP 5

It's important to realize that the Color Settings dialog box in Photoshop 6 and 7 is very different from the color settings in Photoshop 5, which were spread across four different dialog boxes. Photoshop 6 and 7 also differ from version 5 in their ability to have multiple documents open, each with a separate RGB space, and in their ability to easily perform soft proofing. Therefore, if you're using version 5, you'll probably need to review your Photoshop manual to learn more about that version's color settings. If you're using a previous version, now is a good time to upgrade. Earlier versions of Photoshop used a very different, greatly inferior method of color management.

Soft Proofing in Photoshop 7

Here's the payoff for all of this tedious color management theory. With your color settings configured and your profiles assigned, Photoshop can now do a pretty good job of generating a screen image, or *soft proof,* of what your image will look like when it is printed on a particular printer. Although Photoshop's soft proofs won't exactly match your printed page, they'll be pretty close, and most likely will save you a few test prints.

To generate a soft proof, you'll need the appropriate printer profiles. These are most likely available from your printer vendor's Web site or were included in the software that shipped with your printer. Epson, HP, Canon, and many other vendors are diligent about generating profiles for their color printers, and you should install these profiles in the same folder as your monitor profiles.

With the proper profiles installed, open the document you want to soft proof and choose View>Proof Setup from the Photoshop menu bar. In the Proof Setup dialog box, select Custom from the Setup pop-up menu (Figure 10.10). Choose the appropriate printer profile from the Profile pop-up menu. Most printers install separate profiles for each type of paper that the printer supports. For example, if you are using an Epson printer with Epson's Heavyweight Matte Paper, then you'll want to select that profile.

The Intent pop-up menu lets you control how Photoshop will deal with colors that fall outside the gamut of your device's color space. For images with strong saturated colors, choose Perceptual from the Intent menu. For other images, select Relative Colorimetric. If you're not sure which is the best choice, you'll want to try a little experimentation. Odds are, you'll find Perceptual to be the best choice for most images (Figure 10.11).

If you select the Paper White and Ink Black boxes, Photoshop will simulate both the color of the paper and the black point of the paper/ink combination to which you will be printing. These choices usually yield the most accurate soft proof. Click the Save button and give this proof setup the same name as your printer; then click OK.

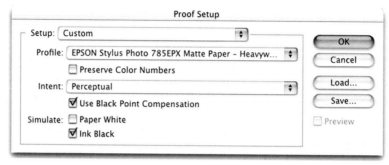

FIGURE 10.10 With the Proof Setup dialog box, you can create special soft proof settings for all of your printers.

Now, choose View>Proof Colors. You should see the colors in your image shift and the resulting image should be closer to what your printed output will look like. Note that you can select a default proof setup by choosing View>Proof Setup when there are no documents open. A discussion of the other Proof Setup settings is beyond the scope of this book, but you can learn more from your Photoshop manual, Photoshop's online help, or by simply checking the settings and doing some test prints to determine which configuration generates the most accurate proof.

Your CMS also comes into play when you print. You'll learn more about this in Chapter 15, "Output."

THE RIGHT PROFILE FOR THE JOB

Note that many vendors include printer profiles designed for specific types of paper. Be sure to choose the profile that matches the type of paper you'll be using, as different types of paper can produce very different colors.

PREPARING YOUR IMAGE

In the next chapter, you will begin to correct and adjust the tone and color of your images. However, there are a few things that you might need to do to your image before you start editing. No matter how many pixels your camera captures, it probably doesn't create files that have a resolution that is right for your printer, and your image as you shot it might not be cropped quite the right way. In this section, you're going to learn how to get your image properly sized and cropped.

New Image Resolutions

Although your camera may capture millions of pixels, it doesn't necessarily create files that have a resolution that is appropriate for your intended output. In imaging terms, resolution is simply the measure of how many pixels fit into a given space. For example, if your image has a resolution of 72 *pixels per inch* (ppi), then the pixels in the image are sized and spaced so that 72 of them lined up alongside each other cover a distance of one inch.

The average computer screen has a resolution somewhere between 72 and 96ppi, so almost all digital cameras output files at 72 dots per inch (dpi). At 72dpi, a 2048 × 1536 pixel image like you'd get from a typical 3-megapixel camera will cover 28.4 × 21.3 inches—far larger than either the average computer screen or printer. Although you can zoom in and out of an image on your screen, for printing you'll need to make some adjustments.

PPI VERSUS DPI

Pixels (short for pixel *elements) are the colored dots that appear on your computer screen. It's very important to understand that, when speaking of printing from your computer, there is a difference between the pixels on your screen—which are measured in pixels per inch— and the dots of ink that your printer creates—which are measured in dots per inch. We'll be discussing this in more detail later. For right now, take note that we're measuring our images in* pixels per inch.

Resizing an Image

Most image editing applications let you resize an image in two ways: you can either *resample* the image, or you can choose to not resample the image.

Let's say you have a 3-megapixel digital camera that outputs an image with dimensions of 2160 × 1440 pixels and a resolution of 72ppi. That is, if you line up 72 of your image's pixels side by side, you will cover one inch of space. At this resolution, 2160 × 1440 pixels will take up 20 × 30 inches. Obviously, this is too big to fit on a piece of paper. (In addition, 72ppi is too coarse for fine printing.)

Let's suppose, though, that you want to print this image out on an 8" × 10" piece of paper at 72 pixels per inch. To do this, you'll have to throw out every third pixel or so to reduce the number of pixels in the image so that the entire picture can fit into a smaller area (Figure 10.11).

Another way to think about this is to imagine your image projected onto a piece of graph paper—a piece of graph paper with 72 little boxes

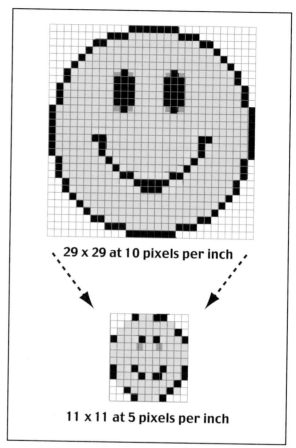

29 x 29 at 10 pixels per inch

11 x 11 at 5 pixels per inch

FIGURE 10.11   To resize an image down to a smaller size with the same resolution, you have to throw out some pixels (or resample) to fit your image into the smaller size

per inch (72 lbpi). To fit the image onto a smaller piece of graph paper—but one with boxes of the exact same size—you must throw out some of the image's pixels.

This process of discarding data is called is called *resampling* (or, more specifically, *downsampling*), because you are taking a sample of pixels from your original image to create a new, smaller image. Resampling can also be used to scale images up, but, just as downsampling requires your computer to throw away data, *upsampling* requires your computer to make up data.

For example, if you have an image that is 4" × 6" at 200dpi and you want to enlarge it to 8" × 10" at 200dpi, then you'll need to resample it upward, which will force the computer to interpolate new pixels to create the bigger images. Most applications offer a variety of interpolation techniques. Photoshop, for example, offers three interpolation methods: *nearest neighbor*, *bilinear*, and *bicubic*. For 99% of your resampling needs, bicubic interpolation is the best choice.

Now imagine the same 20" × 30" image projected onto a sheet of rubber graph paper. If you wanted to shrink this image to 14" × 10", you could simply squeeze the sheet of paper down. You would not throw out any pixels, but now your pixels would be much smaller, and more of them would fit into the same space. That is, the resolution of your image—the number of pixels per inch—would have increased. This is what happens when you resize your image *without* resampling (Figure 10.12).

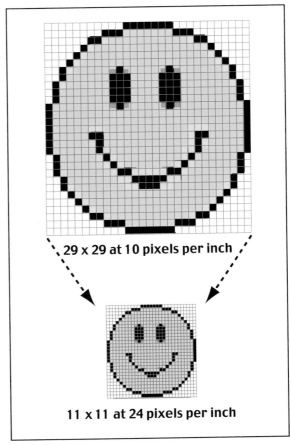

29 x 29 at 10 pixels per inch

11 x 11 at 24 pixels per inch

FIGURE 10.12   If you don't resample an image when you resize, all of its pixels are kept, but they're squeezed closer together, resulting in a smaller, higher-resolution image.

Similarly, if you have a 4" × 6" image with a resolution of 200dpi and you scale it up to 8" × 10" without resampling, then you're effectively stretching the image. Its pixels get larger, and fewer of them fit into the same space—that is, the resolution goes down—as the image gets larger. This is what happens when you resize up without resampling.

Most of the time, when you scale up, you'll want to resize without resampling to prevent the computer from making up new data. However, if your camera did not produce a big enough image to start with, you might not be able to achieve the size you want with the resolution you need unless you resample.

TUTORIAL UNDERSTANDING RESOLUTION

ON THE CD

In addition to providing controls for resizing your images, Photoshop's Image Size dialog box provides a great tool for understanding the relationship between pixel dimensions and resolution. In this tutorial, we're going to take a quick look at this control, and hopefully arrive at a better understanding of resolution, size, and resampling. If you haven't already installed Photoshop (or the Photoshop demo included on the companion CD-ROM), do so now. You'll also need the image flower.jpg image from the Tutorials/Chapter 10/Resizing folder on the companion CD-ROM.

STEP 1: OPEN THE IMAGE

ON THE CD

In Photoshop, open the flower.jpg image, located in the Tutorials | Chapter 10 | Resizing folder on the companion CD-ROM. This image was shot with a Canon D30, a 3-megapixel digital SLR.

STEP 2: OPEN THE IMAGE SIZE DIALOG BOX

From the Image menu, select Image Size (Figure 10.13). For the purpose of this step, make sure the Resample Image checkbox is unchecked. Take a moment to familiarize yourself with the contents of this dialog. In the upper Pixel Dimensions section, you can see the actual pixel dimensions of the image—in this case 2160 × 1440—as well as the total size of the image—8.9MB. Note that, right now, these pixel values are *not* editable.

The lower, Document Size section of the dialog shows the resolution of the image in pixels per inch, and the resulting print size in inches.

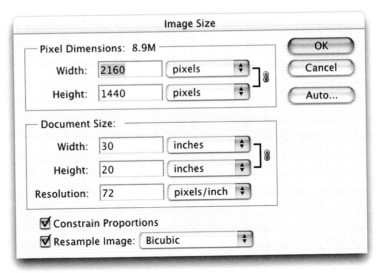

FIGURE 10.13   Photoshop's Image Size dialog shows the actual pixel dimensions of an image, as well as the print size at the current resolution.

STEP 3: RESIZE THE IMAGE WITHOUT RESAMPLING

Notice that width, height, and resolution are linked together by a thick black line. This is to indicate that you cannot change one of these values without changing the others. For example, if we enter 10 in the Width field, and then press the Tab key to apply the entry, Photoshop will automatically calculate a new height of 6.667 inches at 216 pixels per inch (Figure 10.14).

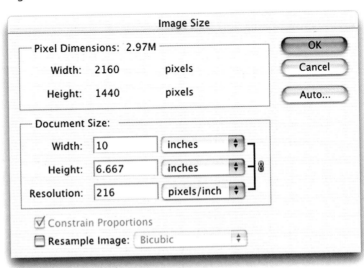

FIGURE 10.14   After entering 10 in the Width field, Photoshop automatically calculates a new height and resolution.

Photoshop has automatically adjusted the height to preserve the aspect ratio of the image, and has calculated a new, higher resolution. Because Resample Image is *not* checked, Photoshop is not allowed to add or remove any data, so the only way it can fit the image into our requested size is to increase the resolution—that is, cram the pixels closer together.

When Resample Image is unchecked—when Photoshop is not allowed to add or remove data—it is as if your image is on a giant rubber sheet that can be stretched and compressed. As it gets compressed, resolution goes up because the pixels get pushed closer together. As it stretches, resolution goes down because the pixels get pulled farther apart.

STEP 4: RESIZE WITH RESAMPLING

As you'll learn later, the optimum image resolution for printing on a typical inkjet printer is 240 pixels per inch. Enter 240 into the Resolution field and press Tab. At that resolution, Photoshop calculates an image size of 90" × 6" for our image. Suppose, though, that you want to print the image at 3" × 5". Enter 5 into the width field and press Tab. Photoshop calculates a new height of 3.3 and a resolution of 432.

This resolution is much too high for our printer, but if you enter 240 in the Resolution field, your print size will change back. This image simply has too much data to print 3" × 5" at 240 pixels per inch.

Check the Resample Image box. Note that the Width and Height fields in the Pixel Dimensions area are now editable. With Resample Image checked, it is now possible to change the number of pixels in the image. Note, too, that Resolution is no longer linked to Width and Height. It is now possible to change the resolution independent of the width and height, because *it is now possible for Photoshop to throw out data if it needs to.*

With your Document Size width still at 5 × 3.3, change your resolution to 240 (Figure 10.15).

Note that several things have happened. First, the pixel dimensions dropped from 2160 × 1440 to 1200 × 800. Our file has gone from 8.9MB to 2.75MB. More importantly, our print size did not change. We now have the width, height, and resolution we want.

When using the Image Size dialog, pay attention to which fields are editable and which are linked together. This will give you a better understanding of how pixel dimensions, print size, and resolution are all interrelated.

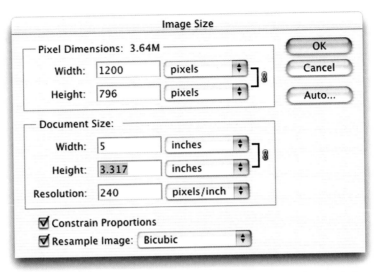

FIGURE 10.15   With Resample Image checked, Resolution is no longer tied to print size because Photoshop is free to add or remove pixels. This lets you change resolution independent of print size.

TUTORIAL   ## CROPPING AND RESIZING AN IMAGE

Because you usually can't get both you and your camera into exactly the right position to frame an image, your pictures usually need to be cropped. Moreover, because most cameras create images at 72dpi, your images usually need to be resized before printing. In this tutorial, we'll cover both topics by cropping and resizing an image for printing.

Although Adobe Photoshop is used in this tutorial, you can use any image editor that provides a Crop tool and a resizing/resampling function.

STEP 1: OPEN THE IMAGE

ON THE CD

The image for this tutorial is included on the companion CD-ROM and is located in the Tutorials/Chapter 10/cropping folder. Open the image *kittycrop.tif* (Figure 10.16). You should be able to open the document in any editor that supports TIFF files.

STEP 2: EVALUATE THE IMAGE

Let's take a quick look at the image so that we can formulate a plan of action. The original intent when we were shooting this image was to frame the picture

FIGURE 10.16 Although this is not the most compelling image, with a little cropping we can make it more interesting, while a little resizing will make it more appropriate for printing.

so that only the window was visible. Unfortunately, our camera—a Canon EOS D30—didn't have a long enough lens to zoom in to this second-story window. Even after zooming to full telephoto, the image area was too large. It will need to be cropped.

Open the Image Size dialog box (Figure 10.17) by choosing Image | Image Size from the menu bar in Photoshop. The image file was taken straight out of the camera and, as you can see, it has a resolution of 72 ppi and an area of 30" × 20". Because we plan to print the image on a desktop color inkjet, we will want it to have a resolution of 240 ppi (Chapter 15 will cover the details of choosing a printer resolution). Obviously, some resizing is in order.

STEP 3: PERFORM THE FIRST RESIZING

Before we do anything else, let's get the image set to the proper printer resolution so we can get an idea of how big it will print without any resampling. If the Image Size dialog box is not still open, open it now.

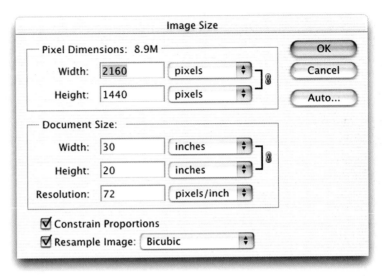

FIGURE 10.17   When the image came out of our 3-megapixel camera, its 3 million pixels were set to a resolution of 72ppi, giving the image an area of 30" × 20".

Make sure that the Resample Image checkbox is *not* checked. We don't want Photoshop to add or remove any pixels, we just want it to squeeze the pixels it has closer together.

Notice that the Image Size dialog box has two areas, Pixel Dimensions and Document Size. When Resample Image is unchecked, we can no longer change the Pixel Dimensions of the image, as changing the number of pixels requires the ability to resample. We simply want to change the document's print size.

Make sure the Units box next to the Resolution field is set to pixels/inch, and then change the Resolution box to 240. Photoshop will immediately calculate a new image size and display the new values in the Width and Height fields (Figure 10.18).

As you can see, at 240dpi our image is now 9" × 6". Click OK to accept the changes.

STEP 4: CROP THE IMAGE

Photoshop provides a couple of ways to crop an image, but the easiest is with the Crop tool. Click on the Crop tool in Photoshop's tool palette. Use your mouse to drag a rectangle that crops out everything outside of the window pane (Figure 10.19).

Image Size

Pixel Dimensions: 2.97M

Width: 2160 pixels

Height: 1440 pixels

OK

Cancel

Auto...

Document Size:

Width: 9 inches

Height: 6 inches

Resolution: 240 pixels/inch

☑ Constrain Proportions

☐ Resample Image: Bicubic

FIGURE 10.18 After changing our resolution to 240 pixels per inch (without resampling), our image goes down to a more reasonable 9 × 6 inches.

kittycrop.tif @ 45% (RGB)

45%   Doc:8.9M/8.9M

FIGURE 10.19 Photoshop's Crop tool shows you a preview of your crop while you're cropping.

When you get the crop the way you like it, press the Enter key on your keyboard, or double-click inside the crop area to perform the crop.

STEP 5: RESIZE AGAIN

As you can see, cropping can make a world of difference. Already, our image is more interesting. (In case you're wondering, those strange black spots in the image are shadows from the camera's flash that are being cast by irregularities in the poured glass window pane.)

Open the Image Size dialog box again to see how big the image is now. After you have cropped, your image should be somewhere around 5.5" × 4". This is a little small, so let's resize the image up a bit.

With Resample Image unchecked, enter 6 inches into the Width field. Because the Constrain Proportions box is checked, Photoshop calculates the appropriate height, which turns out to be approximately 4.3 inches.

However, notice that the resolution of our image has gone down. Because we told Photoshop not to resample the image, as we stretched the image out to make it bigger, our resolution dropped. Let's boost it back up to our requisite 240dpi.

Turn on Resample Image and make certain that the pop-up menu next to Resample Image is set to Bicubic. Notice that the Pixel Dimensions fields are no longer dimmed and can, therefore, be edited. This is because resampling enables us to change the number of pixels in the image (Figure 10.20).

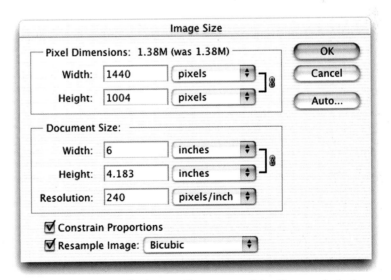

FIGURE 10.20 With your final Image Size command, you'll resample the image up to your desired print size and resolution.

FIGURE 10.21   THE FINAL IMAGE, RESIZED FOR PRINTING.

Enter 240 in the Resolution field. The Pixel Dimensions and Document Size readouts should now be larger. Click OK to accept the changes. Now the image should be ready to print. Figure 10.21 shows the final image as it will print.

Why You Should Resize First

As you learned earlier, many digital cameras use interpolation to increase the resolution of their images. As explained, these interpolation schemes often degrade the quality of an image by introducing artifacts. Simply put, calculating new image data is a tricky, difficult thing to do. When it's done poorly, aliasing artifacts, loss of sharpness, and other image problems can appear.

Photoshop's Bicubic interpolation algorithm is *very* good and you can usually resize your images quite a bit before they noticeably degrade. If you're starting with a 3- or 4-megapixel image, you'll usually find that you can resize to fairly large print sizes—8" × 10" or 11" × 13" with little or no loss in quality.

As you'll see in later chapters, some image editing tasks require painting using digital paint brushes. This is one very good reason to perform all of your cropping and resizing before you do anything else. If you resample your image to its final print size *before* you do any painting effects, then you'll be assured of painting at the optimal resolution.

Moving OnAs you shoot and edit more, you'll find the workflow that works best for you, and transferring and arranging images will become easier and easier. Image sizing is something that is confusing for many beginners, so spend some time getting to know your image editor's resize tools. Remember that your main image editing workflow concern is to avoid recompressing your image.

Obviously, most images will need more adjustments than simple resizing and cropping. In the next chapter, we will begin to improve the quality of an image by performing tonal adjustments.

11

CORRECTING TONE AND COLOR

In This Chapter

- Histograms Revisited
- Levels
- Should You Worry about Data Loss?
- Curves
- Levels and Curves and Color

With your image editing software, you can perform some amazing manipulations (some would say "deceptions") of your images. The most powerful features of your image editor, however, are not its capabilities to alter the content of an image, but to alter the tone and color so that the image—no matter what its content—looks better on the printed page.

In Chapter 8, "Manual Exposure," you learned how you can use the histogram on your camera to make an exposure selection that will allow you to capture an image with more dynamic range. In this chapter, you're finally going to get to take advantage of all that work you did when you were shooting. Using the tools in your image editor, you will be able to use all of that range that you meticulously exposed for to produce images with better contrast and color.

In terms of fundamental image editing, little has changed since the first edition of this book. The main tools you'll use to achieve your adjustments are Levels and Curves controls. Fortunately, most quality image editing programs include these types of controls, so even if you're not using Photoshop, you should have no trouble following along with the concepts and tutorials in this chapter.

To get started, let's quickly revisit the histograms that you saw in Chapter 8 and look at how the information in the histogram is manipulated by the Levels control.

HISTOGRAMS REVISITED

In Chapter 8, you learned about histograms—graphic representations of the tonal values within an image. If you'll recall, a histogram is essentially nothing more than a bar chart of the distribution of different colors or tones in a picture. Some cameras can produce histograms of images you've shot, making it easier to determine if you have over- or underexposed an image while you're in the field.

Your image editor can also produce a histogram of an image. Consider the image in Figure 11.1.

Figure 11.1 is a simple gradient from black to white, created using Photoshop's Gradient tool. The histogram confirms that the image goes from complete black to complete white, with most of the tones distributed at either end of the spectrum. You can also see from the histogram that there is a lot of contrast in this image—that is, the range of black to white covers the entire spectrum of the histogram.

Now look at Figure 11.2.

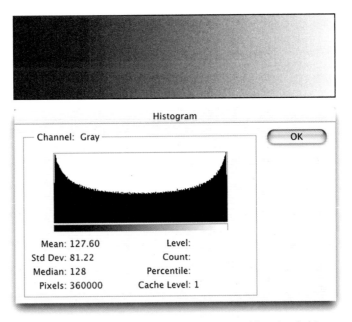

FIGURE 11.1   This gradient from black to white yields a simple histogram.

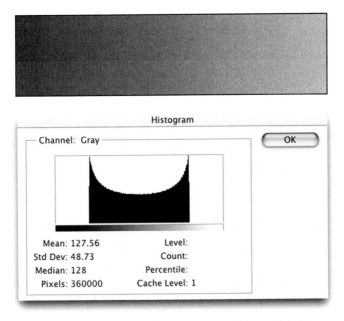

FIGURE 11.2   This grayscale ramp from 80% black to 20% black yields a similar histogram to the one shown in Figure 11.1, but the tones are centered in the middle of the spectrum.

Also created in Photoshop, this gradient was specified as being 80% black to 20% black instead of pure black to pure white. If you look at the histogram, you can see that the tones in the image fall in the middle of the graph. There are no dark or completely black tones, nor are there any really light or completely white tones. In other words, there's not much contrast in this gradient —the range from lightest to darkest is very small.

What if we wanted to adjust this image, though, so that it *did* go from black to completely white? That is, what if we wanted to greatly improve the contrast of this image?

TUTORIAL

CORRECTING AN IMAGE WITH BRIGHTNESS AND CONTRAST (OR TRYING TO, ANYWAY)

Many applications include a brightness and contrast control that is similar to the brightness and contrast dials on a television set. Photoshop is no exception; you can open the control by choosing Image>Adjust>Brightness and Contrast. In this tutorial, you will use Brightness and Contrast to try to correct the grayscale ramp in Figure 11.2 so that it looks like the grayscale ramp in Figure 11.1. As you might have already guessed from the title of this tutorial, you're not going to have much success in this endeavor. Like many less-enjoyable activities, however, you'll probably learn a lot.

STEP 1: OPEN THE IMAGE

ON THE CD

Open the file grayramp.tif, located in the Tutorials/Chapter 11/Brightness & Contrast folder of the companion CD-ROM. Use your image editor's Histogram feature to view a histogram of the image. In Photoshop, you can open the control by choosing Image>Histogram. The histogram should look something like the one in Figure 11.2.

STEP 2: ADJUST THE IMAGE'S BRIGHTNESS

Now, open the Brightness and Contrast control in your image editor. In Photoshop, choose Image>Adjust>Brightness and Contrast (Figure 11.3).

Brightness and Contrast provides two sliders, one for brightness and the other for contrast. By sliding each in either direction, you can increase or decrease either property.

In this image, the black is not black enough, so begin your adjustments by lowering the brightness, to drop the darkest tone down to black. To get full

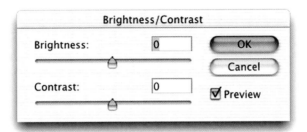

FIGURE 11.3 Photoshop's Brightness and Contrast control.

black using Photoshop's control, slide the Brightness control until it reads approximately –75.

Unfortunately, in doing this, you also lowered the brightness of all the other tones in the image, including the whites (Figure 11.4). Look at the histogram and you'll see that the image has no more contrast than it did before. Rather, the whole tonal range has just been shifted down toward the bottom of the scale.

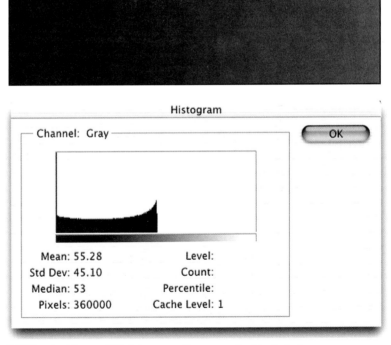

FIGURE 11.4 After a –75 brightness adjustment, the blacks in the gray ramp are darker, but unfortunately, so are all of the grays and whites. All of the tones have been uniformly shifted down the gray spectrum.

This is the main problem with a Brightness and Contrast control: every pixel is adjusted in exactly the same way. Consequently, if you only want to correct the shadows or highlights of an image, you're out of luck. What's more, if you enter a brightness change that is too extreme, some tonal values might get pushed completely off the scale, resulting in clipped highlights or shadows.

STEP 3: ADJUST THE CONTRAST OF THE IMAGE

So far, you've darkened the entire image to restore the blacks to true black. Now you need to try to restore the whites by increasing the contrast of the image. Move the contrast slider to around +66. You have now restored the white to full white, but the image is a far cry from the gray ramp shown in Figure 11.1. A quick check of the histogram (Figure 11.5) shows why.

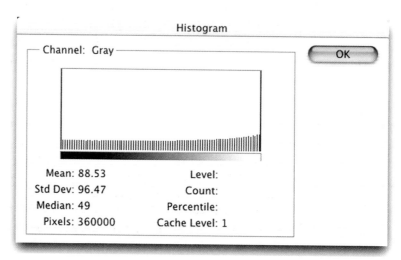

Histogram

Channel: Gray

OK

Mean: 88.53   Level:
Std Dev: 96.47   Count:
Median: 49   Percentile:
Pixels: 360000   Cache Level: 1

FIGURE 11.5 After both brightness and contrast adjustments, the image has lost a lot of tonal information, and the distribution of the remaining tones has been changed.

First, notice how there are far fewer lines in the histogram than there were before. In the process of stretching the tones out to create more contrast, Photoshop has had to throw out some tonal information. In other words, it has had to redistribute the tonal values in the image to make them stretch all the way down to black, and all the way up to white.

Data loss is an unfortunate side effect of any tonal adjustment, and you'll read more about it later. However, a brightness and contrast control is particularly bad with data loss because it doesn't throw out data in a very intelligent manner. Rather, it simply uniformly removes data across the entire tonal range.

What's worse is the distribution of the curve of the histogram. Notice that it no longer has the same shape that it had before. Colors are not predominantly distributed at the top and bottom of the curve, but have been flattened out over the entire range of the curve. The original image had much more black and much more white, while this image has a pretty even distribution of everything. This is why the ramp itself appears less contrasty.

STEP 4: GIVE UP

That's really about the best you can do with Brightness and Contrast. Yes, you could try to not stretch the blacks or whites so far, so that fewer tones would drop out, but there's simply nothing you can do to preserve the original distribution of tones. The fact is, Brightness and Contrast is simply a bad tool (so bad that Adobe didn't even grace it with a keyboard shortcut in Photoshop!). Don't worry, though, there is something better.

LEVELS

In Chapter 8, you saw that different exposure settings let you capture more or less tonal information. Through the use of a histogram on your camera, you saw that it is possible to measure this tonal information, both to determine how much contrast is in an image, and where that contrast lies along the tonal spectrum.

If you followed along with the last tutorial, though, you saw that, when you are correcting and adjusting an image, preserving the distribution of those tones is fundamentally important, as is ensuring that too much data doesn't get thrown out while you are making adjustments. Typically, the problem with a Brightness and Contrast control is that its actions affect the entire tonal spectrum, resulting in edits that are too broad in scope and thus severely alter the tonal relationships within the image.

Fortunately, if your image editor has a Levels control, you have a solution to these problems. Photoshop's Levels control can be opened by choosing Image>Adjust>Levels. It produces the dialog box shown in Figure 11.6.

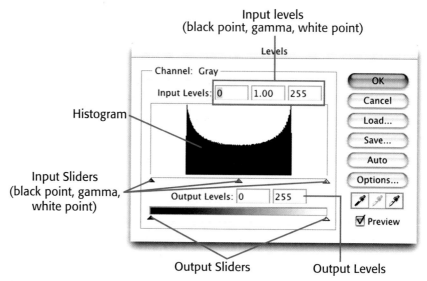

FIGURE 11.6 Photoshop's Levels control offers a number of features. Right now, you'll only be using the Histogram, Input Sliders, and Input Levels fields.

First, you can see that a Levels control is built around a histogram of your image. In Figure 11.6, the histogram is from the grayscale ramp shown in Figure 11.2. Directly beneath the histogram are three input sliders. The leftmost slider shows the position of black in the histogram—that is, it points at the location on the graph that represents 100% black. The rightmost slider shows the position of white, while the middle slider shows the *gamma*, the midpoint of the image. The Input Levels fields above the histogram are simply numeric readouts of the positions of the three input sliders—0 represents black, white is represented by 255, and shades of gray are somewhere in between.

The easiest way to understand what these sliders do is to use them. Therefore, let's go back to the image shown in Figure 11.2 and try again to correct it so that it looks like the one shown in Figure 11.1.

TUTORIAL   ## USING LEVELS INPUT SLIDERS

Once again, we're going to try to correct the grayscale ramp shown in Figure 11.2 so that it has better black and white values and improved overall contrast.

This time, instead of using a Brightness and Contrast control, we're going to use a Levels control. Although we'll be using Photoshop for this example, you can easily follow along in any image editor that provides a Levels control.

STEP 1: OPEN THE IMAGE

ON THE CD

Again, open the same gray ramp image that you used in the Brightness and Contrast tutorial (grayramp.tif, located in the tutorials folder of the companion CD-ROM). Once the image is up, open your Levels control. In Photoshop, you access Levels by choosing Image>Adjust>Levels.

STEP 2: ADJUST THE BLACK POINT

As you can see from the histogram in the Levels dialog box shown in Figure 11.6, the darkest tone in this image is not full black, but is closer to 80% black. Make sure the Preview checkbox in the Levels dialog box is checked. Drag the black triangle at the far left of the histogram to the right until it is directly beneath the leftmost value of the histogram (Figure 11.7). The black point readout should be around 52.

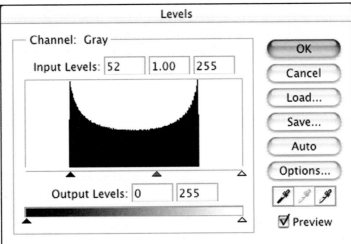

FIGURE 11.7 Setting the black point using the Levels control results in a gray ramp with correct black levels.

Now look at your image. The leftmost side—that is, the black side—of the grayscale ramp should be black. With our Levels adjustment, solid black is no longer at 0 on the histogram, it's now at 52 (remember, the histogram is a graph of values from 0 to 255). Therefore, everything to the left of our new black point is considered black. Notice that our gamma point—the middle slider—has automatically moved to the right to preserve the relationship between black, midpoint, and white.

Now look at the right side of the image. Our lightest value has not changed! Unlike a Brightness and Contrast adjustment, which adjusted every value in the image uniformly, our Levels adjustment has affected only the areas between the black point and the gamma point.

To understand this better, click OK to accept the changes. Now, open the Levels control again to see a new histogram of the image (Figure 11.8).

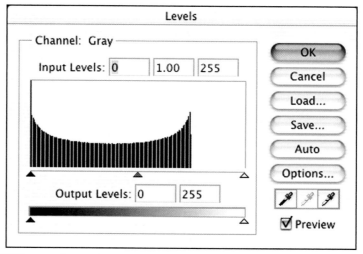

FIGURE 11.8   After our black point adjustment, our histogram looks different. The darker tones have been stretched all the way to black, but the overall shape of the histogram has remained the same.

You might be a little surprised to see that the histogram looks different than it did when you closed the Levels box before. Remember, though, that even after you performed your black point adjustment, the image still had a full range of tones from 0 to 255. This histogram is a graph of those new, adjusted tones.

As you can see, some bars are missing, indicating that we've lost some data. This makes sense when you think about what your black point adjustment did. You moved the black point in to indicate the value that you wanted to be black. The Levels control placed that value at 0 and stretched all of the values between 0 and your midpoint (the gamma slider) to fill the space. Unfortunately, there wasn't enough data to fill the space (if there had been, you probably wouldn't have needed to make this adjustment in the first place), so some tonal values were left empty. Fortunately, Photoshop has spaced these missing tones across the tonal spectrum, so their absence is less noticeable.

The good news is that, so far, the distribution of tones within the image—as represented by the shape of the histogram—is better preserved than it had been with the Brightness and Contrast control.

STEP 3: ADJUST THE WHITE POINT

Now we need to do the same thing to the white point that we did to the black point. Open your Levels control and take another look at your histogram. The white values are not really white, they're light gray.

Drag the white slider to the left so that it points to the rightmost data in the image. The white point display should read approximately 190 (Figure 11.9).

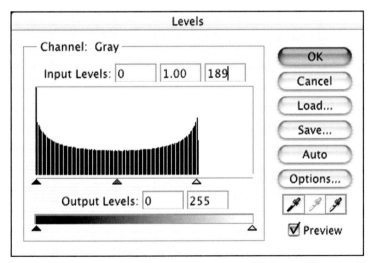

FIGURE 11.9   After adjusting the white point, your Levels dialog box should look something like this.

Now look at the right side of your image. It should be a brighter white. The good news is that your shadows are still nice and dark! As with the black point adjustment, adjusting your white point only affected the values between the white point and the midpoint.

Clicking the Auto button in the Levels dialog box does the same thing that you have just done in these two steps. It moves the black point to the leftmost tonal value in the histogram, and it moves the white point to the rightmost value. Why not just use Auto every time? Because some images might need different adjustments to their white and black points. As you'll see later, sometimes you might want to leave a little "headroom" above and below your tonal range.

The Load and Save buttons allow you to save your Levels adjustments for re-use later. For example, if you find that your camera is consistently off with its white and black points, then you can save a Levels adjustment that can be loaded and applied to all your images.

STEP 4: PLAY WITH THE GAMMA SLIDER

This particular image doesn't need a gamma adjustment, but there are some interesting things to learn by moving it around and observing the results. Slide the gamma slider to the left and watch what happens to your image (Figure 11.10).

As you move it, the midtones in your image become much lighter. Slide it back to the right, past its original location, and you'll see your midtones get darker. As you move the gamma slider, though, your black and white values stay locked down at black and white. Gamma lets you adjust the midtones of your image to shift contrast more toward shadows or toward highlights. With it, you can often bring more detail out of a shadowy area, but you'll never have to worry about your blacks or whites turning gray.

Type 1.0 into the gamma readout (the middle text box above the histogram) to return the gamma slider to its original location.

With the Levels dialog box still open, zoom in on your image (in Photoshop you can do this by pressing Command-+ on a Mac, or by pressing Ctrl-+ if you're using Windows). Now, drag the gamma slider to the left. Again, you'll see your midtones lighten, but now watch what's happening in the shadow areas. If you look closely, you'll probably see some slight banding.

This banding is the result of the data that's being thrown out as the Levels control stretches the tonal values in your image. Drag the slider in the other direction and you'll begin to see banding in the highlights of your image as you darken the midtones, causing the highlights to stretch to fill in the now empty space.

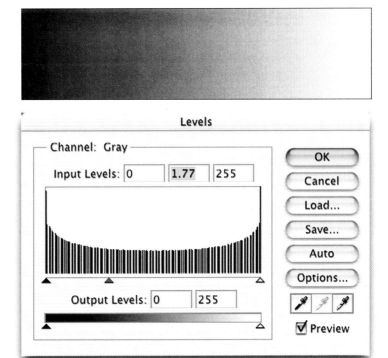

FIGURE 11.10   As we move the gamma slider, the midtones in our image shift toward black or white.

Play around with these controls to get a feel for their effect, and to see how the image changes and degrades. These changes and problems are particularly easy to see in this document, since it is a simple linear gradient.

Should You Worry about Data Loss?

In the last two tutorials you engaged in image editing operations that removed data from your image. That really sounds like something you should be worried about, doesn't it? In some cases it is.

Fortunately, the type of data loss that you saw in the last tutorial was not readily apparent on-screen—you had to make a fairly extreme adjustment and zoom in very close to the image—and the data loss was certainly far too slight to appear in a printout. Most of the printers you'll be using can't generate a complete range of 256 shades of gray anyway, so if you've thrown out 5% of them it won't really matter.

However, if you were to make the change you just made, and then go back and make two or three more edits that also produced some data loss, your image might visibly degrade. This is why it's so important to capture as much data as you can *when you're shooting*. If your image has a lot of tonal range to begin with, then you won't have to make adjustments that are too extreme when you're editing, and your image editor won't have to throw out so much data as it stretches the image's tones. Controlling data loss is just one more reason why it's important to choose a good exposure when you take a picture.

Once you have your image in your image editor, you'll want to think carefully about your edits to minimize your data loss. When you are editing, try to achieve as much as possible with the fewest tonal corrections. In other words, don't use a Levels command to fix your black point, and then go back later to adjust your white point. Make your tonal corrections count by accomplishing as much as you can with each correction.

In addition, watch for *posterization* in your image. Posterization occurs as the number of tones in your image is reduced. If you start to see these types of artifacts, there's a good chance that your tonal corrections have eliminated too much image data (Figure 11.11).

FIGURE 11.11 We adjusted the image on the left to increase the amount of purple in the flowers, to produce the image on the right. However, upon closer examination, you can see that, in the process, we removed a lot of tonal information, resulting in *posterized* color. The posterized flowers have fewer tones, resulting in stair-steppy gradients and large areas of solid purple.

TUTORIAL	**REAL-WORLD LEVELS ADJUSTMENTS**

Hopefully, working in the controlled space of a linear gradient helped you better understand what, exactly, a Levels control does. In this tutorial, we're going to apply that knowledge to an image we looked at earlier.

STEP 1: OPEN THE IMAGE

ON THE CD

Open the street.tif image located in the Tutorials/Chapter 11/Real-World Levels Adjustments folder of the companion CD-ROM (Figure 11.12). As you'll recall from Chapter 8, there was a very particular vision in mind for this image, that of the dark line of the street cutting across the gray and white field of houses. To achieve that goal, this image was intentionally underexposed so as to plunge the street into deep shadow. Unfortunately, the entire image is a little dark.

FIGURE 11.12   Our goal when we were exposing this image was to emphasize the shadowy line of the street. By underexposing, we captured nice, dark shadows. Unfortunately, this exposure resulted in the rest of the image being much too dark.

A quick look at the histogram (Figure 11.13) shows that the image has a good amount of tonal information (dynamic range) even though it doesn't go to completely black or white.

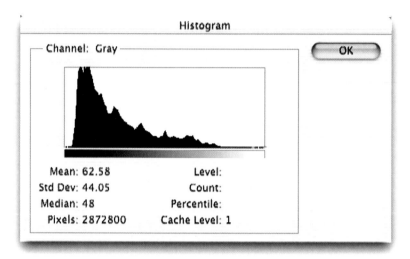

FIGURE 11.13 The histogram shows a good amount of tonal information, but poor highlights.

A second, slightly overexposed image was also shot, and its histogram showed that it had a wider dynamic range. However, its shadow detail was not as strong, making it more difficult to achieve our original intent. Wide dynamic range isn't everything; you have to be sure that your exposure places the tones in your image in the correct tonal zone. For this reason, it's better to choose the underexposed image.

STEP 2: SET THE BLACK POINT

In Photoshop, choose Window>Show Info (Figure 11.14). When it is used in conjunction with Photoshop's Eyedropper tool, the Info palette can provide very handy information about the colors and tones in your image. We'll use this information to refine some of our Levels adjustments. As discussed in Chapter 6, "Building a Workstation," an Eyedropper tool and Info readout are essential image editing tools. If your application doesn't have these, you might consider finding another image editor.

Open the Levels control in your image editor. In the Levels dialog box histogram, you can see that the black levels in the image don't descend all the way to 0. That is, they don't go to complete black, but end at about 10 (or about 4% if you want to think in percentages of black).

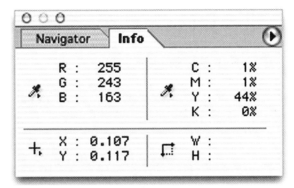

FIGURE 11.14   As you move Photoshop's Eyedropper tool over an image, the Info palette displays the values of each pixel. Pixel values are presented using a number of different measures.

We're going to leave the black level where it is because we intend to print this image. Unfortunately, most images tend to get darker when they go to print so it's a good idea to leave a little room for the shadows to darken up a bit. As you'll see later, the same is true for highlight areas.

STEP 3: SET THE WHITE POINT

There are a couple of simple considerations to make when you are setting the white point for this image. First, we know that we want to generally brighten the image, since it was underexposed. The question is, how far do we want to go?

Drag the white point to the left until it is at the edge of the rightmost histogram data. The white point readout should read about 198.

This definitely removes the underexposed pall that covered the image before (Figure 11.15). Our shadows have brightened up a bit, so let's make a quick gamma adjustment.

STEP 4: ADJUST THE GAMMA

Although our blacks are still nice and black, our white point adjustment did affect enough of the midtones that the image has lost some of the nice dark areas that it had before. Drag the gamma slider to the right until it reads about .83.

This should darken the shadows without affecting our blacks or whites.

STEP 5: READJUST THE WHITE POINT

With the gamma adjusted properly, we have a better idea of what our whites really look like. Your white point should still be set around 198. Although the image looks good with this white point, there are a few considerations to weigh.

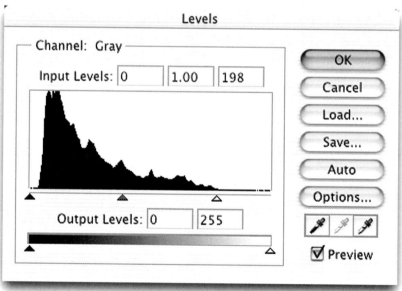

FIGURE 11.15 White point adjustment.

The whitest thing in the image at this point is the white house in the lower-right center of the image. The question to ask at this point is, "Just how white do we want it to be?"

Click on the Eyedropper tool from Photoshop's toolbox and hold it over the white in the house. The K field in the Info palette shows you the actual black value of the pixels in that area (in printing terminology, black is always represented by "K" since "B" usually stands for Blue) (Figure 11.16).

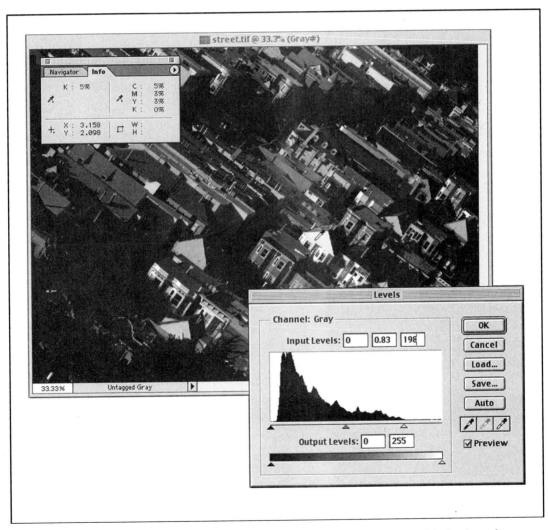

FIGURE 11.16 With the Eyedropper tool and the Info palette, you can find out the exact black values of any pixels in your image. With this information, you can make more intelligent decisions about your tonal adjustments.

The house is reading about 5% black. If you hold the Eyedropper over the door, you'll see that the house is reading 0%, meaning that area will simply be paper white, with no ink.

As bright as it is, the house is a little distracting with this white point. What's more, there is little detail between the house and the door. Pull the white point to around 210. This takes the harsh whiteness out of the house as well as some of the other white details throughout the image. What's more, it restores some contrast between the house and its door. If you measure the house now, you'll see that it reads about 12% while the door is still at 0. The door will now provide a nice specular highlight in the image (Figure 11.17).

FIGURE 11.17   The final image readjusting our white point.

STEP 6: SAVE THE IMAGE

Click OK to accept your Levels changes and you're done for now. Save this adjusted image to your drive. Although the tones are now properly adjusted, the image could use a little sharpening before printing. You'll learn more about sharpening in Chapter 13, "Essential Imaging Tactics."

CURVES

Although the Levels control is very powerful, your image editor probably provides a tool that offers even more control over your tonal corrections: Curves. You can open this control by choosing Image>Adjust>Curves. Although you can achieve the same thing in Curves that you can in Levels, it is not a replacement. Both tools are appropriate for different tasks.

A typical Curves interface (Figure 11.18) is really just a different approach to the same adjustments that you were making with the Levels control.

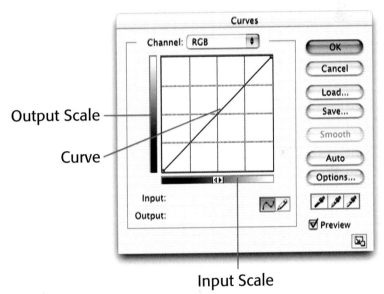

FIGURE 11.18 Photoshop's Curves dialog box is typical of most Curves tools, offering a simple graph of input (before) values to output (after) values.

The Curves dialog box also presents a graph of the data in your image. Instead of graphing distribution of tones, however, it shows a graph of the unaltered versus altered pixels in your image. The horizontal gray ramp along the bottom of the Curves dialog box represents the pixels in your image before they are altered by the Curves command.

The vertical gray ramp along the left side of the Curves dialog box represents the pixels in your image *after* they are altered.

When you first open the Curves control, the Curves graph shows a 45° line from black to white, indicating that the input pixels (the ones along the bottom) are identical to the output pixels (the ones along the top). If you change the shape of the line, you change the correspondence of the input pixels to the output pixels (Figure 11.19).

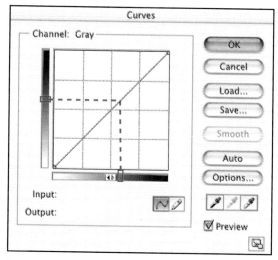

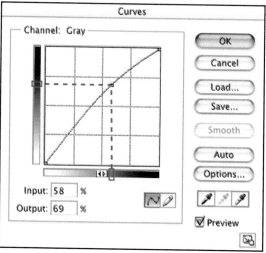

FIGURE 11.19 In the upper diagram, before editing, each point on the input ramp corresponds to the same spot on the output ramp. After adding a point, the corresponding spot on the input graph in the lower diagram is equal to a lighter spot on the output graph. What's more, all of the surrounding points have been altered along a smooth curve.

A QUICK WORD ABOUT TONE

When you are correcting and adjusting color, it's important to remember that when you add more red, green, or blue to an image, you're adding more light—your color will get lighter. In other words, some colors are inherently brighter than others. A light blue, for example, in addition to being a different hue, and having a different saturation, is also lighter than a dark red or dark blue. Therefore, if you perform adjustments that change the color in your image, you might also be changing the overall lightness or darkness of your image.

When you adjusted the black point using your Levels control, you told your image editor that there was a new value that it should consider black. The image editor then stretched and squeezed the values in your image to make your desired adjustment. The curve in the Curves dialog box, which starts out as a straight line, lets you see very clearly how the tones in your image are being stretched and squeezed.

To redefine your black point using Curves, for example, you simply move the black part of the curve to a new location (Figure 11.20). The black point on the input ramp (the vertical ramp) has been remapped to a lighter shade of gray, as indicated by the output ramp (the horizontal ramp). All of the other tones on the curve have been adjusted accordingly.

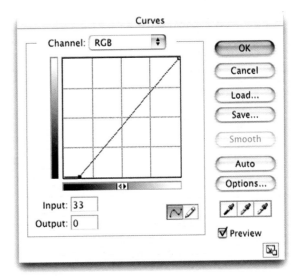

FIGURE 11.20   Black point adjustments in Curves.

The main advantage of Curves is that, while Levels lets you edit the white, black, and midpoints of an image, Curves lets you edit as many points as you want.

TUTORIAL

CORRECTING AN IMAGE WITH CURVES

The easiest way to learn how the Curves control works is to try it out. In this tutorial, we're going to use the Curves tool to make the same types of adjustments we made using the Levels control. As you'll see, Curves will provide us with a little more flexibility for particular edits.

STEP 1: OPEN THE IMAGE

ON THE CD

We're again going to return to an image we shot in Chapter 8. This time, it's the greenhouse image, which presented an interesting exposure challenge in that we wanted to overexpose enough to render the whites as white, but not so much that shadow detail would be lost. Open the image greenhouse.tif located in the Tutorials/Chapter 11/Correcting an Image with Curves folder on the companion CD-ROM (Figure 11.21).

As you can see from the histogram, the image has a good amount of dynamic range. However, as is obvious from both the image and the histogram, the picture lacks contrast and is generally too dark. We need to reset the white and black points.

STEP 2: SET THE BLACK POINT

Open the Curves control. In Photoshop, you can open it by choosing Image>Adjust>Curves, or by pressing Cmd/Ctrl-M (Command if you're using a Macintosh, Control if you're using Windows). The black point on the curve is the point at the bottom of the 45° line. This point indicates that black on the input scale corresponds to black on the output scale. We want to change it so that dark gray—the darkest tone in the image—on the input scale corresponds to black on the output scale. Because the input scale goes horizontally from black to white, we need to move the black point to the right.

Click on the black point and drag it to the right until the Input box reads about 27. Output should stay at 0. With this move, you're saying that values at 27 or lower are equivalent to 0, or black. The dark areas in your image should now look black.

What do those numbers mean? The 27 value that you just selected in the Curves dialog box is equivalent to about 10% black. Remember that, to your

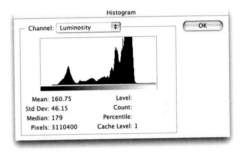

FIGURE 11.21   The histogram confirms what your eyes will tell you: this image is too dark and needs better contrast.

computer, tonal values span from 0 to 255. Therefore, 27 is equal to 27 ÷ 255, or about 10%.

STEP 3: SET THE WHITE POINT

The white point is the point at the other end of the curve, in the upper right-hand corner. Just as you moved the black point directly to the right, you want to move the white point directly to the left to indicate that light gray should become white.

Click on the white point and drag it to the left until the Input box reads about 218 (85%). The Output value should now read 255. In other words, the value 218 has been stretched out to 255 (Figure 11.22). So far, this is no different than the type of adjustment you make when you move the black and white points in the Levels dialog.

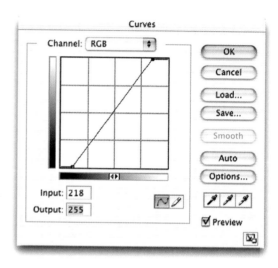

FIGURE 11.22   Black and white points are set in Curves by sliding the end points toward the center of the graph.

STEP 4: ADJUST THE GAMMA

The image is looking better, but it could use a slight gamma adjustment to help the midtones. Right now, the shadow tones in the roof and the misty tones in the sky are a little dark.

The gamma point is the point on the curve in the middle of the graph. Normally, it lies at the intersection of the two middle grid lines, but because of our white and black point adjustments, the midpoint has shifted up and to the left a bit. Move your pointer over the curve until the Input display reads about 124. This is roughly the midpoint. Now, click and drag up and to the right a tiny bit to lighten the midtones. Drag the point until the readouts show roughly Input 119, Output 135 (Figure 11.23).

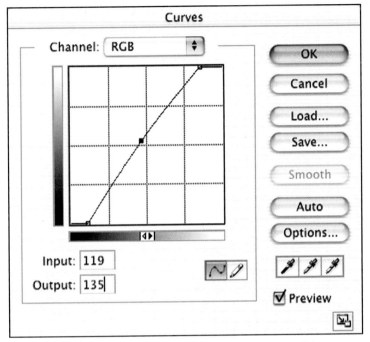

FIGURE 11.23   Gamma is adjusted by dragging the midpoint of the curve to lighten or darken the image.

As you move the point, notice that the curve changes shape. Remember when you tried to use the Brightness and Contrast controls and were hampered by the fact that your adjustments were applied evenly to the entire image? With Curves, as you can see, your adjustments create a smooth curve of change throughout the tonal range. What this means is that in addition to adjusting that single gamma point, you have also adjusted the nearby points by varying degrees. Levels works the same way, but with Curves you can really see how other tones are affected.

STEP 5: MAKE ANOTHER ADJUSTMENT

The image is looking much better now. However, our gamma adjustment, in addition to lightening the rooftop, lightened up the greenhouse, rendering it a little less contrasty. If we were working in Levels we'd be out of luck, as Levels only lets you adjust the black point, white point, and gamma. With Curves, though, we can reshape the curve as much as we want.

With the Curves dialog box still open, move the mouse over the front part of the greenhouse in the image. The mouse pointer should turn into an

Eyedropper. Click the mouse and drag the Eyedropper around. A circle will appear over the parts of the curve that correspond to those tones in your image. You now know which part of the curve you need to adjust.

Click the mouse in the relevant part of the curve (around 98) to create a point, and then drag down slightly, to around 101. This should darken up the greenhouse enough to restore some contrast. Unfortunately, this edit also lightens the sky enough that some of the striations in the mist have been washed out.

STEP 6: ADJUST THE SKY

With one or two final adjustments, we can darken the sky, and increase the contrast of the striations in the fog. Click on the image to determine where the sky falls along the curve. You'll probably find that it registers between 185 and 200. Click somewhere in this area to set a point, and drag down slightly to darken the sky a bit. Now, set different points to target the white and black parts of the streaks in the fog. This should allow you to create a more dramatic sky, as shown in Figure 11.24. Click the Save button to save your final Curves adjustments.

That's it. You're done. Typically, at this point you'd want to do a test print and make refinements to your adjustments. You'll learn more about printing in Chapter 15, "Output."

LEVELS AND CURVES AND COLOR

So far, you've seen how Levels and Curves controls can be used to adjust tone and contrast, whether in color or grayscale images. These tools, however, can also be used to adjust, correct, and change color. In previous chapters you read about many ways in which color can go wrong when you shoot. Levels and Curves are two tools that allow you to fix color problems that arise from bad white balance, improper exposure, or a bad camera.

To understand how Levels and Curves affect color, you have to understand how color is stored in an image. In Chapter 3, "How a Digital Camera Works," you learned that digital cameras make color by combining red, green, and blue information. These separate red, green, and blue components are referred to as *color channels,* or just *channels,* and most

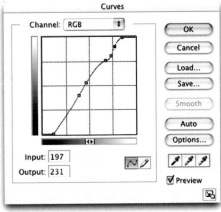

FIGURE 11.24 With our final Curves adjustment, we've selectively altered several tonal areas of the image. This is far more than we could have done with Levels.

image editors allow you to perform corrections and adjustments on these individual channels.

In Photoshop, you can access the different color channels through the Channels palette (choose Window>Show Channels). The Channels palette includes separate rows for the Red, Green and Blue channel as well as for your image—the RGB channel (Figure 11.25). By clicking on each channel, you can view its contents.

If you click on the Red channel in the Channels palette, you'll see a grayscale image that represents all of the red in your image. Why is it grayscale? Because, if you'll recall, one *24-bit image* is made up of three separate *8-bit images*, and with 8-bit images you can have up to 256

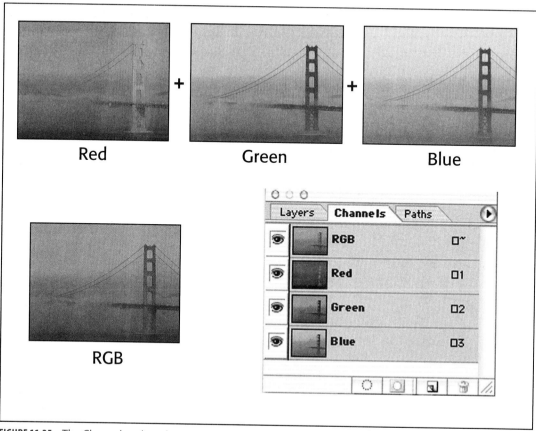

FIGURE 11.25   The Channels palette lets you view and edit the individual Red, Green, and Blue channels that comprise your RGB documents.

shades of gray. Therefore, a bright white pixel in a Red channel equates to full red in your final image (because bright white has a value of 255, the maximum allowed in an 8-bit image). Combine a bright red pixel in a Red channel with identical pixels in the Green and Blue channels and you'll have a white pixel in your final image, because full red, plus full green, plus full blue equals white.

When you view a channel in Photoshop, you can use all of the editing, painting, and manipulation features that you would normally use. This is a very handy feature for digital camera users, since digital cameras often have trouble with specific channels. For example, many cameras produce inordinate amounts of noise in the Red channel of an image. With your image editor, you can try to attack the noise in the Red channel directly by applying special noise reducing filters or blurs—or even painting by hand—directly into the Red channel.

Similarly, many digital cameras have trouble accurately capturing blue. If you find the blues in your image are a little bit off, you can try to correct them by editing the Blue channel directly.

In the next tutorial, you'll see how you can use Levels and Curves corrections in specific color channels.

TUTORIAL

USING BOTH LEVELS AND CURVES TO CORRECT COLOR

Although Curves offers the same functionality as Levels, you'll probably find that it's often easier to use a combination of the two tools. Some adjustments are simply easier to perform in Levels than they are in Curves.

When you are using multiple adjustments, it is important to consider the data loss that we discussed earlier in this chapter. However, if your adjustments are small, and you're only performing a few of them, this type of loss shouldn't be a concern.

In this tutorial, you'll use both a Levels and a Curves adjustment to correct a bad white balance.

STEP 1: OPEN THE IMAGE

ON THE CD

Open the image meerkat.jpg located in the Tutorials/Chapter11/Using both Levels & Curves folder of the companion CD-ROM. This picture was shot with the camera's daylight white balance setting. Unfortunately, the camera had an ultraviolet filter on the front of the lens, which confused the white balance, resulting in an image that's too red (Figure 11.26).

White balance problems can be hard to deal with, as the color troubles typically run through the entire range of colors and tones within the image. Fortunately, this image isn't too bad. Figuring out how to correct this image is further complicated by the fact that both the dirt and the meerkat naturally have a lot of red in them.

The image also needs some simple white and black balance adjustments, both to improve the contrast and to brighten up the image. However, because the white balance problem has botched the tone in the image, let's save the white and black point compensation until after we've corrected the red cast.

STEP 2: TAKE A CLOSER LOOK

We can tell from looking at the image that there's too much red. However, it's interesting to look at some histograms to get a better idea of what's going on. Choose Window>Show Channels to open the Channels palette and click on

FIGURE 11.26 When this image was shot, the camera's daylight white balance preset got confused by a UV filter on the camera's lens and the resulting image came out too red. We can correct this bad white balance using some simple Levels and Curves adjustments.

the Red channel to see just the red information in the image. Now choose Image>Histogram. Because you are only looking at the Red channel, the histogram is limited to graphing the red information. Now look at the histograms for the Green and Blue channels (Figure 11.27).

Sure enough, there's more red data than blue or green data, particularly toward the lighter end of the tonal spectrum. We need to darken the Red chan-

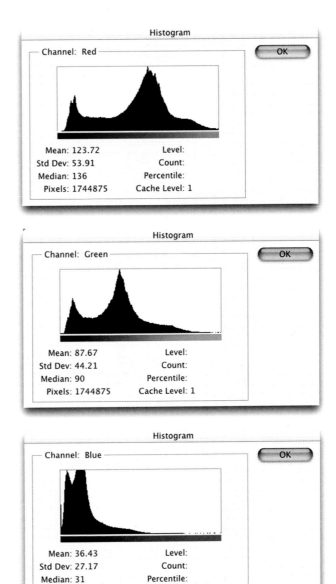

FIGURE 11.27 By looking at the histograms for each color channel, we can get a better idea of what corrections are needed.

nel so that its tonal range slides down to be more like that of the Blue and Green channels.

In the Channels palette, click on the RGB row to return to the full RGB display of the image.

STEP 3: MAKE A CURVES ADJUSTMENT

Open your image editor's Curves control. Notice that there is a Channel box at the top of the dialog box, above the curve graph. Opening this pop-up menu lets you select the channel you want to modify with your Curves adjustment. Open the Channel pop-up menu and select the Red channel.

We want to darken the Red channel, so drag the black point in the lower-right corner of the image to the right until the Input box reads about 33 (Figure 11.28). This should immediately cut a lot of the red from the image.

FIGURE 11.28 Most of the red cast can be removed with a simple Red channel Curves adjustment.

Now, however, the image is too green. Select the Green channel from the Channel pop-up menu at the top of the Curves dialog box. Drag the white point (the point in the upper right-hand corner) to the left until the Input box reads about 247.

This helps the green, but now our image is too blue. Switch to the Blue channel and drag the white point to the left until the Input box reads about 205.

Your image should be looking pretty good now. Yes, there's still a lot of red in it, but most of this is red that was actually in the image. However, we could cut a tiny bit more red from the midtones, both to remove some more red and to improve the contrast of the image.

Switch back to the Red channel and click on the middle of the red curve to create a control point. Click at around Input 168 and drag down to Output 147. This should remove a little more red. If you find that the image is a bit too green, switch to the Green channel and make a similar midpoint adjustment (Figure 11.29).

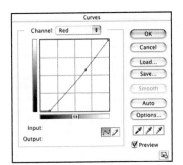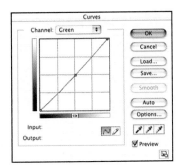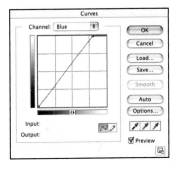

FIGURE 11.29   The final Curves adjustments for each color channel.

Click OK to accept your Curves adjustments. Notice that we were able to make all of these Curves changes with a single command. This is another advantage to operating on individual channels.

STEP 4: MAKE A LEVELS ADJUSTMENT

With our color correction completed, we have a better idea of just how bright or dark our image is. Now we can adjust our white and black points. This type of adjustment is usually easier with Levels, so open the Levels control and drag the white and black points to their appropriate locations. If you think the image needs it, make a slight gamma tweak to improve the midtones (Figure 11.30).

FIGURE 11.30 With a simple Levels tweak to adjust our white and black points, our image is finished.

There you have it, much less red, brighter and better contrast.

By operating on individual color channels, we were able to target particular ranges of color for correction. Also note that we were able to perform many different corrections with a single Curves command. As you learned earlier, fewer color correction operations means less loss of color data.

DON'T TOUCH THAT DIAL

In Chapter 13, you're going to see many more editing and correction techniques, while Chapter 14, "Special Effects," will cover a number of techniques for creating "special" effects. Before heading into those areas, however, there are a few more tools you need to learn. Many of these tools will enable you to perform more sophisticated edits, and will allow you to easily change and undo your edits as you work.

12

BUILDING YOUR EDITING ARSENAL

In This Chapter

- Brushes and Stamps
- Masks
- Layers
- Other Editing Tools

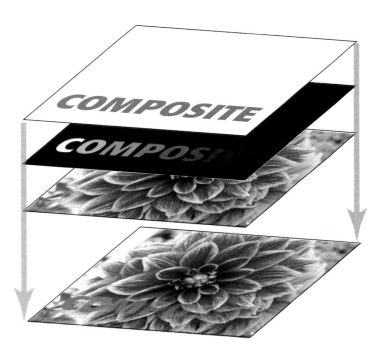

I n the last chapter, you were introduced to the Levels and Curves tools. These are powerful tools. They're so powerful, in fact, that you'll be reading much more about them later. However, there's much more to your image editor than just the Levels and Curves controls, so before moving on to more sophisticated editing, there are a few more tools you need to learn about.

In this chapter, we're going to cover the basic tools and functions that you'll use in all of your everyday—and not so everyday—editing tasks. These are the features you'll turn to again and again—in many different combinations—to perform your corrections, adjustments, and modifications. As in previous chapters, although the examples and tutorials in this chapter are built around Photoshop, any decent image editor should provide equivalent functions. Even if you're using a different set of tools, you should have no trouble translating the workflows and approaches presented in the following chapters to any image editor.

Since the first edition of this book was published, Adobe has released Photoshop Elements, a scaled-down, inexpensive version of Photoshop. For most editing and printing tasks, Elements provides all the image editing power you might need. At the end of this chapter, you'll find a simple comparison between Photoshop Elements and the full version of Photoshop. You might be surprised to find that you don't need to spend the extra money for the full package.

BRUSHES AND STAMPS

Many of the retouching and editing tasks that are performed in a real darkroom are dependent on brushes, masks, and paint. Your image editor is no different, except that your brushes and tools are digital. To get good results from them, you still need a good hand, a trained eye, and well-designed tools—just as in a real darkroom.

The documentation that came with your image editor should offer plenty of information on how to use your editor's tools. In this section, therefore, you're going to learn what each tool is good for. Being able to identify the right tool for a particular job will often save you a lot of time.

Brushes

Hopefully, your image editor includes a good assortment of paintbrushes and airbrushes. A good brush tool is one that offers an easy way of selecting different brush sizes and shapes, has anti-*aliased* (smooth) edges, pressure sensitivity when used with a drawing tablet, and variable opacity (Figure 12.1).

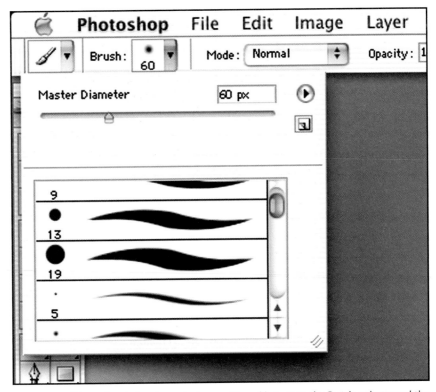

FIGURE 12.1 Photoshop's Brush controls—scattered between the Brush palette and the toolbar—let you select brush size, transfer mode, and opacity.

You'll use these tools for everything from painting out unwanted elements in a scene to performing certain types of color correction, creating masks, and "brushing in" different special effects.

To use a brush tool well you need—obviously—good hand-eye coordination and a feel for the brush. Your brush skills will develop over time and will be greatly aided by the use of a drawing tablet. In addition to providing a more intuitive interface, a drawing tablet is *much* easier on your hand than is a mouse. If you plan to do a lot of image editing, consider investing in an inexpensive pressure-sensitive drawing tablet such as the Wacom tablet shown in Figure 12.2.

You'll also want to spend some time learning the different keyboard shortcuts that augment your brush tool. Learn your brush's features, including parameters such as *spacing* and *repeat rate*.

FIGURE 12.2   A pressure-sensitive drawing tablet such as this Wacom Graphire is a must-have for serious image editing.

Airbrushes

Airbrushes are very similar to normal paintbrushes, the main difference being that they don't lay down a full load of paint with one pass. Instead, they work like a real-world airbrush—they spray on a fine layer of color that can be darkened by repeated strokes. Airbrushes are ideal for very fine shading and detail work. Touching up shadows and highlights, trying to match the color and tone of an existing element in your image, or trying to soften an effect or composite are all potential uses for your application's airbrush tool. In general, the airbrush is ideal for any application where you don't want to "commit" to a particular color or tonal value, but want to build up color or tone with multiple strokes.

The airbrush requires a finer touch than the normal paintbrushes, and the tool's sensitivity can usually be adjusted with simple parameter sliders. As with the paintbrush, learn to control the sensitivity of your airbrush and spend some time practicing to get a feel for how it applies color.

Rubber Stamp or Clone

One of the most powerful—and seemingly magical—tools in your image editing toolbox is a rubber stamp tool (also known as a clone tool), which provides a brush that performs a localized copy from one part of your image to another as you brush (Figure 12.3).

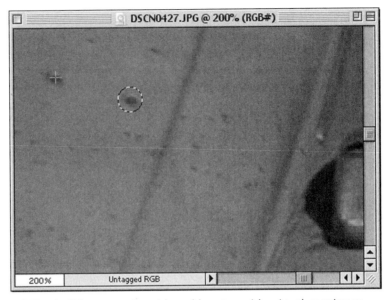

FIGURE 12.3   When you paint with a rubber stamp (clone) tool, your image editor copies paint from your source area (the crosshairs) to your target area (the circle).

You'll use your rubber stamp tool for everything from removing dust and noise to painting things out of your image to painting things in to your image. The advantage of a rubber stamp tool over normal copying and pasting is that the tool's brush-like behavior lets you achieve very realistic composites and edits.

Study your rubber stamp tool's documentation to learn the difference between absolute and relative cloning and to learn how to set the tool's source and destination points. When you rubber stamp an area, you want to be able to quickly select a source area and then start painting, so it's imperative to learn the tool's controls.

Your image editing application provides many more tools and functions, but brushes and stamps are the ones that you'll be using the most. These are also tools that will not be heavily discussed or documented in the rest of this book. For the rest of these tutorials, it is assumed that you know how to follow an instruction such as "Rubber stamp out the telephone wires." If you don't know how to use these tools, consult your manual.

TUTORIAL   ## Cloning Video Tutorial

To learn more about cloning, watch the Cloning Tutorial movie located in the Video/Chapter 12/Cloning folder on the companion CD-ROM (Figure 12.4).

ON THE CD

 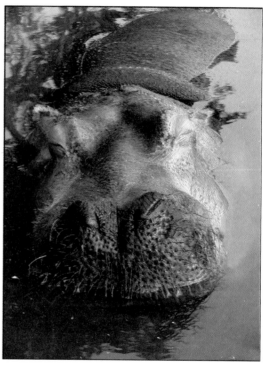

FIGURE 12.4   We used nothing more than Photoshop's Rubber Stamp (or Cloning) tool to remove the wires from in front of this hippo. A cloning tool is a must for even the simplest touch-ups, so make sure you know how to use one. You can see how this image was corrected by watching the Cloning tutorial movie located on the CD-ROM.

Masks

People are often confused by the mask tools provided by their image editor, even though masks are fairly simple to understand and use. A mask is just like a stencil that you would use in a real darkroom or painting studio. The only difference is that digital masks are much, much better.

As in the real world, you'll use digital masks for controlling the extent and range of your edits and adjustments. If you only want to color correct the background of an image, for example, you might build a mask over the foreground elements. You could also use that foreground mask to paste a new background behind your foreground elements (Figure 12.5).

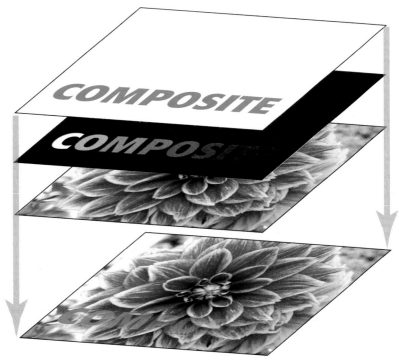

FIGURE 12.5 Masks are used to control which parts of a layer are visible when creating composites. Similar to stencils, digital masks have the advantage of allowing for varying degrees of transparency. Although masks are essential for complex special effects work, they're also useful for basic color corrections and adjustments.

Many photographers feel that masking is not such an important tool because they're not interested in creating weird special effects or wacky composites. Masking, however, can be an essential color correction tool, allowing you to create adjustments and corrections that would otherwise be impossible.

Like many editing tasks, knowing how and when to use a mask is a skill. However, learning the basics of your mask tools is pretty simple once you understand a few simple concepts.

Mask Tools

Most image editing applications offer many tools for creating masks, and you'll often find yourself using these tools in combination. Some tools, for example, are more appropriate for masking complex subjects such as hair or fine detail. Other tools are more appropriate for masking geometric shapes or large areas of color. For building complex masks, you'll freely switch between each of these tools.

Selection Tools

The simplest mask tools are the selection tools—the lasso, rectangular and circular marquees—that let you create simple selections by outlining areas of your image. You might not think of these as mask tools, but the selections they produce work just like a mask. Create a rectangular selection around an object, for example, and your editing tools will only work inside that selection. Everything outside of the selection is masked out.

What makes these mask tools effective is that most applications let you add and subtract from the selections you make. Photoshop, for example, lets you add to a selection simply by holding down the Shift key while you select more image. This allows you to use different tools for different parts of your image. For example, you can use Photoshop's Circle tool to select a curvy section of an object, and then hold down the Shift key and use the Lasso tool to outline the rest of the object (Figure 12.6).

Similarly, Photoshop lets you use the Command key (Control if you're using Windows) to subtract from a selection. The ability to keep

FIGURE 12.6 By holding down the Shift key when you use a selection tool, you can add to a selection. The ability to add to a selection allows you to use different tools to select different parts of an image. In this image, we used the rectangular marquee to select a rectangular-shaped area of the chair, and then the lasso tool to trace around the edge detail.

adding to a selection with different tools is essential for building complex masks.

In the same family as the selection tools are magic wand tools that automatically hunt down similar colors to create selections automatically. As with other selection tools, Photoshop allows you to combine Magic Wand selections with selections made using other tools, by simply holding down the Shift or Command (Control) keys.

Mask Painting

Photoshop's QuickMask mode lets you create a mask by painting. To use QuickMask, you simply click on the QuickMask icon at the bottom of the main tool palette. In QuickMask mode, any areas that you paint black will be selected when you exit QuickMask mode, and any areas that you paint white will be unselected (Figure 12.7).

FIGURE 12.7   In QuickMask mode, you can select areas simply by painting. Areas painted red in QuickMask mode are selected when you switch back to normal mode. QuickMask is an easy way to make odd-shaped selections.

You can switch in and out of QuickMask mode as much as you like, meaning that you can combine its mask selection tools with your image editor's other mask tools.

Color-Based Selection Tools

Many applications provide special tools for automatically selecting certain colors. Photoshop, for example, includes a Color Range command that can automatically select all occurrences of a particular color in an image (Figure 12.8).

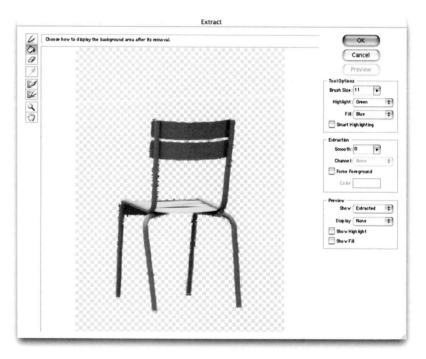

FIGURE 12.8 Photoshop's Color Range command lets you select all of the occurrences of a particular color in your document.

Color Range will almost always select more pixels than you want, but the extra pixels can usually be easily removed with another selection tool.

Special Mask Tools

Some applications include special dedicated tools, such as Photoshop's Extract tool, which can perform complex extractions of difficult subjects like hair or transparent surfaces (Figure 12.9). Extract doesn't create a mask, but it does let you isolate an image for compositing with another image.

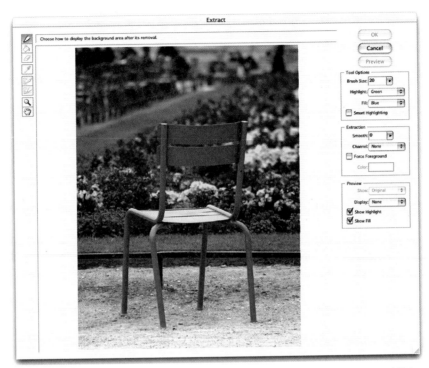

FIGURE 12.9   Photoshop's Extract tool includes sophisticated edge detection capabilities for extracting part of an image. The result can then be composited with other images.

There are also several third-party masking plug-ins that can be added to any image editor that supports Photoshop plug-ins. Programs such as Corel's KnockOut or Extensis' Mask Pro provide a simple way of creating complex masks. If you find yourself consistently trying to mask difficult subjects such as hair or other objects with fine detail or transparency, it might be worthwhile to look into one of these options.

Saving Masks

Once you've used the various tools at your disposal to create a selection, you can save that selection as a mask for later use. In Photoshop, selections can be saved by choosing Select>Save Selection. At any time, you can use the Select>Load Selection command to restore your selection.

In Chapter 11, "Correcting Tone and Color," you saw how separate red, green, and blue channels are used to create a full-color image. You also saw that you can access and manipulate those individual color channels. Selections, or masks, are stored in a similar fashion. When you save a selection, your image editor creates a new channel in your document—called an *alpha channel*—and stores an image of your selection (Figure 12.10).

FIGURE 12.10 When you save a selection, Photoshop stores a grayscale, 8-bit alpha channel. Black areas of the image are masked, while white areas are not. If you load this alpha channel as a selection, then the white area will be selected, just as if you had traced it with a lasso tool.

As you can see, any selection can be represented by a grayscale image—areas within the selection are stored as white pixels, areas outside are stored as black. In Photoshop, you can create as many different selections as you want, and store each in its own alpha channel. From the Channels palette, which you can open by choosing Window>Show Channels, you can access each masks by simply clicking on its name (Figure 12.11).

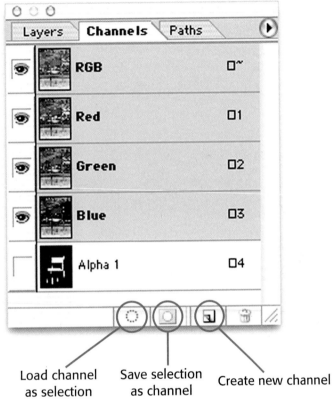

Load channel   Save selection   Create new channel
as selection   as channel

FIGURE 12.11   You can see and access the alpha channel
from Photoshop's Channels palette.

Sort of Masked

So far, we've discussed masks as if they were simple stencils. Digital masks, however, are much more powerful than real-world masks are, because, in addition to masking an area, they can *partially* mask an area. Just as black pixels in a mask are completely opaque, gray pixels are only *partially* opaque, meaning that you can use masks to apply effects and adjustments that vary across an image.

The easiest way to understand masks is to use them. In the following tutorial, you'll use a series of complex masks to alter an image.

| TUTORIAL | **CREATING COMPLEX MASKS** |

Masks are used for everything from constraining painting and filter effects, to controlling how different images composite together. In this tutorial, you'll see that you can also use masks to create complex color corrections and adjustments.

STEP 1: OPEN THE IMAGE

ON THE CD

Open the image tree.jpg, which is located in the Tutorials/Chapter 12/Creating Complex Masks folder on the companion CD-ROM (Figure 12.12). Your goal in this tutorial is to try to emphasize the foreground elements—the tree and the bent wrought-iron cage—by lightening the background. To edit the background without disturbing the foreground, therefore, you need to mask out the tree.

FIGURE 12.12   Because we want to edit the background of this image without disturbing the tree, we need to create a tree mask.

STEP 2: CREATE A MASK

ON THE CD

Using your choice of masking techniques, create a mask for the tree as well as the entire wrought-iron cage that surrounds the tree. Save the mask by choosing Select>Save Selection. To save time, the file *tree with mask.jpg* has been included in the Tutorials/Chapter 12/Creating Complex Masks folder. This image includes a pre-built mask that you can use for the rest of this tutorial (Figure 12.13). (In case you're wondering, this mask was created by simply painting over the tree and fence using Photoshop's QuickMask tool.)

FIGURE 12.13 This mask was built using the QuickMask tool and is included in the Tutorials>Chapter 12>Creating Complex Masks folder.

STEP 3: LOAD THE MASK

Before you can use a mask, you have to load it. Open Photoshop's Channels palette. You should see separate channels for red, green, blue, and your mask (called Alpha 1). At the bottom of the Channels palette are a series of buttons. The far left button is the Load Channel as Selection button (Figure 12.11). Drag the Alpha 1 channel on top of this button, and Photoshop will load the channel as a selection.

Sometimes, after loading a mask, it can be difficult to tell what is selected and what isn't. For example, with the tree mask loaded, it's difficult to tell whether the foreground or background is masked. To find out, click on the paintbrush tool and brush it around on the image. You should see that the paint is only going into the background because the tree is completely masked. Click Undo to remove your brush strokes. (If Undo doesn't undo all the strokes, use the History palette to remove the brush strokes.) If the paint is going into the foreground, then your mask is backward. From the Select menu, choose Invert Selection to reverse your mask. Now when you brush, your paint should go into the foreground.

STEP 4: FADE THE BACKGROUND

With your mask loaded, you can now start manipulating the background. If the goal is to emphasize the foreground, then you should try lightening the background using a simple Levels command.

Choose Image>Adjust>Levels to open the Levels dialog. In previous tutorials, you used the Input controls exclusively, and learned how they allow you to change the distribution of tones within your image. So far, though, your Levels adjustments have redistributed the tones in your image so that they fit between full black and full white.

However, what if your printer can't print full black? Many offset printers can't hold more than 85% black—any more ink and they jam up. Therefore, Levels includes a pair of output sliders that allow you to adjust the limits of the tonal range in your image. The distribution of tones specified by the input levels remains the same.

Let's eliminate many of the darker tones without changing the tonal relationships in our image. Slide the leftmost output slider to roughly the midpoint (around 126) and click OK. This should create a faded background (Figure 12.14).

STEP 5: ASSESS THE CHANGE

Now it's time to assess if this was the right edit. With all of those selection lines marching around, it can be difficult to see the image clearly. Choose Select>Hide Selection to hide the selection lines; the selection is still active, you just can't see it. You can always choose Select>Show Selection if you need to double-check that the selection is still active.

FIGURE 12.14 We've faded everything but the tree. Unfortunately, we've faded more than just what was behind the tree in the scene. The sidewalk in front of the tree has faded as well.

Sure enough, as we planned, the adjustment faded the background. Unfortunately, because we faded everything but the tree, our edit has also caused elements in front of the tree to fade. This is not really the desired effect. Click Undo to remove the Levels adjustment.

What we want is a Levels adjustment that won't affect the entire image uniformly, but will be stronger in parts of the image that appear farther away. It's time to create another mask.

Choose Deselect from the Select menu to deselect the current selection. We don't want anything selected right now.

STEP 6: CREATE A GRADATED MASK

Although you can use any number of selection tools to create masks, you can also paint them by hand, directly into an alpha channel. In the Channels palette, click on the Create New Channels button (the second button from the right). A new channel will be created, selected, and filled with black.

Remember that black areas in a mask are completely opaque, white areas are completely transparent, and gray areas are somewhere in between. We want a mask that fades from fully opaque to fully transparent.

Set Photoshop's foreground and background colors to black and white by clicking on the Black/White switch next to Photoshop's color swatches in the main tool palette (Figure 12.15).

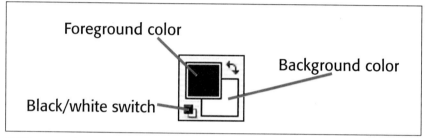

FIGURE 12.15   Photoshop's Black/White switch lets you immediately set the foreground and background colors to black and white, respectively.

Now select the Gradient tool and drag from the top of the image to the bottom. This will create a complete black to white gradient.

STEP 7: TRY THE NEW MASK

Click on the RGB channel in the Channels palette to switch back to full-color view. Now, load the new channel by dragging the Alpha 2 channel to the Load Channel as Selection button. A selection will appear that covers about half the image. Don't worry, Photoshop has loaded the complete mask; it's only choosing to outline areas that are more than 50% masked. Choose Select>Hide Selection to hide the selection and then apply the same Levels adjustment you did in Step 4 (Figure 12.16).

This is the effect we wanted—a lightening of the image that gets stronger from bottom to top. Unfortunately, the effect is no longer confined to just the background. Click Undo to remove the Levels adjustment, and let's make another new mask.

FIGURE 12.16   We get a better fade with a graduated mask, but now our tree is fading along with the background.

STEP 8: CREATE YET ANOTHER MASK

Go back to the Channels palette and delete the Alpha 2 channel by dragging it to the tiny trash can at the bottom of the palette. Now make a new channel.

We want to create a gradient that fills all the document *except* where the tree is. Unfortunately, the Gradient tool will fill the whole channel unless we *use the tree mask we already created*. Load the first mask (the tree) by dragging the Alpha 1 channel to the Load Channel as Selection button. You should see the outline of the tree mask.

Now, click on the Gradient tool and make a top-to-bottom, black-to-white gradient (Figure 12.17). Click on the RGB channel to view your color image.

FIGURE 12.17 This mask provides the gradient we need to create our fade while masking out the tree.

STEP 9: FADE THE BACKGROUND

Now, load your new mask and apply your Levels adjustment. You should see a Levels change that affects only the background, but varies from the bottom to the top of the image!

With this mask, you can now independently edit the foreground and background of your image. Try experimenting with different color corrections and filters. The image in Figure 12.18 has had a more severe Levels adjustment applied to it, as well as some subtle desaturations of the foreground and background.

FIGURE 12.18   Our final tree image includes some extra color desaturations and levels adjustments.

LAYERS

Layers are pretty easy to understand. If your image editor provides a layer facility, you'll be able to stack images—and parts of images—on top of each other within a document. Layers allow for much more than simple collages and composites. A robust layer facility provides you with the ability to more easily make the types of corrections that you saw in the last tutorial, and—if you structure your layers properly—allows you to go back and adjust and tweak your edits later.

Some Layer Basics

If your image editor provides layer controls, you'll need to spend some time learning how they work. Following are some of the basics of using the Layers control in Photoshop. (Note that Layers weren't added to Photoshop until version 3. If you're using an earlier version, it's time to upgrade!)

Creating, Deleting, and Moving Layers

Fortunately, layer management is very simple in Photoshop; you simply use the Layers palette. On the bottom of the palette are all the controls you need to create and delete layers (Figure 12.19). Right now, you only need to worry about the Create layer and Delete layer buttons located on the right side of the palette.

Create adjustment layer   Create new layer   Delete layer

FIGURE 12.19   Photoshop's Layers palette includes simple button controls for creating and deleting layers.

When you create a new layer, it will appear as part of the layer stack in the palette. Because new layers are empty, your image won't look any different. All edits—whether painting, filters, or image adjustments—happen in the currently selected layer. Note that you can turn off the visibility of a layer by simply clicking its Eyeball icon.

Layers that are higher in the Layers palette obscure any lower layers, and you can re-arrange layers by dragging them up or down the stacking order. Note that you cannot change the order of the lowest layer—the Background—unless you double-click on it to turn it into a normal, floating layer.

New layers are completely transparent, while the Background layer is completely opaque. (Obviously, as you paint into a layer, Photoshop changes the opacity of that part of the layer so that your paint is visible.)

Opacity and Transfer Modes

You can change the opacity of the currently selected layer by simply sliding the Opacity control back and forth.

You can also change how the currently selected layer interacts with layers that are lower in the stacking order by selecting a *blending* (or *transfer*) mode from the pop-up menu in the Layers palette. Normally, the pixels in a layer simply overwrite any pixels that are lower down the stack. By changing the blending mode, you can force layers to blend with lower layers. Each pixel in a layer is mathematically combined with the pixels that are lower in the stack to create new pixels (Figure 12.20).

As you work more with blending modes, you'll get a better idea of what they do. At first, don't worry about being able to predict their results. Just start playing around with them until you find the effect you like. To lessen the effect of a mode, lower that layer's opacity.

In addition to creating weird composite effects like those shown in Figure 12.20, you can use layer modes for hand-coloring grayscale images and creating certain types of color corrections (Figure 12.21).

To reduce the colored speckled noise in figure 12.21a, we first added a Hue/Saturation Adjustment Layer to the image and used it to drain the color out of the particularly noisy background areas. We then created a number of separate layers and set the transfer mode of each one to Multiply. Then, using a paintbrush, we simply hand-colored the areas that we had desaturated. The image is not completely free of noise, and the desaturation introduced some smudging artifacts, but these are not as unsightly as the colored speckles that we eliminated.

FIGURE 12.20 A few of Photoshop's blending modes.

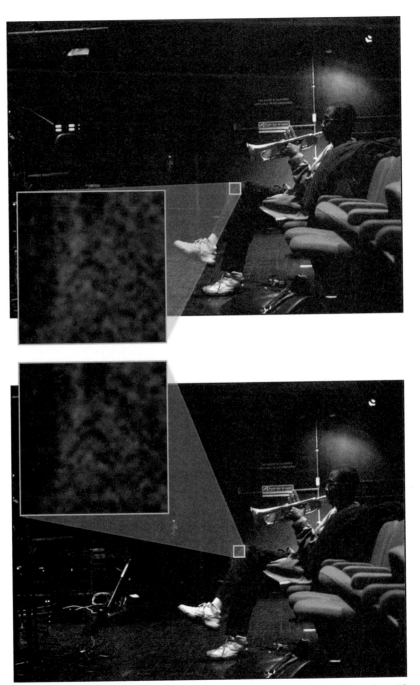

FIGURE 12.21   The low-light, high-ISO image shown above is plagued by noise with bright-colored speckles. Although we can't eliminate the noise, using a blending mode correction technique we can at least eliminate the colored speckles and make the noise look more like texture.

WATCH THAT RAM!

As you add layers to your image, its RAM requirements will quickly skyrocket. Nothing affects Photoshop performance as much as RAM, so if you find your computer getting sluggish, it might be that Photoshop is running out of memory. The easiest way to shrink the RAM requirements of your document is to eliminate extra layers. If you think you've finished editing an individual layer, consider merging it with other layers using Photoshop's Merge Linked or Merge Visible commands, located in the Layers menu.

Adjustment Layers

One of Photoshop's most powerful editing features is its adjustment layers, which let you apply Levels, Curves, and many other image correction functions *as layers.* For example, when you add a Curves adjustment layer to your document, Photoshop presents you with a normal Curves dialog box. You can adjust your image as desired but, when you click OK, instead of applying the Curves adjustment to the image, it stores the adjustment in a new adjustment layer that appears in your Layers palette (Figure 12.22).

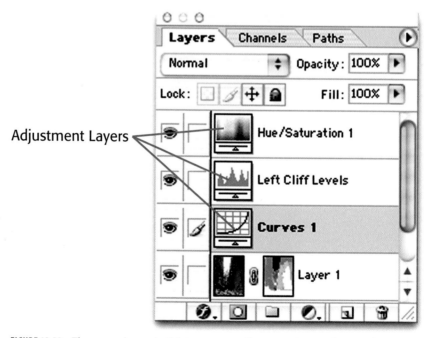

FIGURE 12.22   The upper layers in this image are adjustment layers. They apply, respectively, Hue/Saturation, Curves, and Levels adjustments to the underlying layer. Their settings can be altered or changed at any time.

An adjustment layer affects all of the layers beneath it. The real strength of adjustment layers, though, is that you can go back at any time *and change the adjustment layer's settings*. Therefore, if you decide at some point that you need a different Curves adjustment, you can simply double-click on your Curves adjustment layer and change its Curves parameters. In addition to providing flexible editing, adjustment layers keep you from re-applying effects that result in data loss. You'll be using adjustment layers extensively throughout the rest of this book.

Layer Masks

In the last tutorial, you saw how alpha channels can be used to create masks. As powerful as alpha channels are, there is an easier way to perform many types of masking operations.

Photoshop allows you to attach a layer mask to any layer to create complex mask effects. From the Layers palette pop-up menu (Figure 12.23) you can choose to attach a layer mask to a layer.

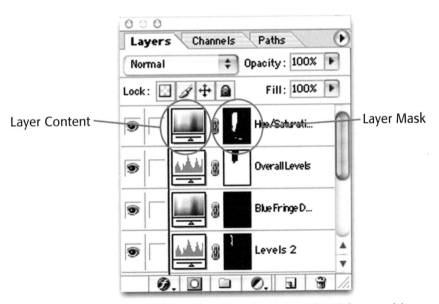

FIGURE 12.23 You can paint masking information directly into a layer's layer mask by clicking on the layer mask thumbnail in the Layers palette.

Each layer entry in the Layers palette has a Document thumbnail and a Layer Mask thumbnail. You can click on these thumbnails to switch editing the layer or editing its layer mask. As you paint or edit a layer mask, you create masking information that works exactly like the alpha channel masks you saw earlier. Paint black into a layer mask and the pixels in that part of the layer will be masked and, thus, invisible.

The complex masking effects that you created in the last tutorial could have also been created using layer masks and adjustment layers. The *Final Tree.psd* document included on the companion CD-ROM includes all of the adjustment layers used to create the image in Figure 12.18.

You'll get a lot of first-hand layer masking experience in the next chapter.

OTHER EDITING TOOLS

Levels and Curves are the most powerful tone and color correction tools that you'll find. In addition to their editing controls, these tools provide clear visual feedback that helps ensure that your edits are not ruining your image by blowing out your highlights, darkening your shadows, or tossing out too much image data.

Although powerful, these tools are not always the easiest options for certain types of corrections. For example, perhaps one part of your image needs to be more purple, or another part has a yellow-green cast. Although Levels and Curves provide controls for editing individual color channels, targeting a specific range of yellow can be difficult when you have to think in terms of red, green, and blue.

Fortunately, most image editors provide other tone and color correction tools. Here is a brief rundown of other tonal correction facilities provided by Photoshop. Each of these functions can be applied through an adjustment layer.

DESTRUCTIVE VERSUS NON-DESTRUCTIVE EDITING

If you open a Levels or Curves control (or any of the other adjustment tools mentioned below) and apply a change to your image, you are actually changing the pixel data in your image. This is called destructive editing *because you are destroying your original image data. As you've seen, this is sometimes a process that degrades your image quality. Adjustment Layers do not effect your original data. Instead, they are adjustments that are applied on-the-fly to your image data as the data is written to the screen or output to a printer. These types of corrections are called* non-destructive edits *because they do not change your original image data.*

Hue/Saturation

Raising or lowering saturation in an image is very difficult to do with Levels or Curves, but it's a snap with the Hue/Saturation control. Just slide the Saturation slider left or right to raise or lower the saturation of your image. Like Levels and Curves, Hue/Saturation can operate on individual color channels, or you can target particular color areas.

If your camera tends to shoot some colors too "hot"—that is, too saturated—or, if it tends to produce images that are undersaturated, you can easily change the saturation with the Hue/Saturation slider. You'll learn more about this tool in Chapter 13, "Essential Imaging Tactics" (Figure 12.24).

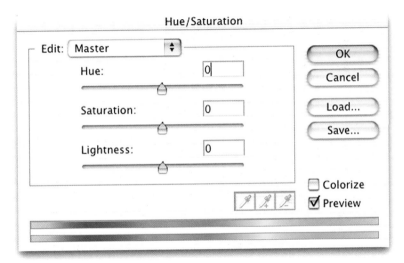

FIGURE 12.24 Photoshop's Hue/Saturation dialog provides another interface for adjusting color. Hue/Saturation is particularly effective at increasing or decreasing color saturation or brightness.

Selective Color

Photoshop's Selective Color control lets you adjust the cyan, magenta, yellow, and black levels of a specific tonal range. The Selective Color dialog box provides a choice of nine different tonal ranges (red, yellows, greens, cyans, blues, magentas, whites, neutrals, and blacks) that can be adjusted using simple sliders.

Because the colors ranges it targets are so broad, Selective Color is not a very subtle tool—you'll almost always need to run this operation through a mask to limit its effects.

Unique Tools

Most image editing applications also include an assortment of additional, special editing tools. Photoshop 7, for example, includes an extraordinary Healing Brush that is something of a super-intelligent Cloning tool. Photoshop Elements, meanwhile, has a special tool specifically designed for removing red-eye. In addition to specialized brushes, many programs include automatic tone and color adjustment features, such as the Variations dialog in Photoshop.

Although all of these tools can be a boon for certain editing tasks, it's still important to understand basic editing concepts and tactics. Such an understanding will help you better use specialized tools, and will afford you a level of "manual override" for times when automated tools don't work, or don't provide the level of control you need to make a particular edit. You will be spending the rest of the book learning these basic editing procedures.

THE RIGHT TOOL FOR THE JOB

These are just a smattering of the tools that you'll find in a high-end image editor like Photoshop. However, with this basic arsenal, you can correct and adjust most of the problems that you'll find in your digital images. In the next chapter, you'll begin to use these tools in combination to tackle the most common digital imaging problems.

ESSENTIAL IMAGING TACTICS

In This Chapter

- Workflow

- Initial Cleanup

- Color and Tone Adjustment

- Saturation Adjustment

- Editing

- Scaling

- Sharpening

Now that you have a handle on how to use some of the tools and functions of your image editor, it's time to put those tools to work. The creative possibilities inherent in a program as powerful as Photoshop—or any other state-of-the-art image editor—are endless. However, as a digital photographer, there are certain issues and problems that you will run into fairly consistently. In this chapter, you'll learn how to handle these problems and how to perform the type of corrections that you'll most certainly need to make during your digital photographic career.

Because every editing task is different, it's difficult to create a comprehensive list of problems and solutions. Consequently, the tutorials in this chapter are intended to provide you with a set of fundamental skills that you can repurpose and recombine to solve other problems that you might run into. In addition to creating a skill set, the tutorials and lessons in this chapter will demonstrate a flexible, non-destructive form of image editing that allows for a great deal of flexibility.

ON THE CD

In addition to the printed tutorials, there are a few new video tutorials included on the CD-ROM. Ideally, these should be viewed in the order presented herein.

WORKFLOW

For maximum flexibility and to preserve image quality, you should perform your edits in a particular order. For example, you almost always want to perform any sharpening operations *after* you've performed all of your other corrections and edits. Because sharpening can be a very destructive operation, you only want to do it once, after you're sure that nothing else in your image will change.

Typically, your image editing workflow will progress something like this:

1. **Initial clean-up.** You will first attempt to remove any excess noise as well as any spots or dirt from the image. By removing these elements first, you won't exaggerate them with later operations. This is also the stage where you'll correct any *barrel* or *pincushion* distortion caused by your camera's lens. You might also crop your image at this stage, and possibly perform an initial resizing to get a better idea of what your final image will look like.

2. **Color and tone adjustment.** Once your image contains only the pixels you're interested in, you can begin to perform your first color and tone adjustments. These operations are typically how you will determine the tonal range of the image. After a few adjustments, you

might find that your shadows have brightened enough to reveal some noise that was not removed earlier. Consequently, color and tone adjustment will sometimes be followed by a little more cleanup.

3. **Saturation adjustment.** Because it's difficult to adjust saturation with a Levels or Curves adjustment (the tools you'll usually use in your color and tone adjustments), you'll often need to tweak the saturation of your image. As you boost saturation, you might find that your colors need further refinement.

4. **Editing.** With all of your colors adjusted, you can begin to perform any additional editing such as compositing, collage work, special effects, or other manipulations. Often, to make these edits blend seamlessly together, you'll need to perform additional color and saturation adjustments.

5. **Scaling.** If you didn't crop and scale your image during the initial cleanup, you can perform those operations after you've finished all of your adjustments and edits. For the Web, you'll probably need to scale your image down, while printing might require sizing up.

6. **Sharpening.** Finally, after everything's finished and your image is the correct size, it's time to apply any requisite sharpening. If you scaled your image down in the previous step, that process probably served to sharpen the image. If you scaled your image up, it could very well need additional sharpening.

 A NOTE ON SAVING

Unless you're shooting in a special Raw or TIFF mode, the images that come out of your camera are compressed using JPEG, a compression scheme that degrades your image. Therefore, once you start editing, you don't want to resave your image as a JPEG file because you'll introduce more degradation. Lock your original JPEG file (think of it as a negative) and, once you start editing, resave your image in Photoshop's native format or in another lossless format such as TIFF. The only time you need to resave your image as a JPEG file is if you're going to post it on the Web or send it via e-mail.

Obviously, this workflow is not carved in stone and, as described previously, you'll often move back and forth between different steps. If you follow the procedures on the following pages, you'll learn how to apply your edits and adjustments so that they remain editable and can be undone at any time, allowing you to easily move back and forth from step to step, and making it simple to go back and make changes to your document later.

INITIAL CLEANUP

No matter how careful you were when you were shooting, your document might have some troublesome artifacts that will need to be removed before you begin more complex edits. These artifacts can include anything from noise to lens flares and dirt.

Removing Noise

Noise is the most troublesome artifact to get rid of and, unfortunately, the most prevalent. Although modern digital cameras are getting much better in their capability to generate images with low noise, most cameras will still generate some noise, particularly in shadow areas and bright skies, and especially when you shoot at higher ISOs.

The problem with trying to remove noise from an image is that it's often very difficult to separate noise from fine detail. Consequently, in removing noise, you'll often end up softening very finely detailed areas. Moreover, depending on the noise reduction method you use, removing noise can also lower the contrast or saturation of your image.

Nevertheless, a slightly softer or less-saturated image is usually preferable to an image covered with distracting, ugly noise. In this section, you'll learn several methods of removing noise. Why so many? Because some methods are more effective against particular types of noise than others. In addition, some methods will be more appropriate to your particular image.

After some experimentation, you'll probably discover that some methods work better than others to eliminate the particular type of noise your camera creates, so don't worry about mastering all of these techniques. Try them all, and then focus on the ones that work best for you.

Identifying Noise

Before you can remove noise, you have to find it. In some images—particularly those shot at high ISOs—the noise will be strong enough that you won't have any trouble identifying it. In other images, noise might be less pronounced. Determining which parts of the image have noise problems will make it easier to develop a plan of attack.

Shadow areas are the most common havens for noise, even the lighter shadows under a person's chin. Because low-light photos have many shadowed areas, you'll find much more noise in low-light images than in daytime images. Nevertheless, daylight skies are sometimes susceptible to noise, as are any flat, colored objects. When you identify noise, pay attention to what the noise looks like. Is it a simple grainy noise, or is it loaded with specks of color?

Some of the individual color channels in your image can have more noise than other channels (Figure 13.1). The Blue and Red channels are very susceptible to noise—daylight sky noise will usually live exclusively in the Red channel, for example—while the Green channel is usually more clear. Examine your image's color channels individually by clicking

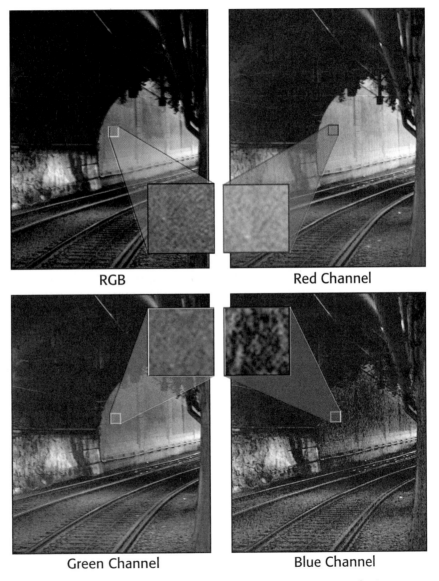

RGB

Red Channel

Green Channel

Blue Channel

FIGURE 13.1   Different color channels will often have different amounts of noise. Consequently, when you remove noise from an image, it's often most effective to attack an individual color channel.

on their names in Photoshop's Channels palette. You can also look at individual color channels by pressing Command-1 for Red, Command-2 for Green, and Command-3 for Blue (substitute Control for Command if you're using Windows). To return to RGB view, press Command-~. Try to get in the habit of looking at the individual color channels and making a note of which channel is noisiest.

As mentioned earlier, because your image has not yet had any tonal or color correction, there might be areas that are so dark that you can't see if they're noisy. You can always apply a Levels adjustment layer to brighten up your image while you remove noise, and then discard the adjustment later. However, don't brighten the image too much. You don't want to bother with removing noise that will be too dark to see in the final image.

Another approach is to remove the noise you can see now, and then go back for another noise removal pass *after* you've made your tonal corrections.

In addition, don't obsess too much about fine-grained noise. Depending on your printer, you might not be able to see the noise anyway. For example, if your inkjet printer produces fairly large, visible ink dots, then these dots will obscure any noise in your image. Similarly, if you shoot with a very high-res camera (4 megapixels or better), you probably don't need to worry about slight noise that becomes visible when you zoom in to 100%. Although it might look bad on-screen, at this size you're able to see noise that is too fine to appear in print. If you're unsure of whether your noise is a problem, do a test print to see how bad the noise might be.

Once you know where the noise is, you can begin to use any combination of the following procedures to remove it.

Noise Reduction with Dust and Scratches, Median, or Despeckle

Photoshop includes a Dust & Scratches filter that averages adjacent pixels that have a sudden contrast change (Figure 13.2). You can set the pixel size of the noise you are targeting and the threshold of contrast that you want the filter to search for.

The Median filter offers a function similar to Dust & Scratches, but without control over the threshold. Despeckle is another similar filter, but lacks any control over pixel size and threshold.

The problem with all three filters is that they tend to soften your images. Although you can sharpen your images to restore some of the detail, this introduces other problems, as we'll see later. These filters are best used with a mask to constrain their effects.

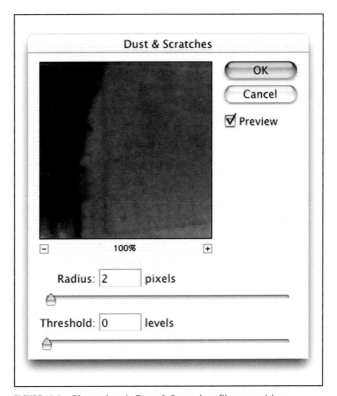

FIGURE 13.2   Photoshop's Dust & Scratches filter provides a simple way to remove artifacts of a particular size. Unfortunately, this filter can soften the fine detail in your image, so you'll want to use it with caution.

For example, perhaps the sky in your image has some pronounced noise that you think could be removed with the Dust & Scratches filter. Using your selection method of choice, select the sky and apply the filter. This will take care of the noise in your sky—the noise for which you've decided Dust & Scratches is appropriate—without affecting the rest of your image.

Noise Reduction Through Selective Blurring

Similar to the previous technique, you can simply select noisy areas of your image and apply a gentle Gaussian Blur or Smart Blur filter. These processes soften the contrast between pixels to create a smooth blur. Because the Gaussian Blur filter provides a very fine control over the pixel size of the blur, you can usually minimize noise without compromising texture (Figure 13.3). However, because a blur effect can soften and destroy fine detail in your image, you must make your selections very carefully.

FIGURE 13.3   With some very selective blurring, we can eliminate a lot of noise without softening fine detail.

If you have bright-colored, noisy specks in your image—bright red dots of noise, for example—a soft blur on the image's Green channel will often eliminate these.

Smart Blur provides a finer degree of control than does Gaussian Blur and is often more intelligent about preserving edge detail. An aggressive Smart Blur—with a Radius of 1.7–2.2 and a Threshold of 7.5–8, High Quality and Normal Mode—applied directly to the Blue channel is often a good solution to Blue channel noise.

Preserving Editability When You Remove Noise

Unfortunately, Photoshop does not offer blurs, despeckle, Dust & Scratches or other filters as adjustment layers. Instead, these filters are *destructive effects*. That is, they actually modify the pixels in your image, so there's no easy way to go back and change their settings or undo their effects if you change your mind about them later.

However, by creating duplicate layers of your source image, you can often isolate these destructive effects so that you can remove or replace them later. For example, let's say you want to use one of the noise reduction techniques described previously to remove some noise from your image. Rather than simply blurring your image, try this:

1. Create a new, duplicate layer of your image by dragging your background layer to the New Layer button in the Layers palette (this is assuming that your image is currently a single-layer image).
2. Apply a noise-reducing blur or filter to the upper layer by selecting the appropriate filter from the Filter menu. Your entire image will now look blurry, and will probably exhibit some loss of fine detail.
3. Now, add a layer mask to your upper, blurred layer. Set the mask to be empty by choosing Layer>Add Layer>Hide All to create the mask. This will create a layer mask that hides your entire blurred layer.
4. With your upper layer active, click on a white paintbrush and begin painting into the layer mask of the upper layer. This will selectively reveal the blurred image and it will appear as if you are painting in the blurred effect (Figure 13.4).

With this technique, you can go in and repaint the mask any time you want to change the blurred area. If you want to change your blur settings, just delete the layer, duplicate your base layer again, re-blur it, and paint a new mask.

You can use this approach for any type of edit or effect. When it is combined with adjustment layers, this approach allows you to keep nearly every editing action discrete and editable. It will, however, result

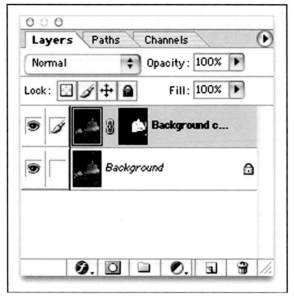

FIGURE 13.4 Once you've duplicated your layer and created your Layer Mask, your Layers palette should look like this.

in huge files and require a good amount of memory. However, when you feel that certain effects are finished, you can merge their layers together to reduce the size of your file.

TUTORIAL

SELECTIVE BLURRING VIDEO TUTORIAL

To learn more about this technique and to see how to create the effect shown in Figure 13.3, watch the video included on the companion CD-ROM in the Video/Chapter 13/Blurring Noise movie.mov.

ON THE CD

Noise Reduction in Lab Mode

As discussed in Chapter 3, "How a Digital Camera Works," Lab mode stores your image as three channels: a Luminance channel and two color channels. Just as you can attack the separate Red, Green, and Blue channels of an RGB image, Lab mode lets you selectively de-noise the color information in your image independent of the luminance. Converting to Lab mode, and back again, does result in a tiny bit of quality loss, but this loss will not be perceptible until you change modes a dozen times or so.

To reduce noise in Lab mode:

1. First, convert your image to Lab by choosing Image>Mode>Lab color.
2. In the Channels palette, switch to the A & B channel.
3. Use a Smart or Gaussian Blur (or any of the averaging filters discussed previously) to attack the noise (Figure 13.5).
4. Now, switch back to RGB.

FIGURE 13.5   If you convert your image to Lab mode, you can attack the color information in your image independently of the lightness or detail of your image.

Using Photoshop's History palette, you can easily jump back to the Blur operation to try different settings. This method of noise reduction often tends to reduce saturation in your image. Once you get back into RGB mode, you can use Hue/Saturation to try to restore lost saturation.

Noise Reduction with a Luminance Copy

In the previous method, we eliminated noise by blurring the color channels independently of the Luminance information. There's another way to do the same thing without having to convert your image to Lab mode.

1. Using Photoshop's Layers palette, duplicate your image by dragging it to the New Layer button at the bottom of the palette. You now have two identical copies stacked on top of each other (Figure 13.6).
2. Use the Blending pop-up menu at the top of the Layers palette to set the blending mode to Luminosity. With this mode, the hue and saturation of the lower layer is preserved, while all luminance information

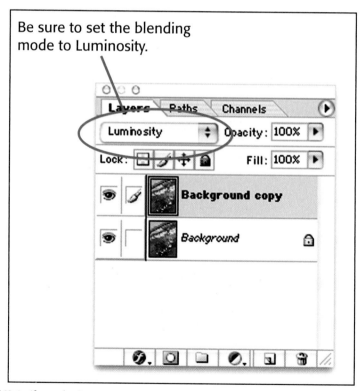

FIGURE 13.6 If you don't want to convert your image to Lab mode, you can target just the color in your image by using the Luminosity blending mode between two identical layers.

comes from the top copy. Luminance equates to brightness, which is a measure of contrast. Therefore, the detail in your image will come from the top layer, while the color will come from the bottom.

3. Now apply a blur filter to the lower layer to eliminate the noise. Because your contrast information is coming from your upper, unblurred layer, your noise-reducing blur shouldn't soften the details in your image.

A quick click on Undo after you apply your Blur filter makes it easy to go back and try different blur settings.

Using Third-Party Utilities to Eliminate Noise

Several programs are specifically designed to eliminate noise. If your camera produces conspicuously noisy images, or if your application demands that your images be very low in noise, then it might be worth an investment in one of these applications.

- **QImage Pro.** If you're a Windows user, you're in luck! QImage Pro is one of the best image editing utilities available for any platform. In addition to excellent noise reduction tools, QImage provides extraordinary white balance correction, sharpening, cataloging, color correction, and batch processing tools.

- **Quantum Mechanic.** Mac and Windows users have an excellent tool in Quantum Mechanic, a Photoshop plug-in that provides excellent noise, artifact, and moiré removal tools.

Dark Frame Subtraction

In Chapter 8, "Manual Exposure," you learned about shooting for dark frame subtraction, a method of removing the excess noise that can happen with long exposures. As you'll recall, on very long exposures (greater than one second), some pixels in your camera's sensor can get stuck "on," appearing as bright white specks in your final image (Figure 13.7). Unfortunately, because your camera interpolates the color of each pixel by examining the color of the surrounding pixels, one stuck pixel can adversely affect the color of several adjacent pixels. Some newer cameras have special *pixel mapping* features that search the image sensor for bad pixels. These pixels are then excluded from the camera's color processing algorithms.

Whether or not your camera has a pixel mapping feature, you can minimize the effects of stuck pixels by using the following technique. In Chapter 8, you learned that when shooting exposures over one second you should shoot a separate frame immediately following the first image, using the exact same exposure settings, but with the lens cap on. The idea is to take a second image of only the noise that appears in the first image.

For that second frame to be useful, you now need to subtract it from the first frame. This won't eliminate the noise from your image, but it will replace the distracting bright white specks with less distracting darker specks.

Open both your image and your corresponding dark frame. Copy the dark frame and paste it into a new layer in your image file. Give the dark frame a slight Gaussian Blur and set its blending mode to Difference. This should remove much of the noise from your image (Figure 13.7).

FIGURE 13.7   The noise in the first image was reduced using the Dark Frame Subtraction technique. Many cameras now offer a "Long Exposure Noise Reduction" facility that performs this operation in-camera.

Removing Dust and Blotches

If you have a digital camera with removable lenses, it is possible for dust to get to your camera's sensor. Sensor dust will appear as dark blotches or spots on your final image. Check your manual for instructions on cleaning your sensor (don't just assume that you can blast it with compressed air!).

Sensor dust sometimes looks just like the artifacts that appear when you have dust on your lens. The easiest way to determine if the problem is with your sensor is to change the lens on your camera. If the artifact is still there, you know it has nothing to do with your lens.

Sometimes, no matter what type of digital camera you have, a pixel or two on the CCD can go bad. If one of the pixels in your camera's sensor dies, your images will consistently have a white or blue spot at the location of the bad pixel (Figure 13.8).

FIGURE 13.8   This image was shot with a Canon PowerShot S100 Digital Elph that, unfortunately, has a bad pixel.

Unfortunately, there's nothing you can do to fix the camera, and most vendors won't replace or repair a camera with only one or two bad pixels. However, just like dirt or smears, you can quickly remove these erroneous pixels with your image editor's clone tool, by simply cloning from the immediately surrounding area (Figure 13.9).

FIGURE 13.9   A quick retouching with a clone tool, and the bad pixel is gone. Also note that we were able to clone away the horizontal lens flare.

TUTORIAL   **CLONING VIDEO TUTORIAL**

To learn more about cloning, watch the Cloning video in the Video/Chapter 12 Folder on the companion CD-ROM.

ON THE CD

CORRECTING BARREL AND PINCUSHION DISTORTION

Barrel and pincushion distortions are simple geometric distortions that occur in images shot with extreme wide-angle or telephoto lenses. If you had to zoom way out when you were shooting your image, then there's a good chance that the lines in your image will be bowed outward. Conversely, if your lens was zoomed in all the way, there's a chance that your image will be bowed inward. If you're using a wide-angle or fisheye attachment on your lens, your images will almost certainly be distorted (unless you're using a very expensive *rectilinear* wide-angle lens on a digital SLR).

These distortions don't occur in all lenses—in fact, the lack of them is the mark of a very good lens. In the following tutorial, you'll see how to correct a simple barrel distortion.

TUTORIAL

CORRECTING BARREL DISTORTION

Your lens might not have a big problem with barrel or pincushion distortion and, even if it does, the distortion might not be visible on all images. Sometimes, if the distortion is slight, it can be hidden by other curves and geometry within the image. Usually, you'll spot the distortion in architectural photos or other images that have very obvious horizontal and vertical lines. In this tutorial, you'll correct an image that was shot with an Olympus C2100UZ. With the lens zoomed out to full wide, the image barreled just a little bit.

STEP 1: OPEN THE IMAGE

ON THE CD

Open the image graphwall.jpg, located on the companion CD-ROM in the Tutorials/Chapter 13/Correcting Barrel Distortion folder. Barrel distortion is easy to spot in this image because of the horizontal and vertical lines painted on the wall of the building. Nevertheless, the distortion is slight, so it's a good idea to create some guides to help in our adjustments.

STEP 2: CREATE GUIDE LINES

To make it easier to gauge the effects of your correction, it's a good idea to create some simple vertical and horizontal guide lines. Choose View>Show Rulers to display Photoshop's rulers at the top and left side of your document.

Click in the top ruler and drag to pull down a guide line. Drop it along the top horizontal line on the wall.

Next, click on the left ruler and drag to the right to place a vertical guide on the left side of the building. With these guide lines in place, all you have to do is correct your image until the painted lines on the wall match up with your guide lines (Figure 13.10).

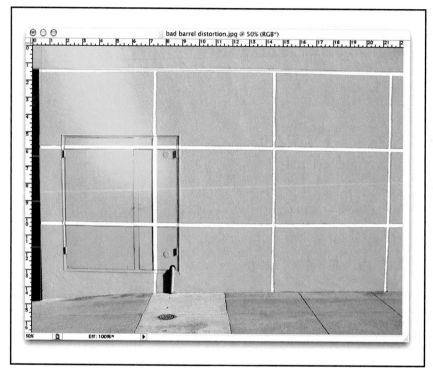

FIGURE 13.10   To begin to correct the barrel distortion in this image, we first add some guide lines to more clearly see true vertical and horizontal.

STEP 3: EXPAND YOUR CANVAS

To correct this distortion, we're going to use a filter that will cause the image to distort to a size that's larger than the current image's canvas size. Therefore, before you can start correcting the image, you need to add a little working room.

With the background color set to white, choose Image>Canvas Size, and set the Width to 10 inches and the Height to 8 inches. This is more canvas than you need, but you can always crop it later.

STEP 4: CORRECT THE IMAGE

Photoshop's Spherize filter can apply a bulging, spherical distortion to your image. Fortunately, it can also create a depressed, bowl-like effect that is ideal for correcting barrel distortion. If you look closely at the graph wall image, you'll see that the distortion radiates from the center of the image in a spherical fashion. You'll also notice that the distortion gets worse toward the edges of the image.

Open the Spherize filter—choose Filter>Distort>Spherize (Figure 13.11).

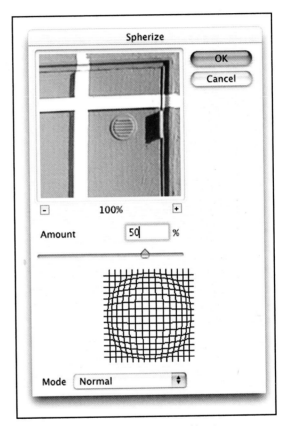

FIGURE 13.11   Photoshop's Spherize filter is a great tool for correcting barrel distortion.

The Spherize filter is very simple. Simply enter a value for the amount of spherification that you want to apply. Positive percentages will cause the image to bulge outward, while negative values will bow the image inward. In other words, positive values will add barrel distortion, while negative values will create pincushion distortion. You're simply going to use the Spherize filter's pincushioning ability to reduce the barrel distortion in the image.

How much spherizing to apply is simply a matter of trial and error. Enter a value of –50 and click OK. Figure 13.12 shows the results.

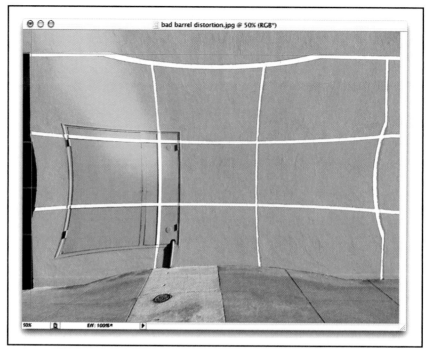

FIGURE 13.12   Well, the image doesn't have any barrel distortion anymore. Apparently, though, our Spherize value was too high.

STEP 5: TRY AGAIN

Obviously, –50 is way too much, but now you should have a good idea of what the filter does. Click Undo and open the Spherize filter again. Let's try something less extreme. This time, enter –10.

Check out the results and you'll probably find that this effect is still a little strong. Keep experimenting, but be sure to examine the entire image when you evaluate your results. Don't just look at the guide lines. You want to find a setting that provides the best results overall, not just a correction along the two guide lines.

A Spherize setting of –6 is probably about right.

STEP 6: CROP

As you can see, the spherizing effect has changed the shape of the image. Click on the Crop tool in the main Tools palette and crop off the curved edges of the image (Figure 13.13).

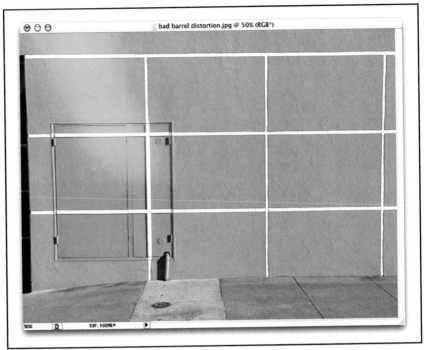

FIGURE 13.13   With a tiny bit of spherizing, and a little bit of cropping, our distortion is gone.

You can correct pincushion distortion in the same way; just use positive values in your Spherize command to add barrel distortion.

COLOR AND TONE ADJUSTMENT

After scrubbing the noise off your image and correcting any optical distortions, you're ready to move on to the correcting the image's color and contrast.

As you saw in the last two chapters, a good image editor provides color correction tools that pack incredible power. However, none of these tools is a "magic bullet" that can fix your image in one shot. Although you might, ideally, like to correct an image with a single, well-crafted Curves adjustment, the reality is that you'll often have to apply several different types of adjustments and corrections to get your image adjusted to your liking.

In the following tutorial, you'll take all of the color correction and masking skills that you learned in the last chapter and apply them to the color correction of an image.

TUTORIAL   COLOR CORRECTION

Figure 13.14 shows a picture of a bald eagle. Although it's an okay image, the picture has some color troubles. First, the "bald" white color of the eagle's head has gone blue. In fact, most of the white tones in the image have gone blue. The file's EXIF information (see Chapter 8) reveals that the image was shot with a Daylight white balance setting. Given that the scene was plainly shadowed, it's obvious that we're facing a bad white balance. Unfortunately, the daylight setting has emphasized the blue of the shadows.

FIGURE 13.14   Because of a white balance problem, this bald eagle really looks a little more blue than bald. In this tutorial, we'll restore the white of his feathers, and make some other adjustments to make him stand out more from the background.

In addition to the color troubles, the bright colors in the background slightly overpower the black and white of the eagle, so we'll want to tone down the background colors. Finally, the image is a bit underexposed and so it will need some black and white point adjustments.

STEP 1: OPEN THE IMAGE

ON THE CD

Open the image eagle.tif, located on the companion CD-ROM, in the Tutorials/Chapter 13/Color Correction folder.

STEP 2: REMOVE THE BLUE CAST

Let's begin by removing the blue cast caused by the bad white balance. We want to begin here in order to have the color as accurate as possible before we begin adjusting white and black points, or before trying to assess the foreground/background troubles.

It's pretty easy to see that this image is too blue. There are a number of ways to handle this problem. We could use a Curves or Levels adjustment targeted at the Blue channel, but we're going to use Photoshop's Hue/Saturation tool, simply because it's very easy to use in a situation like this, where the offending color is so easily identified.

From Photoshop 7's Layers palette, create a new Hue/Saturation adjustment layer. (See Figure 12.19 for a description of Photoshop's Layers palette.)

To remove a color using Hue/Saturation, we first need to target the color. From the Edit pop-up menu at the top of the Hue/Saturation dialog box, select Blues. The color ramp at the bottom of the dialog box will show you the range of colors that Hue/Saturation will target. As you can see, the default target is a little darker than the blues that we're facing. We need a lighter blue.

Move your mouse over the eagle—your pointer should change to an Eyedropper—and click somewhere on the white of the eagle's head in an area that is too blue (Figure 13.15).

The color selector should slide further down the left of the color ramp. The leftmost read-out should read approximately 178°/208°. You have now targeted the proper range of blues in the image.

To remove those blues, simply drag the Saturation slider to the left. A desaturation of about –81 should be all you need. You want to be careful about going too far, as you might posterize some of the bluish tones a little too much.

As you desaturate the blues, the eagle's head will probably darken in tone slightly. Remember, your operation has simply changed the color of those pixels from a heavily blue-hued color to a lightly blue-hued color. In this case, the new light blue color is a little darker than the dark blue color that was there before. To lighten the eagle's head back up a bit, drag the Lightness slider to the right to about +16. Click OK.

That pretty much takes care of the blue. Our bald eagle now looks, well, bald (Figure 13.16).

FIGURE 13.15 Selecting a color range in the Hue/Saturation dialog box.

FIGURE 13.16 After our blue correction adjustment, our eagle is closer to being the right color. His white feathers now appear white instead of light blue.

STEP 3: DESATURATE THE BACKGROUND

The background is still a little too colorful for the black-and-white eagle in the foreground. Let's use another Hue/Saturation layer to desaturate the background.

With your last Hue/Saturation layer selected, create another Hue/Saturation adjustment layer. New layers are created above the currently selected layer, and we want the layers in this image to stack up on top of each other. In other words, we don't want to insert a layer between the background and our first adjustment layer. This time, leave the Edit pop-up menu set to Master to desaturate everything, not just a particular color range. Drag the Saturation slider down to about –61 to drain the color out of the background.

Unfortunately, this will also drain the color out of the eagle, rendering the entire image a little flat. To protect the eagle from the effects of this adjustment layer, you need to mask him. Choose Layer>Add Layer Mask>Reveal All and the mask will be selected for painting.

Click on a big paintbrush, select Black as your foreground color, and begin painting over the eagle. Each brush stroke will appear to brush in more saturated color. This is because each brush stroke is actually *masking out* the adjustment layer's desaturation effect. As you paint, you should also see a thumbnail of your mask appear in the layer mask thumbnail of the Layers palette (Figure 13.17).

After masking, your eagle should be back to his normal level of saturation. This looks better, but now the background looks washed out and the entire image is a little flat. Let's darken the background to lend more weight to the foreground and to boost its colors back up a bit.

STEP 4: ADJUST THE LEVELS OF THE BACKGROUND

Create a Levels adjustment layer (make sure it's the topmost layer) and drag the middle input slider to set the gamma to about 5 (Figure 13.18).

Unfortunately, because the Levels adjustment is affecting the entire layer, it's difficult to see what is a proper adjustment. Add a layer mask to your Levels adjustment layer and paint out the eagle, just as you did in Step 3.

With the eagle masked, double-click on the Levels adjustment layer in the Layers palette to re-open the Levels dialog box. Now you can readjust the levels without affecting the eagle. Try a gamma adjustment of around .7. Click OK when you're finished.

STEP 5: ADJUST THE WHITE POINT AND BLACK POINT

Now that you have the color and contrast right, you can look at brightening the whole image. Add another Levels adjustment layer—this time with no

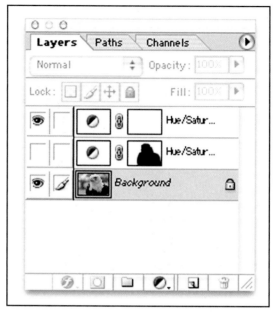

FIGURE 13.17 Photoshop's Layers palette after painting a mask.

FIGURE 13.18 Eagle image with Levels adjustments before any Levels masking information is applied. Without a mask, the Levels adjustment is affecting the entire image.

mask—and adjust the levels to your taste. We used a black point (the leftmost input slider) of 9, gamma (the middle slider) of 1.14, and white point (the rightmost slider) of 229. Click OK when you're finished (Figure 13.19).

FIGURE 13.19   The final eagle image after color correction.

As you can see, performing even simple color corrections on an image can often take several color correction functions filtered through a variety of masks. It's also important to think about the stacking order of your adjustment layers. For example, if you move the first Levels layer you created *below* either of the Hue/Saturation layers, your image will get darker because it will be operating on colors before they've been desaturated.

TUTORIAL

COLOR CORRECTION VIDEO TUTORIAL

The preceding tutorial showed you how to use a variety of color correction techniques to correct bad color in an image. However, you'll often want to color correct to simply improve good color that's already there. In fact, sometimes the color in your image might be fine by one criteria, but not what you had intended when you shot.

In the Color Correction video located in the Video/Chapter 13 folder on the companion CD-ROM, you'll learn how to color correct a decent-looking image to make it look better (Figure 13.20).

FIGURE 13.20   The top image doesn't look bad, but with some subtle color corrections, we can make it look much better. To learn how, watch the Color Correction video on the CD-ROM.

In this video, you'll see how to use the non-destructive editing techniques that you've been learning to improve the overall color of the image, and to make the image more dramatic by emphasizing some highlights and shadows. As you'll see, photo editing often has as much to do with painting as it does with photography.

Removing Red-Eye

Because of their small size, many digital cameras are particularly prone to *red-eye*, that demonic look that can appear in your subject's eyes when the flash from your camera has bounced off their retinas and back into the camera's lens. Although there are ways to avoid red-eye when you shoot (see Chapter 7, "Shooting"), there will still be times when you will face this problem in an image and need to remove it.

There are several effective methods for removing red eye. Which one to use depends mainly on the capabilities of your image editing software.

- **Use a red-eye removal filter or tool.** Many editing programs include special tools and filters for automatically removing red-eye. Although Photoshop 7 lacks such a tool, Photoshop Elements includes a very good red-eye removal tool. There are also some third-party plug-ins for performing red-eye removal.
- **Desaturate the red area**. Since it's the pupil that turns red, and pupils are usually black or very dark brown, simply desaturating the red area will drain it of color and restore it to its normal dark tone. Select the affected area and then use your desaturation method of choice. In Photoshop, you can use the Sponge tool or the Hue/Saturation dialog.
- **Copy the blue channel information.** As with the previous technique, use your selection method of choice to select the red area of your subject's eye. With the selection made, switch to the blue channel and copy, and then switch to the red channel and paste. Because the blue channel contains good data, it's okay to simply paste it into the red channel.
- **Repaint the area by hand**. If there's any natural color visible in your subject's eyes, you can try to select it with the eyedropper tool and repaint the rest of the area with a paintbrush or pencil tool. This is probably the most difficult technique because you will need to be careful to preserve any highlights or catchlights in the subject's eyes. An eye without a glint of light does not look natural. Examine some non-red-eye flash photos to see what this highlight should look like.

Removing Color Fringing

In Chapter 8 you read about weird purple and fringing artifacts that can occur in 2-and 3-megapixel cameras when you shoot high-contrast areas with a wide-angle lens. Although opinions sometimes differ as to what causes these problems, everyone agrees that the results are ugly! Fortunately, there are several methods you can use to eliminate these weird color fringes.

Desaturating Fringe

Most fringing artifacts can be eliminated with a simple Hue/Saturation adjustment layer. The idea is to simply target the color of the fringe and drain the saturation out of it to make it blend better with the background. The trick is to not alter any of the other color in your image.

TUTORIAL DESATURATING A CHROMATIC ABERRATION

Open the image Palace.jpg, located in the Tutorials/Chapter 13/Desaturating aC.Abb. folder on the companion CD-ROM. The chromatic aberrations are not terrible, but they are there. Look between the two rightmost columns and you'll see a nasty red fringe on the left side of the right column, and a bad green fringe on the right side of the left column (Figure 13.21).

FIGURE 13.21 This image suffers from some bad fringing artifacts. In this tutorial, we'll remove them with some simple painting techniques.

Although the fringes aren't huge, the predominant colors in the image are red and green, so you'll have to be careful when you remove the extra colors.

STEP 1: SELECT THE FIRST FRINGE

Using the Marquee or Lasso tool, select the rightmost, red fringe. You don't have to be really precise in this selection (Figure 13.22); your main goal is to protect the other red tones in the image.

FIGURE 13.22   Select the area of bad red fringe in the image.

STEP 2: CREATE A HUE/SATURATION ADJUSTMENT LAYER

With your selection active, use the Layers palette to create a new Hue/Saturation adjustment layer. Notice that the Layers palette shows your adjustment layer with a layer mask that matches your selection.

STEP 3: TARGET THE OFFENDING COLORS

Now you need to select the colors of the fringe. To do this, you'll need to zoom in to your document to see some individual pixels. Press Command-+ (Control-+ in Windows) a few times to zoom in to 200%. Because the fringe is kind of a pinkish red, you want to limit the effects of the adjustment to reds. Select Reds from the Edit pop-up menu at the top of the Hue-Saturation dialog box.

Now you need to sample the color of the fringe in the image. Using the eyedropper, select one of the very light-colored pink dots within the fringe. The color selection scale will shift to the left to encompass the color that you sampled. Because the palace columns contain a lot of red, you want to narrow your red selection so as to not desaturate the columns. The color selection scale has four sliding controls, two on the left and two on the right. The inner sliders control the range of colors to select, while the outer controls create a color selection drop-off to ensure smooth color shifts.

Slide all four sliders inward to create a very tight color selection (Figure 13.23).

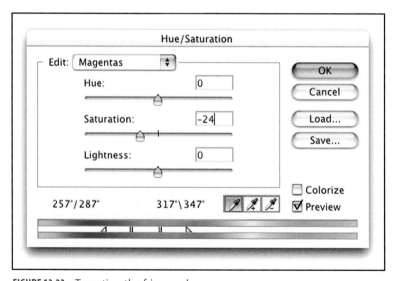

FIGURE 13.23   Targeting the fringe color.

STEP 4: DESATURATE THE FRINGE

Now, drag the Saturation slider to the left to drain some of the saturation out of the selected red tones. As they lose saturation, they might turn gray. If so, try backing off on the desaturation by moving the Saturation slider back to the right, and instead add a little lightening by moving the Lightness slider to the right.

STEP 5: TARGET MORE COLORS

Although the image is probably looking better, there's still most likely a lot of red or pink. You want to now expand the target color range. Click on the middle eyedropper, the one with the + next to it, and click on some of the remaining fringe colors. This will add these colors to the range of colors that is being desaturated. You might have to go deep into the shadows of the columns to get all of the colors. You might also have to adjust your Saturation and Lightness settings after you select more colors.

STEP 6: CHECK THE RESULTS

When you're finished, click OK, and zoom out to check the results. In addition to looking at the quality of the fringe reduction, look closely at the surrounding area of your selection to ensure that you haven't inadvertently desaturated any other parts of the column. If there is still visible fringing, double-click on the adjustment layer to tweak your settings.

When you're all done, do the same with the other fringe, but this time target the greens.

This approach will work for most chromatic aberrations, although you need to be careful. Sometimes the color of your aberration will very closely match the background of your image. For example, you'll frequently run into blue aberrations against a blue sky. Be sure to select and feature your aberration first, to protect the rest of the sky. You'll also probably want to do less desaturation and more lightening to match the hue of the fringe to the sky.

Removing Chromatic Aberration by Hand

Sometimes your aberrations might be bad enough that you simply need to go in and paint them out using a paintbrush or clone tool. With the Clone tool, you can clone in color from the surrounding area, but you'll need a steady hand. Use a very soft-edged brush and set the opacity low. Using a paintbrush is a similar process, but you'll need to sample the paint color by hand using the Eyedropper tool.

You can also use the Blur tool to blur a fringe out of existence. Set the Blur tool's opacity very low—around 15 to 20%—and change its mode to Color. Brush along the fringe and you should see it slowly fade away.

Removing Fringes by Shrinking Channels

Fringes are often very pure red, green, or blue colors. Consequently, they're often confined to an individual color channel. If you examine your individual channels and find this to be true, you can always go in and edit the channels directly.

Fringes sometimes look just like a mis-registration from a printing press. That is, if your image has red fringing, it can often appear as if the Red channel has slipped out of registration with the Blue and Green channels. It hasn't, but you can try to correct it using the same procedures you would use to fix a mis-registration.

1. Select the offending color channel.
2. Shrink it to "scoot" the fringe under the other color channels. You can do this by choosing Edit>Transform>Numeric and entering a tiny value—99.7 or 99.8, for example. This will reduce the size of the channel and hopefully hide the aberration.

After shrinking a channel, be sure to examine your image closely for any new artifacts that might have been introduced by the transformation. In particular, make sure no new fringing has developed in other parts of the image.

Adjusting Tonal Range with Layers

You can also improve the tonal range of an image by stacking a duplicate of the image and using a special blending mode. For example, if you have an underexposed image that lacks punch, duplicate its layer. Then, set the blending mode of the upper copy to Screen. The blending should help boost the tone of the image.

Similarly, if you have an image that's overexposed, stack a second copy and set the blending mode to Multiply (Figure 13.24). If you want to know more about what these transfer modes are doing, Photoshop's Help file has full descriptions.

Correcting White Balance

In Chapter 11, "Correcting Tone and Color," you learned how to use Levels and Curves controls to correct color in an image, and even used the controls to correct an image with an incorrect white balance. There's no set method or rule for correcting a bad white balance, as each situation is unique. Levels, Curves, and Hue/Saturation adjustments will usually be your best tools for white balance correction, and each image will usually have its own correction needs.

In general, though, there are some guidelines to follow when correcting white balance.

FIGURE 13.24   We can make the sky in this panorama much more dramatic by duplicating the base layer and setting the duplicate's blending mode to Multiply.

- **Don't expect to be able to use a single correction to fix a bad white balance.** Although white balance usually affects all areas of an image, it often affects one color range (highlights or midtones, for example) more than another. You might need to use separate adjustments for each color range in your image.
- **Use masks to isolate areas for corrections.** If the color in one area of your image is particularly off, you might have to mask it off and apply a strong color correction to fix it.
- **Don't expect to restore accurate color.** Although you can greatly improve the white balance of an image, you probably won't be able to restore absolute color accuracy. In addition to changes in hue, you'll probably find that it's difficult to achieve full brightness in your colors.

As you might have guessed, the best way to achieve good white balance is when you're shooting. For those, hopefully rare, times when your images are poorly white balanced, the preceding tips should help you on your way to restoring proper color.

Correcting Vignetting

Hopefully, you kept an eye out for *vignetting* when you went shopping for a camera. If not, you'll probably need to develop a method for removing this darkening of the corners of your image (Figure 13.25).

FIGURE 13.25   This image suffers from vignetting, a darkening of the corners.

The easiest way to handle vignetting is to build a mask that mimics the darkening in your image. You can then apply a Levels filter through mask to compensate for the darkening. It might take some time to refine your mask, but once you have one that works, you can probably re-use it for any image with vignetting problems.

You can paint a vignette mask by hand using a large airbrush or a very soft-edged paintbrush, or a gradient tool. Alternatively, you can use a selection tool such as Photoshop's Pen tool or Lasso tool to outline the edges of your vignette corners. Then, apply a strong feather to your selection to fade its edge.

Once you're satisfied with your selection, save it as an alpha channel (Figure 13.26). With your mask still selected, create a Levels adjustment layer and try to lighten the vignettes. If your mask needs adjustment, throw out the adjustment layer, edit your mask, and start over.

FIGURE 13.26   If you have trouble with vignetting, consider building a mask that matches your camera's vignette, like the one shown on the left. By applying a Levels filter to the mask, you can usually correct the darkened corners of your image.

Once you have a mask that works, you can copy it into any image that has a vignetting problem.

SATURATION ADJUSTMENT

Once you've made all of your color adjustments—which you'll typically do with Levels or Curves controls—you'll want to consider a separate pass to adjust saturation. Why not adjust saturation at the same time that you're correcting tone and color? Because it's difficult to change saturation using Levels and Curves and because you don't know what your saturation concerns will be until you've corrected your image and arrived at your final colors.

The easiest way to adjust saturation—whether increasing or decreasing—is through the Hue/Saturation control, which can be applied as a straight, destructive filter, or as an adjustment layer.

When you correct saturation, keep an eye out for posterization and be aware that your monitor can produce images that are much more saturated than what your printer can print. As with color correction, you'll want to make test prints and, ideally, use your color management software to keep an eye on your final results. Increasing saturation is usually the easiest way to push colors out of the printable range of your printer.

Increasing Contrast and Saturation with Layer Stacking

There's another way to increase contrast and saturation without using an adjustment layer or correction function. By stacking and blending copies of an image, you can build up saturation in color images, and contrast in grayscale images (Figure 13.27).

FIGURE 13.27 By duplicating an image layer and setting the Blending mode of the copy to Soft Light, you can create a much higher-contrast image.

To create the effect in Figure 13.27, we duplicated our base layer and set its Blending mode to Soft Light. We then dialed down the opacity to control the degree of saturation increase. Now, just as in an adjustment layer, we can go in and erase or mask parts of the image to control the application of an effect.

Why use this approach over a Saturation command? Because in color images you often get a nice alteration of hues in addition to an increase in saturation.

Decreasing Contrast and Saturation with Layer Stacking

If you want to decrease the saturation of an image, either because your camera goes a little too "hot" on some colors or because you simply prefer muted tones, you can perform a trick similar to the one just discussed.

Create a new layer and fill it with a color. Change its Blending mode to Soft Light or Hard Light, and adjust its opacity to control the intensity of the effect. Depending on the color you choose for your desaturation layer, you can tone or cast the colors in your base image at the same time that you're desaturating them. For even stranger, more pronounced effects, experiment with the other blending modes.

EDITING

Your image is cleaned, your colors are adjusted, and you now have an image that is perfect raw material for your artistic license. Now is the time when you'll begin to create any composites or collages, or any radical touch-ups. Since you know that you've already removed any color fringes or other image artifacts, you can perform all of your artistic edits without concern of duplicating artifacts.

There's also a good chance that the edits you perform are going to lead you to create many new layers in your document. Color correcting can be much more complex when different elements are on different layers, which is just one more reason why it's good to get those operations out of the way (Figure 13.28).

However, after your edits, you might find that you need to tweak your color correction settings or perform another color correction pass to blend and smooth out your edits.

In the next chapter, you'll explore many of the things that might transpire in this editing stage, from compositing to adding texture and tone to your image. For now, let's concentrate on the remaining steps of your image editing workflow.

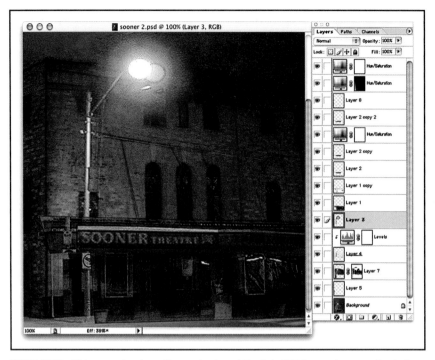

FIGURE 13.28 This complex, heavily manipulated Coolpix 950 image is comprised of over 16 layers, each of which isolates an individual color correction or painted object. This layered approach makes for easier edits and revisions.

SCALING

There are many reasons why you might need to resize your image, and in Chapter 10, "Preparing Your Images for Editing," we discussed the differences in sampling and resampling when scaling. In most cases, it's good to save the scaling step until after you've completed your color corrections and edits because you don't want to enlarge your image if it's full of noise and color artifacts—you'll end up enlarging those along with the image.

If you're stuck working on a low-resolution image, let's say 640 × 480, you might want to enlarge your image some before you start editing because you might need some extra pixels to perform your painting and editing tasks.

When you're finished with all of your edits and adjustments, you'll probably need to change the resolution and size of your image to something more appropriate for your printer (see Chapter 15, "Output"). If your final destination is the Web, you'll definitely need to scale your image down, assuming that you were shooting at one of your camera's higher resolutions.

You'll need to scale up if your image came out of your camera smaller than you'd like to print. You might also need to scale the image up if you're printing to a printer that demands higher resolution. Although your image editor can do a good job of scaling an image up, you can only go so far. Use the following tips for best results.

Scaling Down

If your images need to be output to the Web, video, or for display on a computer, then they most certainly will need to be scaled down, or *down-sampled*.

Downsampling is a fairly worry-free process because your computer is throwing data *away* rather than having to make it up. About the only thing you need to know when you downsample an image for use is what size, in pixels, the final product should be.

Talk to your designer, Webmaster, producer, or whomever is responsible for your final graphics (if you're responsible, then you're on your own) and find out the desired pixel dimensions of your final image.

From Photoshop's Image Size dialog box, check the Resample Image checkbox, enter a Resolution of 72 pixels per inch, and enter your desired pixel dimensions in the Pixel Dimensions fields. Click OK, and then choose File>Save As to save a *copy* of your smaller file with a new filename (be sure to type in a new name or you might overwrite your original!). You never know if you'll need a bigger image someday, so it's a shame to throw away all that extra resolution by writing over your original file.

Scaling Up

As explained in Chapter 10, when you scale an image up, Photoshop has to interpolate new pixels to get the image up to your desired size. Fortunately, Photoshop's bicubic interpolation algorithm is very good at up-sampling images up to about one-and-a-half times their original size. After that, the results can be a little soft. Fortunately, with today's high-resolution cameras, you usually don't have to scale up too much to boost your image up to a fairly big print size.

To scale up, you need to know the target resolution of your printer (more on this in Chapter 15) and your desired print size. Open the Image Size dialog box, be sure that Resample Image is checked, enter the appropriate resolution in the Resolution field, and your desired print size in the

Document Size fields. Click OK, and Photoshop will calculate your new image.

As with sampling down, it's a good idea to save your new, larger image as a copy. Your original size image will be free of sampling artifacts, so you should save it for later use.

After scaling up, you might find that your image has softened somewhat. You'll get a chance to sharpen it in the next stage of the workflow. Poke around your image and look for any other artifacts that might have been exaggerated in the upsampling. In particular, look for *aliasing* (stairstepping) along diagonal lines, as well as exaggerations of any noise or aberrations that might have been left in the original image. These can be retouched using the techniques discussed earlier. Aliasing can usually be handled by brushing over the offending areas with a very small Blur tool.

Bear in mind that you often create a larger image because you want a picture that can be viewed from a greater distance. Consequently, super-fine detail is not so important. If you're creating a big image that will be viewed from several feet away, then be sure to evaluate your prints from several feet away. Don't get hung up on trying to see fine detail at close distance.

WHEN 1.5X ISN'T ENOUGH

Of course, there might be times when you need to blow up an image to colossal proportions. Although you can try pushing Photoshop's bicubic interpolation to larger sizes, you might be disappointed by the results. Fortunately, there are some other solutions.

AltaMira's Genuine Fractals PrintPro uses a technology called *wavelet compression* to convert your image from a series of raster dots into a collection of tiny fractal curves. Because fractals reveal more detail as you expand them, and because they can be mathematically enlarged (rather like vector artwork), you can blow up a wavelet-compressed image by fairly extreme factors.

AltaMira doesn't claim great results on images smaller than 2MB, and yet the program still does a very good job of enlarging digital camera images up to three or four times without great degradation. Wavelet compression can't perform miracles, though. After a point, if you need larger files, you'll have to upgrade to a higher-resolution camera.

SHARPENING

With everything else done and your image at its final output size, you're finally ready to apply any necessary sharpening. As with resizing, you don't want to sharpen too early, as you'll run the risk of accentuating noise and other unwanted artifacts. Moreover, you won't know how much sharpening you need until you've adjusted the image's contrast—after all, a more contrasty image looks sharper—and until you've resized the image. If you shrink an image, it's going to get sharper, while if you enlarge it, it will almost always get softer. Consequently, sharpening should be the last step you take before outputting the image.

Photoshop includes a number of sharpening filters. In addition to these, there are third-party sharpeners as well as procedural techniques you can use to sharpen your image. Unfortunately, Photoshop does not offer editable sharpening layers. Once you apply your sharpening effects, that's it. Consequently, it's a good idea to save a copy of your image before you sharpen, or to duplicate a layer before you sharpen it. By sharpening a duplicate, you can always throw it out and go back to your original if you change your mind.

Your biggest concern when you sharpen, however, is to not sharpen too much. Oversharpening can create a number of undesirable artifacts.

How Sharpening Works

Photoshop, like most image editors, has several sharpening filters: Sharpen, Sharpen More, Sharpen Edges, and Unsharp Mask can all be found under the Filter>Sharpen menu. However, the Unsharp Mask (USM) filter is the only one of these that you ever need to consider. The rest are simply too uncontrollable and destructive for quality sharpening.

Unsharp Mask gets its name from a darkroom sharpening technique wherein a blurry copy of a negative (an "unsharp" copy) is sandwiched with the original negative, and a print is made using a doubled exposure time. The unsharp mask negative and lengthened exposure time serves to darken the dark side of an edge and lighten the light side, causing the edge to exhibit a halo. This renders the edge more pronounced and the image appears sharper.

The USM filter works the same way. When you apply the filter, your image is examined one pixel at a time. Obviously, the filter can't really tell what counts as an edge in your image, so it looks for sudden changes in contrast. If there is a sudden change in value between two adjacent pixels, that's probably an edge. The darker pixel will be darkened and the pixels around it will be ramped down, while the lighter pixel will be lightened and the pixels around it ramped up.

If you look at an edge in an image that has had a USM filter applied, like the one in Figure 13.29, you'll see that one side of the edge is darker, while the other side is lighter. The result is a bit of a halo. As long as this halo isn't distractingly strong, the image will appear much sharper.

FIGURE 13.29   If you look closely at a sharpened image, you can see the halos that the Unsharp Mask process creates along the edges of shapes to make them appear sharper.

The key to good unsharp masking is to know when to quit. Too much sharpening and your image will appear unrealistically sharp, and the edge halos will be bright enough to be distracting.

Photoshop's Unsharp Mask tool provides three controls: Amount, Radius, and Threshold. (Figure 13.30). This is typical of USM controls, so even if you're using a different image editor, its unsharp mask tool probably offers the same options.

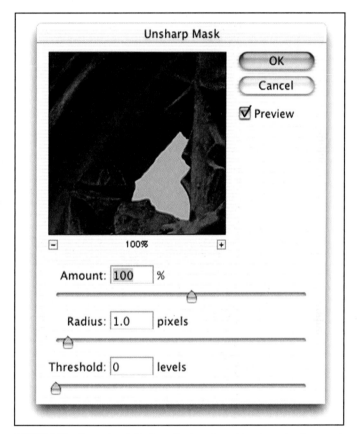

FIGURE 13.30   Photoshop's Unsharp Mask tool provides three simple controls for sharpening your images.

- **Amount** simply controls how much the pixels along an edge will be darkened and lightened. The higher the number, the more the USM filter will change the pixels. Too much of a change and your edge will become unnaturally contrasty and will possibly posterize.
- **Radius** determines the width of the halo that will be created. The wider the radius, the more pixels that will be altered around an edge to create a halo.

- **Threshold** determines what the filter will consider an edge. A higher threshold value requires more contrast between two pixels. With a high threshold, USM will find fewer edges and perform less sharpening.

To learn what makes good sharpening, it's worth spending some time looking at some professional photos. Notice that even images that have lots of detail and contrast are not necessarily razor sharp. Your image editor can actually sharpen an image far beyond what looks realistic (Figure 13.31). At the same time, your eyes like contrast, so it's good to add to add a little more sharpness.

FIGURE 13.31 Although it might seem like more sharpening is better, it is possible to oversharpen an image, resulting in an image with distracting edges that are too contrasty. Oversharpened images tend to have a "hyper-real" look.

When you use a USM filter, start with a high Amount setting—300 to 400% and a very small Threshold. Then, try to find a Radius that produces minimal halos (Figure 13.32). Sharpening is a subjective process, of course, so find a level of halo that suits you. However, be sure to consider your entire image.

Once you've found a Radius that is right, you can back off the Amount and increase the Threshold. Your goal is to use these two sliders to apply your desired radius to the appropriate amount of edge detail in your image.

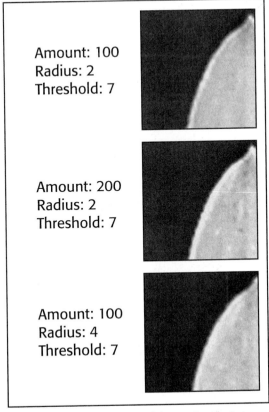

Amount: 100
Radius: 2
Threshold: 7

Amount: 200
Radius: 2
Threshold: 7

Amount: 100
Radius: 4
Threshold: 7

FIGURE 13.32   The right level of sharpening is a balance of all three Unsharp Mask parameters.

ALWAYS SHARPEN AT 100%

Be sure you're looking at your image at 100%, or 1:1, when sharpening. If you've zoomed out from your image, then your image editor is already downsampling its screen image. Sharpening might not be visible.

NOT ALL SHARPNESS IS CREATED EQUAL

Note that some subjects sharpen faster than others. Foliage, and small, very detailed background elements, for example, usually don't stand up to a good deal of sharpening. If these types of objects are mixed with flatter subjects with less detail, consider sharpening these elements separately. Build a mask to separate detailed objects from less complex shapes, and use different levels of sharpening for each. Obviously, you want a mask with a strong feather to ensure a smooth transition.

Similarly, although you might have gone through a lot of noise reduction earlier, there's a chance that shadow areas, skies, and other areas of flat color might still have some noise in them. Because you don't want to exaggerate this noise through sharpening, it's a good idea to mask these areas out before you sharpen.

You can also control the sharpening in your image by sharpening individual color channels. For example, if you have a noisy Blue channel, then leave it alone (or de-noise it, as explained earlier) and sharpen just the Red and Green channels.

Similarly, you can convert your image to Lab mode and sharpen just the L channel to protect any subtle color texture from oversharpening.

Going to the Web? Need small files? Go easy on the sharpening. If small file size is your highest concern, don't sharpen your images too much. As you sharpen, you increase contrast, which means that your files won't compress as small as they will if left a little soft.

Another technique is to upsample your image to about 150% of its regular size using a wavelet compression program such as Genuine Fractals. In Photoshop, apply a very strong Unsharp Mask and then use Genuine Fractals to downsample your image back to its regular size. This is a very aggressive form of sharpening that is not appropriate for most images. If you have a very soft image, though, you might give this method a try.

Shooting VGA and XGA? Don't bother sharpening. To produce lower-resolution VGA or XGA images, many cameras shoot at full-resolution and then downsample the image before storing it. Consequently, images at these resolutions are usually plenty sharp thanks to the camera's downsampling process.

Your sharpening goal at this point should simply be to get your image on-screen to the level of sharpening that you'd normally expect from a photo. Once you start printing, you might find that you need more sharpening (and occasionally, less sharpening). Because too much sharpening can wreck your image, it's a good idea to always apply sharpening to a copy of your image. If you make a mistake, you can always go back to your original.

MORE TOOLS TO COME

The tools and processes covered in this chapter are things you will return to often for all sorts of image adjustments. In the next chapter, we'll build on these tools to create special effects and retouchings.

14

SPECIAL EFFECTS

In This Chapter

- Simulating Depth of Field
- Stitching Panoramas
- Converting Color Images to Grayscale
- Creating "Hand-Tinted" Images
- Adding Texture, Grain, and "Film" Look

nitially, most of your image editing work centered around touching up and adjusting an image to correct problems caused by your camera, or to take advantage of exposure strategies that you might have chosen when you were shooting.

Your image editor is capable of much more than simple tonal corrections, of course. By now, you've probably already played with many of the filters and effects tools in your editing application, and have begun to see just how much you can manipulate an image.

In this chapter, you'll learn some of the typical special effects that, as a digital photographer, you might want to use and explore. The techniques herein should help you get started, and should provide you with a basic set of common special effects procedures. The lessons and examples in this chapter are not intended to help you create "trick photography" special effects. Rather, these techniques are intended to help you make up for deficiencies in your camera, to help you get good results from difficult shooting situations, and to help you make your images more "film-like."

SIMULATING DEPTH OF FIELD

To the experienced photographer, one of the most frustrating things about a typical digital camera is the limited depth of field. As you learned earlier, the tiny focal lengths on most prosumer cameras prohibit shallow depth of field effects. Fortunately, through some clever blurring, you can use your image editor to add a depth of field effect.

One of the most important things to remember about depth of field is that it is a *depth*. That is, the area in focus begins at one point and ends at another and is centered *around* the focal point of the image. A shallow depth of field doesn't simply mean that your background will be blurry; it can also mean that part of your foreground will be blurry. In addition, different planes in your background will be more or less blurry depending on how far away they are.

TUTORIAL   **SHORTENING DEPTH OF FIELD IN AN IMAGE**

Figure 14.1 shows an image with very deep depth of field—everything in the image is in focus. In this tutorial, we're going to create a very, very shallow depth of field that will blur both the foreground and background.

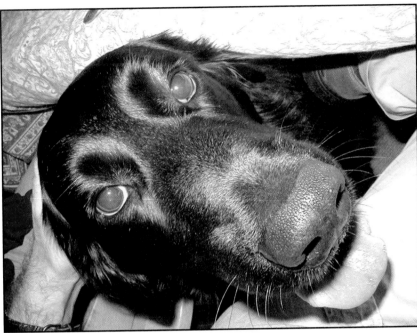

FIGURE 14.1   This image has a very deep depth of field. It's time to make it more shallow.

STEP 1: OPEN THE IMAGE

ON THE CD

Open the image cosmo.tif located in the Tutorials/Chapter 14/DOF folder on the companion CD-ROM. In any portrait, you want the eyes of your subject to be in focus, so we're going to use the dog's eyes as the focal point of this shot. Your goal is to create an effect like the one shown in Figure 14.2.

STEP 2: PREPARE A GRADIENT

The blurring effect is actually very easy; we'll simply use the Gaussian Blur filter. However, we want the blur to increase gradually in both directions as it extends away from our focal point. Consequently, we need to apply our blur filter through a mask.

In Photoshop's Channels palette, create a new channel by clicking on the New Channel button at the bottom of the palette. Our masking needs are very simple for this project. A simple gradient should be all that we need.

Type "D" on your keyboard to select black and white as your default foreground and background colors. Select the Gradient tool from Photoshop's main tool palette (or press G to select it). Click in the gradient sample on the

FIGURE 14.2 With some controlled blurring, we can create a shallow depth-of-field effect.

Photoshop toolbar to open the Gradient Editor. Figure 14.3 illustrates the settings you will need.

You want a gradient that goes from white to black to white. Click on the bottom left stop and change its color to white. Change the bottom right stop to black and drag it toward the center of the gradient. Now click on the right end of the gradient sample to create a third stop, and set its color to white. When you're finished, your gradient should like the one in Figure 14.3. Name the gradient, and click OK to save it.

STEP 3: APPLY THE GRADIENT TO YOUR MASK

With your new channel selected in the Channels palette, click on the eyeball icon next to the RGB channel in the Channels palette. This will allow you to see your full-color image, as well as your alpha channel in red (it's empty so you won't see any red yet, but once you start using the Gradient tool, things will change). Because the Alpha channel is selected (the RGB channels are only "eyeballed"), your actions will only affect your new alpha channel.

Drag the Gradient tool in a diagonal line from upper left to lower right to mask the dog's eyes. Your gradient will appear on-screen as a red tint over your image. Position your gradient so that it looks like Figure 14.4. It might take a few tries, but each time you drag with the Gradient tool, the new gradient will replace the old, so it's easy to quickly try many different gradients.

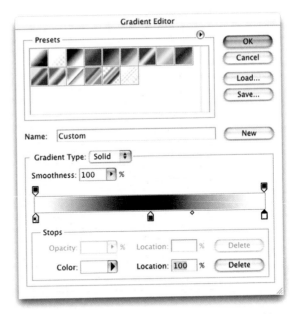

FIGURE 14.3   Use Photoshop's Gradient Editor to build a custom gradient.

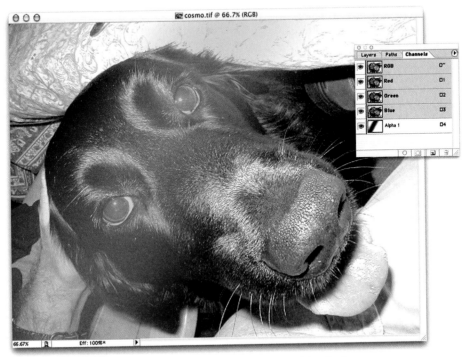

FIGURE 14.4   You want your gradient to blend into and out of the dog's eyes.

STEP 4: APPLY THE BLUR

Remember, at this point, nothing has been selected, you've only created a mask by painting a gradient directly into an alpha channel. Now click on the RGB channel to activate it and drag your new alpha channel to the Load Channel as Selection button at the bottom of the dialog box to load your alpha channel as a selection. Apply a Gaussian Blur filter by selecting Filter>Blur>Gaussian Blur. Enter a Radius of 7 pixels. The foreground and background of your image should go blurry.

Although the effect looks good, the hand in the background looks conspicuously in focus (Figure 14.5). It's on a deeper plane than the dog's eyes and so it should not be in focus. Undo the blur and click on your alpha channel in the Channels palette to select it. We're going to do a little mask alteration.

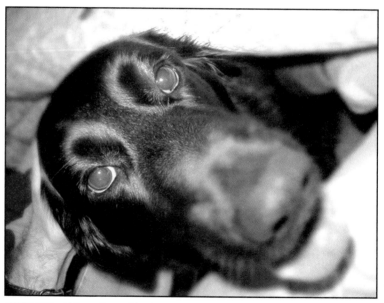

FIGURE 14.5   Although our blur is varying by the same amount, the hand and the dog's eyes are both in focus. Because the hand is actually farther away than the dog's eyes, it should be blurry.

STEP 5: ALTER YOUR MASK

Right now the hand is not being blurred because lies on the same line as our gradient—it is being masked. We want to unmask it so that it will blur. Click the eyeball next to the RGB channel in the Channels palette so that you can see your image and your mask.

The thumb is masked an appropriate amount; we just need to get the rest of the hand to match. Using the eyedropper, click on the thumb to sample its color. This is the color you'll use to paint the rest of your mask. Click on a paint-brush and paint over the hand, up until it bumps the dog. Use a very soft-edged brush.

When you're finished, click off the eyeball next to the RGB layer so that you can see just your mask. It should like something like Figure 14.6.

FIGURE 14.6   After editing, your new mask should look something like this.

STEP 6: APPLY YOUR FINAL BLUR

Load your new mask and re-apply your blur. Now your image should look something like Figure 14.2. With the hand blurred, the depth of field effect is much more realistic.

BLUE EYES?

The dog's eyes are blue because, just as human eyes reflect red when a flash fires directly into them, dog eyes reflect blue. To remove the blue eyes, add a Saturation Adjustment Layer, set it to desaturate completely, and paint a mask to limit the adjustment layer to only the dog's eyes (Figure 14.7).

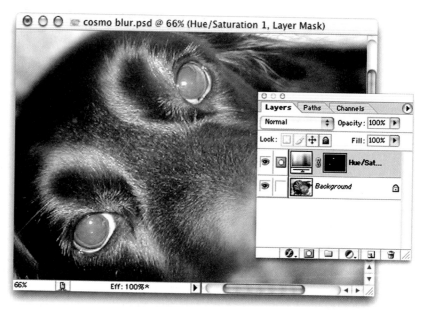

FIGURE 14.7 This dog is suffering from the canine equivalent of "red eye." You can attack the problem just as you would red eye in a human. Use a Desaturation Adjustment Layer to drain the blue color from his pupils.

Create Planes of Depth

Typically, when you choose to shoot with a shallow depth of field (if your camera is capable), the goal is to soften the background to bring more attention to the foreground.

If all of the objects in your background are a good distance behind your subject, then you can usually get away with simply blurring the entire background (Figure 14.8).

If, however, the background elements in your image recede gradually, or in definite planes, from your foreground subject, simply blurring the background will look odd. In Figure 14.9, the blurred background reduces the image to two planes of depth, the foreground and the blurred background. It almost looks as if the woman is standing in front of a blurry backdrop of a street. Because the background recedes into the distance, you need to control the *falloff* of the blur so that it gets stronger for objects that are farther away.

The top image in Figure 14.10 was created using a simple layering process:

FIGURE 14.8 Depth of field can be easily added to this image by blurring the background.

1. Duplicate the base layer (the layer to which you want to add the depth of field effect).
2. Apply a blur to the upper layer. Choose a blur that is appropriate for the farthest elements in your image.
3. Now add a layer mask to the upper layer that reveals the entire layer. Your image will appear blurry.
4. Using the Gradient tool and a paintbrush, mask the blur to reveal the underlying sharp image. In the case of Figure 14.10, a gradient was used to create a depth of field that gets stronger from right to left.

FIGURE 14.9 Simply blurring the background of this image looks odd, because everything in the background is equally defocused. Because the background recedes, the defocusing should increase with distance.

5. Unfortunately, the gradient blended the background tree and buildings by the same amount. In reality, the tree should appear closer (less blurry) than the buildings that are next to it in the image. A paintbrush loaded with 70% gray was used to paint over the tree in the layer mask. This resulted in the tree only getting 70% of the blur.

If your image has very distinct planes in the background, you can use separate layers for each plane, blurring each by different amounts, and building layer masks to reveal the appropriate parts of each layer.Stitching Panoramas

In Chapter 9," Special Shooting," you learned about panoramic images, multiple shots that can be stitched together to create wide, panoramic pictures. Good panoramas require some thought when you shoot, and they sometimes require a little image editing before stitching.

Your camera probably came with stitching software (Figure 14.11), but if it didn't—or if you're not happy with it—then consider a third-party alternative such as RealViz' Stitcher.

No matter what software you use, your images might need a little cleanup before you start stitching. Variations in exposure from one image to the next can cause color banding and shift in your final panorama.

FIGURE 14.10   This depth of field effect works much better because of the more complex, hand-painted mask. In addition to a receding sense of depth, objects at different planes are blurred appropriately.

Hopefully, you tried to compensate for this when you were shooting (see Chapter 9), but even the best laid plans sometimes end up incorrectly exposed.

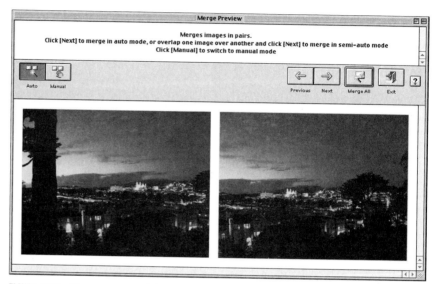

FIGURE 14.11 Many cameras ship with panoramic stitching software such as Canon's Photostitch.

Before you stitch, open up your panoramic shots and examine them for exposure differences. Are some images darker or lighter than others? Skies are particularly susceptible to saturation and hue changes from shot to shot. If you do see variations from one shot to the next, you'll need to color correct your images. Typically, Levels or Curves adjustments are all you'll need. When you correct, consider the following:

- Choose the image you like most as a base image, and correct your other images to match.
- If the first or last image is very over- or underexposed (which sometimes happens because the sun is in the first or last image), consider throwing it out altogether and creating a smaller panorama.
- If you're having trouble matching tones and color from one image to the next, try stitching and then performing corrections on the completed panorama.

Because you typically shoot panoramic images with a very wide-angle focal length, your individual images might suffer from barrel distortion. *Don't* try to correct this before stitching—let the stitching software worry about that.

In addition, don't worry about spotting or removing dust or other aberrations. It's better to do this after you've stitched the panorama.

Most stitching programs offer a combination of automatic and manual controls. If your images were well shot (and after reading Chapter 9, how could they not be?), then your program's automatic functions might be all you need. At other times, though, you might have to resort to manual control.

To use manual stitching controls, you simply find corresponding points within an image. These points are then used to guide the software's stitching efforts. Typically, you need to identify two pairs of points along each seam. Try to pick pairs of points that are close to the top or bottom of the images (Figure 14.12).

FIGURE 14.12   Some programs let you manually specify points for stitching.

Finally, after stitching, your panoramic software might want to crop the image to eliminate uneven boundaries at the top and bottom of the image. These boundaries often create a nice frame and frequently include image elements that you'd like to keep. Rather than letting your stitching software crop your panorama, leave the image uncropped. You can always crop it yourself in your image editor.

KNOW YOUR FOCAL LENGTH

Some stitching programs want to know the focal length of the lens (in 35mm equivalency) that was used to shoot the panorama. If your camera has a fixed zoom lens, then you might not know what the exact focal length was. If you were shooting at full wide (which you should usually do for panoramas), you can simply enter the widest angle that the lens provides (usually around 35mm). To be certain, use an EXIF reader to examine the header information in one of your images (see Chapter 8, "Manual Exposure"). Many cameras store focal length in the EXIF header.

After stitching, you might find that your image needs some more color correction. Again, skies can be especially problematic. If there is a color change from one image to the next, you'll see a short gradation along the seam of your panorama. Odds are that you won't be able to completely match the two images, but you might be able to create a smoother blend by adding a gradated Levels or Curves adjustment. Add the adjustment as an adjustment layer, and use the Gradient tool to create a smooth transition.

This is also the best time to remove dust, spots, or other aberrations.

CONVERTING COLOR IMAGES TO GRAYSCALE

Although your camera might do a great job of reproducing color, there will be times when you'll want to convert your color images to grayscale, either for printing purposes or simply for artistic intent. Photoshop—and most other image editors—allows you to convert an image to grayscale simply by selecting a new color mode (in Photoshop you can do this by selecting Image> Mode>Grayscale). This type of conversion uses a stock recipe for mixing the image's Red, Green, and Blue channels to produce a grayscale result. In theory, the recipe produces an image that is well suited to the eye's different color and luminance sensitivities.

Often, this is the best way to convert your image; however, you might find that the resulting image lacks solid blacks and bright whites. With its color removed, your image might be less punchy. Fortunately, there are several other methods that provide more control and, frequently, better results.

Conversion Methods

Some of the techniques presented next might be better for some images than for others. You'll probably want to try several approaches side by side to see what works best. In addition, be sure that you perform your conversions on a *copy* of your image. Although you might want a grayscale image now, you never know when you might need to go back to your original color version.

Color correct your image before using any of these methods. This might sound strange since you're just going to remove all of the color, but an image with accurate color will usually produce a more pleasing grayscale image.

Figure 14.13 shows an image converted using each of the following methods.

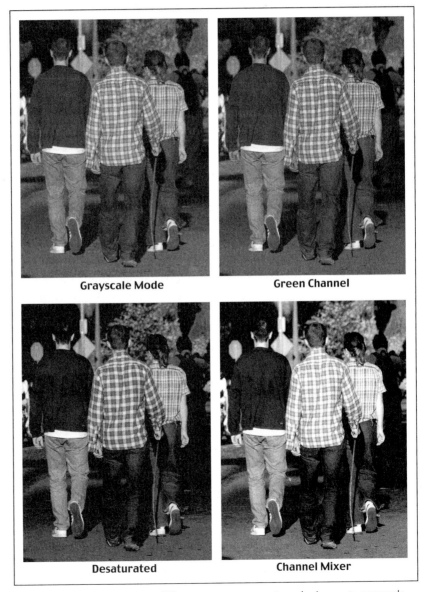

FIGURE 14.13   There are many different ways to convert a color image to grayscale. Here are samples of the four methods discussed.

Channeling

You might have discovered this already, but sometimes one of the individual color channels in your image actually makes for a very good grayscale image. Just click through the individual channels in the Channels palette and see which, if any, looks best. Depending on the color content of your image, any one of the channels might look good, although the Red and Blue channels might suffer from noise.

If you find a channel you like, simply choose Image>Mode>Grayscale, and Photoshop will toss out the other channels, leaving you with a grayscale image of your chosen channel.

Converting to Luminance

Just as you can select a single color channel in RGB mode, you can convert your image to Lab mode and select just the Luminance channel. This will throw out all of the color information in your image. After you convert to Lab mode, click on the Lightness channel in the Channels palette and select Image>Mode>Grayscale.

Desaturating an Image

When you were playing with the Hue/Saturation control, you might have discovered that it is possible to completely desaturate an image to grayscale simply by dragging the Saturation slider all the way to the left. Photoshop provides a Desaturate command (Image>Adjust>Desaturate) that performs the same function.

Mix Your Own Color Formula

As explained earlier, your image editor can convert your image to a Grayscale mode by using a stock formula for combining the Red, Green, and Blue channels in your image. If that formula doesn't produce the image you want, you can always mix your own combination using Photoshop's Channel Mixer (Image>Adjust>Channel Mixer).

The Channel Mixer provides simple slider controls for adjusting how much of each channel (in percentages) will be used to create the final image. Be sure to check the Monochrome text box at the bottom of the dialog box. Be aware that all three channels need to add up to 100%, or you'll lose luminance in your final image. Similarly, if your mixed channels add up to more than 100%, your image will brighten.

CREATING "HAND-TINTED" IMAGES

Hand tinting a photo is a painstaking process involving special tints and a lot of hard work. Fortunately, creating such an effect in your image editor is fairly painless and involves little, or no, painting skill.

The following techniques allow you to create a hand-painted look, or combination grayscale/color images. The following procedures assume that your image is already a grayscale image, either because it was shot that way or because you converted it to grayscale using one of the techniques discussed previously.

Painting with Light Opacity

The simplest way to tint an image is simply to paint over it using a brush with a very light (20% or lower) opacity. You can paint directly on to your image, but it will be very difficult to make changes or corrections later. A better option is to create a second layer to hold the paint. If you choose this approach, set your brush to 100% opacity and change the opacity of the layer to 20%. This won't change the look of your results, but it will make it easier to repaint or change colors. What's more, it makes it possible to resample the colors you're using later (you can simply set the layer opacity to 100% and then sample using the Eyedropper tool). You can even create separate layers for separate colors, making for easy color changes and opacity control of each color.

One problem with this approach is that it tends to lighten up shadow areas and generally lessen the contrast of your image. You can try to put some of that contrast back by stacking a Levels adjustment layer on the very top of your image, or you can choose to use a blending mode for your paint layer. Setting your painting layers to Multiply mode will cause your painted strokes to be multiplied with the underlying tones in your image. Because multiplying usually produces darker tones, your painted colors will darken, so you might have to overcompensate by choosing lighter colors. However, most of the shadow and contrast information in your image will be preserved. Figure 14.14 was hand-painted using multiplied paintbrushes.

Painting Desaturated Images

The easiest way to produce a hand-colored look is to start with a real color picture. Shoot a color image and then add a Hue/Saturation adjustment layer. In the Hue/Saturation dialog box, drag the Saturation slider all the way to the left to desaturate the image to grayscale.

FIGURE 14.14 Originally a grayscale image, this picture was colored by painting into separate layers and adjusting the opacity of each color layer.

With the adjustment layer selected, click on a black paintbrush and begin painting over the parts of your image that you would like to color. The paintbrush will mask those areas of the image, protecting them from the desaturation effect. Consequently, they'll return to their full saturation.

A fully saturated color element in the middle of a grayscale photo can sometimes look a little odd. After resaturating the elements of the image that you want colored, add another Hue/Saturation adjustment layer and apply a little desaturation to the entire image to tone down the color elements. (Alternatively, sometimes it's better to *increase* the contrast between the color and grayscale areas. Use your new Hue/Saturation layer to increase the saturation of the color areas.) (Figure 14.15.)

FIGURE 14.15   The original image on the left lacked some punch. We created the image on the right by boosting the Saturation of the Eiffel Tower, and by Desaturating the sky to render it black and white, thus lending more focus to the foreground elements. Some additional color adjustments were performed to better integrate the foreground and background.

Painting with the History Brush

You can use the History brush to perform a variation of the previous method. Take a color image, convert it to grayscale, and then convert the grayscale image back to RGB. You'll still have a grayscale image, but because it's in RGB mode, it will be able to handle color information.

Select Photoshop's History brush (available from the keyboard by pressing "Y") and begin painting the areas you would like colored. The History brush paints using the information stored in the last History snapshot (the History palette shows a thumbnail view of that snapshot). If you haven't intentionally set a new snapshot, the History snapshot should be your original, color image.

As with the previous coloring scheme, you might end up with an image that has color elements that look a little conspicuous. Consider adding a Hue/Saturation adjustment layer and then dialing down the saturation.

ADDING TEXTURE, GRAIN, AND "FILM" LOOK

After spending all of that time and money choosing the right digital camera, why in the world would you want to go to the trouble of making your images look like they were shot on film? Despite all of the advantages of digital photography, film can have a texture and feel that is more attractive than what your digital camera might produce. Moreover, although they might not be conscious of it, most people are very used to the look of film.

There might also be times when you want to create a film-like look—possibly an old, beat-up film look—for stylistic purposes. Whatever the reason, there are a number of things you can do to make your digital images look more like film.

Before adding any texture or grain, take a look at the color and depth of field in your image. Professional film images are usually shot with larger cameras that afford a fine control over depth of field. Consider using one of the depth of field adjustment methods discussed earlier to shorten the depth of field in your image.

Many films have very particular color and contrast characteristics. Some produce images that are very saturated, while others yield colors that are more pastel. Most of the time you can choose a color quality based on personal taste. However, if the image will be presented with images shot with a specific type of film, you might want to study that film with an eye toward mimicking its color characteristics. If you are trying to represent the look of a black-and-white film, then you'll most likely want to use the Channel Mixing method of grayscale conversion. You might also have to spend some time adjusting contrast with Levels and Curves.

All color and tone adjustments need to be performed before you add any texture or grain, as these effects can complicate your correction process.

Adding Grain

Film images have a noticeable grain caused by the clumps and particles of silver halide that are used to form the image. Films with faster ISOs have more grain, and different brands and formulations of film have different quantities and qualities of grain. Grain might sound like a bad thing, but it can actually be very beautiful, both for its inherent texture and because it serves to make the image a little more abstract, allowing the viewer's imagination to kick in.

The simplest way to add grain is with a noise filter. Photoshop includes a simple Add Noise command (Filter>Noise>Add Noise) that allows you to dial in different amounts of noise (Figure 14.16).

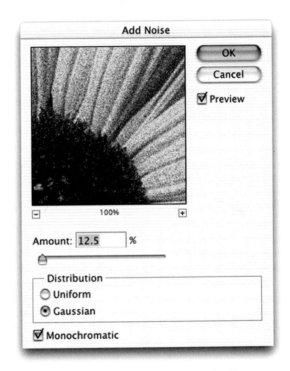

FIGURE 14.16   With your image editor's noise filters, you can create simple film-like grain.

Add Noise is a good choice for adding grain, but it does have limitations. First, it affects the entire image uniformly. Consequently, the resulting image can often look like it's being viewed through a simple "screen" of noise. Second, once you add noise, it's there to stay. As you saw in the last chapter, removing noise is very difficult.

ADDING GRAIN TO AN IMAGE

Although a simple Add Noise filter will let you add a layer of grain to an image, there is a better, more flexible method of achieving film-like noise in your digital pictures. Pick an image to which you would like to add grain, and then step through the following procedure.

STEP 1: CREATE A LAYER OF NOISE

First, you need some grain. Create a new layer in your document and fill it with 50% gray. You can do this in Photoshop by pressing Command-A (Control-A in Windows) to select the entire layer, and then choosing Edit>Fill. In the Fill dialog box, select 50% Gray from the Contents pop-up menu.

Now choose Filter>Noise>Add Noise. Select Gaussian Noise and check the Monochrome checkbox. The amount of noise to use depends partly on the size of your image and on how grainy you want the image to look. In general, though, 25 to 30% should be plenty.

After clicking OK, your image should look like a gray image full of noise (Figure 14.17).

FIGURE 14.17   A better way to add grain is to create a special noise layer and composite it with your document. This will afford you more noise control and editability, including the option to later remove the noise.

STEP 2: CHANGE THE BLENDING MODE

As discussed earlier, simply adding noise to your image applies the same amount of noise to every pixel, no matter how bright or dark. What's more, the noise added by the Add Noise filter is often a little too contrasty. The noise can end up looking like a layer of pixels sitting on the top of your image. We want to create a texture that will blend in with the pixels in your image.

With your noise layer selected, choose Soft Light from the Blending mode pop-up menu of the Layers palette. You should now see a very noisy version of your image.

STEP 3: LOWER THE NOISE OPACITY

As a last step, drop the opacity level on your noise level to about 25%. You should now have a very realistic-looking level of grain (Figure 14.18). You can

FIGURE 14.18   After compositing the noise layer using a Soft Light blending mode and an opacity adjustment, the image has a very realistic, film-like grain.

also change the grain level by simply readjusting the opacity slider. Want to simulate a higher ISO film? Just increase the opacity. Note that you can also turn the noise off altogether by unchecking the noise layer's eyeball icon, or by deleting the layer altogether.

Adding Texture and Damage

You can add more complex textures to your images using a method similar to the one described in the previous tutorial. First, you need a texture such as paper, wood, or stone. The best source for textures, of course, is your digital camera. Although no substitute for a good scanner, it can still do a fine job of photographing paper textures, wood surfaces, or stone. Clip-art libraries of these types of textures are also available from stock photo agencies.

Once you've imported a texture into your image editor, place it on a layer above your image and use a Hard Light, Soft Light, or Multiply Blending mode to merge the texture into your image. You'll typically need to set a very low opacity for your texture. If your texture is too strong, it will overpower your image.

Scratches, dirt, and other "damage" can be added by painting layers of damage onto a white canvas and then blending them into your image using a Multiply blending mode.

COMPOSITING

Compositing—the collage-like process of layering multiple images together—is a mainstay of special effects work. Using the simple selection and layering tools discussed throughout this book, you can create all sorts of fantastic or surreal composites. In addition to doctoring photos, you can also use compositing tools to solve more practical photographic concerns.

The images in Figure 14.19 were shot at the bottom of a canyon using a Canon PowerShot G2. Because the canyon was very deep and underlit, the camera had to overexpose, resulting in harshly overexposed skies. However, if we metered off of the sky, then the canyon was underexposed and we lost all of the detail in the image.

FIGURE 14.19   Canyon source images.

To solve the problem, we shot two identical frames with different exposures with the idea of compositing them to create a final image (Figure 14.20).

The same layer stacking tricks you learned in previous chapters were used to create this composite. After stacking the two images on top of each other, and positioning them so that they were properly registered, we simply added a Layer Mask to the upper layer and began painting into it to control which parts of our upper image were visible. Several other adjustment layers were added to improve the effect, and to provide color and tone correction.

FIGURE 14.20 Canyon sandwich with layers palette.

PREPARING TO PRINT

Photoshop is capable of much more than the few effects shown in this chapter. Hopefully, though, these tutorials provided you with a few starting points for creating more complex effects and introduced you to some effects that digital photographers frequently need to perform.

By this point, you probably have some finished images that are ready for output. Whether your destination is paper, Web, or video, the next chapter should help you with all of your outputting concerns.

OUTPUT

In This Chapter

- Choosing a Printer
- Printing
- Web Output

At some point, you're going to be ready to get your pictures out of your image editor and into the real world. Whether you plan to deliver your images in print or via the Web, CD-ROM, or video, you will need to take some care when you create your output. As you saw in Chapter 10, "Preparing Your Images for Editing," color can vary widely between devices, and you'll almost certainly find yourself returning to your color correction techniques to adjust your images for the vagaries of your target output device.

Although output technology does not tend to advance as quickly as digital camera technology, there have been some important improvements in printers and software since the first edition of this book, from new seven-color printers to software that makes your output workflow easier. In this chapter, you'll learn how to adjust your media for particular types of outputs, whether print or electronic.

CHOOSING A PRINTER

After all of the work you've done in the preceding pages, you should be well prepared for a discussion on printing. Fortunately, most of the color theory that you learned when you were working with your camera will apply to your printer as well. This section begins with a discussion of the issues and questions that you'll face when you buy a printer. Following that, you'll learn more about how to adjust and prepare your images for printing.

Your digital photography system isn't complete without a way to make prints, of course. Fortunately, today you can buy a very high-quality color printer for very little money. Even if most of your images are intended for a magazine, newspaper, or other professionally printed media, you'll still probably want some type of desktop printer for proofing and correction.

There are many different ways to print a color image on a piece of paper, so your first choice when you shop for a printer is to choose a printing technology.

Laser Printers

You're probably familiar with using a laser printer to print text or simple graphics. If you already have a laser printer, or if you use one at work or at a service bureau, then you already know that laser printers are very speedy, quiet, and can produce very high-quality output.

Most laser printers also only print in black and white. If black-and-white output is your only concern, then a laser printer isn't a bad choice.

However, your black-an-white laser printed output will be a far cry from a black-and-white photographic print—you won't be able to print on glossy paper and your image will not be *continuous tone*. That is, you will be able to see the dots and patterns that the printer uses to create shades of gray. Even though the dots and patterns on a modern, high- resolution laser printer will be very difficult to discern, the overall print quality will still be far inferior to a photo-quality output process. However, if you regularly need to make photocopies of your printed output, a laser printer might be your best choice for an output device.

If you are considering a black-and-white laser printer, you'll want to select one with a high resolution—at least 600dpi, preferably 1200. Many laser printers also include special internal software for adjusting and correcting gray tones when you print. This built-in correction can prevent banding and other laser printing artifacts and usually results in a much smoother print.

If you're hoping to use your laser printer to create Xerox-able or printable masters, then you'll want a printer with software that allows you to change the printer's line screen (more on line screens later). You'll also want to be able to deactivate any of the special gray tone correction routines inside the printer.

Color laser printers have been available for years, and have recently come down in price. Just like any other color printing process, color laser printers create a full-color image by combining four different primary colors. While an inkjet printer will lay down all four colors at once, a laser printer prints each color in a separate pass. In other words, the printer moves the paper through the print mechanism up to four times, and applies a different color during each pass. Until recently, color laser printers produced output with a very characteristic "sheen" that smacked of color copying. Current printers do a much better job, even on plain paper, and can produce an image that looks like it was pulled out of a magazine. Even a magazine-quality photo is a far cry from a photographic print, though, in terms of texture, finish, and image quality.

Unfortunately, one of the most notable characteristics of a laser printer is price. Even a black-and-white laser printer will be much more expensive than an inkjet, and a color laser printer will cost you several thousand dollars. On the upside, your cost per print will be much lower than inkjet printing, so if mass production is your goal, a laser printer might be worth the extra money.

Whether you are buying a color or a black-and-white laser printer, your main concern should be image quality. Look at lots of output samples and pay attention to how well the printer reproduces color, and make sure that it can reproduce all color ranges (reds, blues, purples, etc.)

accurately. Also look for artifacts—dots and patterns—throughout the print, but especially in the highlights and shadows. Finally, you'll want to check compatibility with your operating system, hardware, and image editing software, and, if you have any special networking concerns (for workgroup use, for example), you'll want to evaluate the printer's networking options.

Laser printers are good choices for business printing or mass production. For fine art or hobbyist photography, they're really not appropriate.

Dye-Sublimation Printers

Sublimation is the process of converting a solid into a gas without passing it through a liquid stage (dry ice sublimes at room temperature, melting from a solid block into vapor without becoming liquid). A dye-sublimation printer (also called a *dye-sub*) works by using special solid dyes that can be sublimed into a gas that adheres to special paper. As with any other printing technology, these primary color dyes are combined during the sublimation process to create full-color images.

The advantage of a dye-sub printer is that it is truly continuous tone. That is, no dots or patterns will be visible in your final print because the ink hits the paper in a diffuse, gaseous form. Dye-sub paper also looks like real photo paper, giving your prints a true "photo finish."

The downside to dye-sub printers is that their prints can lack sharpness. The same soft, diffuse property that creates continuous tone also means that it's difficult for a dye-sub printer to produce a very hard edge. Dye-sub printers are also a tad slow when you compare them to inkjets or laser printers, and they typically have a high cost per print because of their expensive, proprietary media. In addition, if you're looking for a printer that can be used for other tasks—printing text, for example—then a dye-sub is definitely not for you.

That said, a dye-sub printer is a great way to go if photo quality is your highest concern. In addition to their photo-like appearance, many dye-sub printers coat their prints with a special ultraviolet layer to protect the prints from fading and discoloring.

As with other printing technologies, when you shop for a dye-sub printer, image quality should be your highest concern. Try to look at a variety of samples that cover a full range of color and detail levels as well as a full assortment of light and shadow. Dye-sub resolutions are typically lower than laser printer or inkjet resolutions due to the nature of their printing method—300 and 400dpi printers are common and perfectly acceptable.

These days, most dye-sub printers are small, portable affairs (some can even run off batteries) that produce a maximum print size of 4" × 6". Most of these printers, such as those made by Olympus and HP, can be attached directly to a camera, providing you with a Polaroid-like facility for getting instant prints from your digital camera. Because the media is somewhat pricey, these can be expensive prints and, of course, you have no option to color correct when you print directly from your camera.

As with purchasing any printer, make sure the printer provides the necessary connections for your computer, and that its driver software is compatible with your operating system.

Inkjet Printers

The best all-around photo printing solution is a color inkjet printer. Inkjets work by shooting tiny (*really* tiny—most inkjets use a drop that is only a few picoliters) drops of ink out of a nozzle. As with any color printing technology, different colored drops are combined to create full-color images.

Inkjet printers have a number of advantages over other printing technologies. They typically have a bigger color gamut than a laser printer, they can produce sharper images than a dye-sub printer, and they can print many more types of media than either a laser or dye-sub printer can. They're also often faster than laser or dye-sub because they can lay down a full-color image in a single pass. With the right paper, a good inkjet printer can create an image that's indistinguishable from a photographic print.

Inkjet printers are typically far cheaper than a laser or dye-sub printer, although their cost per print can be expensive—up to $2 per page for a photo-quality 8" × 10" print. However, because of their capability to handle different media, you can also create lower-quality, less-expensive prints by using cheaper media.

Inkjet printers can currently be divided into two major categories: four-color printers and six-color printers. Four-color printers use the same cyan, magenta, yellow, and black colors that an offset printing press uses. Six-color printers add an extra cyan and extra magenta cartridge to beef up the dark tones and provide smoother light tones.

At the time of this writing (summer, 2002), a few companies are just beginning to release seven-color printers, which augment the normal six-color ink complement with an additional, lighter shade of black. In addition to providing smoother tones when printing gray areas, the extra black should also provide for better grayscale printing. If you're very serious about printing photo-quality output, you'll want to keep an eye on this technology.

Your first decision when you choose an inkjet printer is to decide what type of printing you want to do. If you want a general-purpose printer capable of printing good images and text, you'll need to go with a four-color printer. If photo-quality printing is your highest concern, then you'll definitely want to go with a six- or seven-color printer. If this sounds like a difficult choice, be aware that a four-color printer can do a very good job of printing photo-quality prints, especially when it is used with quality paper. However, a six-color printer will be able to do a better job of printing lighter colors and will be able to achieve better dynamic range in the darker tones.

If you choose a six-color printer, you'll next need to decide if you want a printer that can produce archival-quality prints. The dye-based inks used by the typical inkjet printer are not very durable. If you print an image and hang it in direct sunlight, it will be noticeably faded and discolored within a few weeks. Even if you stick the image in a photo album it will still discolor and fade, as dye-based inks are greatly affected by humidity.

Pigment-based inks are far more durable and are typically shown to last anywhere from 20 to 200 years. If fine-art printing is your primary application—and certainly it is if you hope to sell your prints—then it's worth spending the extra money for an archival-quality printer. If you are more of a hobbyist—that is, if you'll be making prints for your own enjoyment and for giving to family and friends—then a non-archival, dye-based inkjet should be fine.

You'll also want to consider paper size when you choose an inkjet. Although most printers offer standard letter-size printing, you can also get models (with four or six colors, dye-based or archival) that print larger. Larger desktop inkjet printers typically support sizes up to 13″ × 19″ (also known as A3 or SuperA3 size). Although a standard letter-size printer is capable of printing an 8″ × 10″ print, if you're interested in fine-art printing you might want to go for a larger printer. You'll pay more for the extra size, of course—usually about twice as much.

REALLY BIG PRINTING

If you need to print images with print sizes over 13″ × 19″, then you'll need to go with a large-format printer. These giant inkjet printers range in size from 24″ wide to over 50″ wide and typically accept sheets or rolls of paper, allowing you to create huge images. They also come with huge price tags. Don't expect to get a large-format printer for under $2,000. For more information, check out vendors such as Epson, Hewlett-Packard, and Encad.

Inkjet printers come in a number of different resolutions and, certainly, a higher resolution is often better. However, as with cameras, don't get hung up on the printer's resolution as the final arbiter of print quality. There are many things that affect the quality of a printer's output, and a printer with a higher resolution won't necessarily do a better job than a lower-resolution competitor.

When shopping for a printer, look at a lot of output, including prints on different types of media. Try to find samples printed on the paper you think you're most likely to use. If you suspect that you're going to do most of your printing on ordinary copier paper (not the best choice), then you'll want to look closely at the printer's plain-paper printing ability. If quality is your highest concern, then you should examine output printed on photo-quality glossy paper. If you have special printing needs—the ability to print on watercolor paper or cloth, for example—then examine output on those media as well. Just because a printer prints well on one type of media doesn't mean it will perform as well on another.

Of course, you'll want to determine if the printer provides the type of connectivity and networking that your computer requires, and you'll want to be sure that it includes a driver for your operating system. Print speed can vary greatly from model to model and from quality setting to quality setting, so if you think you have speed concerns (perhaps you need to print a high volume), then you'll want to assess the printer's print speed.

Some printers provide cable connections or media slots that allow you to connect your camera, or insert your camera's media, directly into the printer. These models let you print directly, without hassling with a computer. Some even include tiny LCD screens for selecting images and performing simple edits. The downside to this type of printing, of course, is that you cannot perform any color corrections or retouching.

Once you have a printer, you'll then want to consider the various ink and paper choices available. Typically, you should experiment with different types of media, as each will have its own imaging characteristics.

Media Selection

You can, of course, stick any old paper in your printer, including the normal 20-pound copier paper that one typically uses for office correspondence. However, paper choice can have a huge bearing on the quality of your final image. In addition to providing a more photo-like finish, different papers respond very differently to your printer's ink. For example, some papers absorb more ink than others, resulting in colors that are more muted and muddy than what you'd get from a paper with a more "opaque" finish.

Some papers are also brighter than others, which will often yield brighter prints, while other papers will have a gloss or finish that results in a more continuous tone print and a more photo-like finish. Finally, there are papers with unique, complex textures such as watercolor paper or handmade papers. These papers typically produce prints with darker colors and strange color textures. In addition to the texture of the paper itself, coarser papers typically absorb ink in unique ways, resulting in smears and smudges that can be very attractive.

In general, you'll want to experiment with your paper selections to find out what works best for your intended output. Be *sure* to read your printer's manual before you shove an experimental piece of paper through your printer. Most printers have thickness limits, and many printers—particularly archival-quality printers—can be damaged if you use media that wasn't specifically designed for the printer.

To get the best quality, you'll want to stick with a paper that is specially formulated for your printer. Epson printers, for example, include settings for specific types of Epson-manufactured paper. Because the printer driver knows exactly what type of paper you're using, it can do a much better job of laying down a good image.

If archival quality is your highest concern, you'll want to choose an archival paper. Print longevity is not determined only by the ink you're using. Special archival papers will also greatly extend the life of your prints. If longevity is your greatest concern, then shop for an appropriate paper.

Ink Choice

In general, you should always buy ink manufactured and certified by your printer manufacturer. There are cheaper, third-party inks available, and these frequently work just fine. However, it's important to know that your printer head can be damaged by the ink that passes through it. More importantly, though, to get accurate color your printer driver needs to know that the ink formulations in your printer will mix and blend in a particular way. If you use a third-party ink, there's no guarantee that they mixed their ink correctly.

There are, however, some third-party inks that work very well and are worthy of consideration. Special archival inks manufactured by Lysen (www.completedigitalphotography.com/archivalinks) let you upgrade certain non-archival printers to archival quality. In addition to their longevity, these inks offer very good color gamuts, and performance that is often equal to the manufacturer-branded inks they're replacing.

If you do a lot of black-and-white printing, you might want to consider a set of quad-tone inks. Typically, the black ink included in a normal four- or six-color printer doesn't allow for a full range of grayscale printing. Printer manufacturers get around this by trying to blend all four (or six) ink colors to create shades of gray. Unfortunately, this approach usually doesn't yield a full range of gray, and often produces an image with a bad color cast.

High-quality black-and-white commercial printing—the kind used to print black-and-white photography books, for example—often uses combinations of multiple shades of black or gray ink. Such ink sets are also available for desktop inkjet printers. Typically, these quad-tone ink sets provide four shades of black ink and special drivers for printing black and white images. Check out www.completedigitalphotography.com/quadtone for more info on this type of printing.

PRINTING

Once you've color corrected, edited, adjusted, tweaked, and obsessed over your image, you might be ready to try printing it out to see what it looks like on paper. Although you can simply load your printer with paper and choose the Print command in your image editor, to get the best results, you're probably going to need to print a few test prints and do a little fussing with your image.

In Chapter 13, "Essential Imaging Tactics," you learned that you should resize your image after you've performed all of your edits, but before you've sharpened. (If you're unsure of how to resize an image, you might want to re-read the section on scaling in Chapter 13.) What size to make your image, though, depends largely on your printer. You can simply decide "I want an 8″ × 10″ image." However, depending on the needs of your printer, your camera might not provide enough resolution to print at that size. To determine the optimal print size for your image then, you need to know the optimal resolution for your printer.

Choosing a Resolution

Before you can resize an image (as discussed in Chapter 13), you need to know the best resolution for your printer. Different printing technologies have different resolution requirements, so calculating optimal resolution differs from printer type to printer type.

No matter what type of printer you use, it's important to remember one fundamental difference between your computer monitor and your printer: your computer monitor can display a single pixel that can be any one of millions of colors; your color printer, on the other hand, can print a single dot that is any one of *four* colors. In other words, there is not a one-to-one correspondence between a pixel on your screen and a dot printed on paper. If a pixel on your screen is defined as being dark purple, your printer has to print a combination of 50 different cyan, magenta, yellow, and black dots, all in a special pattern, to reproduce that one purple dot from your monitor.

Therefore, although your printer might claim to have 1200 dots per inch of resolution, those are 1200 printer dots, not 1200 pixels. Choosing a resolution, then, is dependent on how much information your printer needs to do its job.

Choosing a Resolution for a Laser Printer

Laser printers generate different tones—both gray tones and color tones—through a process called *halftoning*, the same method used to generate images in your local newspaper. Using traditional methods, halftoning is performed by shooting a photo of an image through a special halftone screen. The resulting photo gets broken down by the screen into a pattern of dots that can be easily printed using a single ink. For color printing, four pictures of the image are taken, each through a halftone screen and color filter. The result is four plates that can each be printed using a different color of ink.

Halftoned images are really just huge conglomerations of small patterns of dots. For example, to represent 40% gray, a special pattern of dots are used; for 60% gray, a different pattern (Figure 15.1). When you stand far enough from the image, the dots blur together into smooth patterns of tone. How big the dots are depends on the frequency of the screen — that is, how tightly the screen is woven.

When you print an image on your laser printer, the computer sends the printer its color pixel information. The printer (or the printer driver software) then figures out how to represent each dot of color using a halftone dot pattern.

Just as traditional, photo-based halftoning uses a halftone screen of a particular frequency, your laser printer bases its halftone calculations on a *line screen frequency*. For high-resolution printing (1200dpi or higher), this screen frequency is typically 133 or 166 lines per inch. This is a very fine screen that produces a magazine-quality image.

Lower-resolution printers (300 to 600) typically use a much coarser screen, usually around 85 to 100 lines per inch. Many laser printers (and most high-resolution image setters) let you specify a line screen.

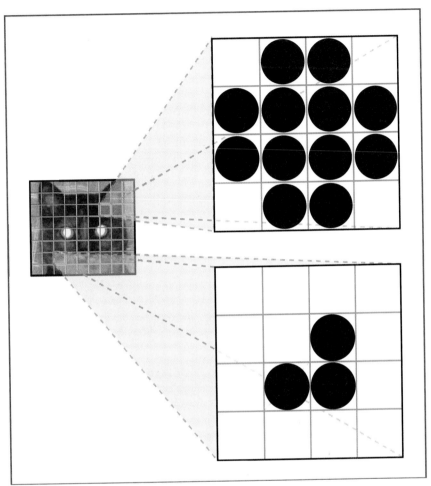

FIGURE 15.1 A single pixel in your image corresponds to a pattern of dots on your printer. Each of these halftone patterns is used to represent a pixel of a particular gray shade or color.

Why does this matter? Because different line screens require images of different resolutions. Typically, the rule for resolution (as measured in ppi) is that your image should be 1.5 to 2 times your line screen. In other words, if your printer uses a 133 line screen, then your image needs to have a resolution of 200 to 266 pixels per inch.

For example, if you have a laser printer that requires 200ppi images (because it uses a 133 line screen) and you have a 2-megapixel camera that produces 1600 × 1200 pixel images, then you can print your image at 8″ × 6″ at 200 dots per inch—1600 ÷ 200 = 8 inches wide; 1200 ÷ 200 = 6 inches high.

Let's say, though, that you want to print an image that can be copied on a photocopier. Images for photocopying typically need to be printed with a much coarser line screen, usually around 85 lines per inch, which means that your image only needs to be around 150dpi. At this resolution, the same 2-megapixel image could be printed at 10.5″ × 8″. (An 85 line screen is also appropriate for newspaper or phone book printing.)

Remember that, when you print to a laser printer, it's best to turn off any special gray tone correction features the printer might have.

Choosing a Resolution for an Inkjet Printer

Inkjet printers don't use the halftone screens that a laser printer uses. Rather, they use special mezzogram patterns that are much more random than halftone screens. As such, an inkjet printer doesn't really have a screen frequency. Fortunately, you can usually follow a very simple rule for determining resolution: a 1400dpi, six-color inkjet printer, your image resolution doesn't need to be any higher than 240 pixels per inch. Although you can send a higher resolution image to the printer, you probably won't notice any difference in quality, and your print times will be much longer. Note that you can often go lower than this, sometimes as low as 180 to 200ppi without a serious loss in image quality. (The number 240 derives from dividing the resolution of the printer by its six primary colors, so $1400 \div 6 = 240$.)

At 240 dots per inch, your 2-megapixel image drops to a 5″ × 6″ print size. However, since you can usually go down as low as 200 dots per inch with hardly any loss in quality, you should be able to coax an 8″ × 10″ image from your 2-megapixel camera.

Paper quality is also a contributing factor to resolution choice. If you're printing on poor-quality paper, you might be able to get away with going to a much lower resolution. The lack of resolution will often be hidden by the fact that the ink will bleed and smear when it hits the paper. Conversely, if you're using a higher-quality paper that does a better job of holding a dot, then you'll need to stick with a higher-resolution image.

HIGHER PRINTER RESOLUTION = MORE TRIPS TO THE INK STORE

Some inkjet printers offer even higher resolutions, usually 2880 dots per inch. It is generally agreed that there is no discernable difference in quality between 1440 and 2880, and that these modes are simply provided by printer manufacturers in an effort to get you to buy more ink.

Using Your Color Management System When You Print

If you've been using a color management system for your editing work (see Chapter 10 for more information), then you should have an appropriate printer profile installed and configured. You can use this profile for generating soft proofs as explained in Chapter 10, and you can also use it when you print from Photoshop to help ensure that the colors that come out of your printer match what's on your screen.

After selecting Print, simply set the Source Space to Document, set the Output Space and Intent to the same settings you chose in the Proof Setup dialog (Figure 15.2).

FIGURE 15.2 If you've been using your computer's Color Management Settings, you'll want to pick the appropriate profile and other settings to ensure that your print more closely matches the soft proof that you generated on-screen.

Finally, it's very important to turn off any color correction routines that might be built in to your printer driver. Many vendors, including Epson and Canon, include their own color correction routines in their printer driver. Unfortunately, if Photoshop is already manipulating the color in your image before it sends it to the printer driver, the last thing you want to have happen is for that driver to then manipulate the data further. The Print dialog for your printer should have a command for de-activating the printer's built-in color correction (Figure 15.3).

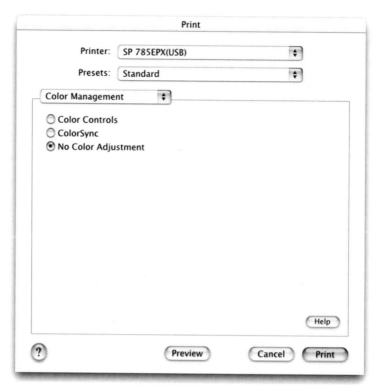

FIGURE 15.3 If you're using a color management system, be sure to deactivate any color correction that might be built in to your printer driver. Shown here is the Epson printer driver running under Mac OS X. A similar option should be provided with any Epson driver running under any OS.

Correcting Your Image for Print

When you print your image, whether or not you're using a color management system, you'll probably find that its colors don't exactly match what you see on your computer screen. This is simply a result of the difficulty of translating colors of light into colors of ink. No matter how hard you try, how meticulous you are, and how good your hardware is, you will rarely get a print right the first time. Just as a darkroom photographer usually has to try many different exposure and development strategies when printing a picture, the digital photographer usually has to perform lots of printer-specific color corrections, and print several pages before a print looks correct.

Therefore, if you find yourself printing many different versions of a print to get the color you like, don't worry, you're not doing anything wrong. However, there are some things you can do to improve your chances of getting a good print, and to reduce your number of failed attempts.

After printing an image, you need to determine which areas of the print appear wrong. Perhaps the image has an overall color cast. Perhaps it has lost contrast or saturation. Perhaps some colors are outright wrong. Once you've identified the problem, you can start trying to concoct a correction that will eliminate it.

After you've performed the initial color corrections and adjustments on your image, but before you start printing, it's a good idea to save a copy of your image. This copy will be something like a negative. It is the original adjusted image that you can use as a base on which to add corrections for your specific printer and media. It is very likely that you will eventually end up with several versions of an image—your original corrected image, and separate copies for each type of media on each type of printer that you print it on.

There are a couple of ways to make adjustments to your image when printing. If you're working in Photoshop, you can simply throw an adjustment layer (or two) on top of your image. As you create test prints and refine your corrections, you can easily go back and tweak your adjustment layers, or even build sets of adjustment layers that are specific to particular types of media.

There's a very good chance that your printer's color issues will be consistent. For example, perhaps a particular type of paper always prints with the same degree of color cast. If this is the case, then you can always assume that you will need a correction for that cast. If you make the correction using an adjustment layer in one image, you can simply copy that layer to other images that will be printed on the same media.

PRINTING APPLICATIONS

There are a number of excellent applications designed specifically for printing images. Although most lack color correction and editing tools, they provide simple layout controls that make it easy to print multiple images on a page. These applications allow you to quickly print multiple copies of the same image, or groups of different pictures on one page. If you're printing smaller than 8″ × 10″, the ability to gang small images (3″ × 5″ or 4″ × 6″, for example) on a single page can be a great media saver (Figure 15.4). Most of these programs also include simple media cataloging features.

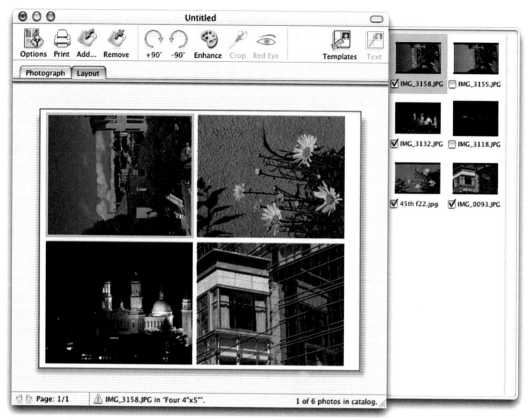

FIGURE 15.4 Included on the companion CD-ROM are a collection of printing applications for Mac and Windows that make it easy to print out complex layouts of prints.

  A collection of printing applications for both Mac and Windows is included on the CD-ROM in the Applications directory.

ON THE CD

Preparing Your Image for Professional Printing

If you are preparing images for professional, offset printing—for a professionally printed catalog, book or mailer, for example—then you will need to perform some extra editing steps to ensure that your images print well. You've probably already done a bunch of work to get the tone and contrast range of your image adjusted. Although the black point, white point, and gamma adjustments that you learned about in Chapter 13 have probably produced images that look good on your screen, they don't necessarily represent a contrast and tonal range that a professional printer is capable of printing. Fortunately, there's a pretty simple way to compress or *target* the tonal range of your image to fit the needs of a commercial printer.

As you've already seen, your computer monitor can display a bigger gamut of colors than most printers can print, and this holds true for commercial printers. Simply put, there are limits to the lightest and darkest dots that a printer can print. Some tones on your monitor are simply lighter than the printer's lightest shade of ink, while others are so dark that the printer cannot lay down enough ink to reproduce that tone. If the shadow and highlight tones in your image are beyond the limits of what your printer can print, highlights will posterize and shadows will turn to mud (Figure 15.5).

FIGURE 15.5   The upper image in this figure was not targeted for this book's printing press. The lower image was.

In Chapter 12, "Building Your Editing Arsenal," you used the Output sliders in Photoshop's Levels dialog box to lighten an image to create an effect. We're going to return to the Output sliders now to compress the tonal range of the image into a range that is acceptable for a printer.

TUTORIAL

TARGETING AN IMAGE

Although your images might look great on-screen, your printed images might often leave you unpleasantly surprised. Unfortunately, your computer monitor is capable of displaying many more colors than your printer can print. Through targeting, you can adjust the tonal range in your image so that it better matches the capability of your printer.

In this tutorial, you're going to target an image for an offset printing press.

STEP 1: OPEN THE IMAGE

ON THE CD

We're going to return to an image you worked with in Chapter 11, "Correcting Tone and Color." Open the greenhouse.psd image located in the Tutorials/Chapter 15/Targeting an Image folder on the companion CD-ROM.

Figure 15.6 shows the untargeted image. If you look at the image on-screen, you'll see that it is not nearly as dark as this printed version and has much better tone and contrast range. The printing process darkened up the image and in the process messed up the contrast.

STEP 2: TALK TO YOUR PRINTER

At this stage, you would want to find out from your printer the minimum and maximum ink densities that their offset printing press can hold. In other words, what are the lightest and darkest dots that the press can print? Typically, they'll respond with something like 5% and 95%. That is, the lightest tone the printer can print is 5% gray, while the darkest is 95% gray. Anything brighter than that will simply be the white of the paper. If you're printing to newsprint or another low-quality paper, you might see numbers more like 15% and 85%.

Paper white is fine for the *specular highlights* in your image—the bright white glints and reflections that occur on very shiny surfaces and on the edges of objects. However, if the brightest spot a printer can make is 15%, then there will be a sudden change from 15% gray to paper white, which will appear as posterization in the highlights of your image. It's better to keep your white areas confined to what's printable so as to maintain control of the highlights in your image.

FIGURE 15.6   Before targeting, the shadows in this image are way too dark.

STEP 3: TARGET THE IMAGE

The image already has two adjustment layers that serve to correct and adjust its tonal values. Add a Levels adjustment layer to the top of the layer stack. As you've already learned, the histogram in the Levels dialog box is a graph of the 256 tones in your image. We want to set the black Output slider (which currently has a value of 0) to 95%, or 13 (255–(255 × .95)). Drag the left Output slider until it reads 13 (Figure 15.7).

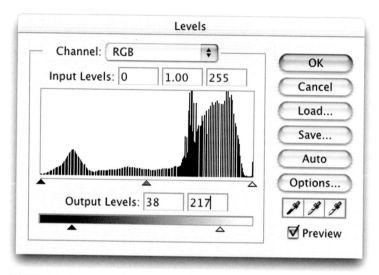

FIGURE 15.7   After targeting, your Levels adjustment layer should look like this.

The white Output slider should be 5%, or 243 (255–(255 × .05)). Slide it into place.

STEP 4: EVALUATE THE IMAGE

You might think that the image looks rather flat now and, certainly, it will have much less contrast than it had before. However, when it is printed, all of the tones are going to go darker at the low end, as the ink is absorbed into the paper. At the high end, this adjustment will hopefully protect your highlights (white points) from posterizing and blowing out to completely white (Figure 15.8).

On many images, you will be able to perform your tonal adjustments and targeting with a single Levels command—that is, you will perform your tonal corrections with the Input sliders and your targeting with the Output sliders. In this image, though, we needed a Curves adjustment between our tonal correction and image targeting.

FIGURE 15.8   After targeting, the image prints much better.

Web-Based Printing

There are a number of Web sites that offer photo printing services. After you upload your images to these sites, they will print the images and mail them back to you. These services typically use pictrographic processes—traditional chemical-based printing processes that expose a piece of photographic paper using a laser or LED device.

The advantage to these services is that they offer you a path to true photo quality—photo paper and continuous tone—from your digital camera. In addition, these prints are more archival than what will come out of a desktop printer, and will usually offer a lifespan of 20 years or so.

The downside is that you have to wait for your prints, and you don't know what type of color and tonal corrections the service will make to your images. In other words, what you see on your screen might not be close to what you get in your prints. Typically, a particular printing service will be consistent about the type of adjustments they make to their images. Therefore, once you've figured out a particular service's idiosyncrasies, you can adjust your images accordingly before you submit them.

Pay close attention to a service's cropping guidelines. Some services will blow up your image to fill an entire print. If your original was a different aspect ratio than the final print, your image will be cropped. Most services allow the option of blowing up to full print size, or padding the image to preserve your original aspect ratio.

Most services also provide photo-sharing facilities. When you upload images for printing, you are usually allowed to create one or more photo albums. You can then send the address of these albums to other people who can view your images and, if they want, order prints. This can be a much faster way to distribute photos to a group of people over the Web, as you only have to upload your images once. It can also save you the hassle of preparing prints for a bunch of people—they can simply order their own. Check out www.completedigitalphotography.com/webprinting for links to Web printing services that are currently available.

WEB OUTPUT

Fortunately, Web output is much simpler than outputting to print. Unfortunately, this is because there simply are no color controls for the Web. Because there's nothing you can do but post your images and hope that your viewers are using decent monitors, you don't need to spend any time adjusting or preparing the color in your images.

Your main concern when you prepare an image for the Web (or for e-mail) is file size. You probably already know what it's like to wait for a large image to download, either from the Web or from your mail server. Don't inflict the same data glut on other people by posting or e-mailing really large files. Obviously, if you and your recipient have high-speed connections, you can probably get away with creating larger files. Be aware, however, that the mail servers provided by many Internet service providers put a limit on the maximum size of an e-mail attachment. If you absolutely *have* to e-mail a large image to someone, consider segmenting it using a file compression utility.

Fortunately, images for the Web tend to be very small. Most users don't have screens that are wider than 800 pixels, and most Web images clock in around 300 or 400 pixels wide. Save a copy of your image (be careful not to recompress it) and resize it to an appropriate pixel size. Be sure to set the resolution to 72dpi.

The two most common graphics file formats on the Web are GIF and JPEG. For photos, JPEG is really the only format you need to use. JPEG allows for varying degrees of compression, and the more compression, the greater your image quality will degrade. Fortunately, Photoshop offers an excellent Save For Web option that lets you experiment with different JPEG compression ratios and compare the effects of different compression settings side by side (Figure 15.9).

FIGURE 15.9 Photoshop's Save For Web feature makes it easy to try out different JPEG settings to balance size and quality.

If you're sending your images to others to post on their Web site, consider sending them an uncompressed image. They might have their own size and compression requirements, and so will want to perform their own resizing and compression. If you send them an uncompressed file, they'll be able to compress it to their specifications without introducing further image degradation.

If you'd like to have your own photo Web site, but don't have access to any Web space, consider using a photo-hosting Web site. Many of these sites offer template-based Web page creation and links to printing services. If you do a Web search for "photo hosting" or "image hosting," you should find plenty of free photo-hosting services.

The advantage of posting photos on a Web page is that you only need to mail the Web address to your interested parties. This saves upload time on your end, and allows them to view the images when they're ready, without having to be inconvenienced by hefty downloads.

Conclusion

Once you start using a digital camera, it's becomes difficult to imagine that film cameras have much of a future. Not because film cameras produce inferior results, but simply because digital cameras provide such enormous creative flexibility. Hopefully, this book helped you understand more about the specific issues and concerns that you'll face when you shoot digital, as well as provided you with solutions for working around those concerns.

Your next step? Start shooting and editing! Your skill with both your camera and image editor will greatly improve as you shoot more and more pictures. Take your camera with you wherever you go and don't hesitate to fire away.

If you'd like to read some more about photography in general, take a look at the suggested reading list in Appendix A, "Suggested Reading."

SUGGESTED READING

The following list will provide you with further reading on the "artistry" of photography, and on more specifics of digital editing and retouching.

The Camera (Ansel Adams Photography, Book 1) **by Ansel Adams, Robert Baker.** Excellent coverage of camera and photography basics. If you want to know more about exposure—particularly the zone system—this is a great place to start.

Examples: The Making of 40 Photographs **by Ansel Adams.** Whether or not you like his photos, reading details about his photographic process can be an invaluable way to learn how to think and see like a photographer.

The Ansel Adams Guide: Book 1: Basic Techniques of Photography **by John P. Schaefer.** Written by one of the trustees of the Ansel Adams archives, this book provides a thorough overview of the entire photographic process from cameras to developing to printing.

On Photography **by Susan Sontag.** An excellent series of essays discussing the effects that photography has had on our way of seeing the world. A must-read for any would-be photographer.

Understanding Comics **by Scott McCloud.** Essential reading for anyone who engages in any type of visual storytelling. In the form of a 200-page comic book, McCloud covers the basics of the visual literacy of comics and, in the process, presents a lot of valuable information for photographers.

Real World Photoshop **by David Blatner and Bruce Fraser.** If you want to know more about color management and printing, this is the book to read. Provides technical details for preparing your images for printing on any type of output device.

B

ABOUT THE CD-ROM

Whether you're a Mac or Windows user, you shouldn't have any trouble finding your way around the *Complete Digital Photography, Second Edition* CD-ROM.

IMAGES Folder contains many of the images found in the book. These images can be viewed on-screen, or printed out for closer examination. Most of the figures are in JPEG or TIFF format and can be viewed using the Adobe Photoshop Elements demo found in the Applications folder. Unfortunately, there is not enough room on the CD-ROM to include all of the images, so images which would benefit from closer inspection – either to reveal subtle color corrections, editing techniques, or artifact troubles – have been selected. Images are arranged in folders by chapter, and are labeled with the same figure numbers as shown in the book. Also included in the Images folder is an Image Comparisons folder, which contains sample images from a number of different cameras. Most of these images were shot within minutes of each other, and all were shot using each camera's full automatic mode.

TUTORIALS Folder contains all of the files you need to complete the book's tutorials. As with the images, the tutorials are grouped into folders by chapter.

VIDEO Folder contains QuickTime movies that demonstrate several image-editing techniques. These movies are referenced from the main text, and they will make the most sense if you watch them after reading the relevant sections of the book. Whether you use Mac or Windows, you will need QuickTime 6 (or any other MPEG-4 player) to view the movies. You can download QuickTime 6 from *www.apple.com/quicktime*.

APPLICATIONS Folder contains demo versions of many popular applications. Most of these application files need to be decompressed before you can install them. Inside each folder is a Web link that will take you to each application's home page. There, you can learn more about each program, as well as read detailed system requirements and installation instructions.

Macintosh

- **Adobe Photoshop Elements 2.** If you don't already have a copy of Photoshop or Photoshop Elements, you can use this demo to follow along with the tutorials in the book.
- **Image Buddy.** This application for OS 9 or OS X provides image cataloging, printing, and simple retouching tools. A great alternative to iPhoto.
- **iView MediaPro.** This excellent image cataloging app provides pro-level features for archiving and searching through your digital photos.
- **Photo Rescue for OS X.** If you accidentally erase an image, or even an entire card full of images, Photo Rescue can help you recover your lost pictures.
- **Portraits & Prints.** This OS X-only app provides an excellent, speedy interface for cataloging and printing your pictures. A great tool for printing lots of different images on one page.
- **Quantum Mechanic.** A powerful Photoshop plug-in for correcting many common image problems.

Windows

- **Adobe Photoshop Elements 2.** If you don't already have a copy of Photoshop or Photoshop Elements, you can use this demo to follow along with the tutorials in the book.
- **Photo Rescue.** If you accidentally erase an image, or even an entire card full of images, Photo Rescue can help you recover your lost pictures.
- **Qimage Pro.** Professional level image cataloging and correction.
- **Quantum Mechanic.** A powerful Photoshop plug-in for correcting many common image problems.

Recommended System Requirements

Macintosh

PowerPC-based Mac with 128 MB of RAM and 350 MB of free disc space; System 9.1, 9.2.x, or Mac OS X v10.1.3 or later; Color monitor and video card capable of displaying thousands of colors; Monitor resolution of 800 x 600 or greater; CD-ROM drive

Windows

Pentium processor with 128 MB of RAM and 150 MB of free disk space; Windows 98, Windows 98 Second Edition, Windows Millennium Edition, Windows 2000, or Windows XP Home/Professional; Color monitor and video card capable of displaying thousands of colors; Monitor resolution of 800 x 600 or greater; CR-ROM drive

GLOSSARY

1-bit image An image composed of pixels that are either black or white. Called 1-bit (or single-bit) because only one bit of information is required for each pixel.

8-bit image An image that uses 8 bits of data for each pixel. Because you can count from 0 to 255, a pixel can be any one of 256 different colors.

24-bit image An image that uses 24 bits of data for each pixel. Because you can count from 0 to roughly 16-and-a-half million, a pixel can be any one of 16.5 million colors.

32-bit image An image that uses 24 bits of data to store the color of each pixel and an additional 8 bits of data to store how opaque each pixel is. This transparency information is called an *alpha channel*.

35mm equivalency What a lens would be equivalent to in terms of a standard 35mm SLR camera. Used as a standard for discussing the field of view and magnification power of a lens. In 35mm equivalency, lenses over 50mm are telephoto, while lenses below 50mm are wide-angle or fisheye.

aberrations Irregularities in a piece of glass that cause light to be focused incorrectly. Aberrations produce artifacts and anomalies in images.

Acquire plug-in A special type of *plug-in* that allows for communication between your image editing application and your digital camera.

action-safe area The area of a video image that will most likely be visible on any video monitor. Essential action should be kept within the action-safe area, as action that falls outside might be cropped by the viewer's screen. See *title safe*.

active autofocus An autofocus mechanism that achieves focus by transmitting something into the scene, usually infrared light or sonar.

additive Light mixes together in an *additive* process whereby, as colors are mixed, they get brighter; that is, light is added as the colors are mixed. Additive colors eventually produce white. Red, green, and blue are the primary additive colors that can be used to create all other colors.

Adjustment layers Let you apply Levels, Curves, and many other image correction functions as a layer, allowing you to remove or adjust the effect at any time.

aliasing The stair-stepping patterns that can appear along the edges of diagonal lines in an image.

alpha channel Extra information stored about the pixels in an image. Alpha channels are used to store transparency information. This information can serve as a mask for compositing or applying effects.

analog As regards photography, light in the real world travels in a continuous wave. To record those continuous analog waves, your digital camera must first convert them into a series of numbers, or digits.

aperture An opening that is used to control the amount of light passing through the lens of a camera. Typically constructed as an expanding and contracting *iris*.

Aperture priority A shooting mode on a camera. Aperture priority lets you define the camera's aperture. The camera will then calculate a corresponding shutter speed based on its light metering.

APS Advanced Photography System. A fairly new format of film and cameras.

artifacts Image degradations caused by image processing operations. Compressing an image, for example, often results in the creation of many image compression artifacts. Different image processing tasks create different types of artifacts.

ASA A measure of film speed. See also *ISO*.

aspect ratio The ratio of an image's length to its width. Most computer screens and digital cameras shoot images that have an aspect ratio of 4:3. 35mm film and some digital cameras shoot in a 3:2 aspect ratio.

aspherical A lens that contains some elements that are not perfect hemispheres. These non-spherical elements are used to correct certain types of aberrations.

auto-bracketing Some cameras include special functions that cause them to automatically shoot a series of bracketed images when you press the shutter release.

autofocus assist lamp See *focus assist lamp*.

automatic exposure A feature that will automatically calculate the appropriate shutter speed, aperture, and sometimes ISO at the time you take a picture.

backs In a medium, or large-format camera, the film is held in the back of the camera. The back can be removed and replaced with other backs, including digital backs.

barrel distortion A type of distortion caused by a lens. Causes the edges of an image to bow outward. Most prevalent in wide-angle and fish-eye lenses. See also *pincushion distortion*.

Bayer pattern The most common color filter array.

bicubic interpolation A method of interpolation used in a resampling process. Usually the best interpolation choice when you scale an image.

bilinear interpolation A method of interpolation used in a resampling process.

bit depth A measure of the number of bits stored for each pixel in an image. Images with higher bit depths contain greater numbers of colors. Also known as *color depth*.

black and white In the film world, "black and white" is used to refer to images that lack color; that is, images that are composed of only shades of gray. In the digital world, it's usually better to refer to such images as "grayscale" as your computer is also capable of creating images composed only of black and white pixels.

blending mode A setting that determines how the pixels in composited layers blend together. Also known as *transfer mode*.

blooming A flaring, smearing artifact in a digital photo caused by a photosite on the camera's CCD getting overcharged. The extra charge spills into the neighboring photosites and creates the artifact.

boot time How quickly (or slowly, depending on the camera) the camera will be ready to shoot after powering up.

bracketing The process of shooting additional frames of an image, each over or underexposed. By intelligently bracketing your shots, you stand a better chance of getting the image you want.

bulb mode A special shutter mode that opens the shutter for as long as you hold down the shutter release button.

burst See *drive*.

catchlight The white highlight that appears in people's eyes.

CCD Charge-coupled device, the image sensor used in most digital cameras.

center-weight metering A light metering system similar to using a *matrix meter*, but that lends more analytical weight to the center of the image.

channel One component of a color image. Different channels of color are combined to produce a full color image. For example, red, green, and blue channels are combined by your monitor or digital camera to create a full-color picture. Also known as *color channel*.

chromatic aberrations Color artifacts caused by the inability of a lens to evenly focus all frequencies of light. Usually appears as colored fringes around high-contrast areas in a scene. See also *purple fringing*.

chrominance Color information.

clipping When highlights or shadows suddenly cut off to completely white or black in an image, rather than fading smoothly.

clone See *Rubber Stamp*.

CMOS Complimentary Metal Oxide Semiconductor. A type of image sensor. Not yet widely used, but offers the promise of better image quality, lower cost, and lower power-consumption than a CCD.

CMS See *color management system*.

CMYK Cyan, magenta, yellow, and black, the primary subtractive colors that are used by a printing process to create all other colors. Although cyan, magenta, and yellow are subtractive primaries, it is impossible to create perfectly pure pigments. Therefore, black ink must be added to create true blacks and darker colors.

coating Special chemicals applied to a lens that serve to reduce flares and reflection.

color calibration The process of calibrating your input and output devices, as well as your monitor, so that color is accurately displayed on each.

color channel See *channel*.

color depth See *bit depth*.

color filter array The colored filters that are placed over the photosites on an image sensor. Because image sensors can only "see" in grayscale, a color filter array is required for them to capture color information.

color gamut The range of colors that can be described by a particular color model. Also known as *gamut* or *color space*.

color management system (CMS) A set of software components that work together to compensate for the differences in your monitor, printer, and scanner so that your images appear as accurately as possible on your display.

color matching engine The software component of a color matching system that performs the translations from one color space to another.

color model A method of representing color. RGB, CMYK, and Lab are all color models and each takes a different approach to representing color. See also *color gamut*.

color space See *color gamut*.

color temperature Different lights shine at different temperatures, measured in degrees Kelvin (°K). Each temperature has a different color quality.

CompactFlash A type of reusable, removable storage. The most common form of storage used in digital cameras.

compositing The process of layering images on top of each other to create composite images. Compositing is used for everything from creating simple collages to performing complex image correction and adjustment.

continuous mode See *drive.*

continuous autofocus An autofocus mechanism that constantly refocuses as new objects move into its focusing zone.

continuous tone A printed image that is made up of continuous areas of printed color. Photographic film prints are continuous tone. Inkjet printers, laser printers, and offset presses use printing methods that don't print continuous tone. If you look closely at a print from one of these devices, you can see that it is made up of small patterns of dots.

contrast detection An autofocus mechanism that determines focus by measuring contrast in a scene. The mechanism assumes that maximum contrast means sharpest focus. Contrast detection is a method of *passive autofocus.*

contrast filters Filters that you can add to the end of a lens to increase contrast in an image.

contrast ratios The ratio of the darkest to lightest tones in an image. The higher the ratio, the more contrast there is in the image.

CRT Cathode Ray Tube.

dark frame subtraction A method of reducing noise in long-exposure digital photos.

demosaicing The interpolation process that a CCD uses to calculate color. The color of any individual pixel is determined by analyzing the color of the surrounding pixels.

depth of field A measure of the area of an image that is in focus. Measured as depth from the focal point of the image.

destructive effects Filters that actually modify the pixels in your image. Unlike non-destructive effects, there's no easy way to go back and change a destructive effect's settings, or undo its effects if you change your mind about it later.

device-dependent color space A color space that represents colors as combinations of other colors. RGB and CMYK are device-dependent color spaces because accurate color representation in these spaces is dependent on the quality of your primary colors.

device-independent color space A color space (such as Lab color) that records what a color actually looks like, rather than how it is made.

device profile A description of the color qualities of a particular device, such as a printer, scanner, digital camera, or monitor. Also known as *profile* or *ICC profile*.

digital photography In this book, the term *digital photography* is used to refer to images shot with a digital camera.

digital zoom A feature on many digital cameras that creates a fake zoom by capturing the center of an image and blowing it up to full image size.

digitizing The process of converting something into numbers (digits). In a digital camera, an image sensor captures an image that is then converted into numbers, or digitized.

diopter An optical control that lets you adjust the viewfinder on a camera to compensate for nearsightedness.

downsample The process of reducing the size of an image by throwing out data.

DPI Dots per inch, a measure of resolution.

drive A special shooting mode for shooting a sequence of images in rapid succession. Also known as *burst* or *continuous mode*.

drybag A sealable, waterproof bag that will keep your camera dry even if it gets submerged.

dual-axis focusing zone An autofocus mechanism that measures contrast along both horizontal and vertical axes.

dynamic range The range of colors that a device can represent. A digital camera with larger dynamic range can capture and store more colors, resulting in truer, smoother images.

effective pixel count The actual number of pixels that are used on an image sensor. In many digital cameras, some of the pixels on the camera's sensor are masked away or ignored.

electron gun The image on a CRT screen or television screen is created by three electron guns that paint the screen with three different streams of electrons. Separate guns are provided for the red, green, and blue components of a color image.

electronic TTL viewfinder An eyepiece viewfinder that uses a tiny LCD screen instead of normal optics, and looks through the lens. (This is the same mechanism you'll find on most video camcorders.)

element One individual lens. Most camera lens are composed of many different elements.

emulsion The light-sensitive chemical coating on the surface of a piece of film.

EXIF Exchangeable Image File. A digital image file format used by most digital cameras. Notable because it includes special header information where all of an image's parameters (shutter speed, aperture, etc.) are stored.

exposure The combination of aperture, shutter speed, and ISO settings that determine how much light will be recorded at the focal plane.

exposure compensation A mechanism for adjusting the exposure on your camera that is independent of any particular exposure parameter. In other words, rather than specifically changing the aperture or shutter speed, you can simply use exposure compensation to over- or underexpose an image. The camera will calculate the best way to achieve the compensation.

exposure lock A mechanism that lets you lock the exposure on your camera independently of focus.

external flash sync connection Allows you to connect an external flash (usually a specific model) to the camera using a small cable.

falloff How quickly an effect changes. For example, a depth of field blur might have a quick falloff, meaning that the blur goes from sharp to blurry very quickly.

fast shutter mode Forces a large aperture to facilitate a fast shutter speed. Sometimes called *sports mode*.

feather The process of blurring the edge of a selection to create a smoother blend between an edit and the rest of an image.

fill flash Allows you to force the flash to fire to provide a slight fill light. Also known as *force flash*.

film A quaint nineteenth-century analog technology for recording images. Requires lots of hazardous chemicals, a lot of patience, and doesn't offer cool features such as Levels dialog boxes or Rubber Stamp tools. Not for the impatient. Does have the advantage that the recording and storage mediums are included in the same package.

filter factor Most lens filters are documented with a filter factor, which will inform you of the exposure compensation (in stops) required when you use that filter.

filters Either colored plastics or glass that you can attach to the end of your camera's lens to achieve certain effects, or special effects that you can apply to your image in your image editing program. See *plug-ins*.

FireWire A type of serial connection provided by many computers and digital cameras. Can be used for transferring images between camera and computer. Much faster than USB. Also called *IEEE-1394* or *i.Link*.

fisheye An extremely wide-angle lens that creates spherical views.

flash compensation A control that allows you to increase or decrease the intensity of your camera's flash. Usually measured in stops.

flash memory A form of nonvolatile, erasable memory. Used in digital cameras in the form of special memory cards.

focal length The distance, usually measured in millimeters, between the lens and the focal plane in a camera.

focal length multiplier Many digital SLRs use an image sensor that is smaller than a piece of 35mm film. If you attach a lens to one of these cameras, its 35mm equivalency will be multiplied by the focal length multiplier. For example, if your digital SLR has a focal length multiplier of 1.6x, a 50mm lens mounted on your camera will have an effective focal length of 80mm.

focal plane The point onto which a camera focuses an image. In a film camera, there is a piece of film sitting on the focal plane. In a digital camera, a CCD sits on the focal plane.

focus assist lamp A small lamp on the front of the camera that the camera can use to assist autofocusing. Also known as *autofocus assist lamp*.

focus ring The ring on a lens that allows you to manually focus the lens. Most smaller digital cameras lack focus rings, which can make them difficult to manually focus.

focus tracking An autofocus mode provided by some cameras that can track a moving object within the frame and keep it in focus. Sometimes called *servo focus*.

focusing spot See *focusing zone*.

focusing zone An area in the camera's field of view in which the camera can measure focus. Most cameras only have one focusing zone. The camera will focus on the object in this zone. Some cameras have multiple zones.

force flash See *fill flash*.

f-stop Sometimes synonymous with *stop*, more specifically a measure of the size of the aperture on a camera. F-stop values are the ratio of the focal length of the lens to diameter of the aperture.

gamma The midpoint (between black and white) in a tonal range.

gamut See *color gamut*.

gels Thin pieces of plastic that are usually placed in front of lights to create colored lighting effects.

grayscale An image composed entirely of shades of gray, rather than color. (Basically, a fancy name for "black and white.")

group Multiple elements cemented together in a lens.

halftoning A process used for printing photos that begins by shooting a photo of an image through a special halftone screen. The resulting photo gets broken down by the screen into a pattern of dots that can be easily printed using a single ink. Your computer can generate halftone output from a laser printer, allowing you to skip the photographic halftoning step.

hardware calibration Special devices that measure the color of an output device. The data gathered by the device is then used to create a color profile of the device. This profile is, in turn, used by color management software to ensure accurate color output.

histogram A graph of the distribution of tones within an image.

hot shoe A mount for attaching an external flash to a camera.

ICC profile See *device profile*.

i.Link Sony's name for *FireWire*.

IEEE-1394 The official name for *FireWire*.

image buffering The capability of a camera to temporarily store images in an internal memory buffer before writing them out to a memory card. A large image buffer facilitates the rapid shooting of multiple frames, as the camera doesn't have to stop shooting to offload images to storage.

image stabilization Some telephoto camera lenses offer special optics that can stabilize the tiny shakes and jitters that can be caused by your hand.

interpolation The process of calculating missing data in an image based on data that is already there.

iris A mechanism that can expand and contract to create circular apertures to control the amount of light passing through a lens.

ISO A measure of a film's "speed" or light sensitivity. The higher the ISO, the more sensitive the film. The sensitivity of digital camera sensors is also rated using the ISO scale.

JPEG Joint Photographic Experts Group. More commonly, the name of a popular lossy image compression scheme.

L*A*B color See *Lab color*.

Lab color A color model created by the Commission Internationale de l'Éclairage. Lab color describes colors as they actually appear, rather than by how they are made. As such, Lab color makes a great reference space for performing color management and calibration.

latitude How far colors in an image can be pushed or pulled.

LCD Liquid Crystal Display.

lens flares Bright color artifacts produced in a lens by reflections within the lens itself.

line screen frequency The density of the screen that is used in a halftoning process. A screen with more density yields an image with smoother tones and more detail.

L-Ion Lithium Ion. A type of rechargeable battery.

linear array A digital camera mechanism that uses a single row of sensors that makes three separate filtered passes over the imaging sensors to create a full-color image.

lossless Indicates that a particular process does not result in any loss of quality.

lossy Indicates that a particular process results in loss of quality.

luminance Brightness information.

macro A special type of lens used for photographing objects at extremely close distances.

manual mode A shooting mode on a camera that allows you to set both the aperture and shutter speed, giving you full control over the camera's exposure.

matrix meter A light meter that analyzes many different areas of your scene to determine proper exposure.

megapixel A million pixels. Usually used as a measure of the resolution of a digital camera's sensor.

Memory Stick A type of reusable, removable storage developed by Sony, not yet adopted by any other camera vendors.

metering The process of measuring light with a light meter (or by eye) so as to determine proper exposure for a shot.

MicroDrive A tiny hard drive that fits in a Type II CompactFlash slot on a camera. Note that a camera usually has to be approved for use with a MicroDrive.

mirror lock-up The ability to lock a camera's mirror into the "up" position to reduce vibration when shooting long exposure images. Some higher-end cameras also provide a lock-up feature to aid in cleaning the camera's sensor.

multiple array A digital camera mechanism that uses three separate CCDs for capturing a color image, one each for red, green, and blue.

multi-segment meter See *matrix meter.*

multi-spot focus An autofocus mechanism on a camera that can focus on one of several different places within an image.

nearest neighbor A method of interpolation used in a resampling process.

neutral density filter A filter that cuts down on the light entering your camera's lens, without altering the color of the light. Enables you to use wider apertures or faster shutter speeds in bright light.

NiCad Nickel Cadmium. A type of rechargeable battery. Not recommended for use in a digital camera.

NiMH Nickel Metal Hydride. A type of rechargeable battery.

nodal point The optical center of a camera's lens.

noise The bane of all digital photographers. Noise appears in an image as very fine-grained patterns of multicolored pixels in an area. Shadow areas are particularly susceptible to noise as are images shot in low light. Noise is very different looking than the grain found in film photos. Unfortunately, it's also far less attractive.

normal lens A lens that has a field of view that is equivalent to the field of view of the human eye. Roughly 50 mm.

overexposed An image that was exposed for too long. As an image becomes more overexposed, it gets brighter and brighter. Highlights and light-colored areas wash out to completely white.

parallax The easiest way to understand parallax is simply to hold your index finger in front of your face and close one eye. Now close the other eye and you'll perceive that your finger has jumped sideways. As you can see, at close distances, even a change of view as small as the distance between your eyes can create a very different perspective on your subject. A camera that uses one lens for framing and another for shooting faces the same problems. Parallax is not a problem at longer ranges, as the parallax shift is imperceptible.

passive autofocus An autofocus mechanism that achieves focus by analyzing the camera's view of the scene.

PC Card adapter A special adapter that lets you insert a storage card from your camera into the PC card slot of your computer.

PC Cards Small, credit-card-sized peripheral cards that can be inserted into a PC Card slot on a laptop computer, or into a special PC Card drive on a desktop computer. PC Card adapters are available for most types of digital camera media, allowing you to insert media directly into your PC Card slot.

PCMCIA See *PC Cards*.

phase detection See *phase difference*.

phase difference An autofocus mechanism that uses measurements taken through different parts of the camera's lens to determine focus. Also known as *phase detection*.

photosite A tiny electrode that sits on the surface of an image sensor. There is one photosite for each pixel on a sensor.

picture elements The smallest area of color information that can be displayed on a computer monitor. Also, the smallest area of color information that can be detected by a digital imaging sensor. Also known as *pixels*.

pincushion distortion A type of distortion caused by a lens. Causes the edges of an image to bow inward. Most prevalent in telephoto lenses. See also *barrel distortion*.

pixel See *picture elements*.

pixel mapping A feature included on some digital cameras. When activated, the camera examines all of the pixels on the camera's image sensor and creates a map of which ones are bad. It then excludes these pixels from all color calculations. The pixel map is stored and used for all shots until you execute the pixel mapping again. Some cameras lose their pixel maps when you change the camera's batteries.

pixellate Sometimes, the individual pixels in an image can become visible, a process called pixellation.

plug-ins Special bits of code, usually effects or image processing filters that can be added to your image editing application. Most plug-ins conform to the Photoshop plug-in standard.

polarizers Special filters that can be fitted onto the end of a lens. Polarizers only allow light that is polarized in a particular direction to enter your lens. Polarizers can completely remove distracting reflections from water, glass, or other shiny surfaces. Polarizers can also be used to increase the contrast in skies and clouds.

posterization Reduction of the number of tones in an image. As a particular tonal range gets posterized, it will appear more "flat."

PPI Pixels per inch, a measure of resolution.

prefocus The process of autofocusing, metering, and white balancing that occurs when you press your camera's shutter release button halfway.

prefocus time How long it takes a camera to perform its prefocus steps (autofocus, metering, and white balance).

prime lens A lens with a fixed focal length.

profile See *device profile*.

proportional zoom control A zoom control whose rate of zoom changes depending on how far you push or pull the control.

prosumer A marketing term for a camera that sits somewhere between the professional and consumer market.

purple fringing A color artifact specific to digital cameras with resolutions greater than two megapixels. Appears in an image around the edges of high-contrast objects, usually shot with wide-angle lenses. Usually confined to the edges of the screen. See also *chromatic aberrations*.

quantization In JPEG compression, the process of averaging the colors in one 64-pixel square area.

quantizing The process of assigning a numeric value to a sample. Part of the digitizing process.

rangefinder A viewfinder mechanism on a camera. A fixed-focus or zoom lens is used for imaging, while a separate optical viewfinder is used for framing your shot.

Raw data Pixel data that comes directly from the CCD with no further processing. Processing is usually performed later using special software. Raw files offer quality equivalent to an uncompressed image, but require much less space.

read-out register The mechanism that reads the signals from each row of photosites on an image sensor. The read-out register amplifies the signals from the photosites and sends them to the camera's analog-to-digital converter.

reciprocity Exposure parameters have a reciprocal relationship so that different combinations of parameters produce the same exposure. For example, setting your camera to a shutter speed of $1/250^{th}$ of a second at f8 is the same as setting it to $1/125^{th}$ at f16.

rectilinear A type of wide-angle lens that includes corrective elements that prevent barrel distortion.

recycling The time it takes a camera to reset itself and prepare to shoot another shot.

red-eye reduction A special flash mode that attempts to prevent red-eye by firing a short initial flash to close down the irises in your subject's eyes.

red-eye When the flash from a camera bounces off a subject's eyes and back into the camera's lens, the subject will appear to have bright red eyes. Most prevalent in cameras where the flash is very close to the lens.

registration When primary color channels are positioned over each other so that a full-color image is produced, the images are said to be "in registration."

refraction The process of slowing and bending light using a transparent substance such as air, water, glass, or plastic.

refractive index The amount of refraction produced by a substance.

refresh rate How often the image on a camera's LCD viewfinder is redrawn. An LCD with a higher refresh rate will produce an image with smoother motion.

resampling The process of computing new pixel information when resizing a document in your image editing application. If you are resizing upward, the resampling process will generate new pixels. If you are resizing downward, the resampling process will discard pixels.

resolution In a monitor or digital camera, the number of pixels that fit into a given space. Usually measured in pixels per inch (ppi) or dots per inch (dpi). In a printer, the number of printer dots that fit into a given space, usually measured in dots per inch (dpi).

RGB Red, green, and blue, the additive primary colors that are used by your computer monitor and digital camera to produce all other colors.

Rubber Stamp An image editing tool that works like a paint brush but that copies image data from one part of your image to another. A staple retouching tool.

sampling The process of analyzing something to determine its content. A digital camera samples light to determine how much, and what color the light is, at any given point in a scene.

saturation A characteristic of color. Colors that are more saturated are typically "deeper" in hue and often darker. As saturation increases, hue shifts slightly.

SCSI Small Computer System Interface. An older, high-speed computer interface for attaching hard drives, scanners and other peripherals.

servo focus See *focus tracking.*

sharpening The process of using software to increase sharpness in a digital image. Sharpening can happen inside a digital camera or through post-processing on your computer.

shutter A mechanism that sits in front of the focal plane in a camera and can open and close to expose the image sensor or film to light. Many digital cameras do not have physical shutters, but instead mimic shutter functionality by simply activating and deactivating their image sensors to record an image. Cameras that do have shutters typically use a two-curtain mechanism. The first curtain begins to slide across the focal plane to create a gap. It is followed usually very quickly by a second shutter that closes the gap. As the gap passes across, the entire CCD is exposed.

shutter lag A delay between the time you press the shutter release button on a camera and the time it actually shoots a picture.

shutter priority A shooting mode on a camera. Shutter priority lets you define the camera's shutter speed. The camera will then calculate a corresponding aperture based on its light metering.

shutter speed The length of time it takes for the shutter in a camera to completely expose the focal plane.

single array system A digital camera mechanism that uses a single image sensor for imaging. Sometimes called a *striped array.*

single lens reflex A camera whose viewfinder looks through the same lens that your camera uses to make its exposure. Also known as *SLR.*

single-axis focusing zone An autofocus mechanism that measures contrast along a single axis only, usually horizontal.

slow sync mode A special flash mode that combines a flash with a slow shutter speed to create images that contain both still and motion-blurred objects.

SLR See *single lens reflex.*

SmartMedia A type of reusable, removable storage.

soft proof An on-screen proof of a color document.

specular highlights The bright white glints and reflections that occur on very shiny surfaces and on the edges of objects.

sports mode See *fast shutter mode*.

spot meter A light meter that measures a very narrow circle of the scene.

sRGB An RGB color space defined by Microsoft and Hewlett-Packard. It is intended to represent the colors available on a typical color monitor. A little too small for digital photography work.

step-up ring An adapter that attaches to the end of a lens and allows for the addition of filters or other lens-attachments. Serves to change the thread size of the lens.

stitching The process of joining and blending individual images to create a panoramic image.

stop A measure of the light that is passing through a camera's lens to the focal plane. Every doubling of light either through changes in aperture, shutter speed, or ISO is one stop. See also *f-stop*.

striped array See *single array system*.

subtractive Ink mixes together in a *subtractive* process whereby as colors are mixed together they get darker; that is, light is subtracted as the colors are mixed. Subtractive colors eventually produce black. Cyan, magenta, and yellow are the primary subtractive colors that can be used to create all other colors.

telephoto A lens with a focal length that is longer than a *normal lens*. As a lens gets more telephoto, its field of view decreases.

TFT See *Thin Film Transistor*.

Thin Film Transistor A technology used to create LCD screens. Typically used for the LCD viewfinder/monitors included on the backs of many digital cameras.

three-shot array A digital camera mechanism that uses three *single arrays*, one each for red, green, and blue.

through the lens See *TTL*.

title safe A guide similar to the *action-safe area*. The title-safe area is slightly smaller.

transfer mode See *blending mode*.

trilinear array A digital camera mechanism that uses three *linear arrays* stacked on top of each other to create a full-color image in a single pass over the image sensor.

TTL A viewfinder mechanism that looks through the same lens that is used to focus the image onto the focal plane. Short for *through the lens*.

underexposed An image that was not exposed enough. In an underexposed image, dark, shadow areas turn to completely black.

upsample The process of enlarging an image by calculating (interpolating) new data.

USB Universal Serial Bus. A type of serial connection provided by many computers and digital cameras. Can be used for transferring images between camera and computer.

VGA resolution 640 × 480 pixels. *VGA* is a computer video standard.

Video LUT Animation A feature available in some versions of Photoshop that allows for real-time, on-screen viewing of color corrections and changes.

video RAM The memory in a computer that is used for displaying images on-screen. The more video RAM, the larger your images can be, and the greater the bit depth they can have. Also known as *VRAM*.

vignetting A darkening of the image around the edges.

virtual reality movie See *VR movie*.

VRAM See *video RAM*.

VR movie A digital movie that lets you pan and tilt in real time to explore and navigate a virtual space.

wavelet compression A new fractal-based compression scheme. Converts your image from a series of raster dots into a collection of tiny fractal curves.

white balance A color calibration used by a camera. Once a camera knows how to accurately represent white, it can represent all other colors. Because white can look different under different types of light, a camera needs to be told what white is, a process called *white balancing*.

wide-angle A lens with a focal length that is shorter than a *normal lens*. As a lens gets more wide angle, its field of view increases.

XGA resolution 800 × 600 pixels. *XGA* is a computer video standard.

zone system A method of calculating exposure.

zoom lens A lens with a variable focal length.

INDEX

A

Accessories, 122–123, 145–146, 260

Action safe areas, 164

Adobe Photoshop Elements, 138–142

Advantages of digital photography, 2, 20

Airbrushing, 352

Aliasing, 17–18, 420

Alpha channels, 360

AltaMira, Genuine Fractals software, 143, 420

Aperture
  controls, 48–51
  depth of field and, 202
  priority modes, 105, 150–151, 222
  sharpness and, 206

APPLICATIONS folder, 479–480

Aqua, 131

Arrays
  in charge-coupled devices (CCDs), 30, 35–36
  color filter arrays, 32

Artifacts, 13, 16–17, 34
  compression and, 38

enlargement and, 62

interpolation and, 65

lenses and, 43, 83–84

purple fringing (sensor bloom), 17, 59–60, 235–237, 407–411

sensor dust, 393

Aspect ratios, 67–69

Astro-photography, 273–274

Auto-bracketing features, 126

Autofocus, 90–91, 166–170
  phase detection and, 174–175

B

Banding, in panoramic photos, 256

Barrel distortion, 83–84, 395–399

Batteries, 123–125
  LCD cameras, 76–77
  power management, 192–194
  temperature, 194

Beam-splitters, 75

Best-shot selection features, 126

Bicubic interpolation, 299

Bilinear interpolation, 299

Bit depth, 7
Black and white photography,
  27, 108, 140
  converting color images to
    grayscale, 440–442
  hand-tinted color effects,
    443–446
  histograms and, 212–217
  tonal control in, 207–212
  zone system, 244–247
Blur filters, 141
BMP format, 141
Boot times, 69, 109–110
Bourke-White, Margaret, 148
Boyle, Willard, 28
Bracketing, 233–235
Brightness and contrast, Photo-
  shop correction tutorial,
  314–317
Brushes
  airbrushing, 352
  editing tools, 350–352
  Healing Brush, 378
  History Brush, 445–446
  Paintbrush tools, 140
Bulb-mode, shutter control, 92

C
Cameras
  accessories, 122–123
  auto-bracketing feature, 126
  batteries, 123–125
  best-shot selection feature,
    126
  body construction of, 78–80
  components and features,
    54–55
  design issues, 69–82
  in-camera effects features,
    126
  LCD-only cameras, 76–77
  noise reduction features, 126

performance considerations,
    109–110
  pixel mapping features, 126
  playback options, 112–113
  point-and-shoot cameras,
    69–71
  prosumer and prosumer SLR
    cameras, 71–76
  remote computer controls,
    125
  resolution and selection of,
    56–64
  selection checklist, 128
  settings for, 148
  SLR cameras pro, 77–78
  status LCDs, 80
  time-lapse features, 125
  tripod mounts, 81–82
  video cameras, 77–78
  voice annotation, 126
Cards, 64–65, 116–118
Cataloging images, 279–281
  software for, 143–144
CD-R and CD-RW drives, 134
CD-ROM
  contents, 479–480
  Images folder, 12–13
Center-weight metering, 101
Channels
  alpha channels, 360
  color channels, 26–27, 140,
    338–341
Charge-coupled devices (CCDs),
    24
  arrays, 30, 35–36
  color filter arrays, 32
  interpolation, 30–36
  operation of, 28–39
  photosites in, 29–30
  pixel masking, 35
Chromatic aberrations, 17,
    59–60, 235–237, 407–411

Chrominance, 38

Clean-up, 380, 381–399
    distortion reduction, 395–399

Clone tool, 352–353
    video cloning Photoshop tutorial, 34

Clone tools, 140

CMOS sensors, 37

CMSs (color management systems),
    283–295
    configuring, 285–295

CMYK color, 140, 281–282, 286

Collins, Michael, 240

Color
    additive process, 26
    adjustment, 380
    artifacts, 16–17
    bad white balance, 16
    black, 281–282
    channels, 26–27, 140, 338–341
    chromatic aberrations, 407–411
    CMYK color, 140, 281–282, 286
    color-based selection tools, 358
    color casts, 15–16
    color depth, 7
    color filter arrays, 32
    color management systems (CMSs),
        283–295
    color matching engines, 285
    color spaces, 28, 140, 284
    color temperature, 100, 153–157
    color theory, 24–28
    converting to grayscale (black and
        white), 440–442
    correction tutorial, 400–406
    Curves control and, 341–347
    gamuts (ranges of color), 284
    hand-tinted effects, 443–446
    histograms and, 212–217
    Hue / Saturation control, 377
    incorrect color, 15
    L*A*B color, 28, 140, 286
    lenses and aberrations in, 43

Level control and, 338–347
    luminance, 179
    monitors and, 134–135
    operating systems and, 130–131
    Photoshop 7 settings, 290–292
    RGB color, 26, 140, 286
    Selective Color control, 377
    sharpness and saturation controls,
        103–104
    subtractive process, 25–26
    tonal controls, 207–212
    tone and, 333

Color channels, 26–27, 140, 338–341
    fringes removed with, 411–412
    grayscale conversions and, 442

Color depth, 7, 134

Color management systems (CMSs),
    283–295
    configuring, 285–295

ColorSync, 130–131

CompactFlash cards, 116–118

Compositing, 450–451

Compression, 37–39
    image transfer and, 279
    lossless, 66
    resolution and, 64–66
    size of image, 151–152
    wavelet compression, 143

Continuous shooting mode, 106

Contrast, 157–158
    contrast detection systems, 168–170
    layers and, 415–417
    Photoshop correction tutorial, 314–317

Contrast detection systems, 168–170

Costs, photography equipment, 3, 20–21

Cropping
    Photoshop tutorial, 303–308
    in workflow, 381

Curves control
    color correction Photoshop tutorial,
        341–347
    described, 331–334

Curves control (*cont.*)
    Photoshop correction tutorial,
        334–338

D
Dark frame subtractions, 199,
    391–392
Data loss during editing,
    323–324
Deleting images, 113
Demosaicing, 33
Depth of field, 150, 202–205
    creating planes of depth,
        434–440
    focal length multipliers and,
        204
    macro photography and,
        242–243
    shortening, tutorial, 432–434
    shutter speed and, 205–206
    simulating, 428
Despeckle filter, 384–385
Digital photography
    advantages of, 2
    vs. analog photography, 7,
        20–21
    costs of equipment, 3
    defined, 6
Digital Wallets, 195
Diopter adjustments, 96–97
Dirt, 270
Distortion
    barrel distortion, 83–84,
        395–399
    cleanup of, 395–399
    geometric distortion and
        lenses, 165–166
    pincushion distortion, 84,
        395–399
Downsampling, 298, 419
Dpi measurements, 297
Drives, media drives, 122, 145

Dust, 270
    removing artifacts caused by,
        393–394
    sensor dust, 393
Dust & Scratches filter, 384–385
Dye-sublimation printers,
    456–457

E
Editing
    brushes, 350–352
    cloning tools, 352–354
    color-based selection tools,
        358
    color theory and, 281–295
    complex mask tutorial,
        362–369
    Curves control, 331–338
    destructive *vs.* non-destruc-
        tive, 376
    filters as destructive edits, 387
    Healing Brush tool, 378
    Hue / Saturation, 377
    layers, 370–376
    Levels control, 318–322,
        326–331
    mask painting, 357–358
    masks, 354–369
    preparing images for, 296–300
    red-eye phenomenon, 407
    selection tools, 356–357
    Selective Color control, 377
    soft proofing in Photoshop 7,
        295–296
    stamps, 352–354
    tone adjustments, 412
    vignetting corrections,
        414–415
    in workflow, 381, 417–418
Elements in lenses, 43–44
Enlargements
    artifacts and, 62

large format prints, 458
wavelet compression and, 143
in workflow, 419
Environmental issues, 270–272
Epson equipment and software, 115
Exchangeable Image File (EXIF) format,
    225–226
EXIF format, 225–226
Exposure, 46–51
    adjusting, 220–233
    aperture controls, 48–51
    automatic reciprocity, 223
    banding, 256
    compensation, 101, 220–222
    fast shutter setting, 103
    irises and, 91–92
    landscape setting, 103
    locks, 172–175
    locks (panoramic), 102
    manual override controls, 222–223,
        231–233
    metering and, 100–101
    motion control and, 198–205
    night setting, 103
    pan-focus setting, 103
    portrait setting, 103
    practice exercises, 225–233
    preset modes, 103
    priority and manual modes, 222–223
    problems, 18–19
    reciprocity, 49–51
    shutters and shutter speed, 48–50, 91–92
    tonal controls and, 207–212
    white balance and, 99–100
    see also Light meters
Extensions for lenses, 269–270
Extract tool, 358–359
Eyedropper tools, 140

F
Falloff, planes of depth and, 434
Fast-shutter exposure setting, 103

Field of view, 44, 202
File formats, support for, 141
File recovery software, 144–145
Film, ISO ratings and, 50–51
"Film" look, adding, 446–450
Filters
    Add Noise filters, 448–450
    contrast filters, 267
    cost and quality of, 265–266
    Despeckle filter, 384–385
    as destructive edits, 387
    Dust & Scratches filter, 384–385
    editing filters, 141
    effects filters, 267
    Gaussian Blur filter, 385–387
    gels as, 269
    gradient neutral density filters, 210
    infrared photography and, 249
    for lenses, 87
    Median filter, 384–385
    neutral density filters, 205
    polarizers, 267
    sharpening filters, 421
    Smart Blur filter, 385–387
    step-up rings and, 265
    ultraviolet filters, 267, 269
    white balance and, 157
FireWire ports, 114
Flashes
    cancel feature, 188
    compensation, 187–188
    continuous flash shots, 106
    fill mode, 187, 191
    flash modes, 186–190
    flash white balance, 191–192
    force flash mode, 187
    hot shoe (external flash) connections,
        111
    intensity control, 112
    modes of, 111–112
    position of, 111
    range of, 110

Flashes (*cont.*)
red-eye phenomenon and, 187, 188
Floppy disks, 119–120
Focal lengths, 44–45, 85–86, 162–165, 204, 439–440
macro photography and, 241
Focal planes, 24, 434–444
Focus, 90–91
autofocus, 166–170
details and contrast, 217–220
focal length, 162–165
macro photography and, 242
manual focus, 91, 176
spots or zones, 171–174
tracking, 167–168
Focus assist lamps, 90–91, 170
4- and 5-megapixel cameras, 60–62
Framing images, 99
F-stop values, 48

G
Gamma slider of Input Levels control, 318, 322–323
Gaussian Blur filter, 385–387
Genuine Fractals software (AltaMira), 143, 420
Geometric distortion and lenses, 165–166
GIF format, 141, 475
Glossary, 483–498
Gradient neutral density filters, 210
Grain, adding, 446–450
Grayscale, 27
converting color images to grayscale, 440–442
see also Black and white photography

H
Halftoning, 462
Hand-tinted effects, 443–446
Healing Brush tool, 378
Histograms, 113, 212–217, 233–235, 312–314, 445–446
History Brush, 445–446
Hot shoe (external) flash connections, 111
Hue / Saturation, 377
hand-tinted effects and, 443–445

I
Image buffering, 105–106
Images
organizing, 279–281
saving, 381
IMAGES folder, 479
Image transfer, 114–115
In-camera effects features, 126
Infrared photography, 247–250
Inkjet printers, 457–459, 464
Inks, 460–461
Interpolation, 30–36, 65
methods in Photoshop, 299
Irises, 91–92
ISO ratings and controls, 50–51, 101–102, 159–161, 206, 223–225
bright light and, 202
noise and, 200

J
JPEG format, 38, 65–66, 141, 475

L
L*A*B color, 28, 140
Landscape exposure setting, 103

Laptops
  as storage devices, 195
  as workstations, 137–138
Laser printers, 454–456, 462–464
Layers
  adjustment layers, 374–375
  creating, deleting, and moving layers,
    370–371
  layer masks, 375–376
  opacity and transfer modes, 371–373
  saturation and, 415–417
  tone adjustment with, 412
LCD-only cameras, 76–77
Lenses, 42–46
  artifacts caused by, 83–84
  caps for, 88–89, 166
  elements in, 43–44
  extension and retraction, 87–88
  extensions for, 269–270
  filters for, 87
  flares, 44, 85, 165
  focal length, 44–45
  geometric distortion and, 165–166
  image stabilized lenses, 207
  interchangeable, 86–87
  lens speed, 50
  portrait lenses, 164
  prime lenses, 45–46
  quality and testing of, 82–87
  threaded lenses, 87
  wide-angle lenses, 170
  zoom lenses, 45–46
Lens flares, 44, 85, 165
Levels, tone information and, 317–323
Levels and Curves controls, 139
Levels control
  adjustments, Photoshop tutorial,
    326–331
  color and, 338–347
  color correction Photoshop tutorial,
    341–347

Levels Input sliders Photoshop tutorial,
    318–322
Levels Input sliders, Photoshop tutorial,
    318–323
Light meters
  automatic exposure mode, 184–186
  center-weighted metering, 181–182
  matrix (multi-segment) metering, 181
  reading and using, 177–180
  spot metering, 182–184
Light Opacity, 443
Linear arrays, 35
Locks, panoramic or exposure locks,
    102
Look-up tables (LUTs), 135
Luminance, 33, 38, 179, 442
LUTs (look-up tables), 135
Lysen (ink source), 460

M
Macintosh systems
  applications for, 480
  Mac OS operating system, 130–131
  monitor profiles and color
    management, 286–287
  system requirements, 481
Macro photography, 240–244
Manual mode, 105
Masks
  color-based selection tools and, 358
  complex mask tutorial, 362–369
  described, 354–355
  layer masks, 375–376
  mask painting, 357–358
  mask tools, 355
  saving masks, 359–361
  selection tools, 356–357
  Unsharp Masks (USM) filters, 141,
    421–425
Matrix (multi-segment metering), 100
Maxwell, James Clark, 24–25

Media. *See* Inks; Memory (storage); Papers, selecting for printing
Median filter, 384–385
Memory Sticks, 118–119
Memory (storage)
  care and storage of media, 121
  CDs, recordable, 134
  CompactFlash cards, 116–118
  flash memory cards, 116–118
  floppy disks, 119–120
  input / output, 113–121
  Memory Sticks, 118–119
  PC Cards, 119
  SmartMedia cards, 118
  storage cards, 64–65
  3" CDs, 119–120
  in workstations, 132, 133–134
  zip disks, 196
Meters and metering, 157
  exposure and, 100–101
  see also Light meters
Modes, automatic shooting modes, 149
Moisture, 270–271
Monitors, 134–138
  calibration tips, 289
  color management systems and, 285–295
  LCD monitors, 136
  Macintosh color management, 286–287
  Windows monitor profiles, 288–289
Moon, photography on, 240
Moore's Law, 3
Motion control, 198–205
Movie mode, 106–108
Multiple arrays, 35–36
Multi-segment metering, 100

N
Names, for image files, 279–280
Nature photography, 69
Nearest neighbor interpolation, 299
Neutral density filters, 205
Night exposure setting, 103
Night shooting, 103, 200–201
Nodal points, 253–254
Noise, 13–15
  adding grain and texture with, 447–450
  blurring to reduce, 385–387
  dark frame subtraction, 391–392
  Despeckle filter, 384–385
  Dust & Scratches filter, 384–385
  exposure time and, 200–201
  features to reduce, 126
  identifying prior to removal, 382–384
  Luminosity to reduce, 390–391
  Median filter, 384–385
  Noise filters, 14
  QImage Pro utility, 391
  Quantum Mechanic utility, 391
  reduction features on cameras, 126
  selective blurring tutorial, 388–390

O
Opacity mode, layers, 371–373
Operating systems, selection of, 130–131
Organizing image files, 279–281
Overexposure, 19

P

Paintbrush tools, 140
Pan-focus exposure setting, 103
Panoramas, 251–260
    attachments for, 260
    exposure and, 256–257
    stitching software, 251–256, 436–440
Panoramic locks, 102
Panoramic software, 142, 251–256,
        436–440
Papers, selecting for printing, 459–460
PC Cards, 119
PhotoRescue software, 144–145
Photoshop 7
    color settings, 290–292
    vs. Photoshop 5, 294–295
    policies, setting, 292–295
    soft proofing in, 295–296
Photoshop Elements (Adobe), 138–142
Photosites in CCDs, 29–30
Pincushion distortion, 84, 395–399
Pixel mapping features, 126, 391–392
Pixels, 7, 297
Playback options, 112–113
Plug-ins
    masking plug-ins, 359
    support for, 140–141
Point-and-shoot cameras, 69–71
Portrait exposure setting, 103
Portrait lenses, 164
Posterization, 324
Ppi measurements, 297
Prefocus times, 110
Prime lenses, 45–46
Printers
    choosing a printer, 454–461
    dye-sublimation printers, 456–457
    inkjet printers, 457–459, 464
    laser printers, 454–456, 462–464
Printing
    applications for, 467

    correcting images prior to, 466–467
    inks, 460–461
    paper selection, 459–460
    professional printing, 468–470
    resolution for, 461–464
    targeting tonal range tutorial, 470–474
    see also Printers
Prosumer and prosumer SLR cameras,
        71–76
Purple fringing, 17, 59–60, 235–237,
        407–411

Q

QImage Pro utility, 391
Quad-tone inks, 461
Quality of digital photographs, 12–21
Quantum Mechanic utility, 391
Quartz, 131
QuickTime, 479–480

R

RAM (random access memory), 132
Random access memory (RAM), 132
Rangefinders, 71–72
Raw data mode, 66
    white balance and, 156–157
RealViz Stitcher, 436
Reciprocity and exposure, 49–51
Reciprocity failure, 13
Recycling, 110
Red-eye phenomenon, 16, 433–434
    removal of, 142, 407
Refraction, 42
Remote camera controls, 108–109, 206
Remote computer controls, 125
Resampling
    in Photoshop resolution tutorial, 302
    resizing and, 297–300
Resizing
    Photoshop tutorial, 303–308
    in workflow, 381

Resolution, 7
  aspect ratios and, 67–69
  categories of, 57–63
  changing image resolution, 297
  compression, 64–66
  dpi *vs.* ppi measurements, 297
  enlarging images and, 62
  4- and 5-megapixel cameras, 60–62
  Photoshop tutorial, 300–302
  for printing, 461–464
  single-megapixel cameras, 58
  6-megapixel cameras, 60–62
  sub-megapixel cameras, 57
  3-megapixel cameras, 59–60
  2-megapixel cameras, 58–59
  VGA and XGA resolution, 64
  for Web images, 260
RGB color, 140
Rubber stamps, 252–253

S

Sampling, 7
Sand, 270
Saturation, 157–158
  adjustment, 381
  control of, 103–104, 207–212
  grayscale conversion and, 442
  hand-tinted effects and, 443–445
  Hue / Saturation, 377
  Layers and, 415–417
Saturation controls, 103–104
Saving images, 381
Scaling, in workflow, 381, 418–420
Self timers, 108–109, 206
Sensor blooming, 17, 34, 59–60, 235–237, 407–411
Servo tracking, 167
Shadows

histograms to evaluate, 213–214
  noise in, 13–15
Sharpness, 19, 157–158
  controls for, 103–104
  filters for, 421
  increasing, 206–207
  in workflow, 381, 421–426
Shooting modes, 105–109, 149–151
Shutter lag, 110, 167
Shutter priority modes, 105, 149–150, 222
Shutters and shutter speed, 48–50, 91–92
  shutter lag, 110, 167
  shutter priority modes, 105, 149–150, 222
Shutter speed, depth of field and, 205–206
Single-megapixel cameras, 58
6-megapixel cameras, 60–62
Size of images, 151–152
  resizing, 297–300
  for the Web, 261–263
Sleep modes, 193
Slow sync exposure setting, 103
SLR cameras
  professional, 77–78
  prosumer, 72–76
Smart Blur filter, 385–387
SmartMedia cards, 118
Smith, George, 28
Snell, Willebrord, 42
Soft proofing, 284, 295–296
Software
  image editing applications, 138–142
  stitching software (panoramic software), 142, 251–256
Special effects, in-camera features, 126

Speed
  ISO ratings (film speed), 50–51
  of workstation processor, 132–133
Split-body cameras, 69, 74
Spot metering, 101
Stamps, 352–353
Stitching software (panoramic software),
      142, 436–440
Stops (f-stops), 48
Storage (memory)
  Digital Wallets, 195
  laptops as storage devices, 195
Sub-megapixel cameras, 57
Sutton, Thomas, 24
System requirements, 481

T
Telescopes, using cameras with, 273–274
Temperature, 194, 271–272
      see also Color temperature *under* Color
Texture, adding, 446–450
3" CDs, 119–120
3-megapixel cameras, 59–60
Thumbnail views, 112
TIFF format, 141
  compression, 65–66
Time-lapse features, 125
Title safe areas, 264
Tone
  adjustment, 380
  color and, 333
  Curves tool and, 331–338
  histograms and, 113, 212–217,
      233–235, 312–314
  Layers to adjust range, 412
  posterization and, 324
  tonal controls, 207–212
  zone system and, 244–247
Transfer mode, layers, 371–373
Transferring images, 278–279
  trouble moving images, 294
Transfer software, 114–115

Trilinear arrays, 35
Tripods, 206
  motion and, 201
  mounts for, 81–82, 255
  panoramic shooting and, 253–255
TUTORIALS folder, 479
TWAIN drivers, 114
2-megapixel cameras, 58–59

U
Underexposure, 18
  intentional, 228–231
Unsharp Mask (USM) filter, 141, 421–425
Upsampling, 298, 419
USB ports, 114
  hubs and, 145–146
USM (Unsharp Mask) filter, 141, 421–425

V
VGA and XGA images, 64, 151, 426
Video
  input / output, 115
  LUT animation, 135
  shooting for, 263–264
Video cameras, 77–78
VIDEO folder, 479
Viewfinders, 71–72, 92–98
  electronic TTL viewfinders, 97
  LCD viewfinders, 93–94
  optical viewfinders, 95–97
  SLR viewfinders, 97–98
Vignetting, 83, 414–415
Virtual reality movies, 251
Voice annotation features, 126

W
Water, 270–271
Weather, coping with cold, heat and
      moisture, 270–272
Web
  outputting images for, 474–476
  resolution for, 64

sharpness for, 426
shooting for, 260–263
Web addresses
    Lysen (ink source), 460
    QuickTime, 480
White balance, 99–100,
    153–157
    correcting, 412–413
Wide-angle lenses, 170
Windows operating systems,
    131
Windows systems
    applications for, 480
    system requirements, 481

Workflow, suggested steps,
    380–381

X
XGA resolution, 64, 151, 426

Z
Zip disks, 196
Zooming
    digital zooms, 89, 263
    proportional zoom, 89
    zoom ranges, 85–86
Zoom lenses, 45–46
Zooms, playback options, 113